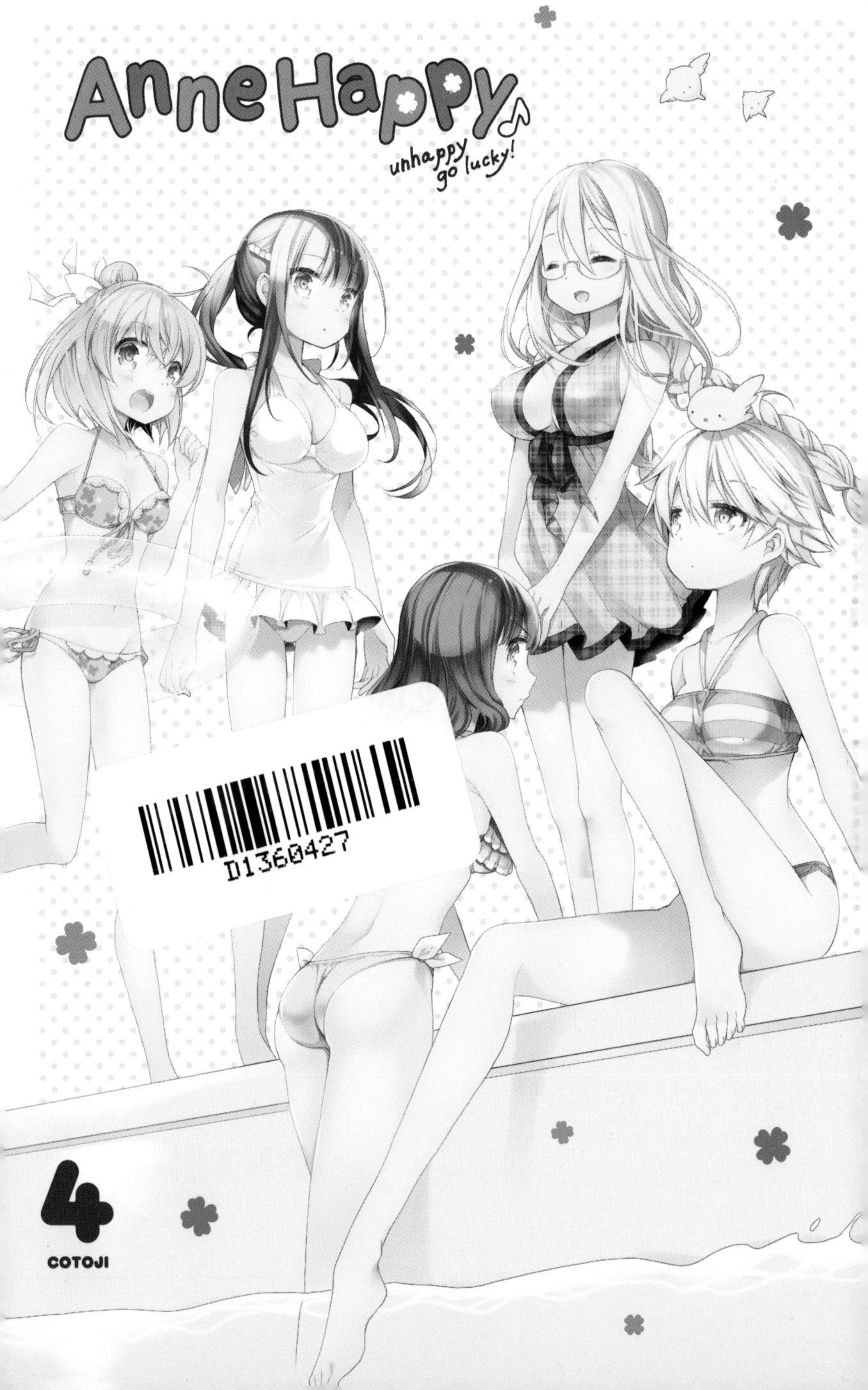
Anne Happy
unhappy go lucky!
4
COTOJI

CONTENTS
ANNE HAPPY
VOLUME FOUR
COTOJI

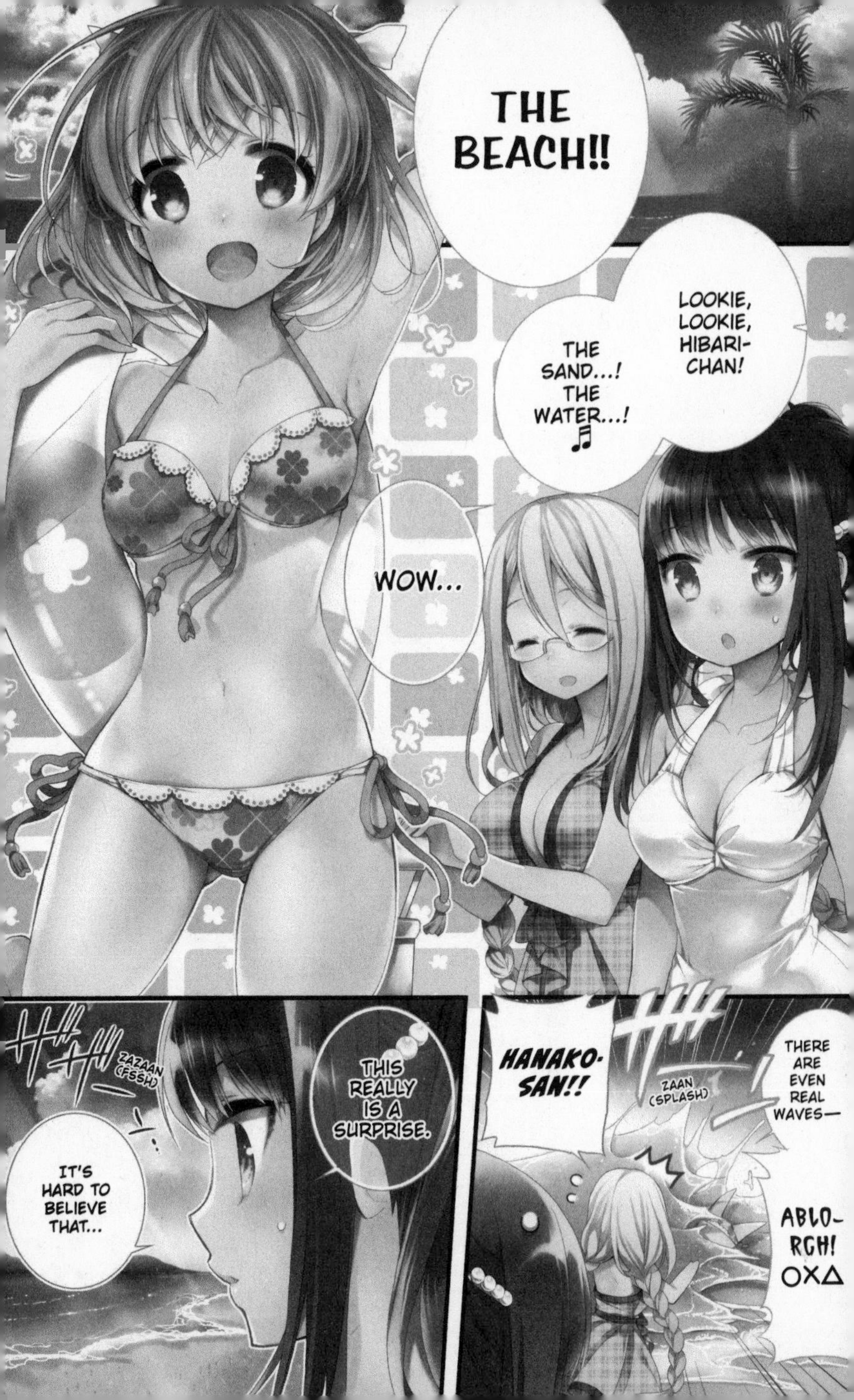
THE BEACH!!
LOOKIE, LOOKIE, HIBARI-CHAN!
THE SAND...! THE WATER...! ♬
WOW...
THERE ARE EVEN REAL WAVES—
ZAAN (SPLASH)
HANAKO-SAN!!
ABLO-RGH! ○×△
THIS REALLY IS A SURPRISE.
ZAZAAN (FSSH)
IT'S HARD TO BELIEVE THAT...

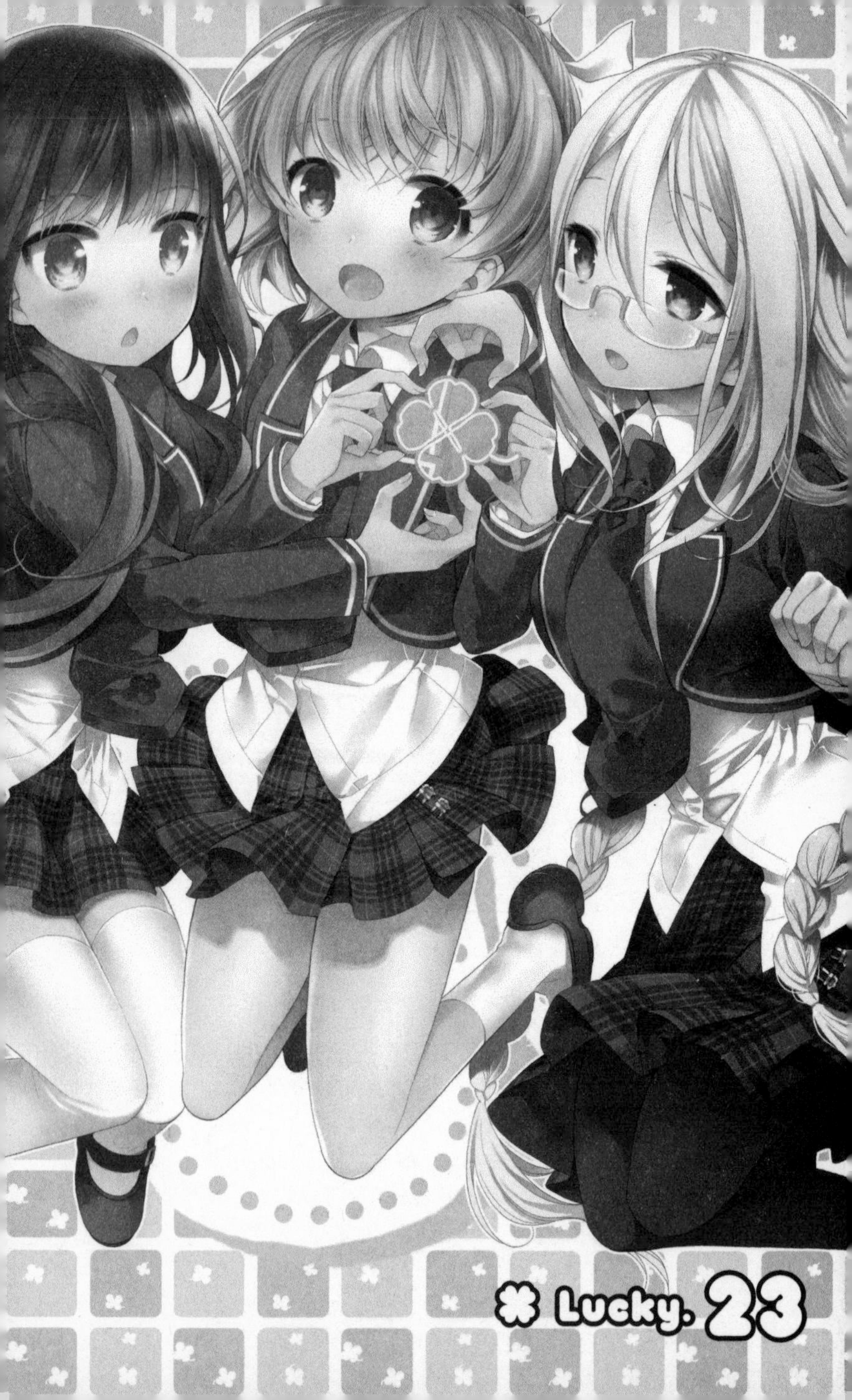
Lucky. 23

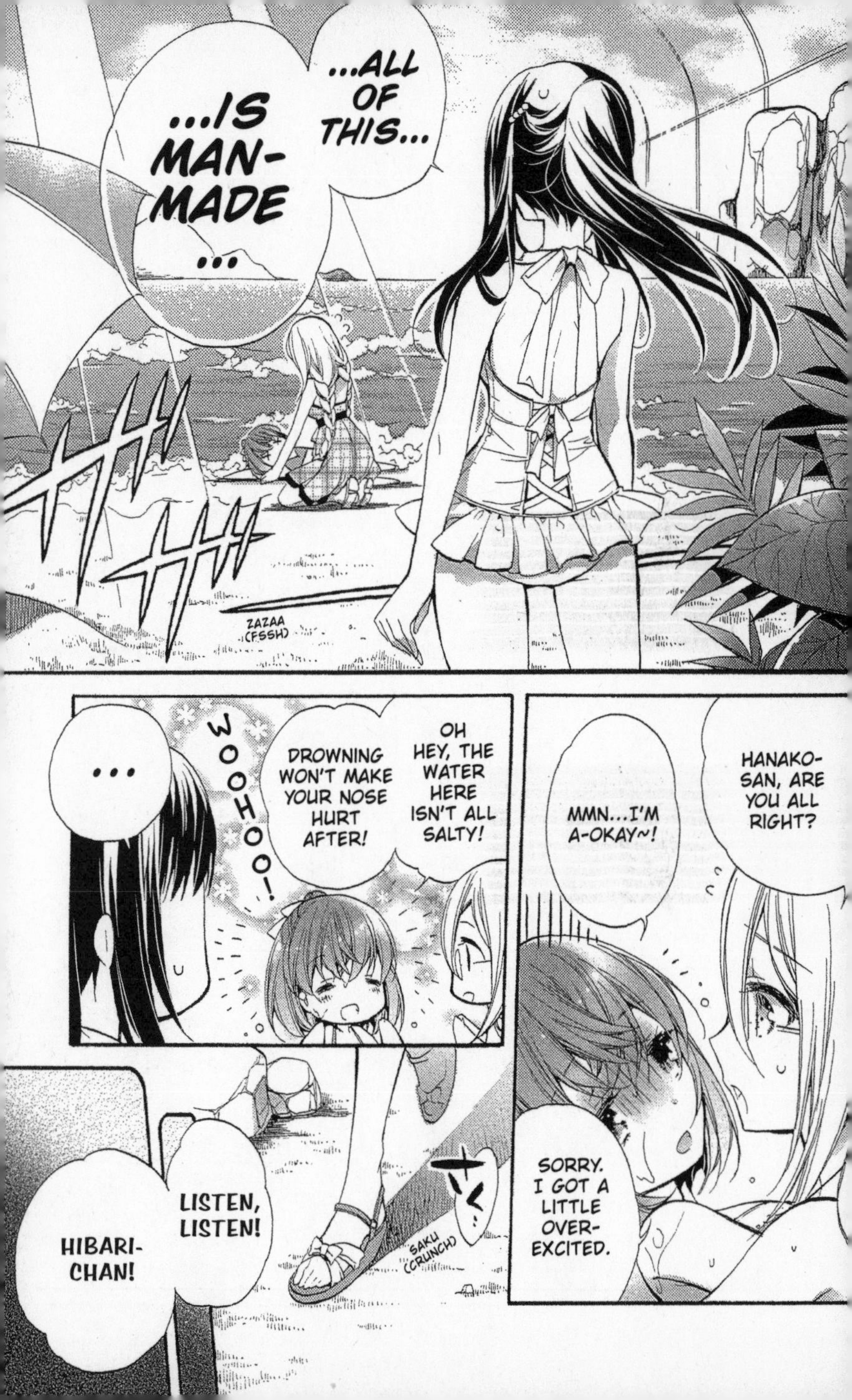

...ALL OF THIS...
...IS MAN-MADE...
ZAZAA (FSSH)
HANAKO-SAN, ARE YOU ALL RIGHT?
MMN...I'M A-OKAY~!
SORRY. I GOT A LITTLE OVER-EXCITED.
OH HEY, THE WATER HERE ISN'T ALL SALTY!
DROWNING WON'T MAKE YOUR NOSE HURT AFTER!
WOOHOO!
...
SAKU (CRUNCH)
LISTEN, LISTEN!
HIBARI-CHAN!

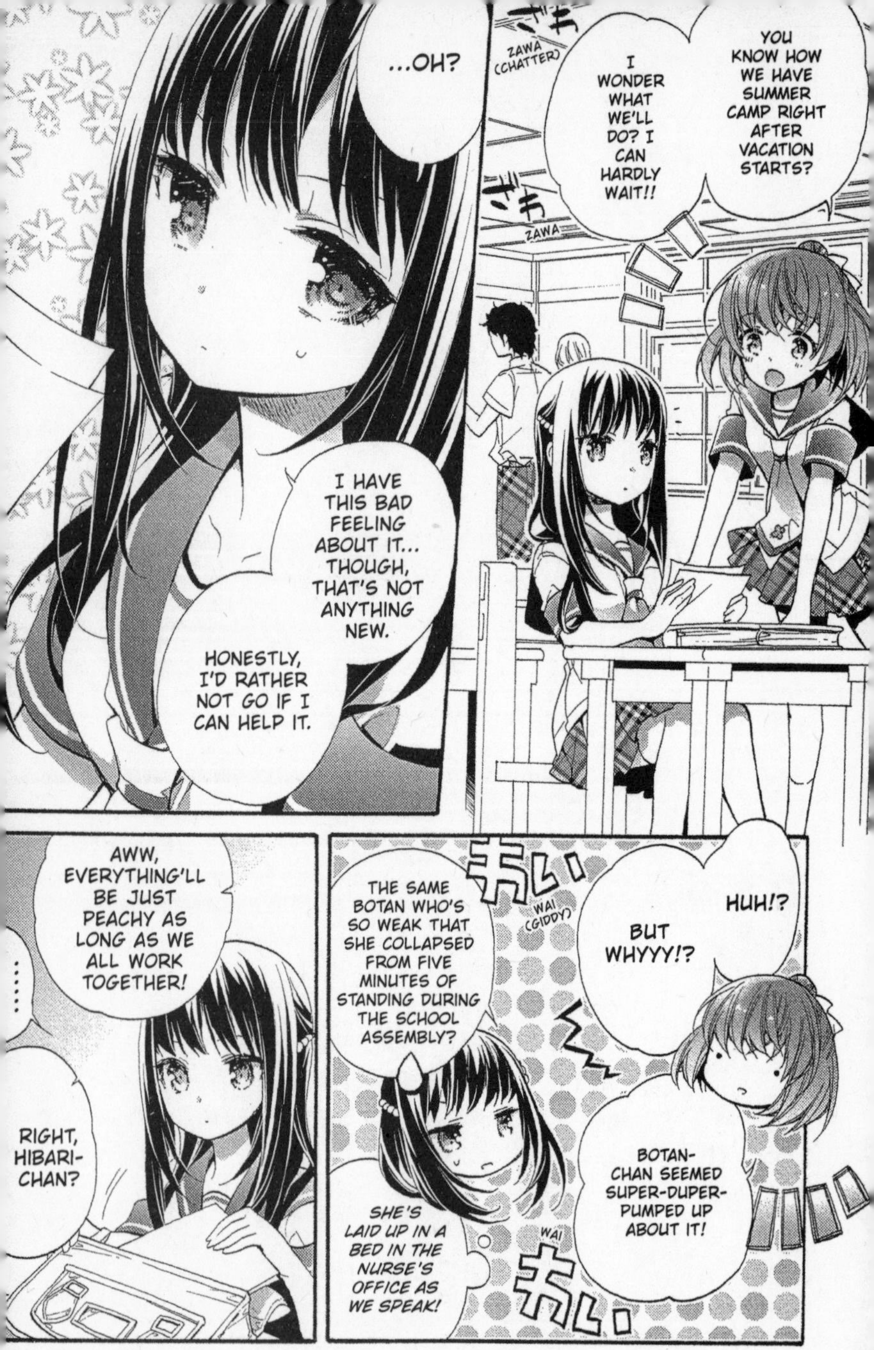
ZAWA (CHATTER)
YOU KNOW HOW WE HAVE SUMMER CAMP RIGHT AFTER VACATION STARTS?
I WONDER WHAT WE'LL DO? I CAN HARDLY WAIT!!
ZAWA
...OH?
I HAVE THIS BAD FEELING ABOUT IT... THOUGH, THAT'S NOT ANYTHING NEW.
HONESTLY, I'D RATHER NOT GO IF I CAN HELP IT.
HUH!?
BUT WHYYY!?
WAI (GIDDY)
THE SAME BOTAN WHO'S SO WEAK THAT SHE COLLAPSED FROM FIVE MINUTES OF STANDING DURING THE SCHOOL ASSEMBLY?
BOTAN-CHAN SEEMED SUPER-DUPER-PUMPED UP ABOUT IT!
WAI
SHE'S LAID UP IN A BED IN THE NURSE'S OFFICE AS WE SPEAK!
AWW, EVERYTHING'LL BE JUST PEACHY AS LONG AS WE ALL WORK TOGETHER!
......
RIGHT, HIBARI-CHAN?

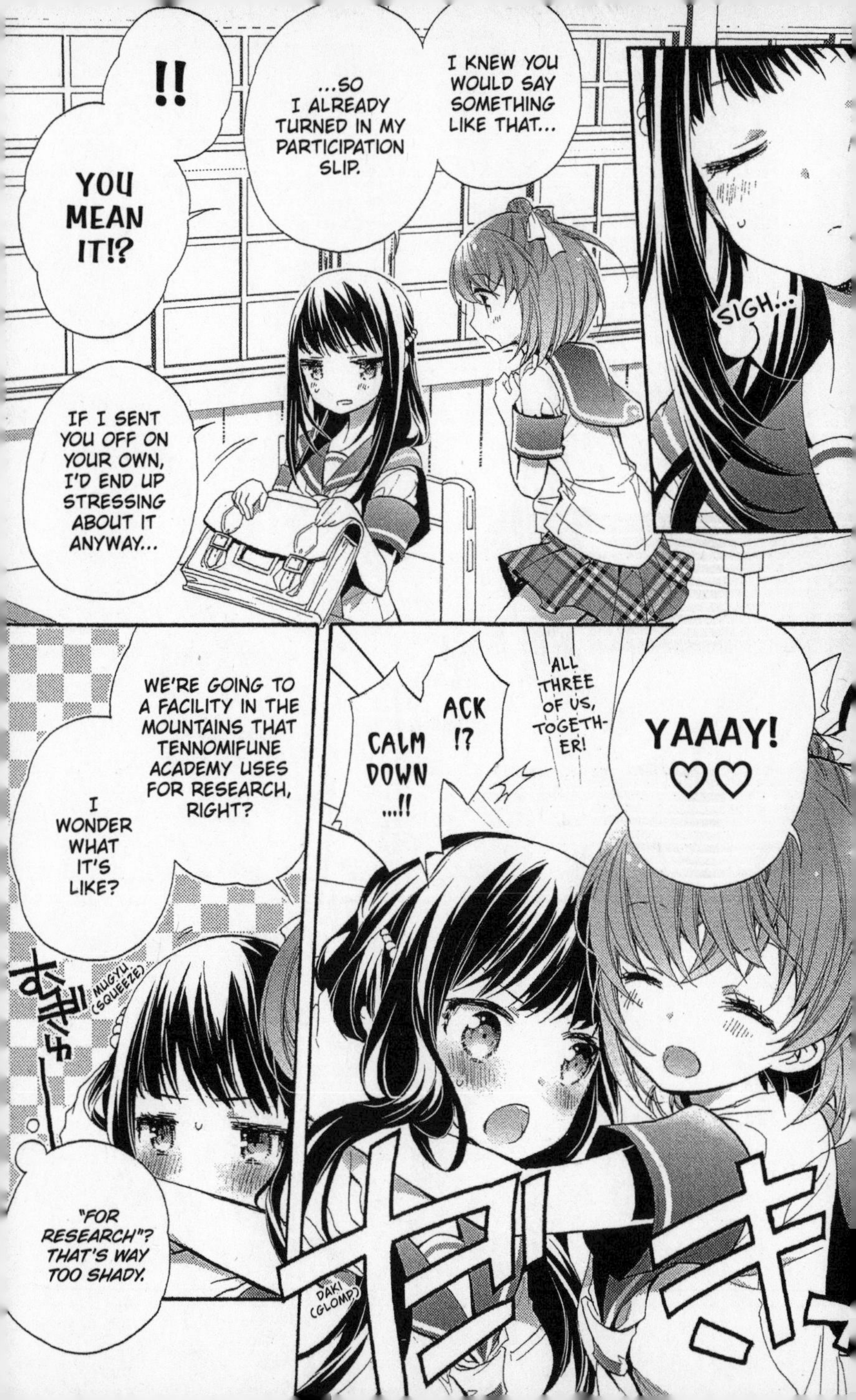
SIGH...
I KNEW YOU WOULD SAY SOMETHING LIKE THAT...
...SO I ALREADY TURNED IN MY PARTICIPATION SLIP.
!!
YOU MEAN IT!?
IF I SENT YOU OFF ON YOUR OWN, I'D END UP STRESSING ABOUT IT ANYWAY...
YAAAY! ♡♡
ALL THREE OF US, TOGETHER!
ACK !?
CALM DOWN ...!!
DAKI (GLOMP)
WE'RE GOING TO A FACILITY IN THE MOUNTAINS THAT TENNOMIFUNE ACADEMY USES FOR RESEARCH, RIGHT?
I WONDER WHAT IT'S LIKE?
MUGYU (SQUEEZE)
"FOR RESEARCH"? THAT'S WAY TOO SHADY.

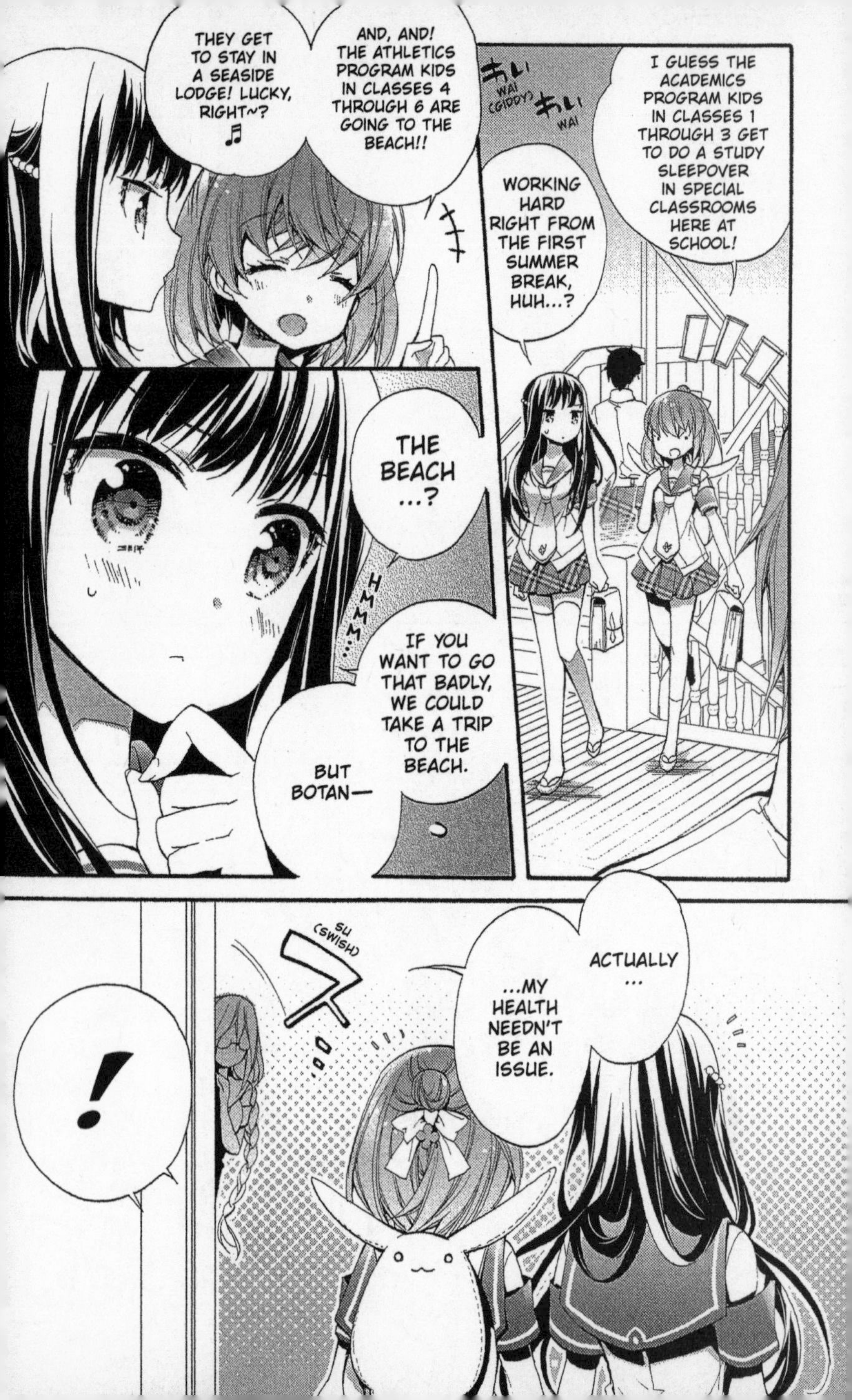
I GUESS THE ACADEMICS PROGRAM KIDS IN CLASSES 1 THROUGH 3 GET TO DO A STUDY SLEEPOVER IN SPECIAL CLASSROOMS HERE AT SCHOOL!
WAI (GIDDY) WAI
WORKING HARD RIGHT FROM THE FIRST SUMMER BREAK, HUH...?
AND, AND! THE ATHLETICS PROGRAM KIDS IN CLASSES 4 THROUGH 6 ARE GOING TO THE BEACH!!
THEY GET TO STAY IN A SEASIDE LODGE! LUCKY, RIGHT~? ♫
THE BEACH ...?
HMMM...
IF YOU WANT TO GO THAT BADLY, WE COULD TAKE A TRIP TO THE BEACH.
BUT BOTAN—
ACTUALLY ...
...MY HEALTH NEEDN'T BE AN ISSUE.
SU (SWISH)
!

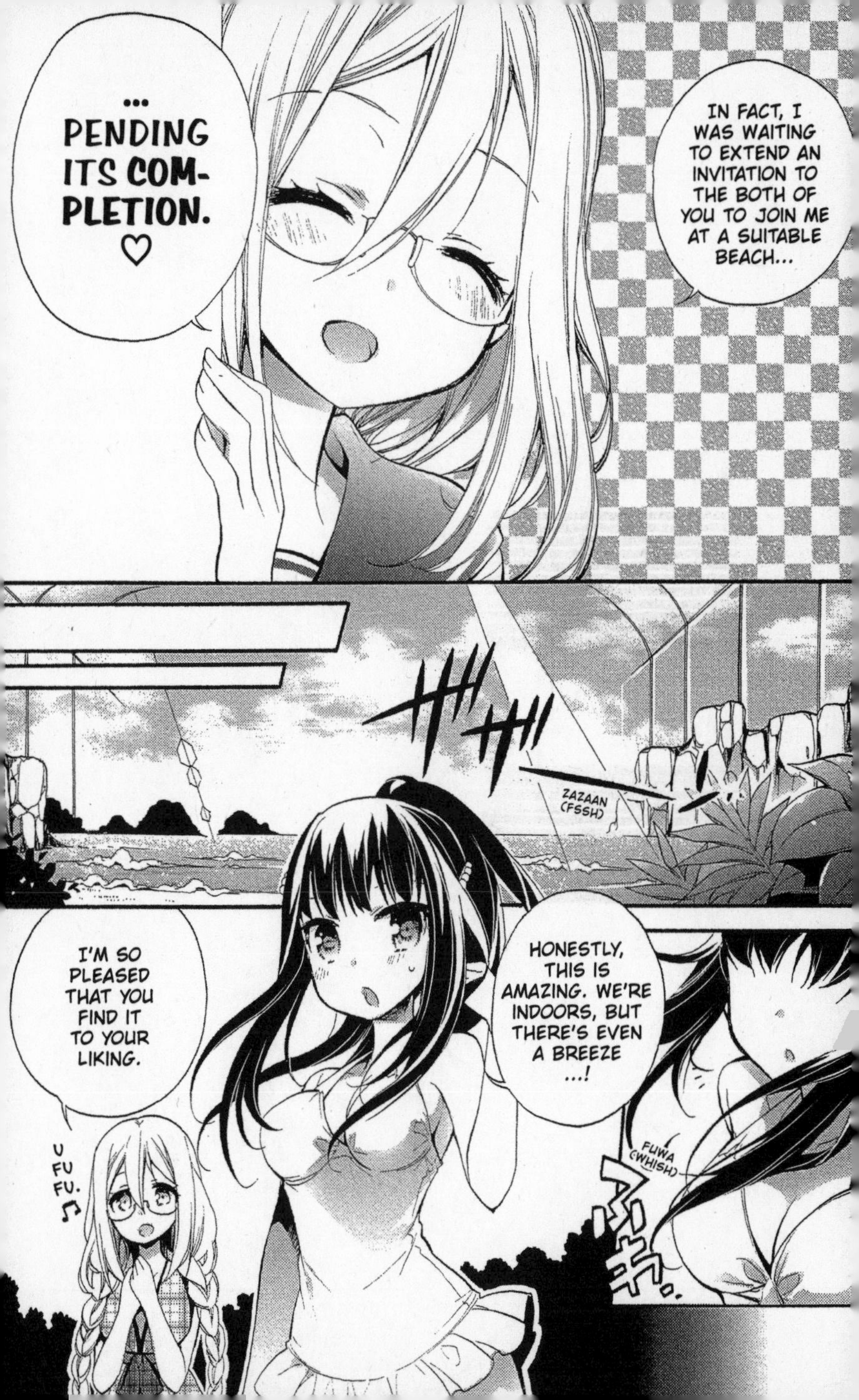
IN FACT, I WAS WAITING TO EXTEND AN INVITATION TO THE BOTH OF YOU TO JOIN ME AT A SUITABLE BEACH...
...PENDING ITS COMPLETION. ♡
ZAZAAN (FSSH)
HONESTLY, THIS IS AMAZING. WE'RE INDOORS, BUT THERE'S EVEN A BREEZE ...!
FUWA (WHISH)
I'M SO PLEASED THAT YOU FIND IT TO YOUR LIKING.
U FU FU. ♪

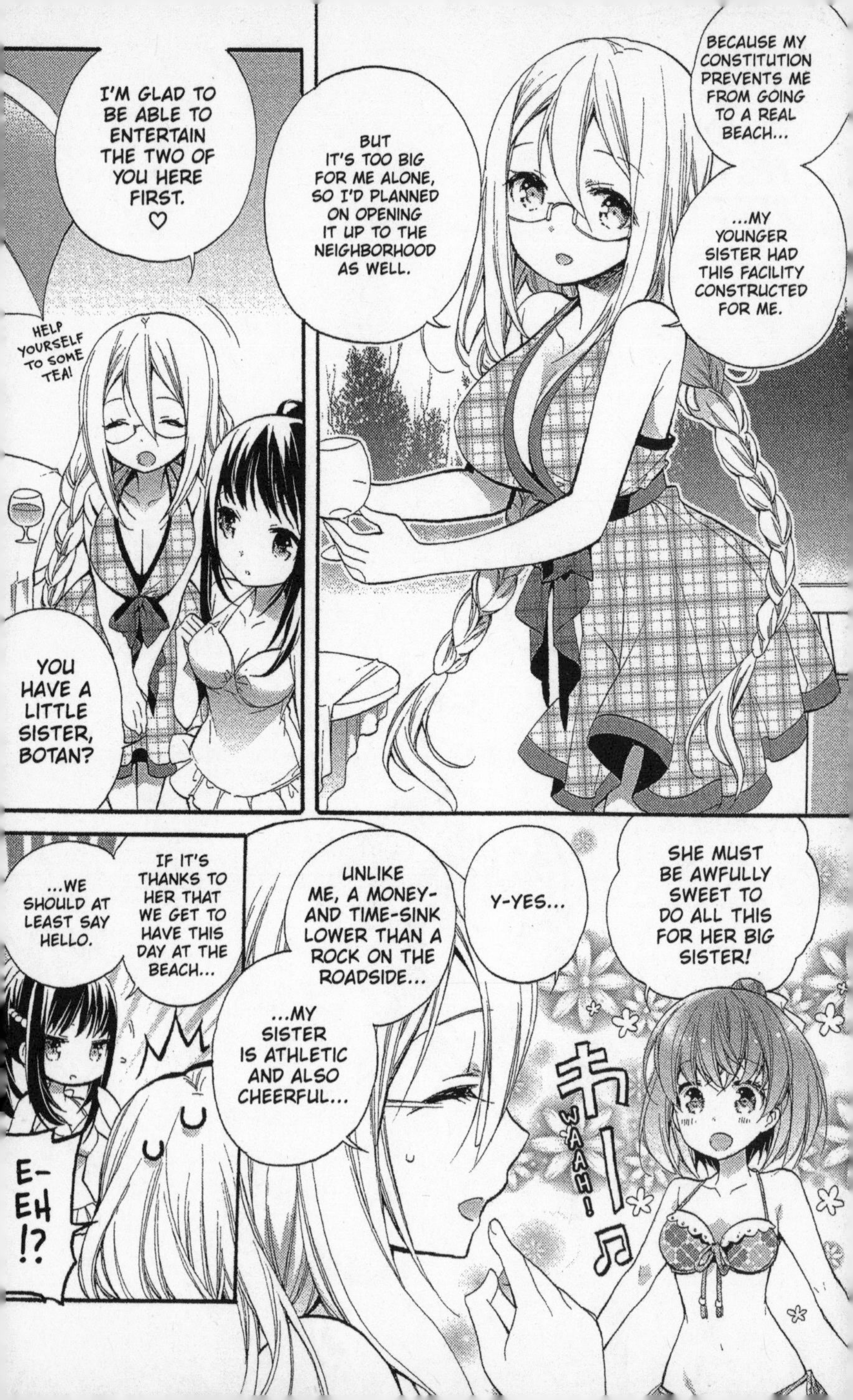
BECAUSE MY CONSTITUTION PREVENTS ME FROM GOING TO A REAL BEACH...
...MY YOUNGER SISTER HAD THIS FACILITY CONSTRUCTED FOR ME.
BUT IT'S TOO BIG FOR ME ALONE, SO I'D PLANNED ON OPENING IT UP TO THE NEIGHBORHOOD AS WELL.
I'M GLAD TO BE ABLE TO ENTERTAIN THE TWO OF YOU HERE FIRST. ♡
HELP YOURSELF TO SOME TEA!
YOU HAVE A LITTLE SISTER, BOTAN?
SHE MUST BE AWFULLY SWEET TO DO ALL THIS FOR HER BIG SISTER!
WAAAH! ♫
Y-YES...
UNLIKE ME, A MONEY- AND TIME-SINK LOWER THAN A ROCK ON THE ROADSIDE...
...MY SISTER IS ATHLETIC AND ALSO CHEERFUL...
IF IT'S THANKS TO HER THAT WE GET TO HAVE THIS DAY AT THE BEACH...
...WE SHOULD AT LEAST SAY HELLO.
E-EH!?

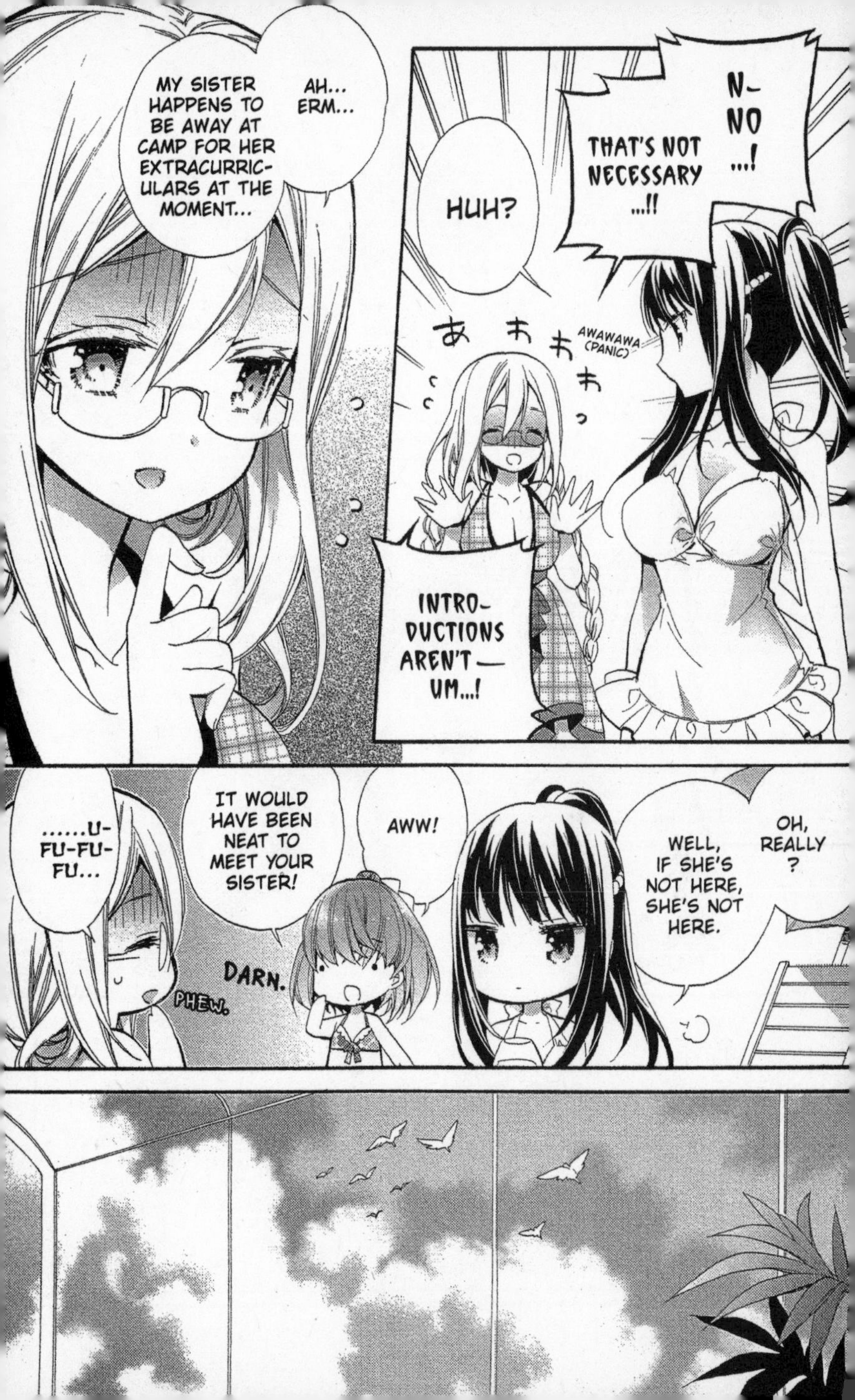
N-NO ...!
THAT'S NOT NECESSARY ...!!
HUH?
あわわわ
AWAWAWA (PANIC)
INTRO-DUCTIONS AREN'T— UM...!
AH... ERM...
MY SISTER HAPPENS TO BE AWAY AT CAMP FOR HER EXTRACURRIC-ULARS AT THE MOMENT...
OH, REALLY ?
WELL, IF SHE'S NOT HERE, SHE'S NOT HERE.
AWW!
IT WOULD HAVE BEEN NEAT TO MEET YOUR SISTER!
DARN.
......U-FU-FU-FU...
PHEW.

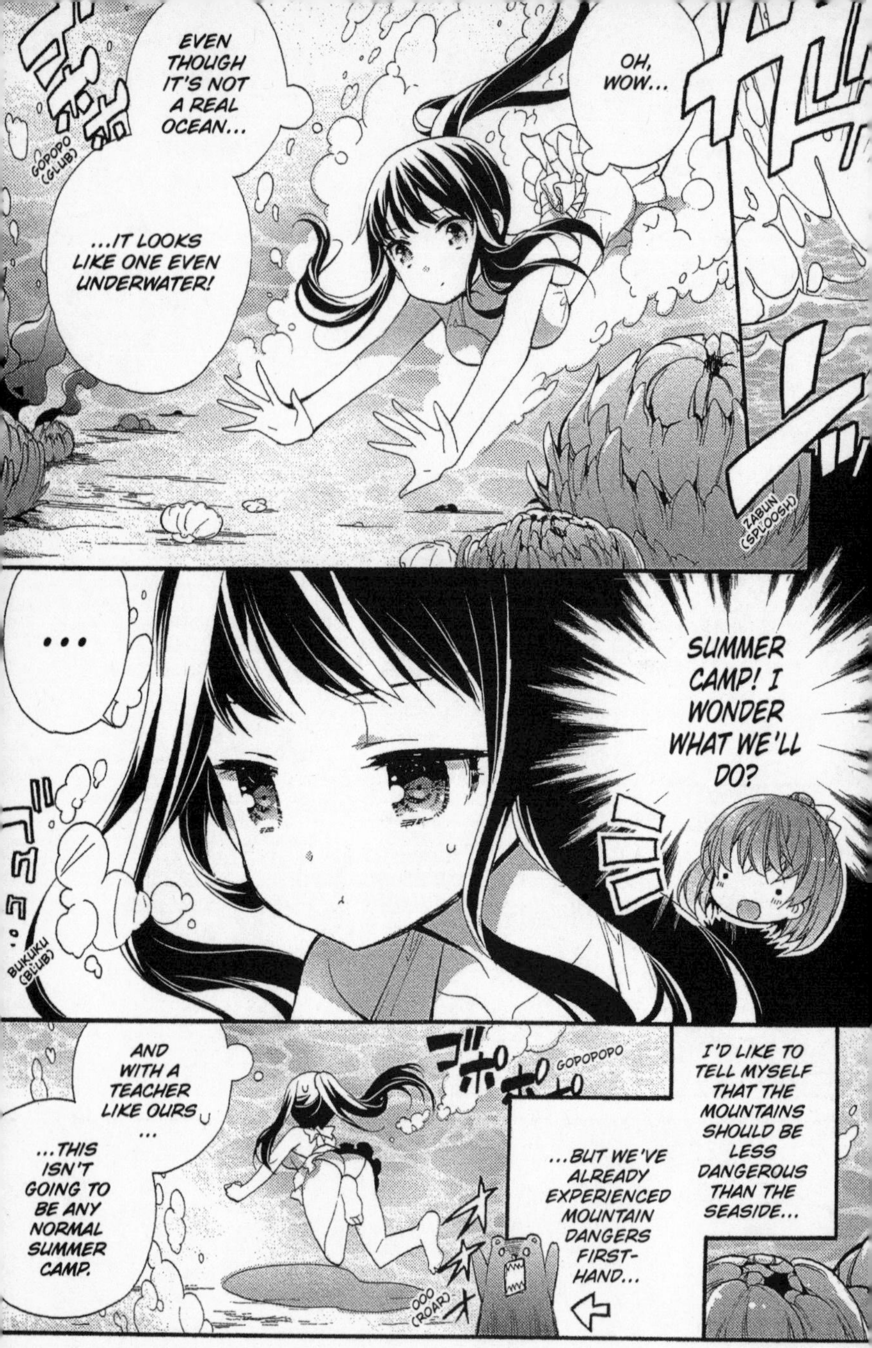
OH, WOW...
EVEN THOUGH IT'S NOT A REAL OCEAN...
GOPOPO (GLUB)
...IT LOOKS LIKE ONE EVEN UNDERWATER!
ZABLIN (SPLOOSH)
SUMMER CAMP! I WONDER WHAT WE'LL DO?
...
BUKUKU (BLUB)
I'D LIKE TO TELL MYSELF THAT THE MOUNTAINS SHOULD BE LESS DANGEROUS THAN THE SEASIDE...
...BUT WE'VE ALREADY EXPERIENCED MOUNTAIN DANGERS FIRST-HAND...
OOO (ROAR)
GOPOPOPO
AND WITH A TEACHER LIKE OURS...
...THIS ISN'T GOING TO BE ANY NORMAL SUMMER CAMP.

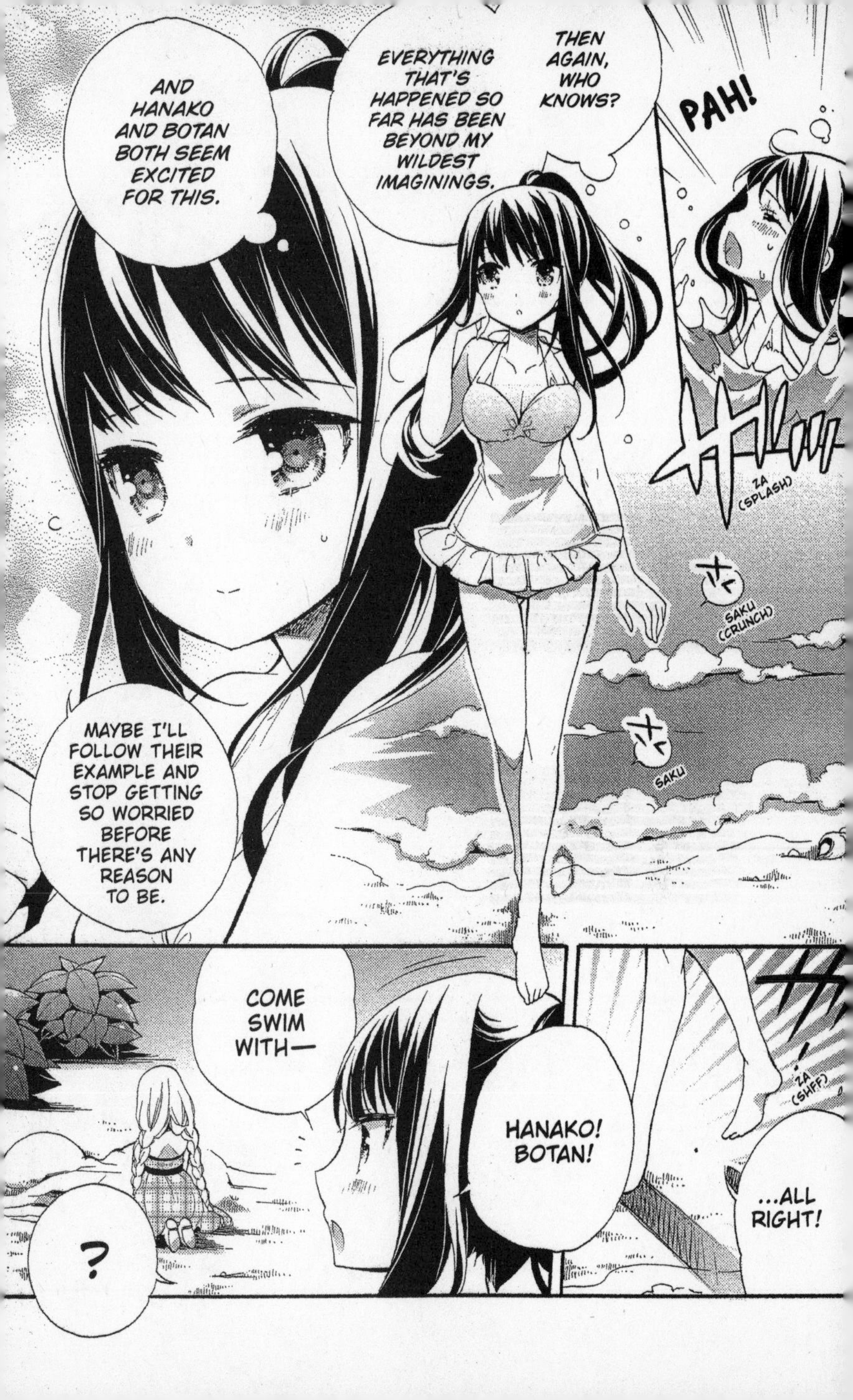

PAH!
ZA (SPLASH)
EVERYTHING THAT'S HAPPENED SO FAR HAS BEEN BEYOND MY WILDEST IMAGININGS.
THEN AGAIN, WHO KNOWS?
SAKU (CRUNCH)
SAKU
AND HANAKO AND BOTAN BOTH SEEM EXCITED FOR THIS.
MAYBE I'LL FOLLOW THEIR EXAMPLE AND STOP GETTING SO WORRIED BEFORE THERE'S ANY REASON TO BE.
ZA (SHFF)
...ALL RIGHT!
HANAKO! BOTAN!
COME SWIM WITH—
?

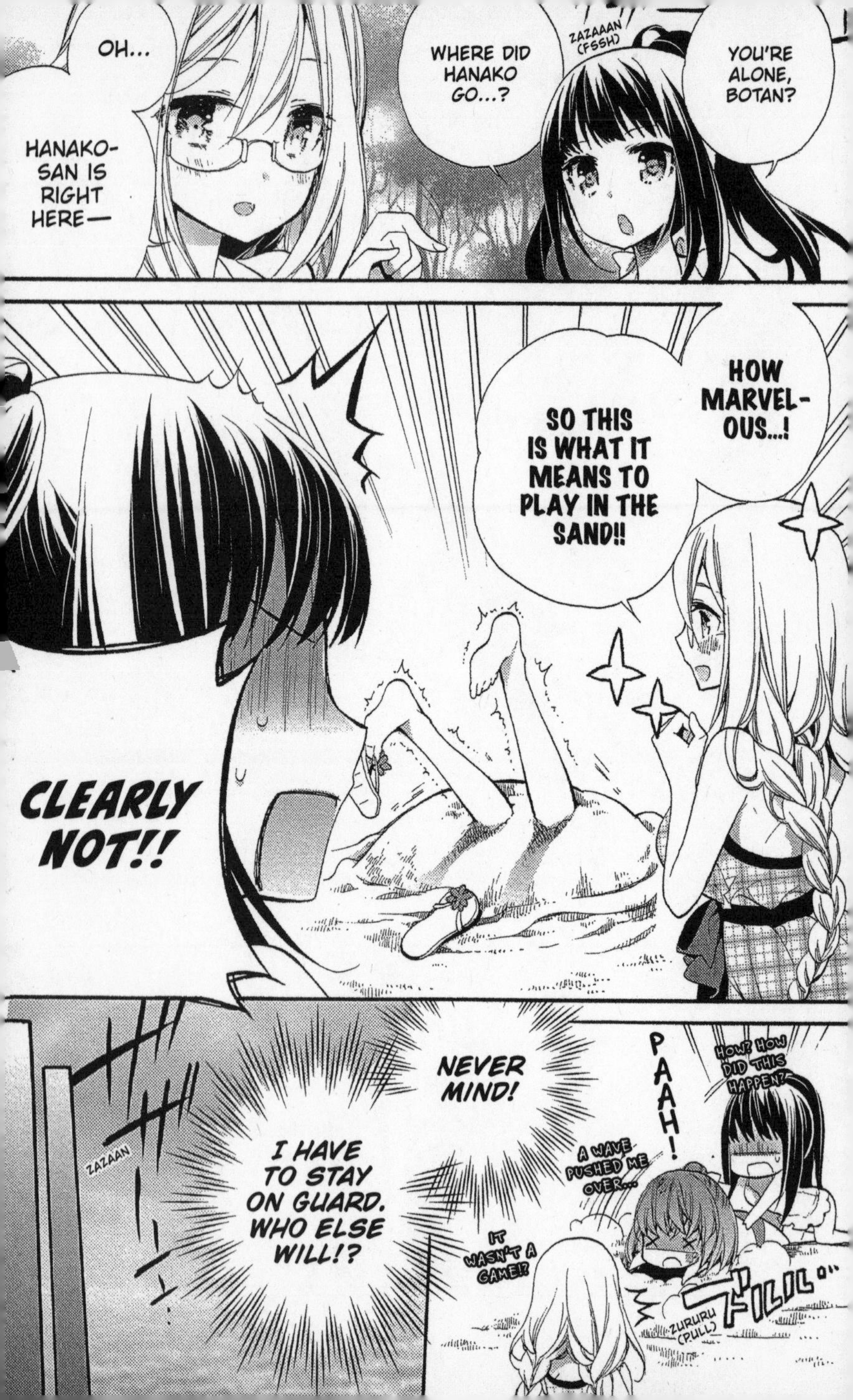
YOU'RE ALONE, BOTAN?
ZAZAAAN (FSSH)
WHERE DID HANAKO GO...?
OH...
HANAKO-SAN IS RIGHT HERE—
HOW MARVELOUS...!
SO THIS IS WHAT IT MEANS TO PLAY IN THE SAND!!
CLEARLY NOT!!
HOW? HOW DID THIS HAPPEN?
PAAH!
A WAVE PUSHED ME OVER...
IT WASN'T A GAME!?
ZURURU (PULL)
NEVER MIND!
I HAVE TO STAY ON GUARD. WHO ELSE WILL!?
ZAZAAN

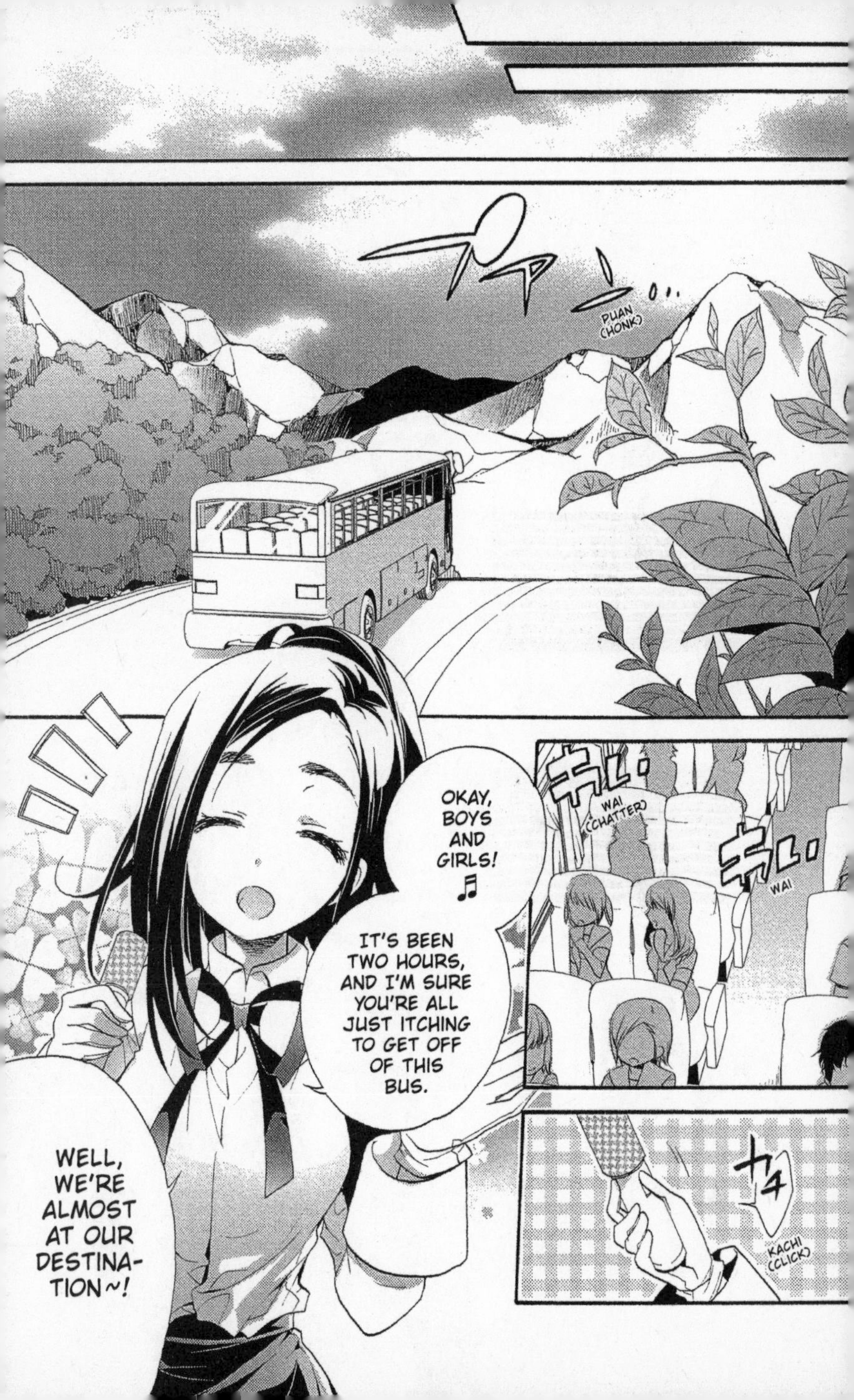
PUAN (HONK)
WAI (CHATTER)
WAI
KACHI (CLICK)
OKAY, BOYS AND GIRLS! ♬
IT'S BEEN TWO HOURS, AND I'M SURE YOU'RE ALL JUST ITCHING TO GET OFF OF THIS BUS.
WELL, WE'RE ALMOST AT OUR DESTINA-TION~!

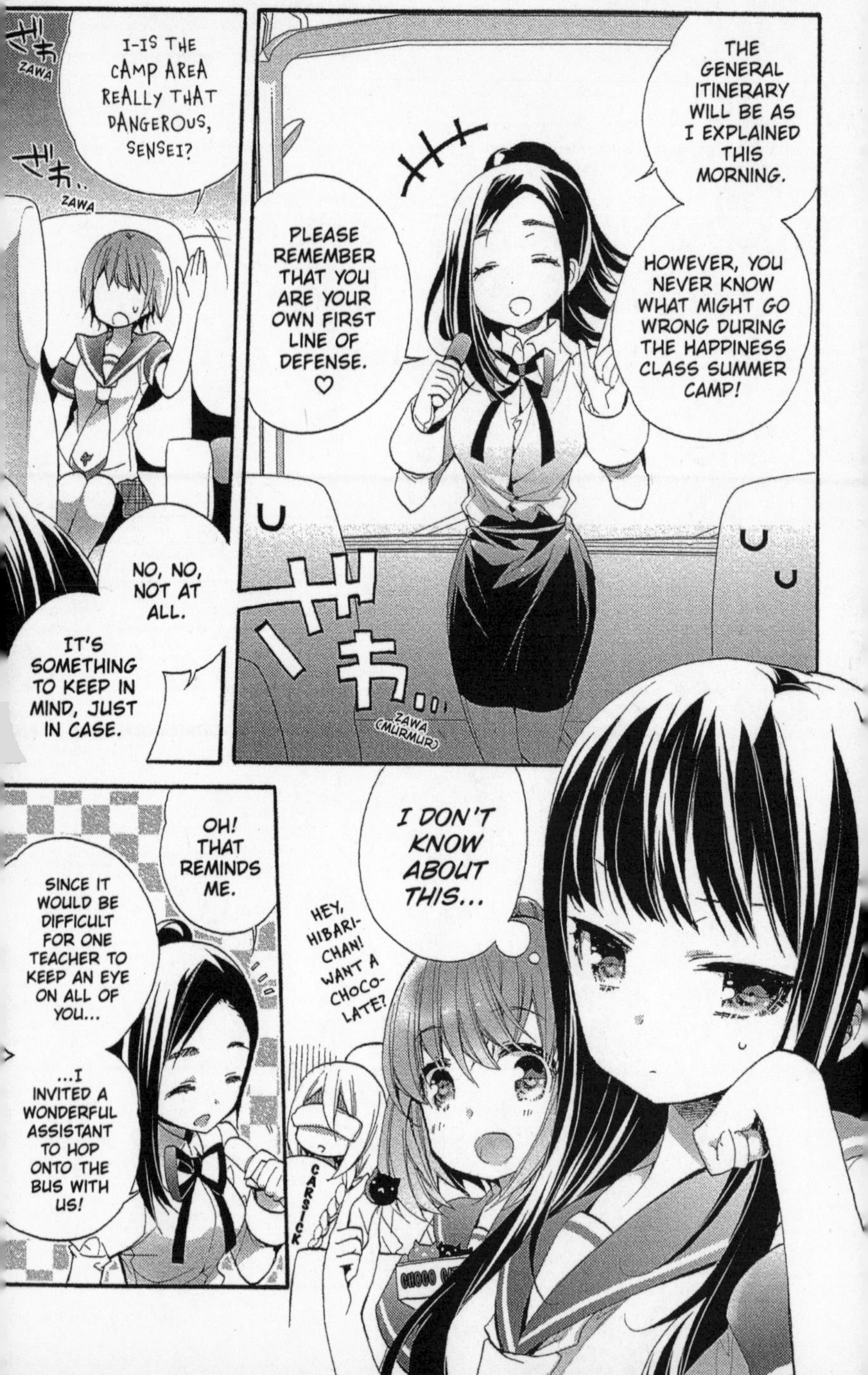
THE GENERAL ITINERARY WILL BE AS I EXPLAINED THIS MORNING.
HOWEVER, YOU NEVER KNOW WHAT MIGHT GO WRONG DURING THE HAPPINESS CLASS SUMMER CAMP!
PLEASE REMEMBER THAT YOU ARE YOUR OWN FIRST LINE OF DEFENSE. ♡
ZAWA (MURMUR)
ZAWA
I-IS THE CAMP AREA REALLY THAT DANGEROUS, SENSEI?
ZAWA
NO, NO, NOT AT ALL.
IT'S SOMETHING TO KEEP IN MIND, JUST IN CASE.
I DON'T KNOW ABOUT THIS...
HEY, HIBARI-CHAN! WANT A CHOCOLATE?
CARSICK
OH! THAT REMINDS ME.
SINCE IT WOULD BE DIFFICULT FOR ONE TEACHER TO KEEP AN EYE ON ALL OF YOU...
...I INVITED A WONDERFUL ASSISTANT TO HOP ONTO THE BUS WITH US!

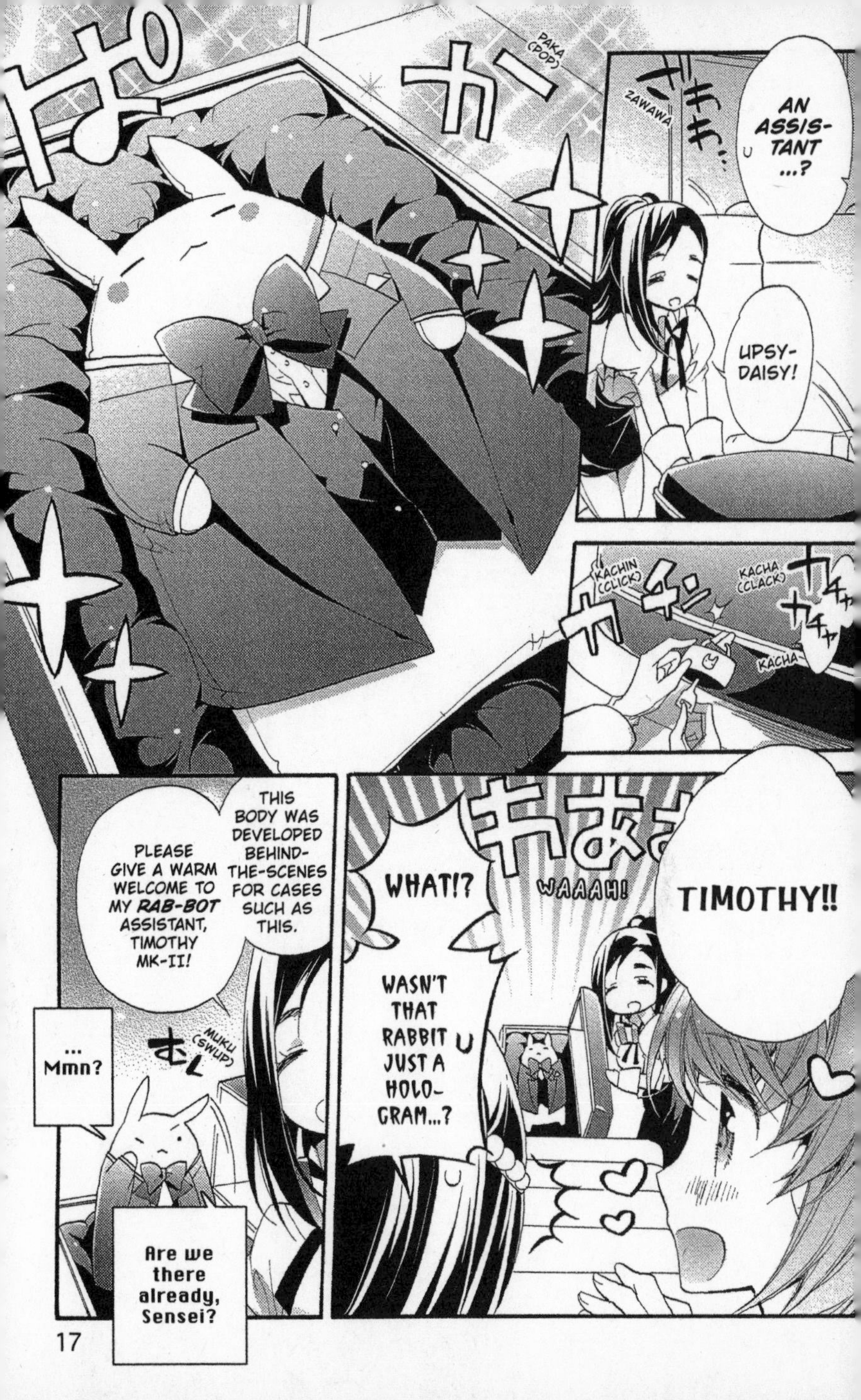
AN ASSISTANT...?
ZAWAWA
UPSY-DAISY!
KACHA (CLACK)
KACHIN (CLICK)
KACHA
PAKA (POP)
TIMOTHY!!
WAAAH!
WHAT!?
WASN'T THAT RABBIT JUST A HOLOGRAM...?
THIS BODY WAS DEVELOPED BEHIND-THE-SCENES FOR CASES SUCH AS THIS.
PLEASE GIVE A WARM WELCOME TO MY RAB-BOT ASSISTANT, TIMOTHY MK-II!
MUKU (SWUP)
... Mmn?
Are we there already, Sensei?

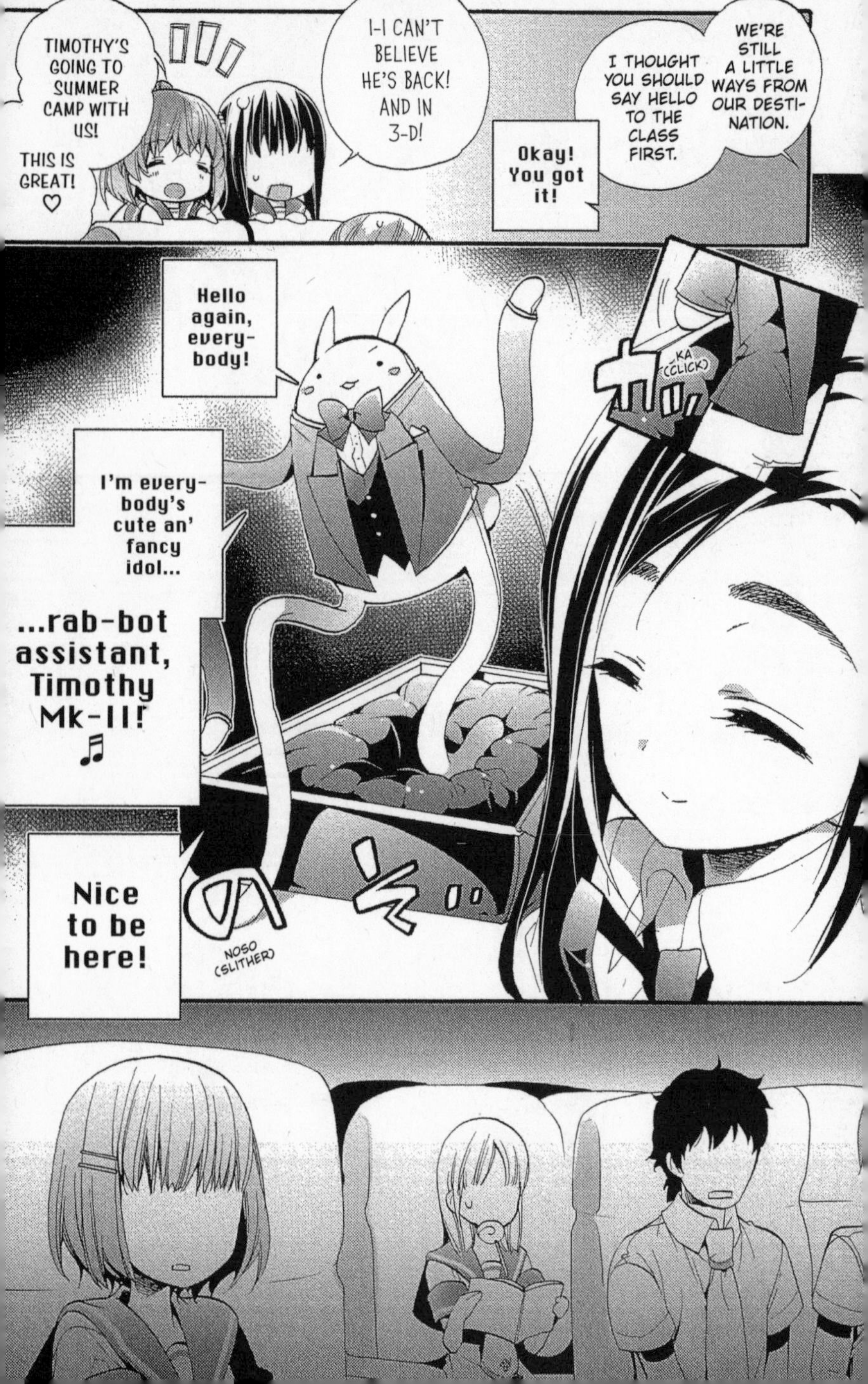
WE'RE STILL A LITTLE WAYS FROM OUR DESTI-NATION.
I THOUGHT YOU SHOULD SAY HELLO TO THE CLASS FIRST.
Okay! You got it!
I-I CAN'T BELIEVE HE'S BACK! AND IN 3-D!
TIMOTHY'S GOING TO SUMMER CAMP WITH US!
THIS IS GREAT! ♡
KA (CLICK)
Hello again, every-body!
I'm every-body's cute an' fancy idol...
...rab-bot assistant, Timothy Mk-II! ♫
NOSO (SLITHER)
Nice to be here!

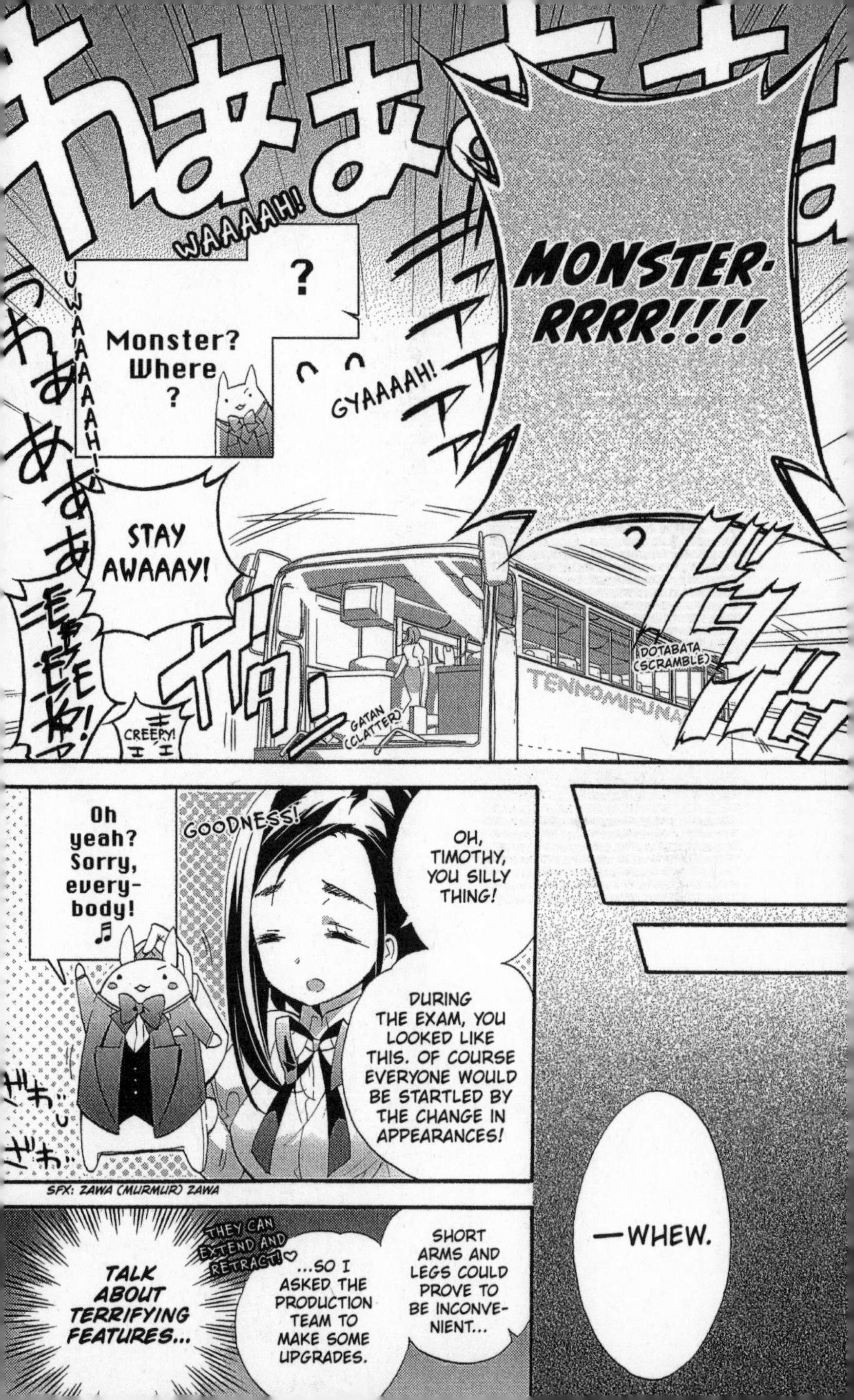
MONSTER-RRRR!!!!
GYAAAAH!
?
WAAAAAH!
Monster? Where ?
UWAAAAAAH!
STAY AWAAAY!
DOTABATA (SCRAMBLE)
TENNOMIFUNA
GATAN (CLATTER)
CREEPY!
—WHEW.
OH, TIMOTHY, YOU SILLY THING!
GOODNESS!
DURING THE EXAM, YOU LOOKED LIKE THIS. OF COURSE EVERYONE WOULD BE STARTLED BY THE CHANGE IN APPEARANCES!
Oh yeah? Sorry, every-body! ♫
SFX: ZAWA (MURMUR) ZAWA
SHORT ARMS AND LEGS COULD PROVE TO BE INCONVE-NIENT...
...SO I ASKED THE PRODUCTION TEAM TO MAKE SOME UPGRADES.
THEY CAN EXTEND AND RETRACT!♡
TALK ABOUT TERRIFYING FEATURES...

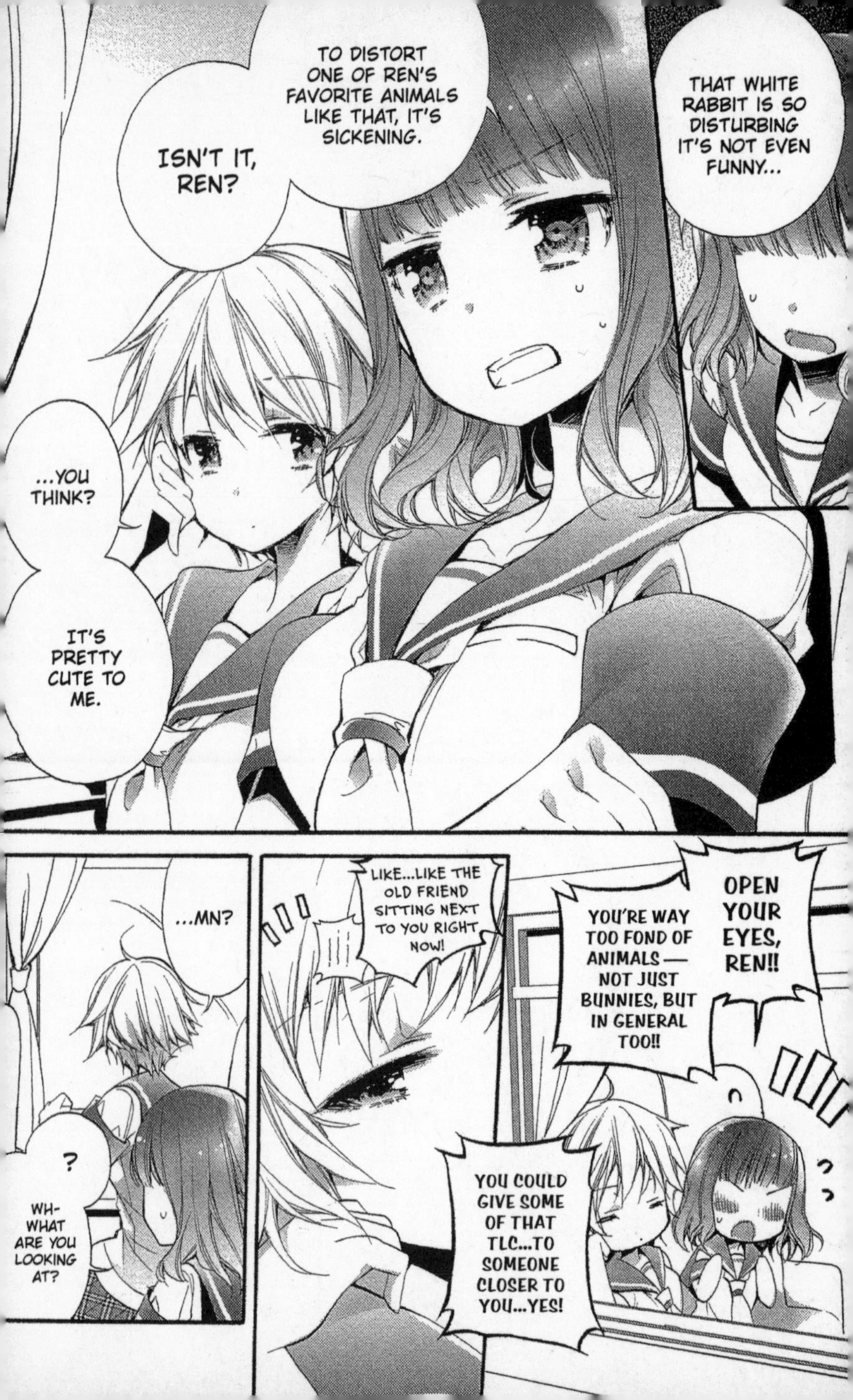
THAT WHITE RABBIT IS SO DISTURBING IT'S NOT EVEN FUNNY...
TO DISTORT ONE OF REN'S FAVORITE ANIMALS LIKE THAT, IT'S SICKENING.
ISN'T IT, REN?
...YOU THINK?
IT'S PRETTY CUTE TO ME.
OPEN YOUR EYES, REN!!
YOU'RE WAY TOO FOND OF ANIMALS—NOT JUST BUNNIES, BUT IN GENERAL TOO!!
YOU COULD GIVE SOME OF THAT TLC...TO SOMEONE CLOSER TO YOU...YES!
LIKE...LIKE THE OLD FRIEND SITTING NEXT TO YOU RIGHT NOW!
...MN?
?
WH-WHAT ARE YOU LOOKING AT?

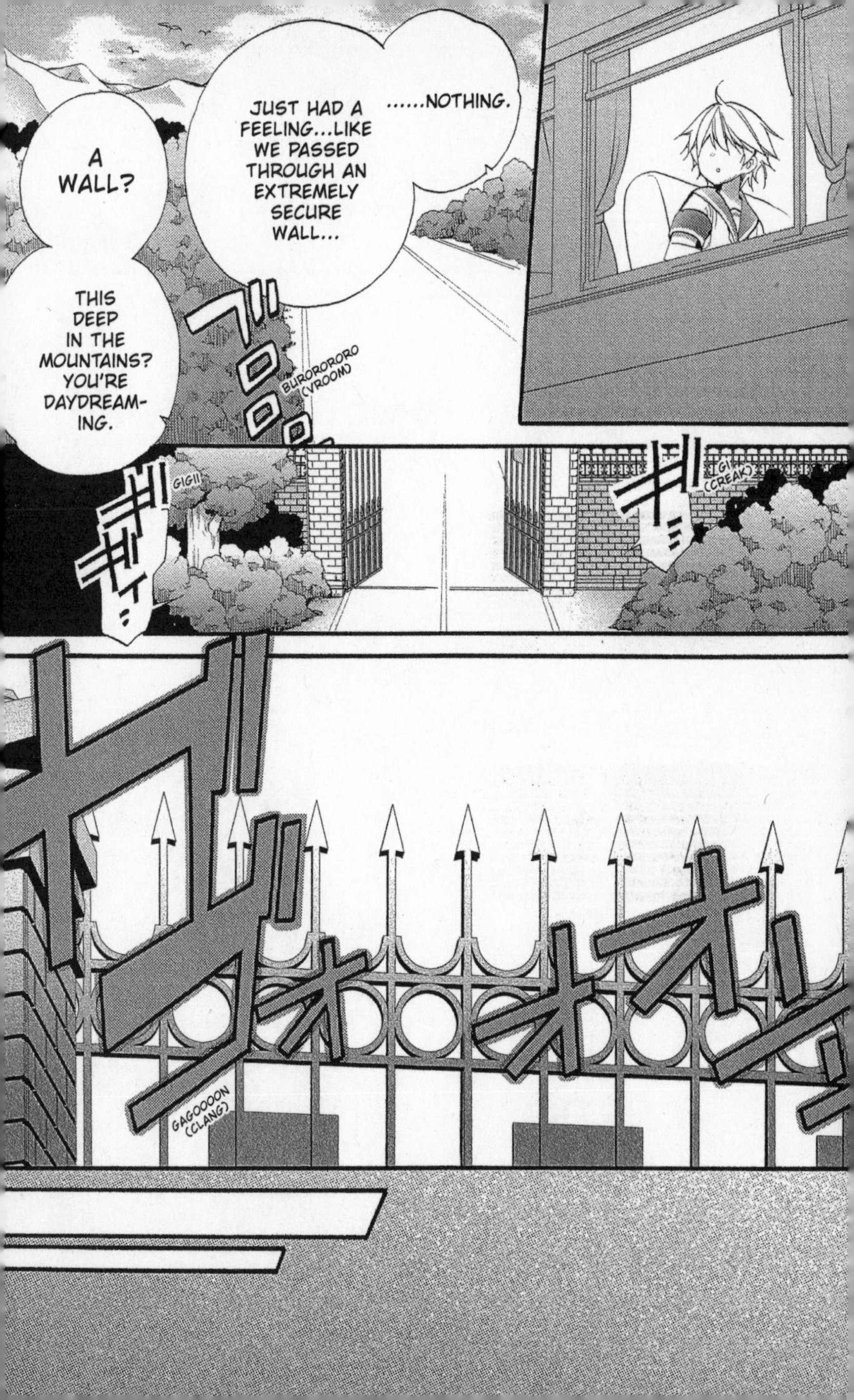

......NOTHING.
JUST HAD A FEELING...LIKE WE PASSED THROUGH AN EXTREMELY SECURE WALL...
A WALL?
BURORORORO (VROOM)
THIS DEEP IN THE MOUNTAINS? YOU'RE DAYDREAM-ING.
GI (CREAK)
GIGII
GAGOOOON (CLANG)

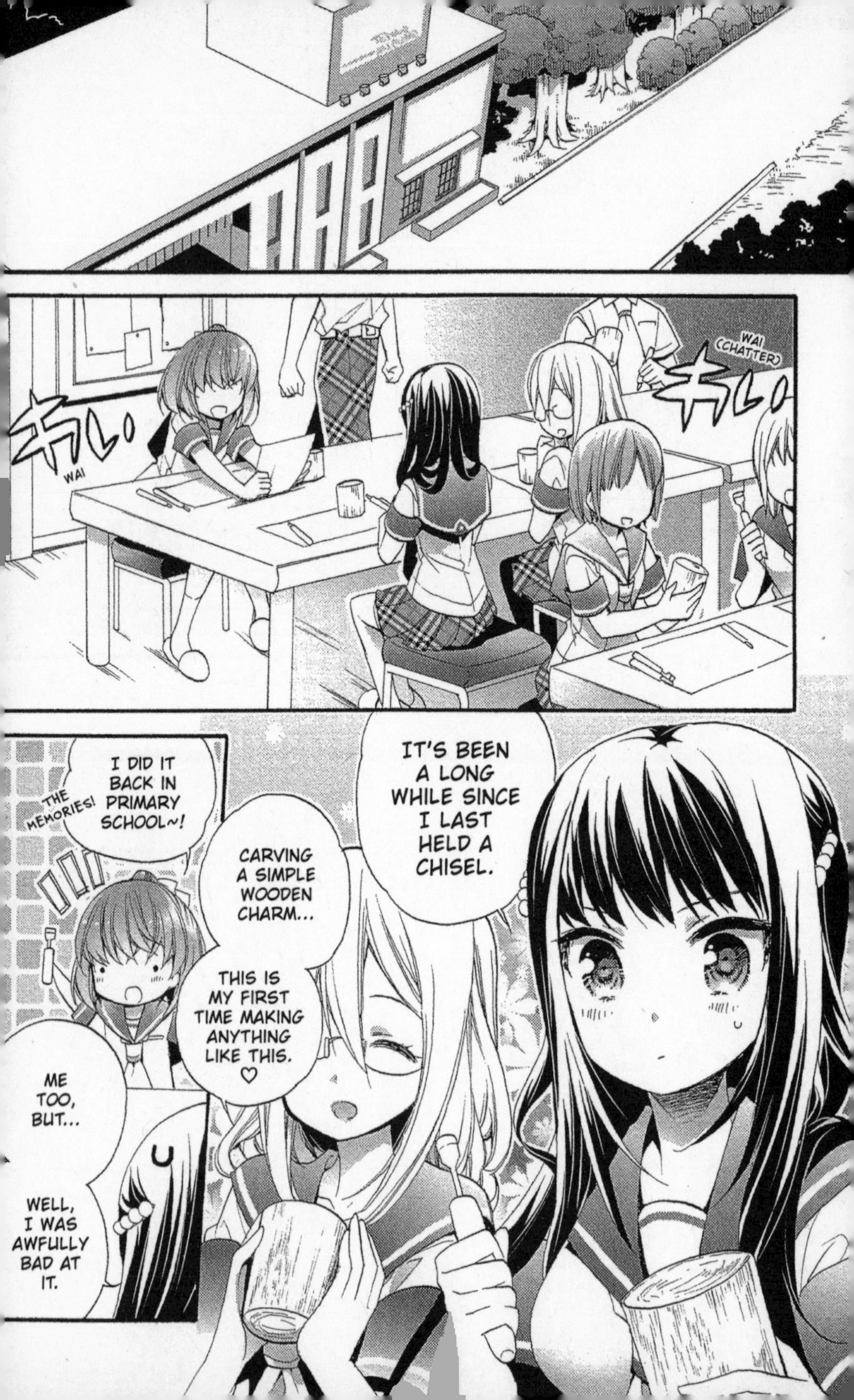
WAI (CHATTER)
WAI
IT'S BEEN A LONG WHILE SINCE I LAST HELD A CHISEL.
CARVING A SIMPLE WOODEN CHARM...
THIS IS MY FIRST TIME MAKING ANYTHING LIKE THIS. ♡
I DID IT BACK IN PRIMARY SCHOOL~!
THE MEMORIES!
ME TOO, BUT...
WELL, I WAS AWFULLY BAD AT IT.

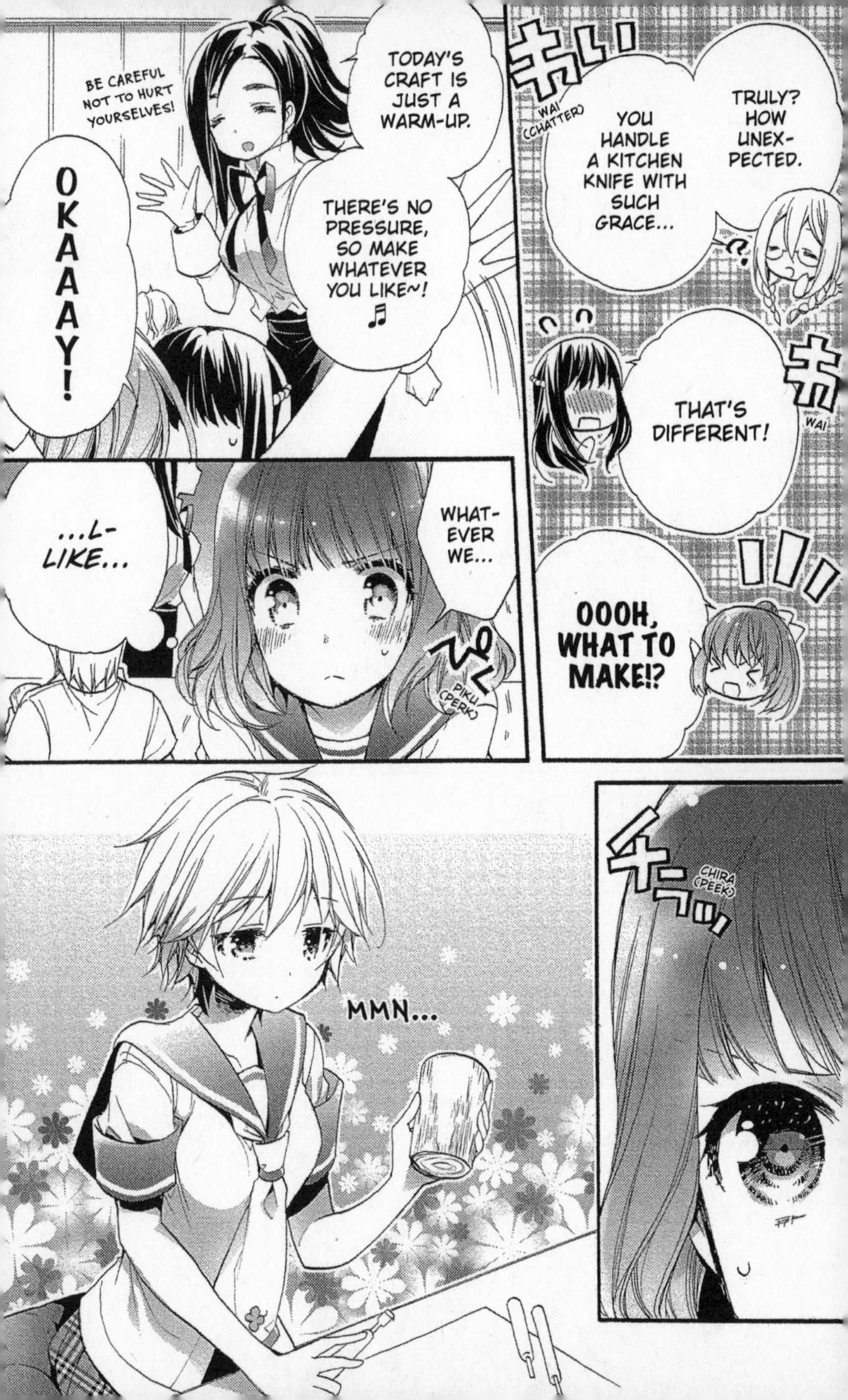
WAI (CHATTER)
TRULY? HOW UNEXPECTED.
YOU HANDLE A KITCHEN KNIFE WITH SUCH GRACE...
WAI
THAT'S DIFFERENT!
OOOH, WHAT TO MAKE!?
TODAY'S CRAFT IS JUST A WARM-UP.
THERE'S NO PRESSURE, SO MAKE WHATEVER YOU LIKE~! ♬
BE CAREFUL NOT TO HURT YOURSELVES!
OKAAAAY!
WHATEVER WE...
PIKU (PERK)
...L-LIKE...
CHIRA (PEEK)
MMN...

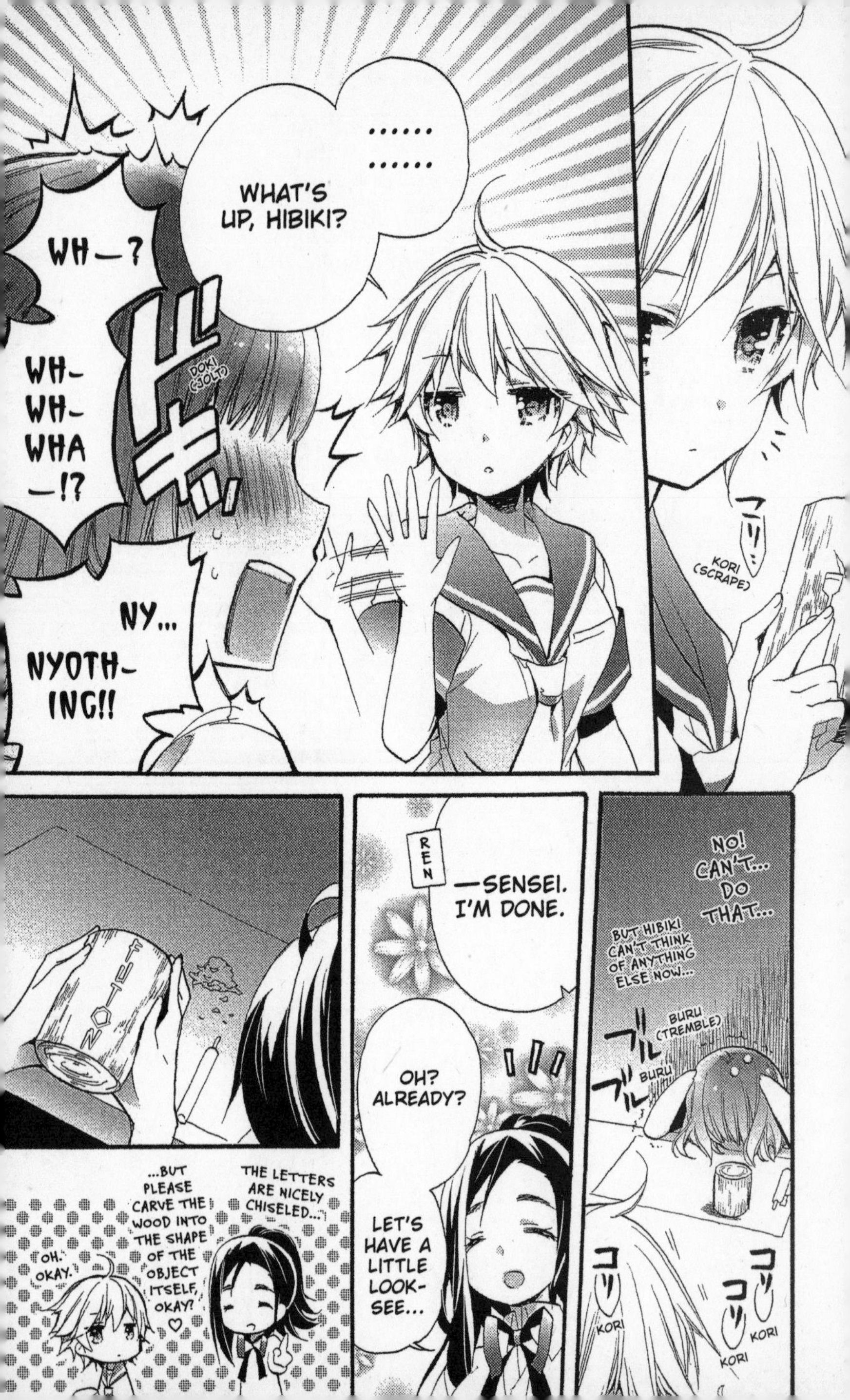
KORI (SCRAPE)
......
......
WHAT'S UP, HIBIKI?
WH—?
DOKI (JOLT)
WH-WH-WHA—!?
NY...
NYOTHING!!
NO! CAN'T... DO THAT...
BUT HIBIKI CAN'T THINK OF ANYTHING ELSE NOW...
BURU (TREMBLE)
BURU
KORI
KORI
KORI
REN
—SENSEI. I'M DONE.
OH? ALREADY?
LET'S HAVE A LITTLE LOOK-SEE...
FUTON
THE LETTERS ARE NICELY CHISELED...
...BUT PLEASE CARVE THE WOOD INTO THE SHAPE OF THE OBJECT ITSELF, OKAY? ♡
OH. OKAY.

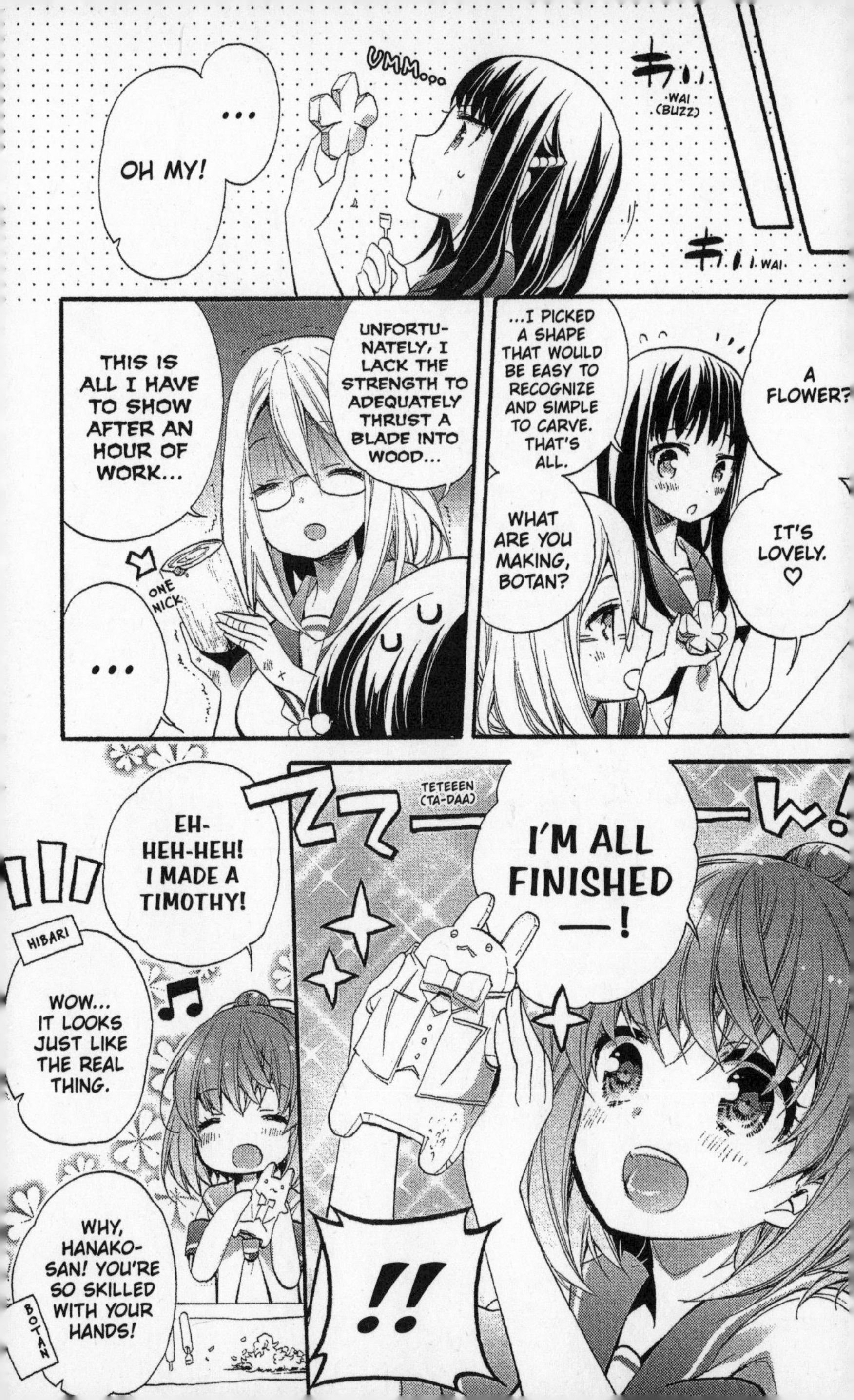
·WAI· (BUZZ)
UMM...
·WAI·
... OH MY!
A FLOWER?
IT'S LOVELY. ♡
...I PICKED A SHAPE THAT WOULD BE EASY TO RECOGNIZE AND SIMPLE TO CARVE. THAT'S ALL.
WHAT ARE YOU MAKING, BOTAN?
UNFORTUNATELY, I LACK THE STRENGTH TO ADEQUATELY THRUST A BLADE INTO WOOD...
THIS IS ALL I HAVE TO SHOW AFTER AN HOUR OF WORK...
ONE NICK
...
TETEEEN (TA-DAA)
I'M ALL FINISHED —!
!!
EH-HEH-HEH! I MADE A TIMOTHY!
HIBARI
WOW... IT LOOKS JUST LIKE THE REAL THING.
WHY, HANAKO-SAN! YOU'RE SO SKILLED WITH YOUR HANDS!
BOTAN

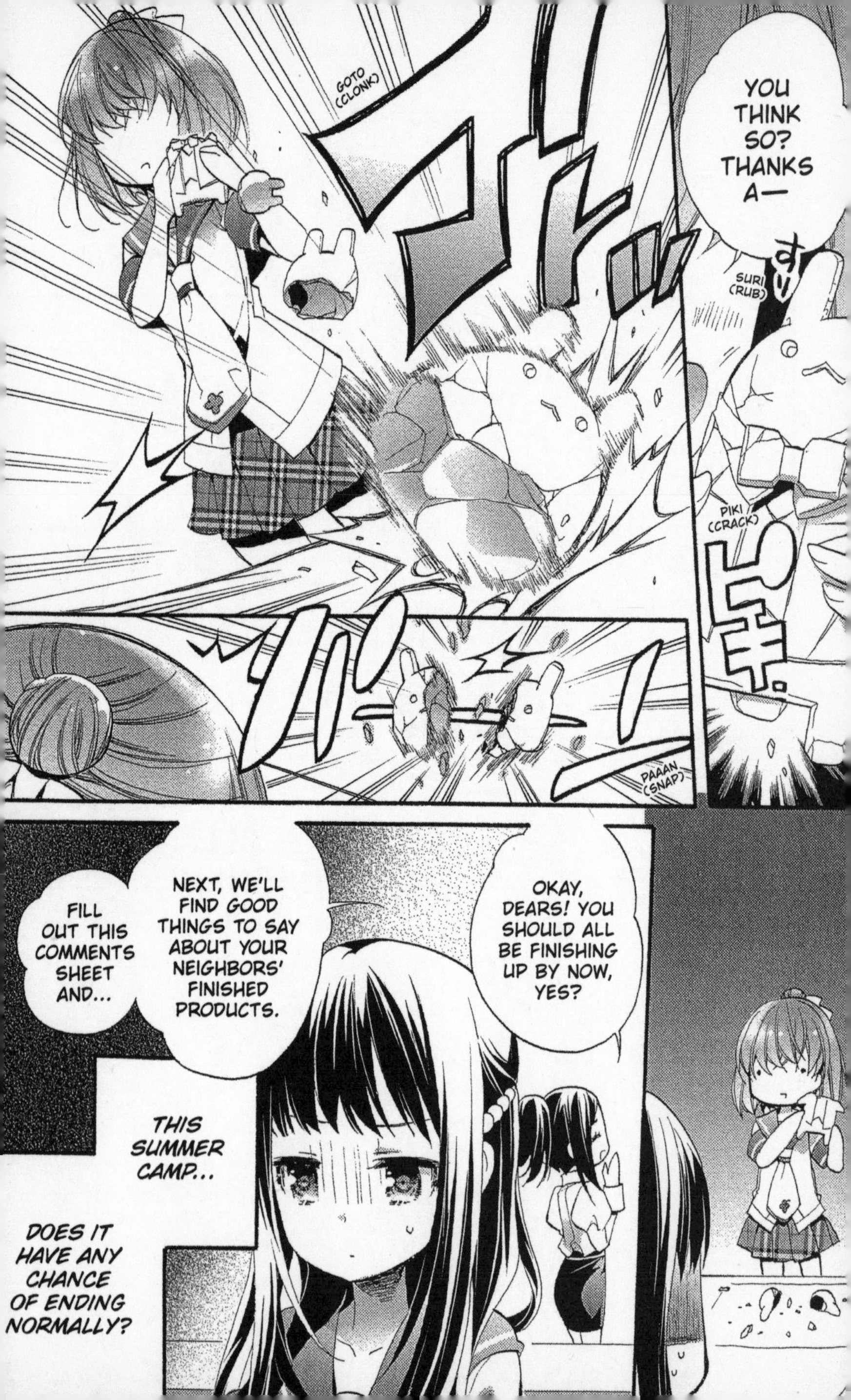
YOU THINK SO? THANKS A—
SURI (RUB)
PIKI (CRACK)
GOTO (CLONK)
PAAAN (SNAP)
OKAY, DEARS! YOU SHOULD ALL BE FINISHING UP BY NOW, YES?
NEXT, WE'LL FIND GOOD THINGS TO SAY ABOUT YOUR NEIGHBORS' FINISHED PRODUCTS.
FILL OUT THIS COMMENTS SHEET AND...
THIS SUMMER CAMP...
DOES IT HAVE ANY CHANCE OF ENDING NORMALLY?

Anne Happy♪

unhappy go lucky!

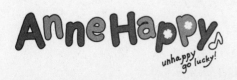

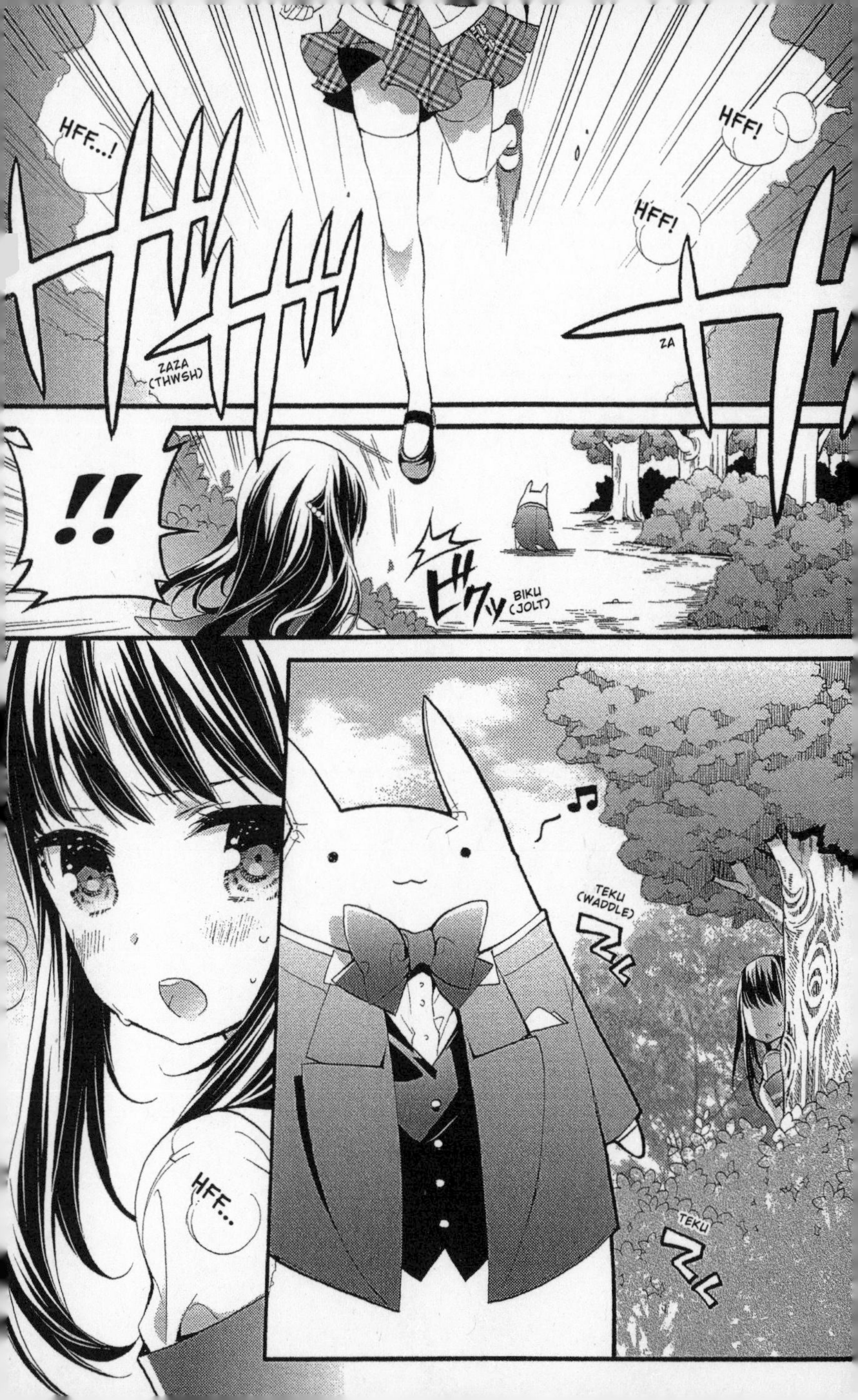
HFF!
HFF!
HFF...!
ZA
ZAZA (THWSH)
ビクッ
BIKU (JOLT)
!!
♪
TEKU (WADDLE)
TEKU
HFF...

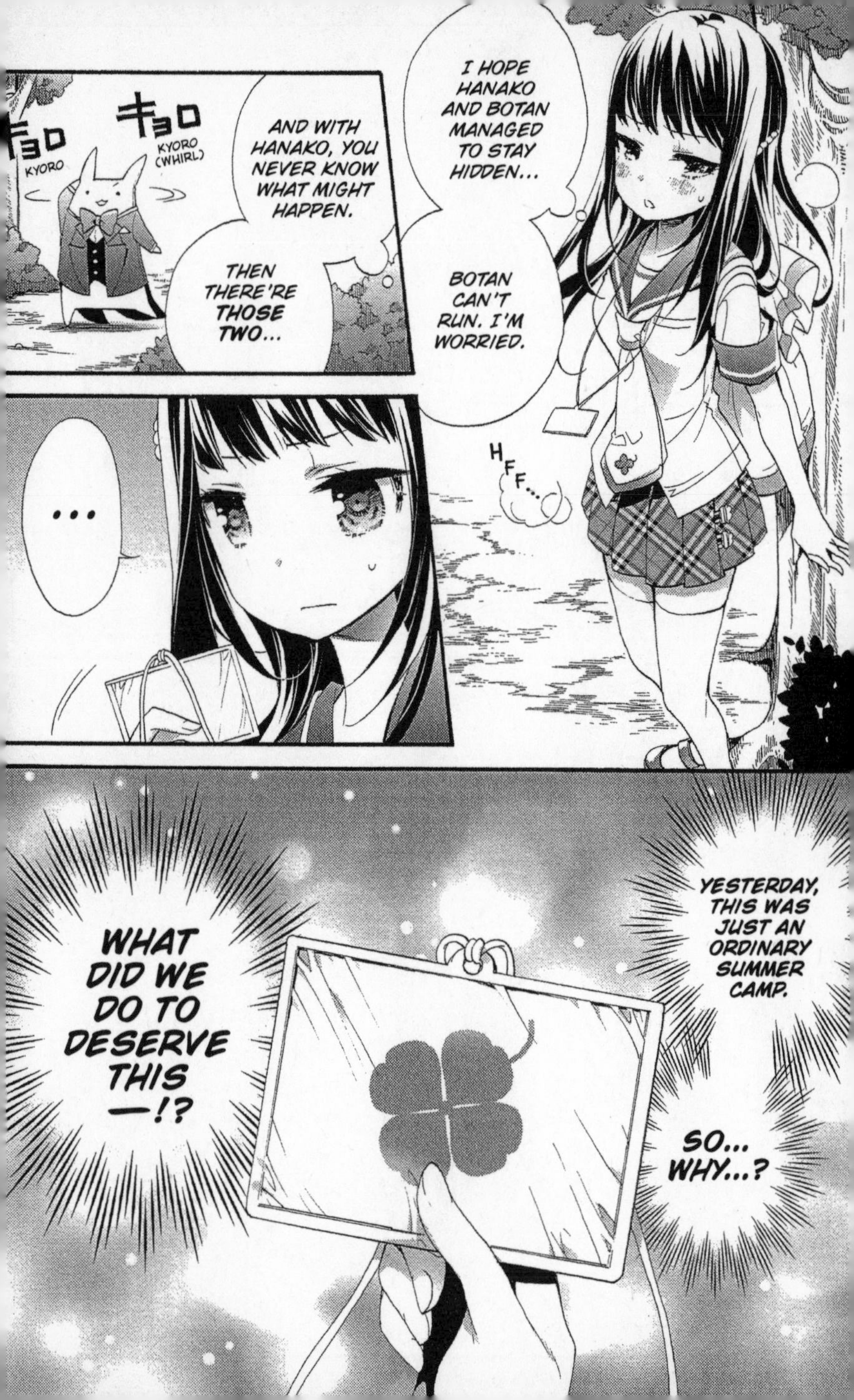

I HOPE HANAKO AND BOTAN MANAGED TO STAY HIDDEN...
BOTAN CAN'T RUN. I'M WORRIED.
HFF...
AND WITH HANAKO, YOU NEVER KNOW WHAT MIGHT HAPPEN.
THEN THERE'RE THOSE TWO...
キョロ
KYORO (WHIRL)
キョロ
KYORO
...
YESTERDAY, THIS WAS JUST AN ORDINARY SUMMER CAMP.
SO... WHY...?
WHAT DID WE DO TO DESERVE THIS—!?

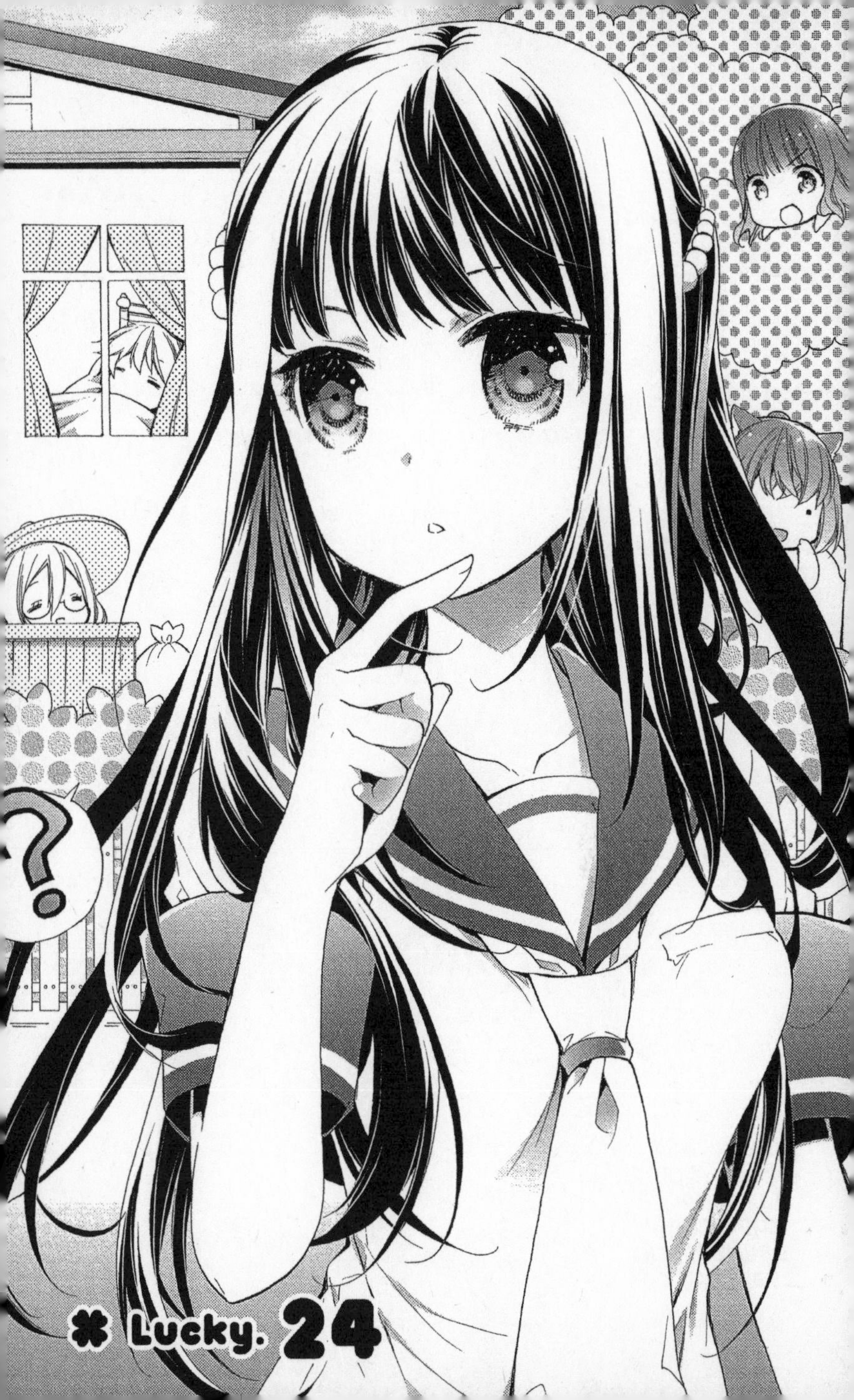
?
✽ Lucky. 24

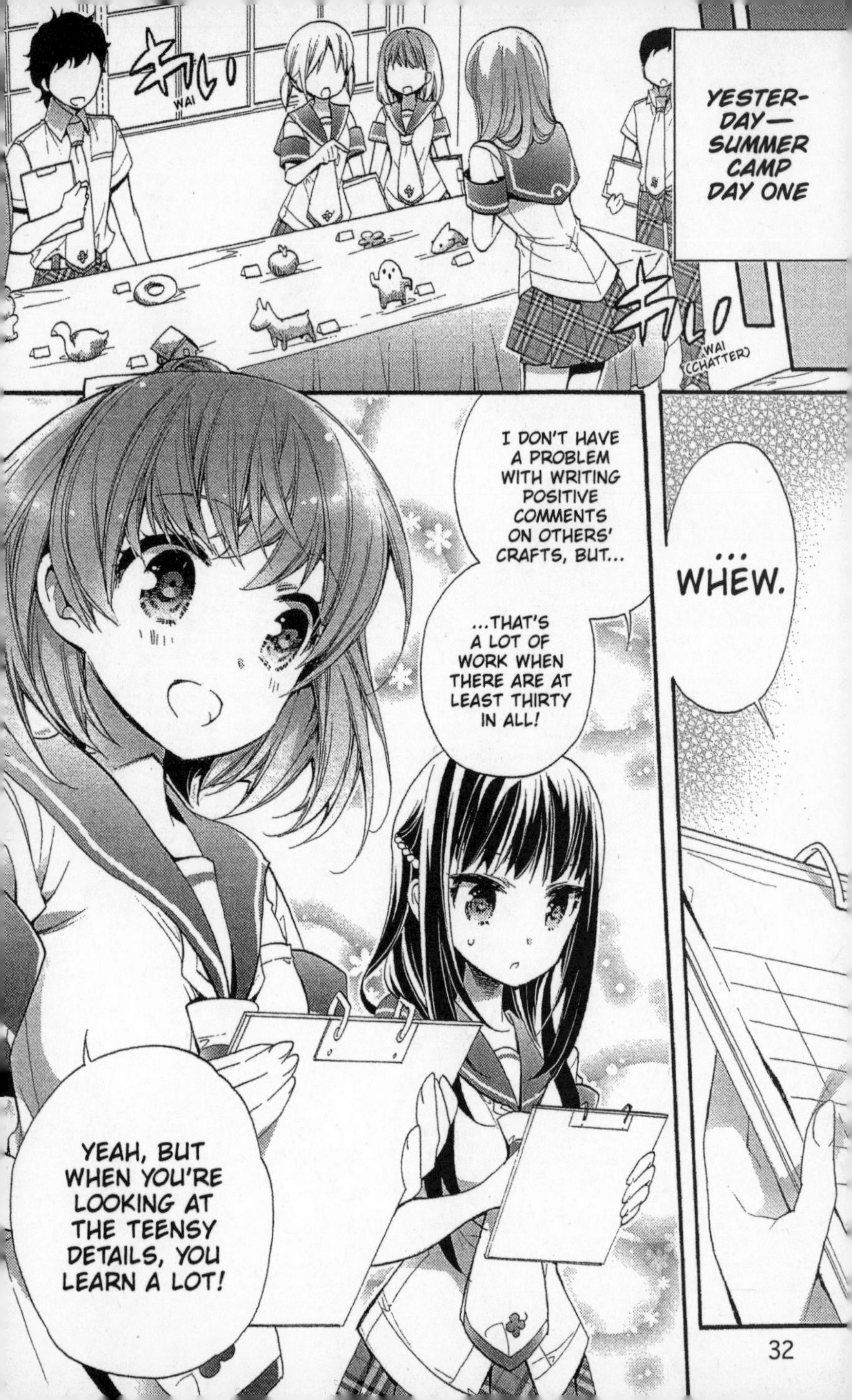

YESTER-DAY— SUMMER CAMP DAY ONE
WAI (CHATTER)
WAI
... WHEW.
I DON'T HAVE A PROBLEM WITH WRITING POSITIVE COMMENTS ON OTHERS' CRAFTS, BUT...
...THAT'S A LOT OF WORK WHEN THERE ARE AT LEAST THIRTY IN ALL!
YEAH, BUT WHEN YOU'RE LOOKING AT THE TEENSY DETAILS, YOU LEARN A LOT!

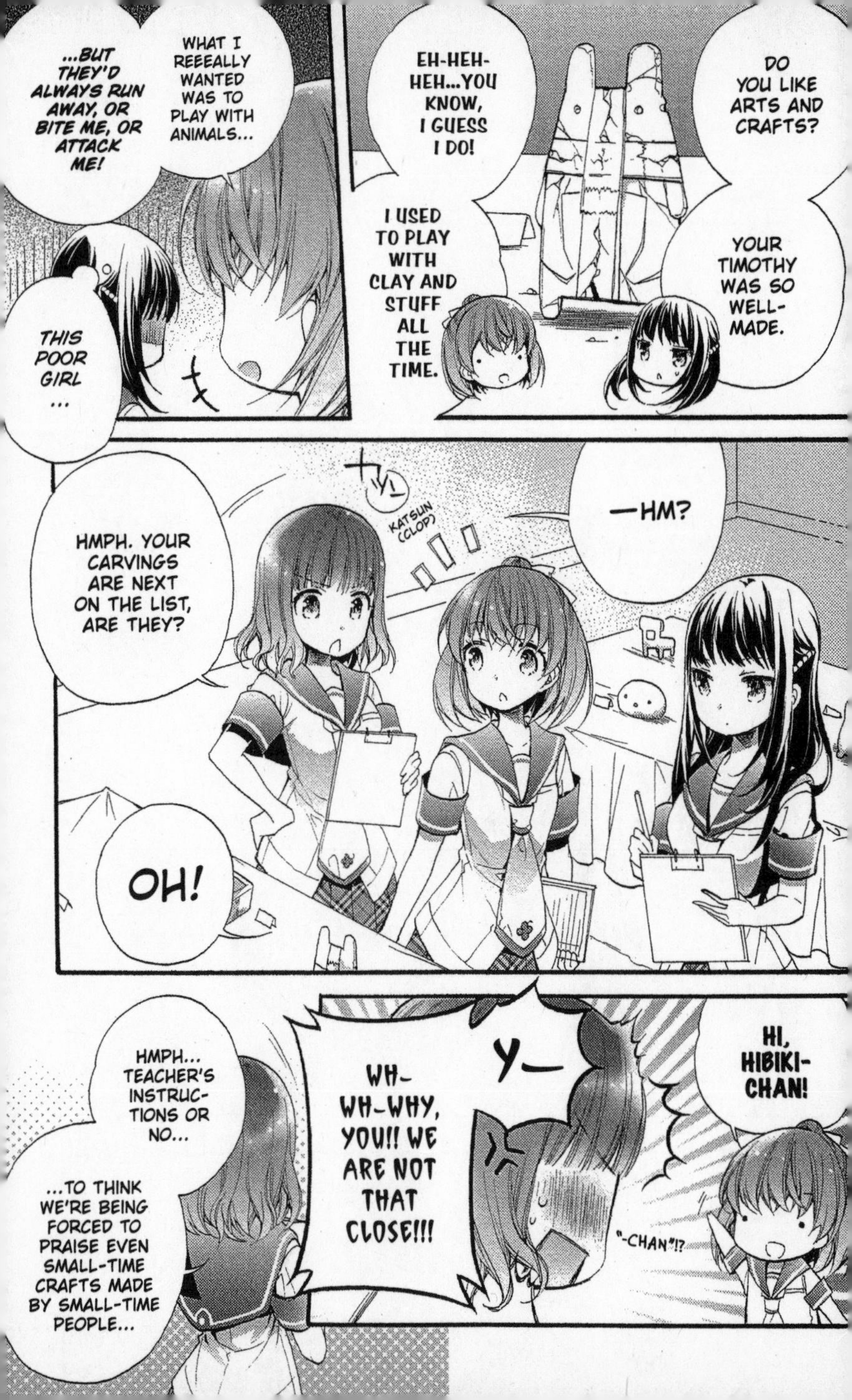
DO YOU LIKE ARTS AND CRAFTS?
YOUR TIMOTHY WAS SO WELL-MADE.
EH-HEH-HEH...YOU KNOW, I GUESS I DO!
I USED TO PLAY WITH CLAY AND STUFF ALL THE TIME.
WHAT I REEEALLY WANTED WAS TO PLAY WITH ANIMALS...
...BUT THEY'D ALWAYS RUN AWAY, OR BITE ME, OR ATTACK ME!
THIS POOR GIRL...
—HM?
KATSUN (CLOP)
HMPH. YOUR CARVINGS ARE NEXT ON THE LIST, ARE THEY?
OH!
HI, HIBIKI-CHAN!
"-CHAN"!?
Y—
WH-WH-WHY, YOU!! WE ARE NOT THAT CLOSE!!!
HMPH... TEACHER'S INSTRUCTIONS OR NO...
...TO THINK WE'RE BEING FORCED TO PRAISE EVEN SMALL-TIME CRAFTS MADE BY SMALL-TIME PEOPLE...

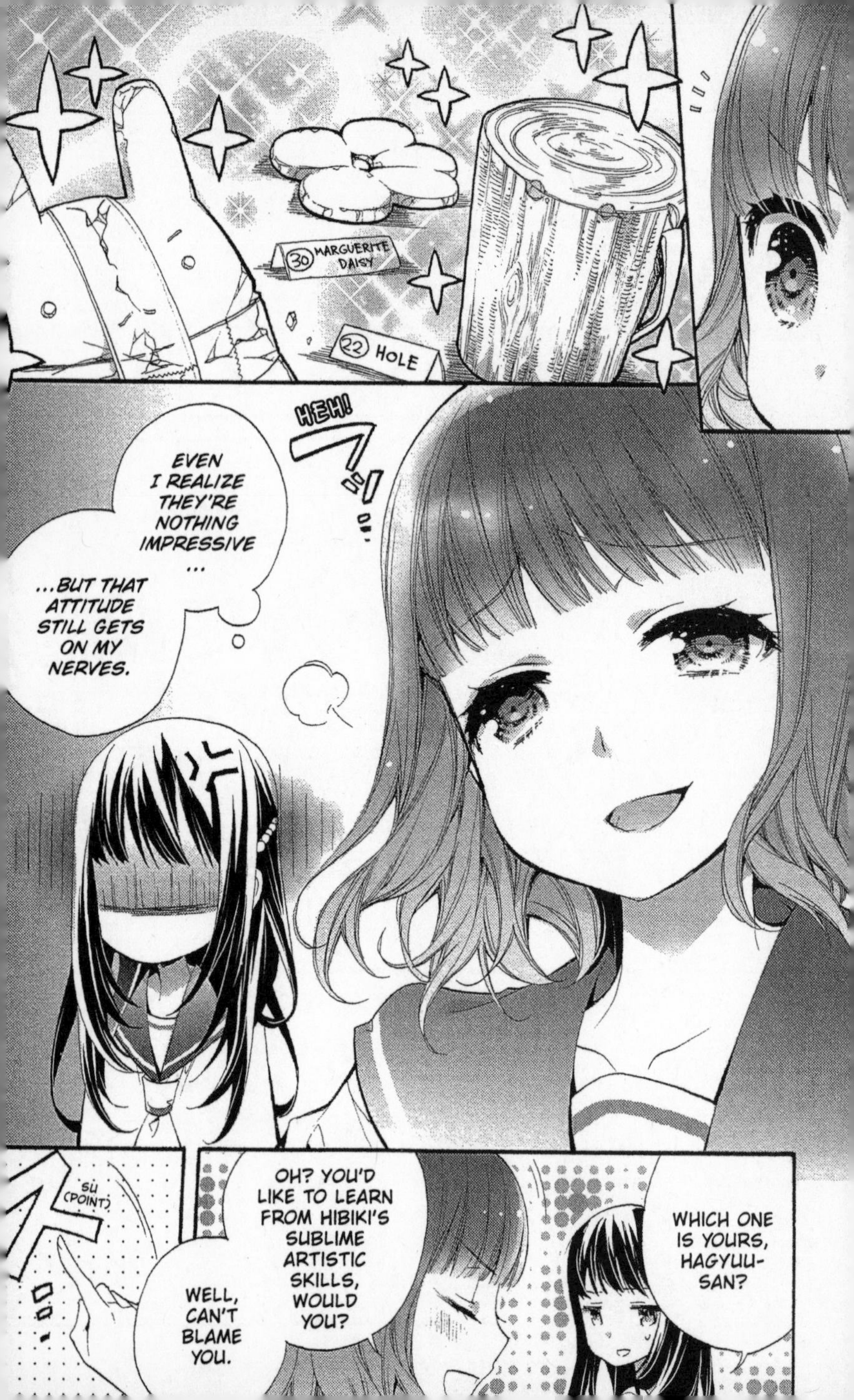
30 MARGUERITE DAISY
22 HOLE
HEH!
EVEN I REALIZE THEY'RE NOTHING IMPRESSIVE...
...BUT THAT ATTITUDE STILL GETS ON MY NERVES.
WHICH ONE IS YOURS, HAGYUU-SAN?
OH? YOU'D LIKE TO LEARN FROM HIBIKI'S SUBLIME ARTISTIC SKILLS, WOULD YOU?
WELL, CAN'T BLAME YOU.
SU (POINT)

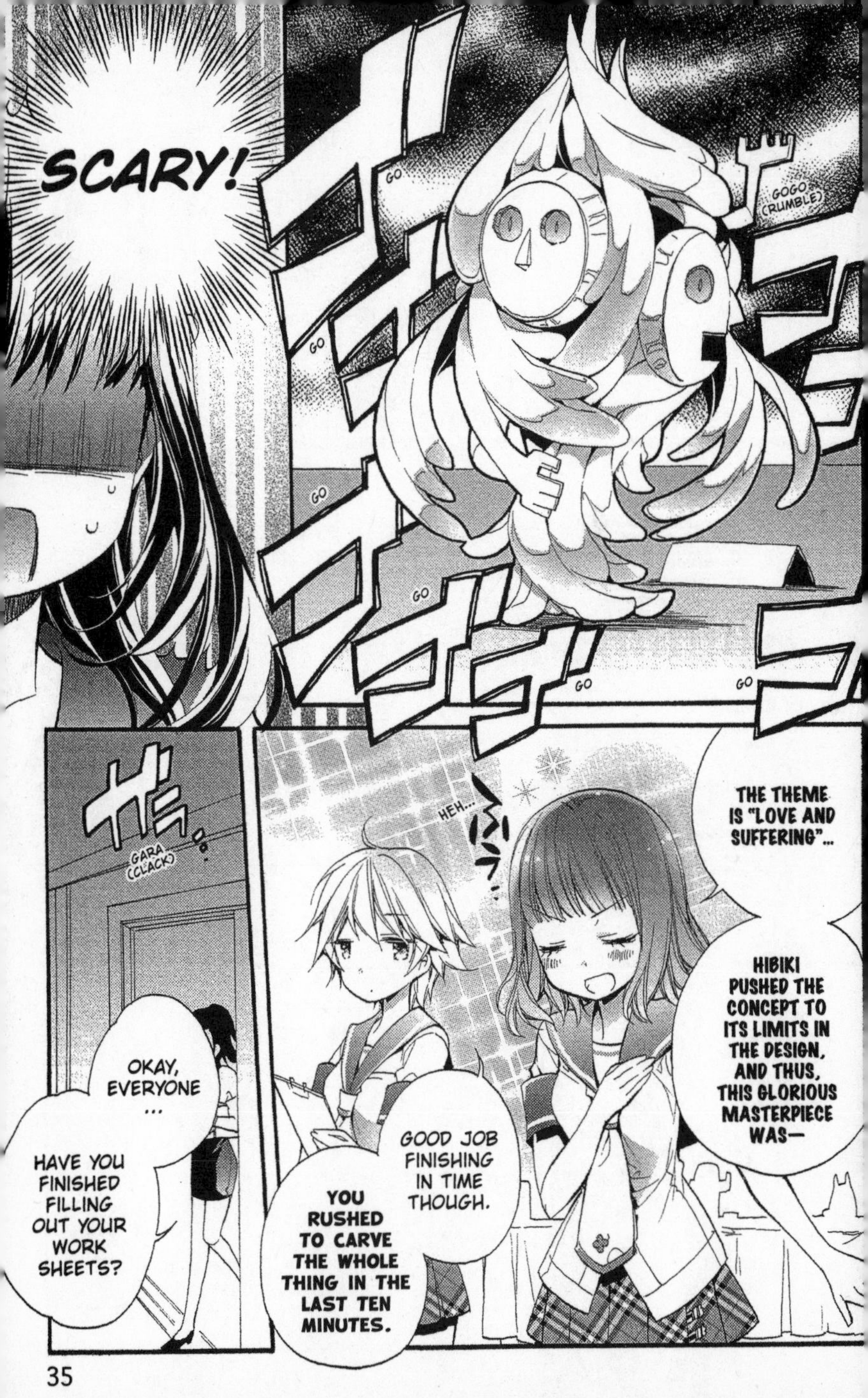
GOGO (RUMBLE)
GO
GO
GO
GO
GO
GO
SCARY!
HEH...
THE THEME IS "LOVE AND SUFFERING"...
HIBIKI PUSHED THE CONCEPT TO ITS LIMITS IN THE DESIGN, AND THUS, THIS GLORIOUS MASTERPIECE WAS—
GOOD JOB FINISHING IN TIME THOUGH.
YOU RUSHED TO CARVE THE WHOLE THING IN THE LAST TEN MINUTES.
GARA (CLACK)
OKAY, EVERYONE ...
HAVE YOU FINISHED FILLING OUT YOUR WORK SHEETS?

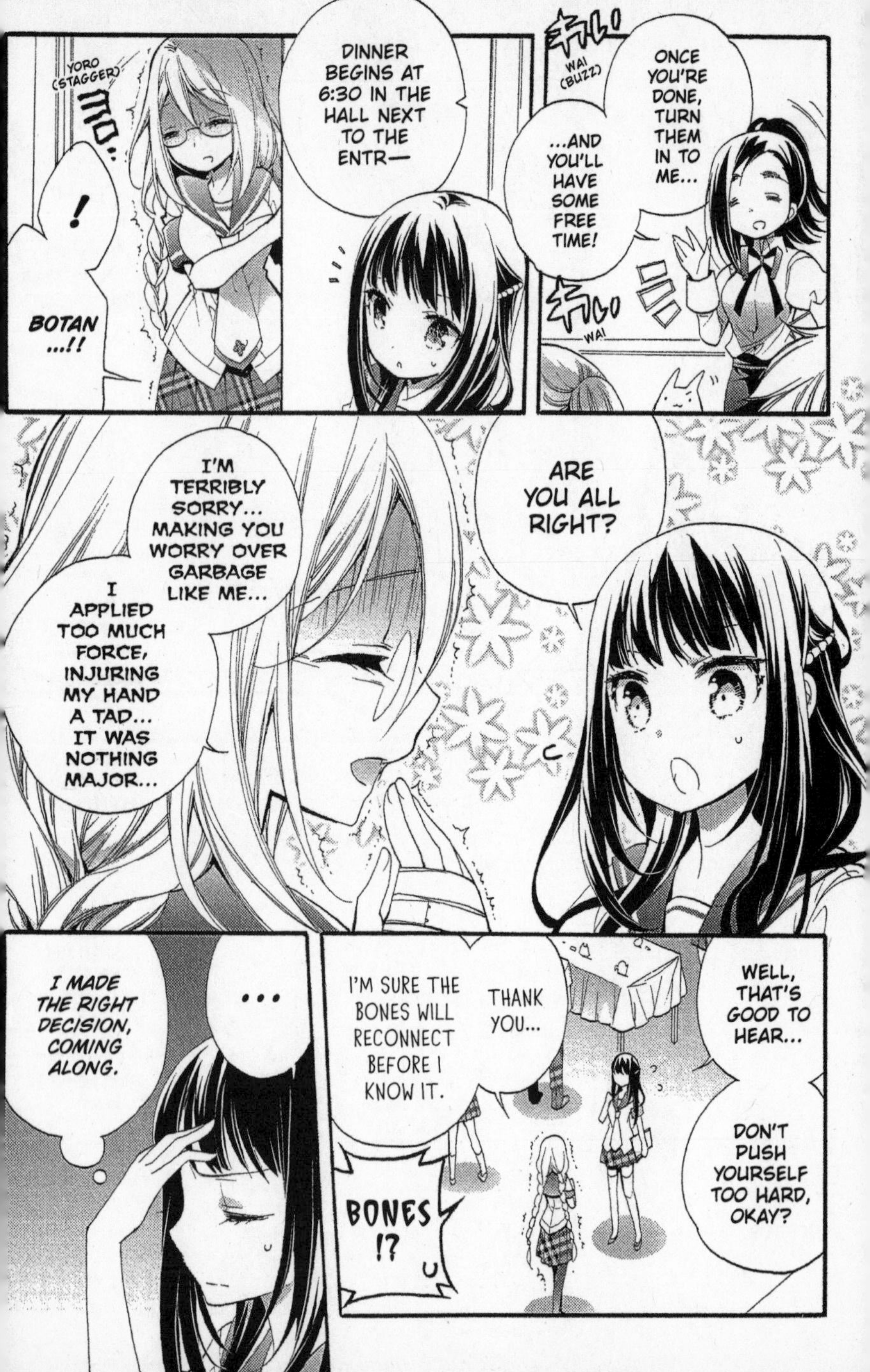
WAI (BUZZ)
ONCE YOU'RE DONE, TURN THEM IN TO ME...
...AND YOU'LL HAVE SOME FREE TIME!
WAI
DINNER BEGINS AT 6:30 IN THE HALL NEXT TO THE ENTR—
YORO (STAGGER)
!
BOTAN ...!!
ARE YOU ALL RIGHT?
I'M TERRIBLY SORRY... MAKING YOU WORRY OVER GARBAGE LIKE ME...
I APPLIED TOO MUCH FORCE, INJURING MY HAND A TAD... IT WAS NOTHING MAJOR...
WELL, THAT'S GOOD TO HEAR...
DON'T PUSH YOURSELF TOO HARD, OKAY?
THANK YOU...
I'M SURE THE BONES WILL RECONNECT BEFORE I KNOW IT.
BONES !?
...
I MADE THE RIGHT DECISION, COMING ALONG.

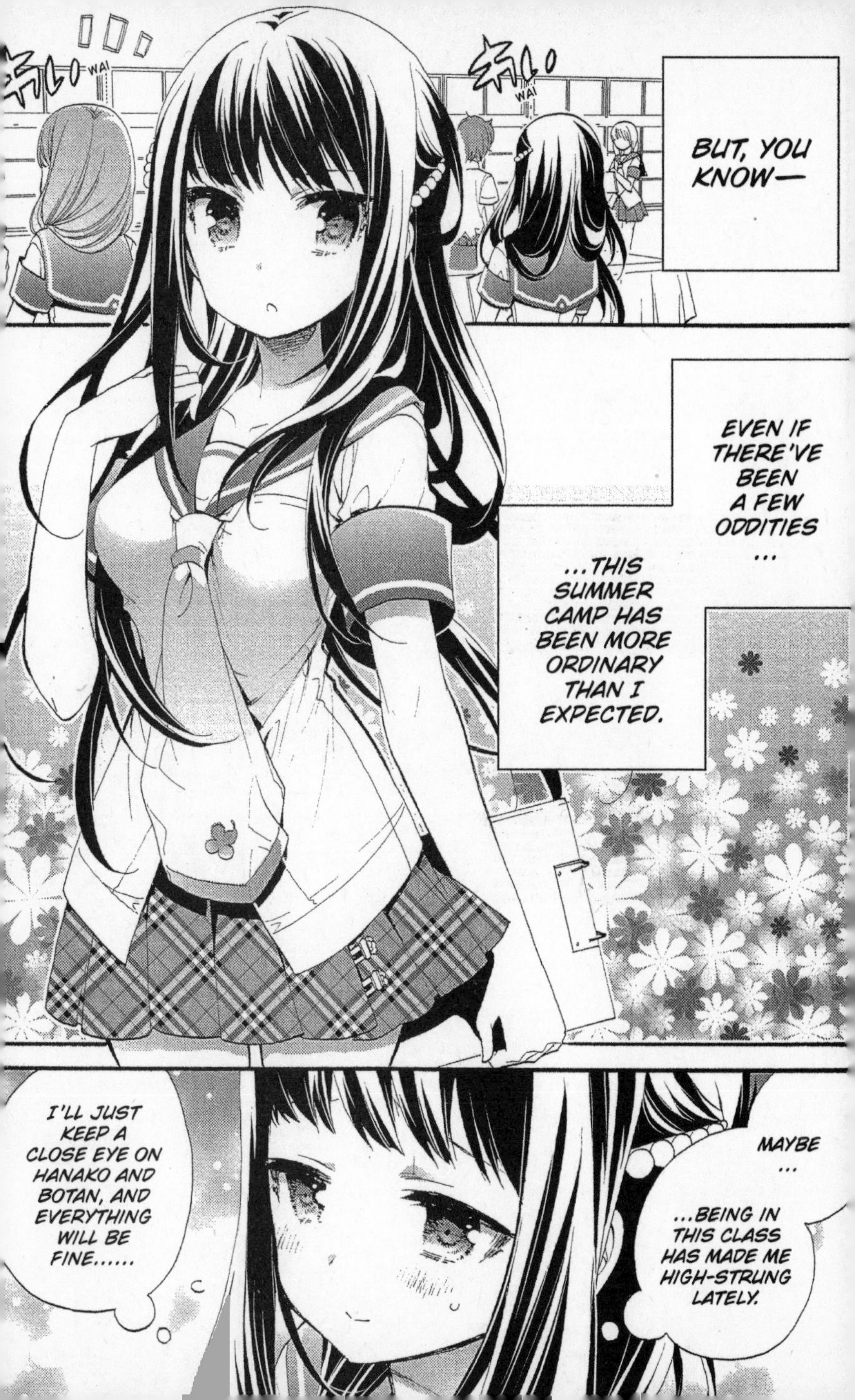
BUT, YOU KNOW—
WAI
WAI
EVEN IF THERE'VE BEEN A FEW ODDITIES ...
...THIS SUMMER CAMP HAS BEEN MORE ORDINARY THAN I EXPECTED.
MAYBE ...
...BEING IN THIS CLASS HAS MADE ME HIGH-STRUNG LATELY.
I'LL JUST KEEP A CLOSE EYE ON HANAKO AND BOTAN, AND EVERYTHING WILL BE FINE......

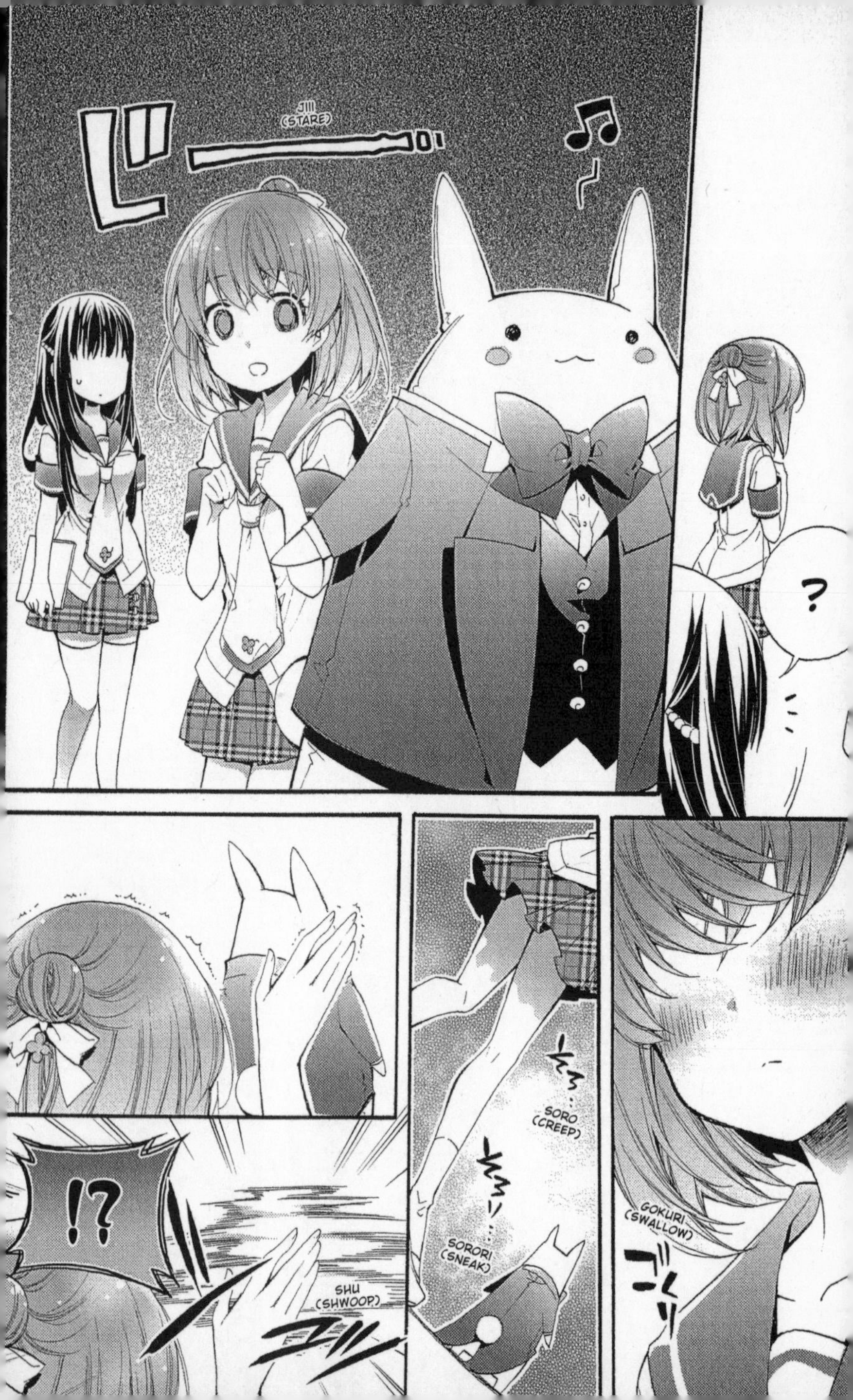
?
JIII
(STARE)
♪
GOKURI
(SWALLOW)
SORO
(CREEP)
SORORI
(SNEAK)
!?
SHU
(SHWOOP)

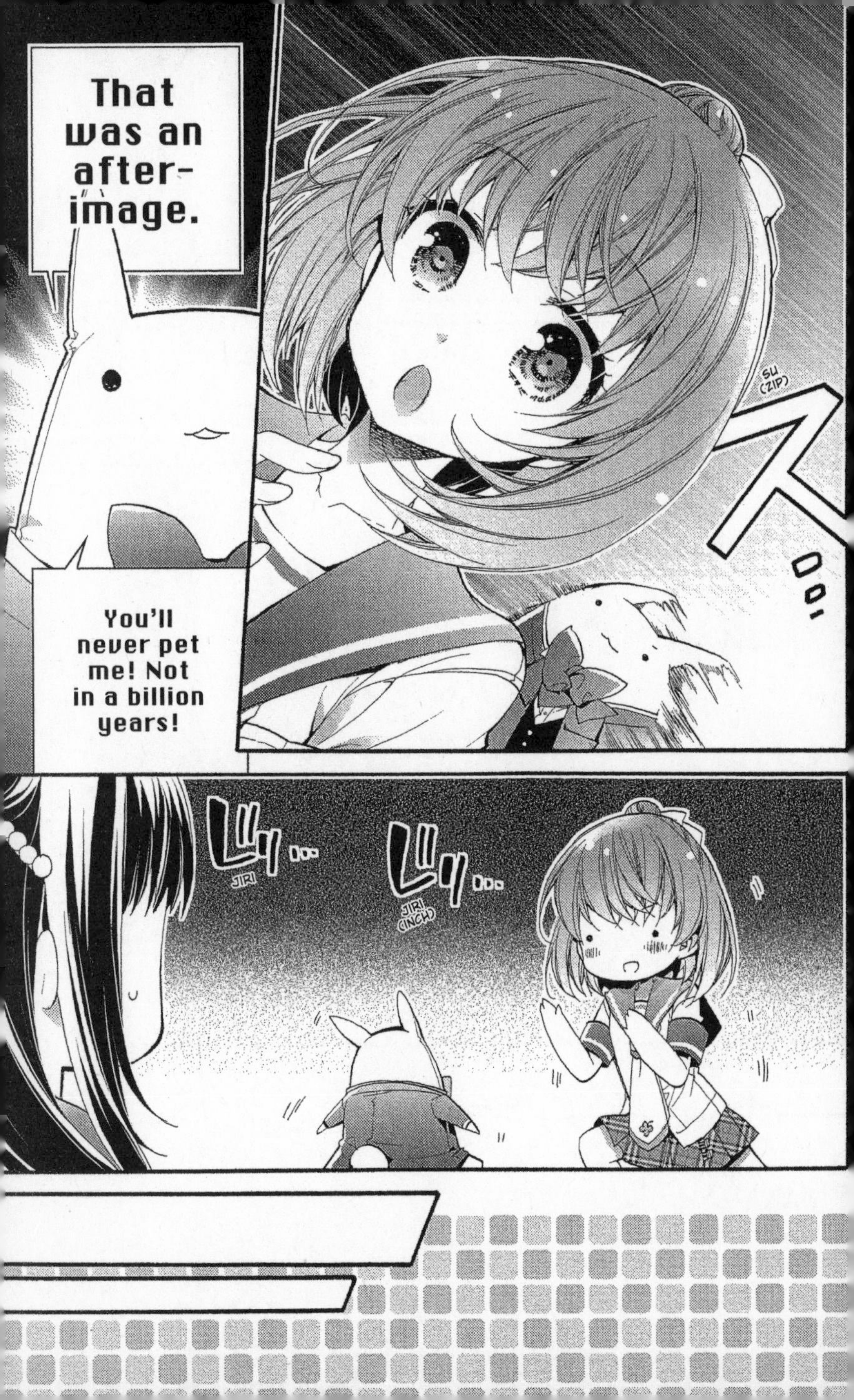
SU (ZIP)
That was an after-image.
You'll never pet me! Not in a billion years!
JIRI (INCH)
JIRI

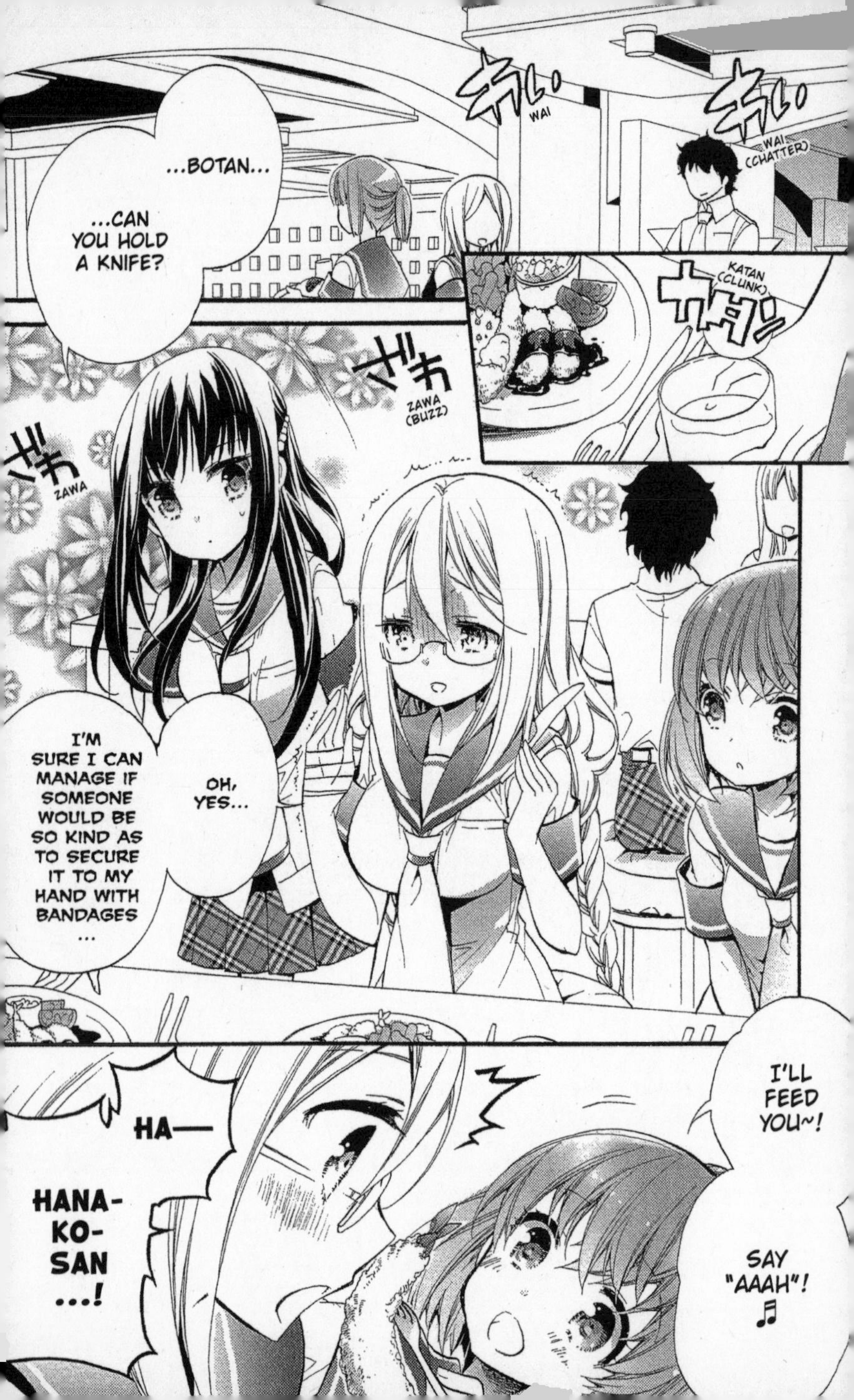

WAI (CHATTER)
WAI
...BOTAN...
...CAN YOU HOLD A KNIFE?
KATAN (CLUNK)
ZAWA (BUZZ)
ZAWA
OH, YES...
I'M SURE I CAN MANAGE IF SOMEONE WOULD BE SO KIND AS TO SECURE IT TO MY HAND WITH BANDAGES ...
I'LL FEED YOU~!
SAY "AAAH"! ♪
HA—
HANA-KO-SAN ...!

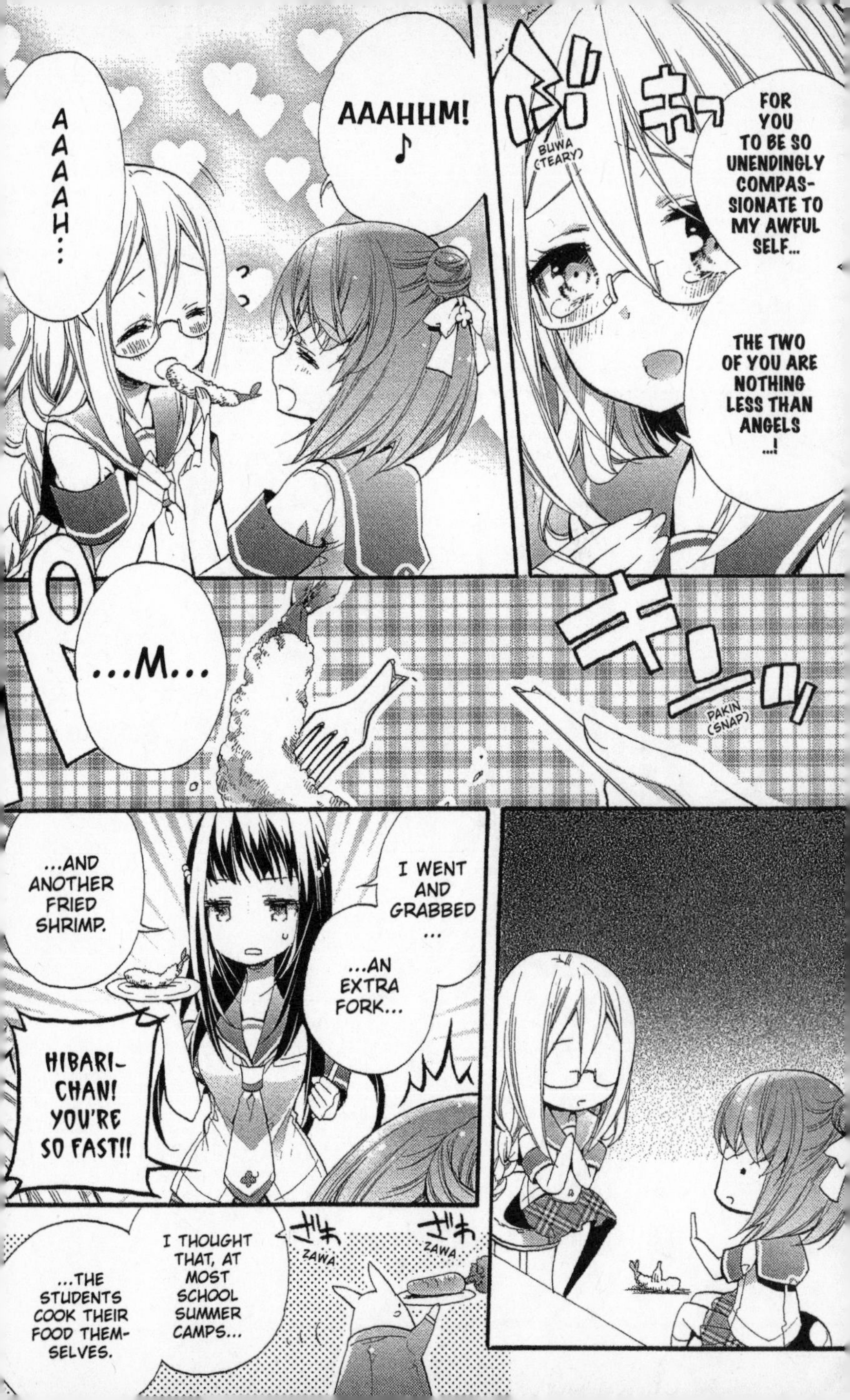
BUWA (TEARY)
FOR YOU TO BE SO UNENDINGLY COMPAS-SIONATE TO MY AWFUL SELF...
THE TWO OF YOU ARE NOTHING LESS THAN ANGELS ...!
AAAHHM! ♪
AAAAAH...
PAKIN (SNAP)
...M...
I WENT AND GRABBED ...
...AN EXTRA FORK...
...AND ANOTHER FRIED SHRIMP.
HIBARI-CHAN! YOU'RE SO FAST!!
ZAWA
ZAWA
I THOUGHT THAT, AT MOST SCHOOL SUMMER CAMPS...
...THE STUDENTS COOK THEIR FOOD THEM-SELVES.

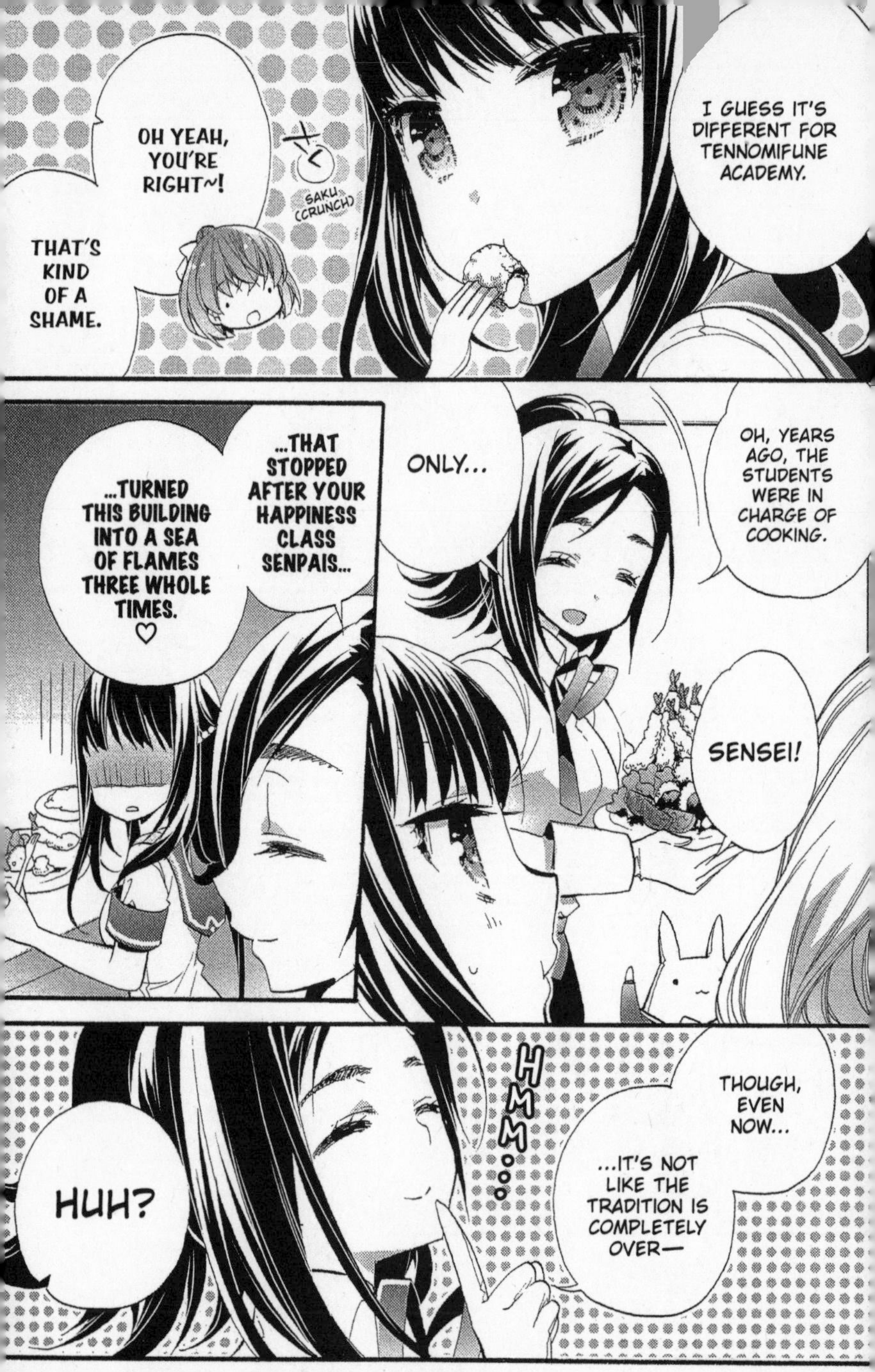
I GUESS IT'S DIFFERENT FOR TENNOMIFUNE ACADEMY.
SAKU (CRUNCH)
OH YEAH, YOU'RE RIGHT~!
THAT'S KIND OF A SHAME.
OH, YEARS AGO, THE STUDENTS WERE IN CHARGE OF COOKING.
ONLY...
SENSEI!
...THAT STOPPED AFTER YOUR HAPPINESS CLASS SENPAIS...
...TURNED THIS BUILDING INTO A SEA OF FLAMES THREE WHOLE TIMES. ♡
THOUGH, EVEN NOW...
HMM...
...IT'S NOT LIKE THE TRADITION IS COMPLETELY OVER—
HUH?

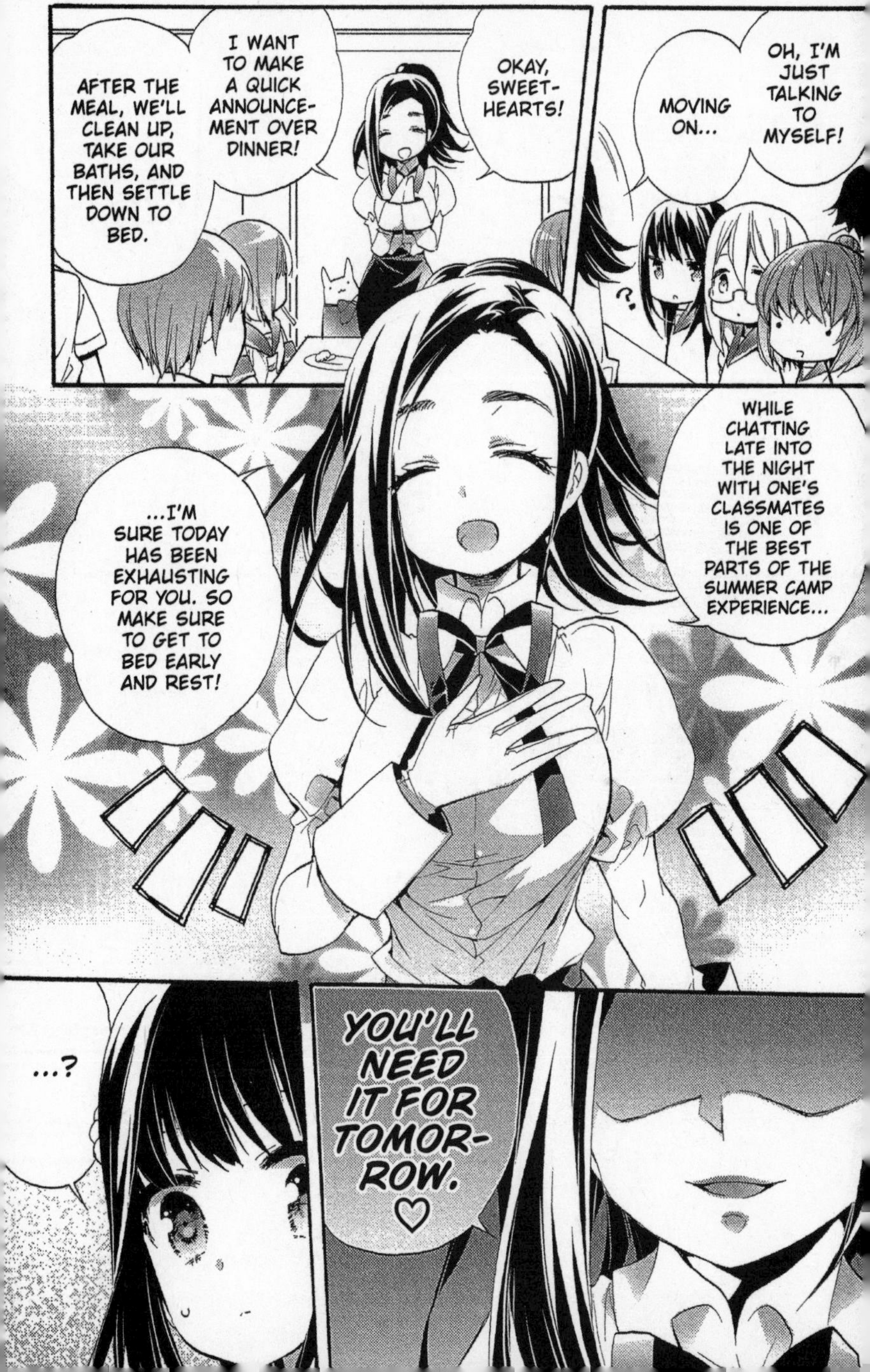
OH, I'M JUST TALKING TO MYSELF!
MOVING ON...
OKAY, SWEET-HEARTS!
I WANT TO MAKE A QUICK ANNOUNCE-MENT OVER DINNER!
AFTER THE MEAL, WE'LL CLEAN UP, TAKE OUR BATHS, AND THEN SETTLE DOWN TO BED.
WHILE CHATTING LATE INTO THE NIGHT WITH ONE'S CLASSMATES IS ONE OF THE BEST PARTS OF THE SUMMER CAMP EXPERIENCE...
...I'M SURE TODAY HAS BEEN EXHAUSTING FOR YOU. SO MAKE SURE TO GET TO BED EARLY AND REST!
YOU'LL NEED IT FOR TOMOR-ROW. ♡
...?

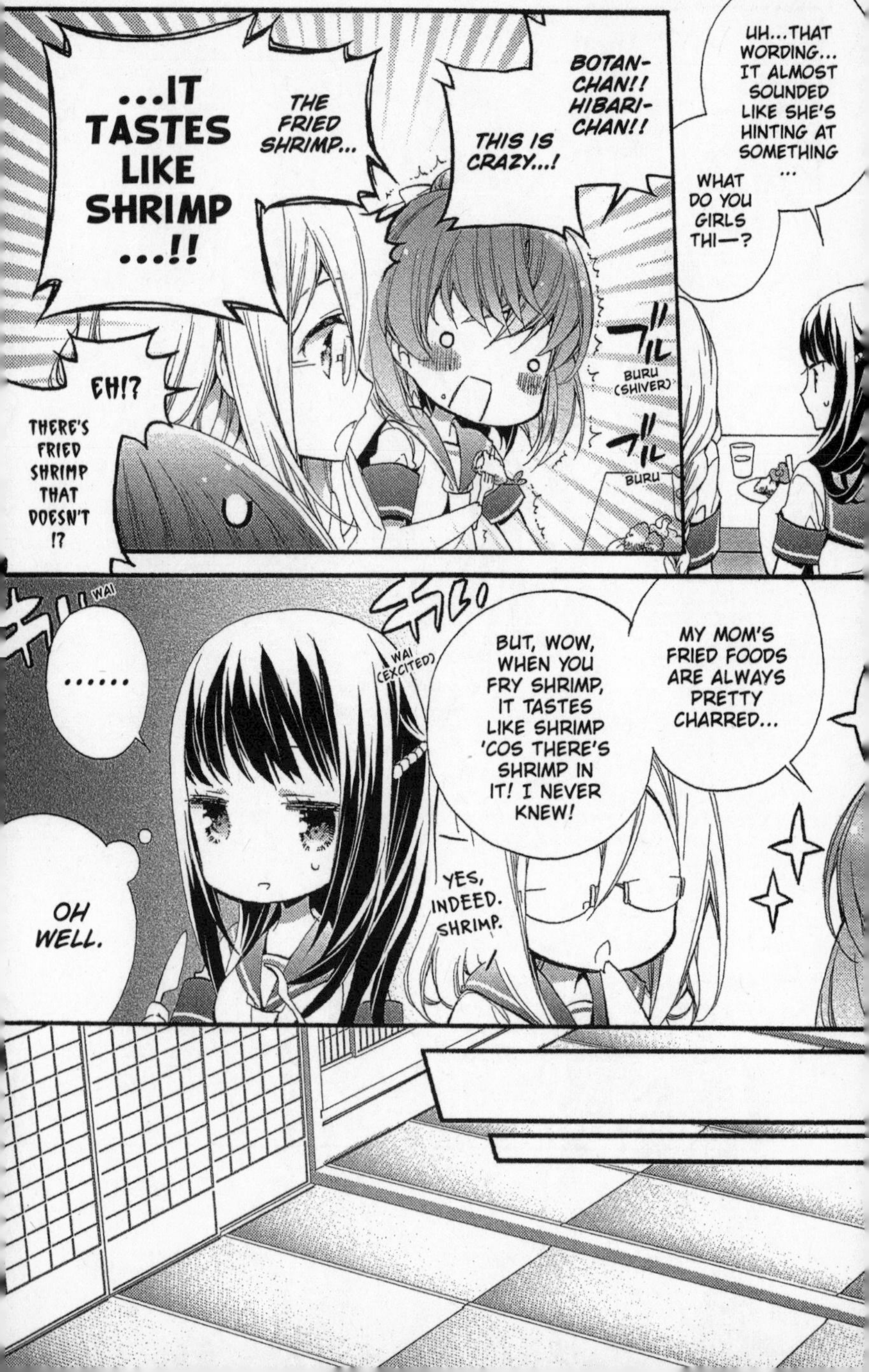
UH...THAT WORDING... IT ALMOST SOUNDED LIKE SHE'S HINTING AT SOMETHING...
WHAT DO YOU GIRLS THI—?
BOTAN-CHAN!! HIBARI-CHAN!!
THIS IS CRAZY...!
BURU (SHIVER)
BURU
THE FRIED SHRIMP...
...IT TASTES LIKE SHRIMP...!!
EH!?
THERE'S FRIED SHRIMP THAT DOESN'T!?
MY MOM'S FRIED FOODS ARE ALWAYS PRETTY CHARRED...
BUT, WOW, WHEN YOU FRY SHRIMP, IT TASTES LIKE SHRIMP 'COS THERE'S SHRIMP IN IT! I NEVER KNEW!
WAI (EXCITED)
WAI
YES, INDEED. SHRIMP.
......
OH WELL.

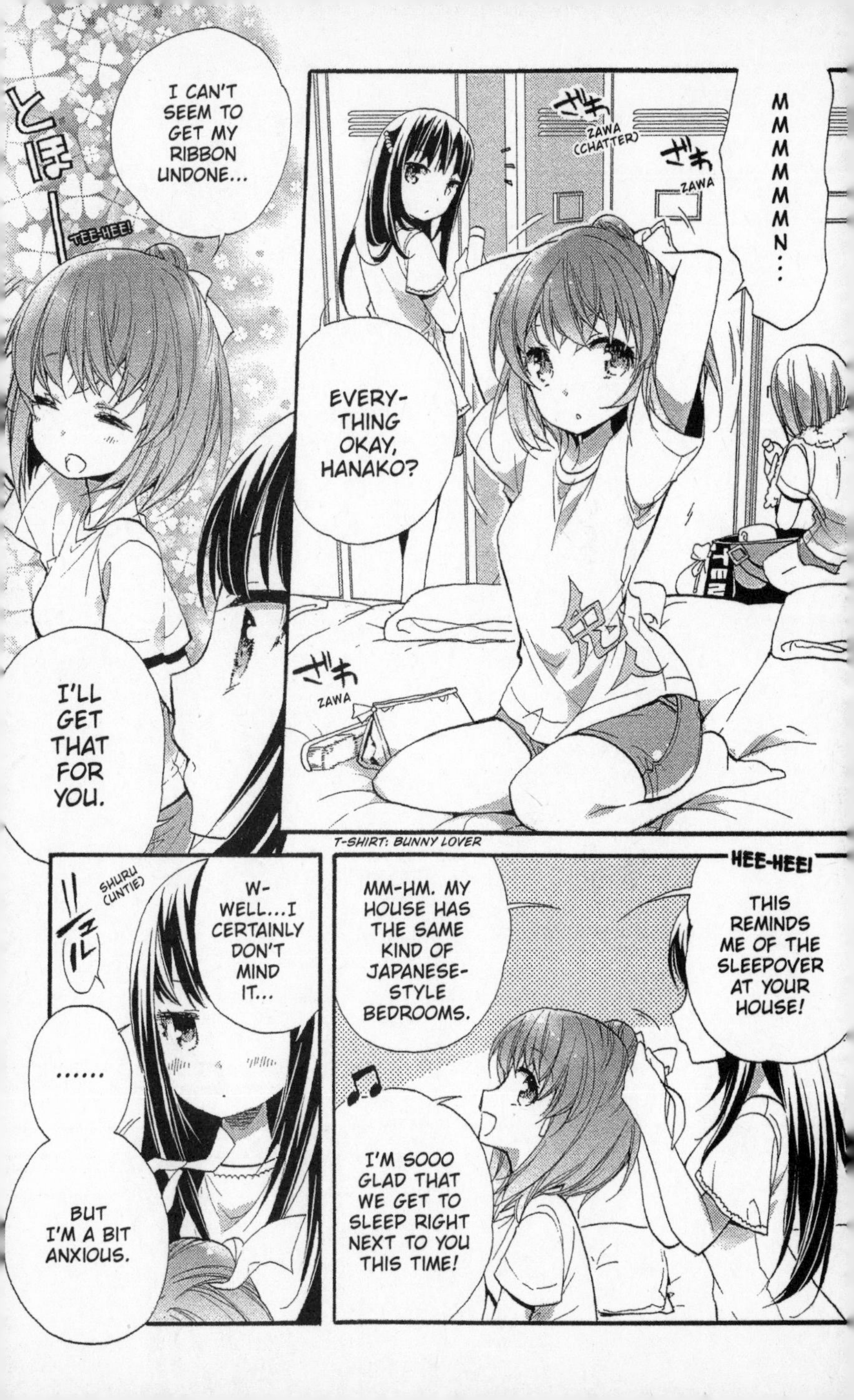
MMMMMMN...
ざわ
ZAWA (CHATTER)
ざわ
ZAWA
EVERYTHING OKAY, HANAKO?
ざわ
ZAWA
T-SHIRT: BUNNY LOVER
とほー
TEE-HEE!
I CAN'T SEEM TO GET MY RIBBON UNDONE...
I'LL GET THAT FOR YOU.
HEE-HEE!
THIS REMINDS ME OF THE SLEEPOVER AT YOUR HOUSE!
MM-HM. MY HOUSE HAS THE SAME KIND OF JAPANESE-STYLE BEDROOMS.
I'M SOOO GLAD THAT WE GET TO SLEEP RIGHT NEXT TO YOU THIS TIME!
シュル
SHURU (UNTIE)
W-WELL...I CERTAINLY DON'T MIND IT...
......
BUT I'M A BIT ANXIOUS.

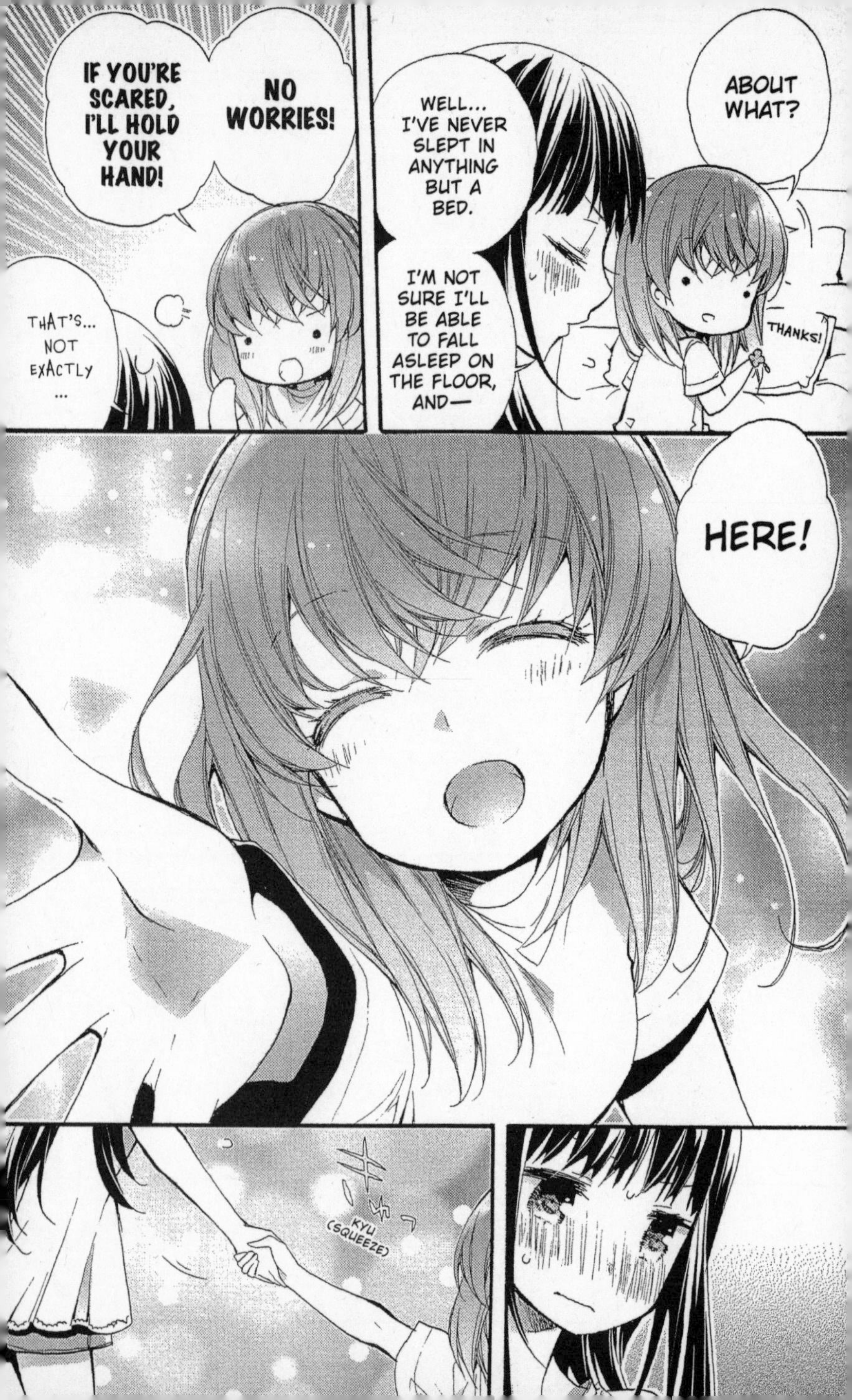
ABOUT WHAT?
WELL... I'VE NEVER SLEPT IN ANYTHING BUT A BED.
I'M NOT SURE I'LL BE ABLE TO FALL ASLEEP ON THE FLOOR, AND—
THANKS!
NO WORRIES!
IF YOU'RE SCARED, I'LL HOLD YOUR HAND!
THAT'S... NOT EXACTLY...
HERE!
KYU (SQUEEZE)

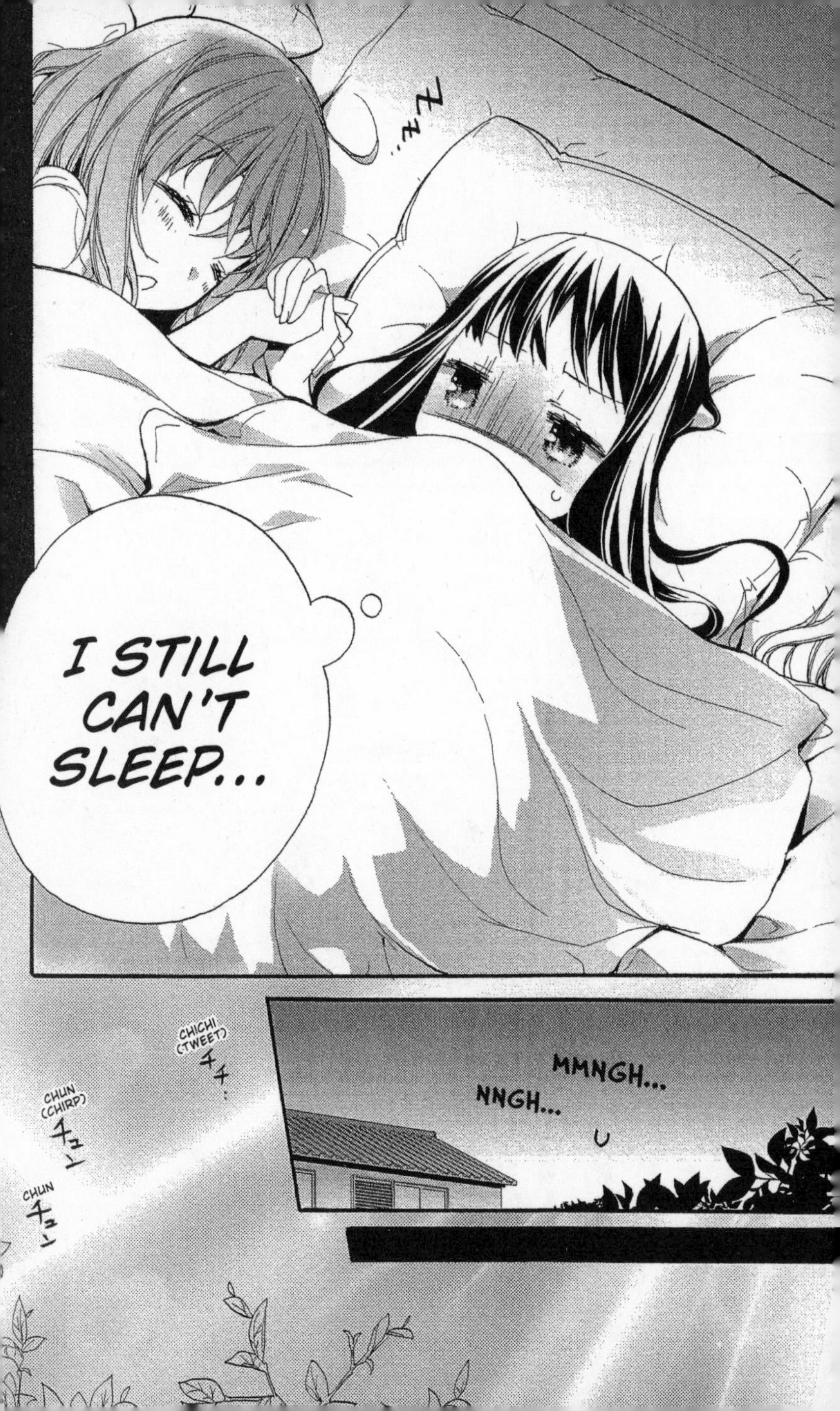

スー…
I STILL CAN'T SLEEP...
MMNGH...
NNGH...
CHICHI (TWEET)
チチ…
CHUN (CHIRP)
チュン
CHUN
チュン

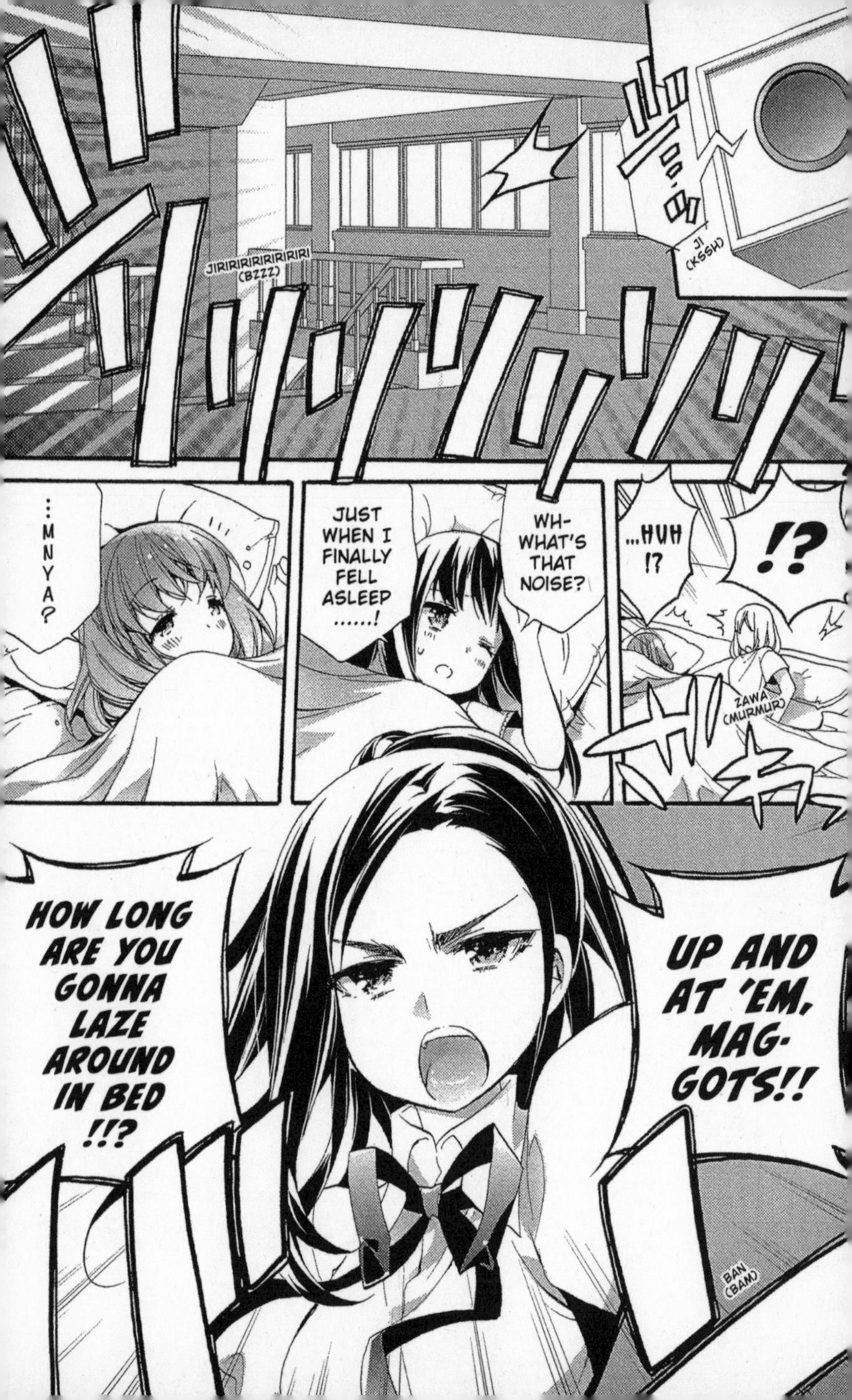
JI (KSSH)
JIRIRIRIRIRIRIRI (BZZZ)
!?
...HUH !?
ZAWA (MURMUR)
WH-WHAT'S THAT NOISE?
JUST WHEN I FINALLY FELL ASLEEP ......!
...MNYA?
UP AND AT 'EM, MAG-GOTS!!
HOW LONG ARE YOU GONNA LAZE AROUND IN BED !!?
BAN (BAM)

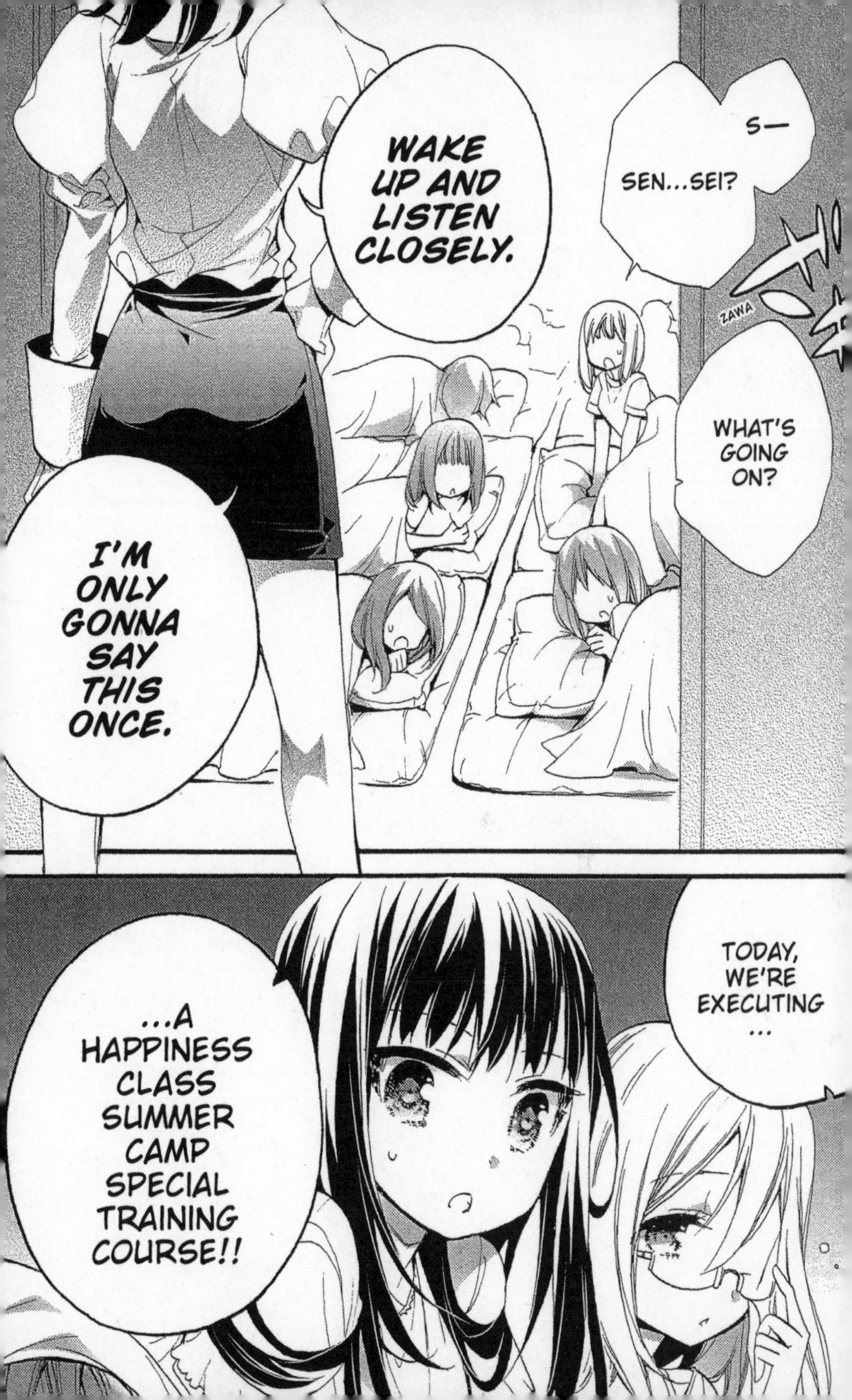
S—
SEN...SEI?
ZAWA
WHAT'S GOING ON?
WAKE UP AND LISTEN CLOSELY.
I'M ONLY GONNA SAY THIS ONCE.
TODAY, WE'RE EXECUTING ...
...A HAPPINESS CLASS SUMMER CAMP SPECIAL TRAINING COURSE!!

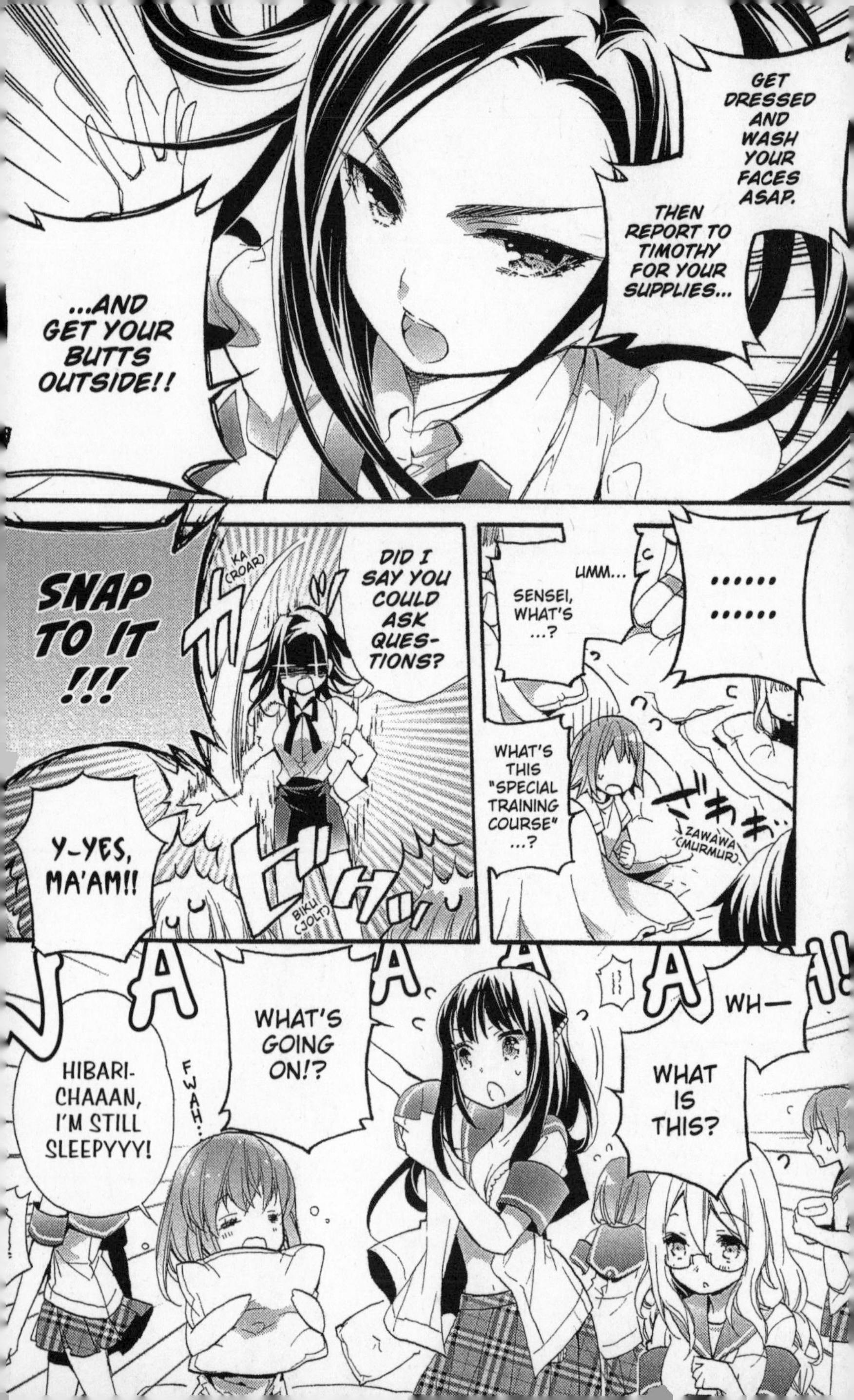

GET DRESSED AND WASH YOUR FACES ASAP.
THEN REPORT TO TIMOTHY FOR YOUR SUPPLIES...
...AND GET YOUR BUTTS OUTSIDE!!
......
......
UMM...
SENSEI, WHAT'S ...?
WHAT'S THIS "SPECIAL TRAINING COURSE" ...?
ZAWAWA (MURMUR)
DID I SAY YOU COULD ASK QUES-TIONS?
KA (ROAR)
BIKU (JOLT)
SNAP TO IT !!!
Y-YES, MA'AM!!
WH—
WHAT IS THIS?
WHAT'S GOING ON!?
FWAH...
HIBARI-CHAAAN, I'M STILL SLEEPYYY!

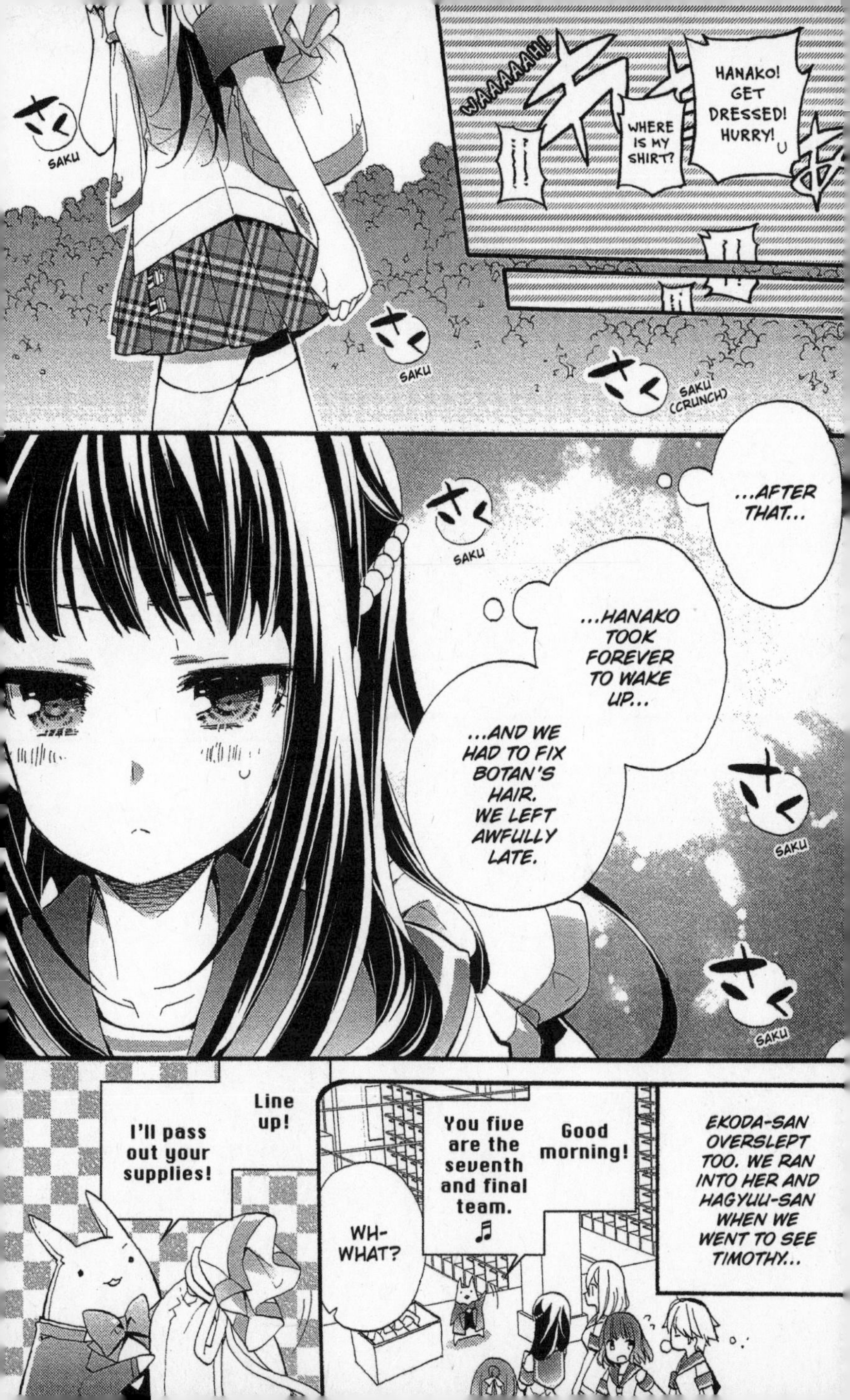

HANAKO! GET DRESSED! HURRY!
WHERE IS MY SHIRT?
WAAAAAAH!!
SAKU
SAKU
SAKU (CRUNCH)
...AFTER THAT...
...HANAKO TOOK FOREVER TO WAKE UP...
...AND WE HAD TO FIX BOTAN'S HAIR. WE LEFT AWFULLY LATE.
SAKU
SAKU
SAKU
EKODA-SAN OVERSLEPT TOO. WE RAN INTO HER AND HAGYUU-SAN WHEN WE WENT TO SEE TIMOTHY...
Good morning!
You five are the seventh and final team. ♪
WH-WHAT?
Line up!
I'll pass out your supplies!

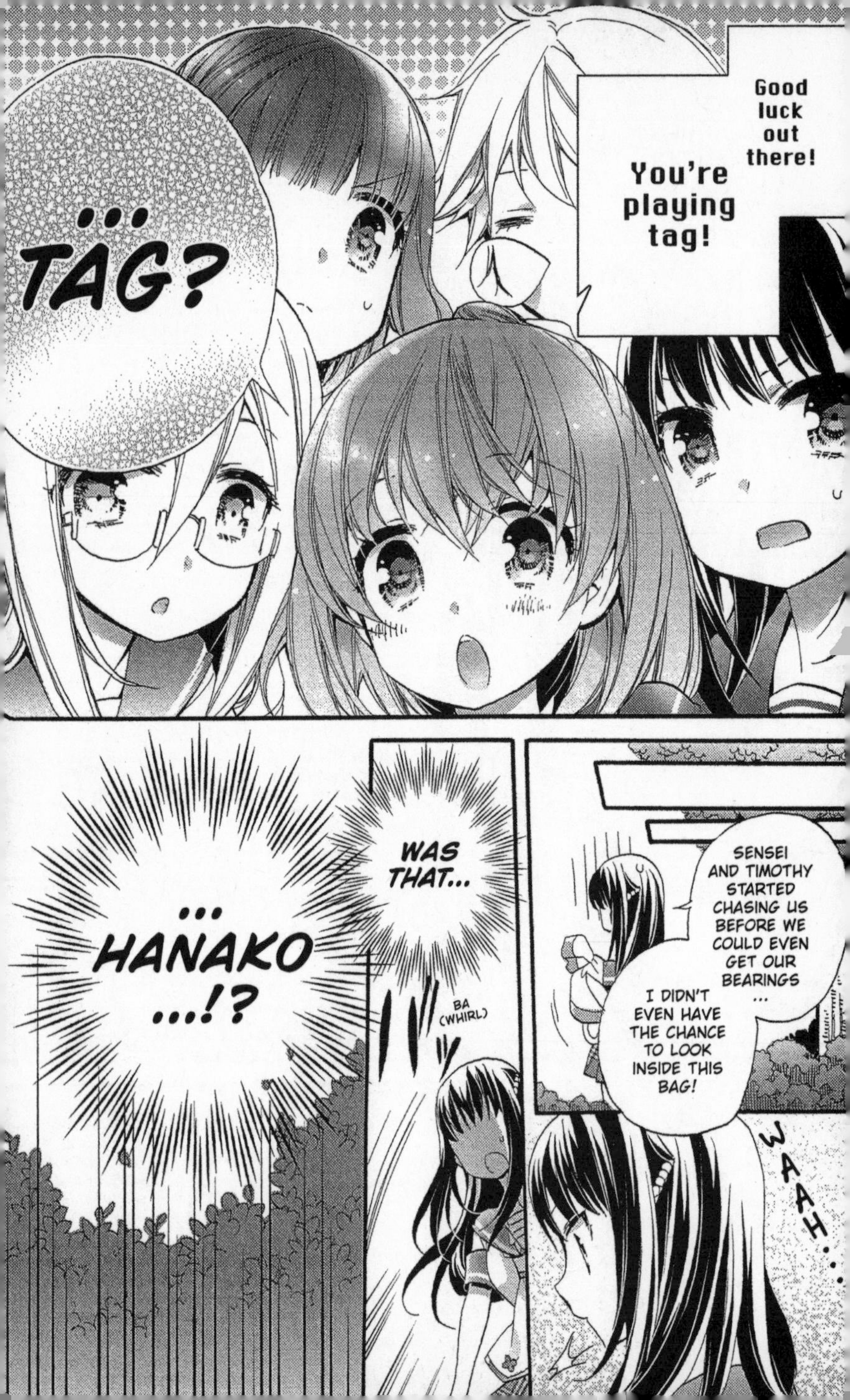
Good luck out there!
You're playing tag!
...TAG?
SENSEI AND TIMOTHY STARTED CHASING US BEFORE WE COULD EVEN GET OUR BEARINGS ...
I DIDN'T EVEN HAVE THE CHANCE TO LOOK INSIDE THIS BAG!
WAAH...
BA (WHIRL)
WAS THAT...
...HANAKO ...!?

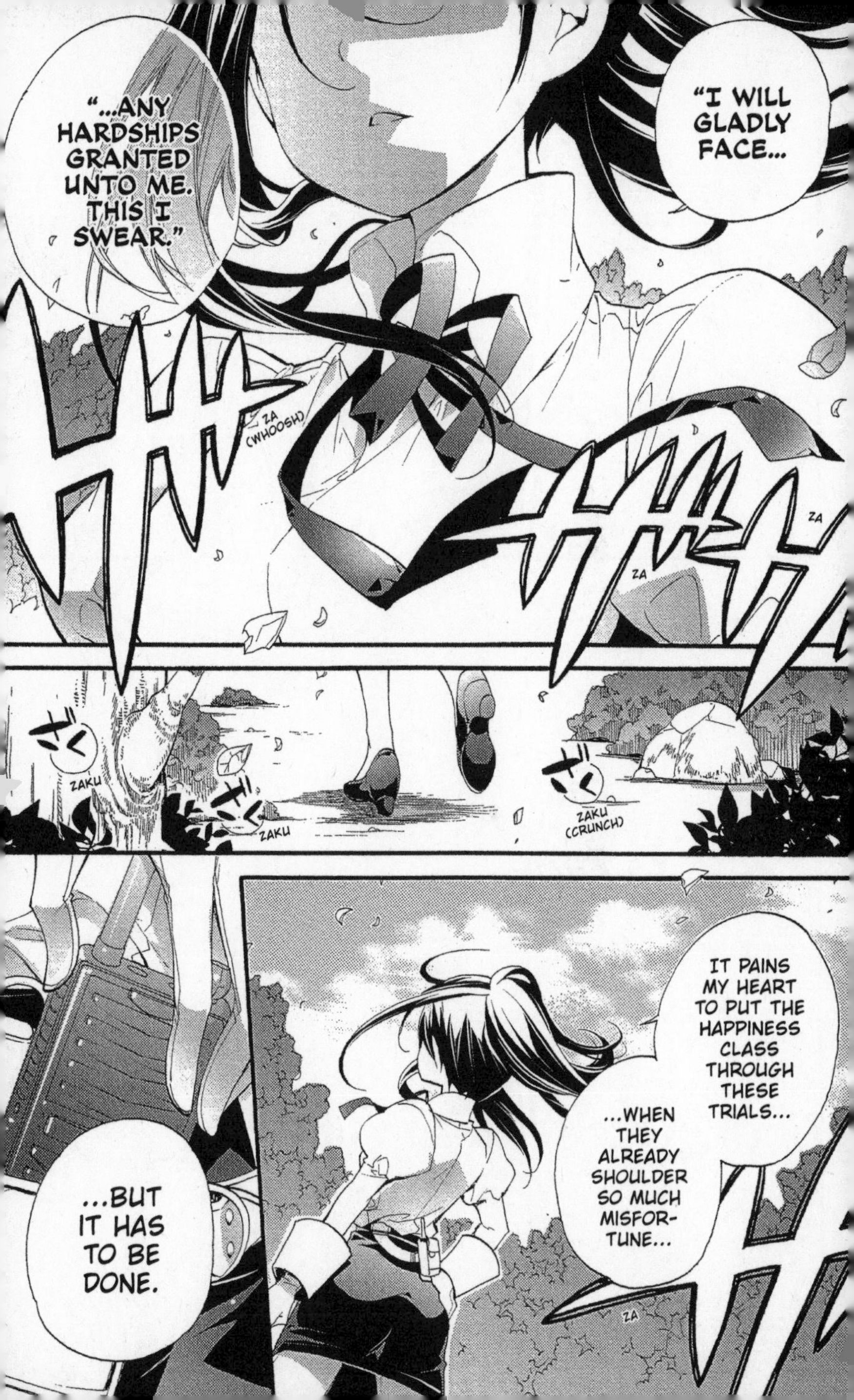
"I WILL GLADLY FACE...
"...ANY HARDSHIPS GRANTED UNTO ME. THIS I SWEAR."
ZA
ZA
ZA (WHOOSH)
ZAKU (CRUNCH)
ZAKU
ZAKU
IT PAINS MY HEART TO PUT THE HAPPINESS CLASS THROUGH THESE TRIALS...
...WHEN THEY ALREADY SHOULDER SO MUCH MISFOR-TUNE...
ZA
...BUT IT HAS TO BE DONE.

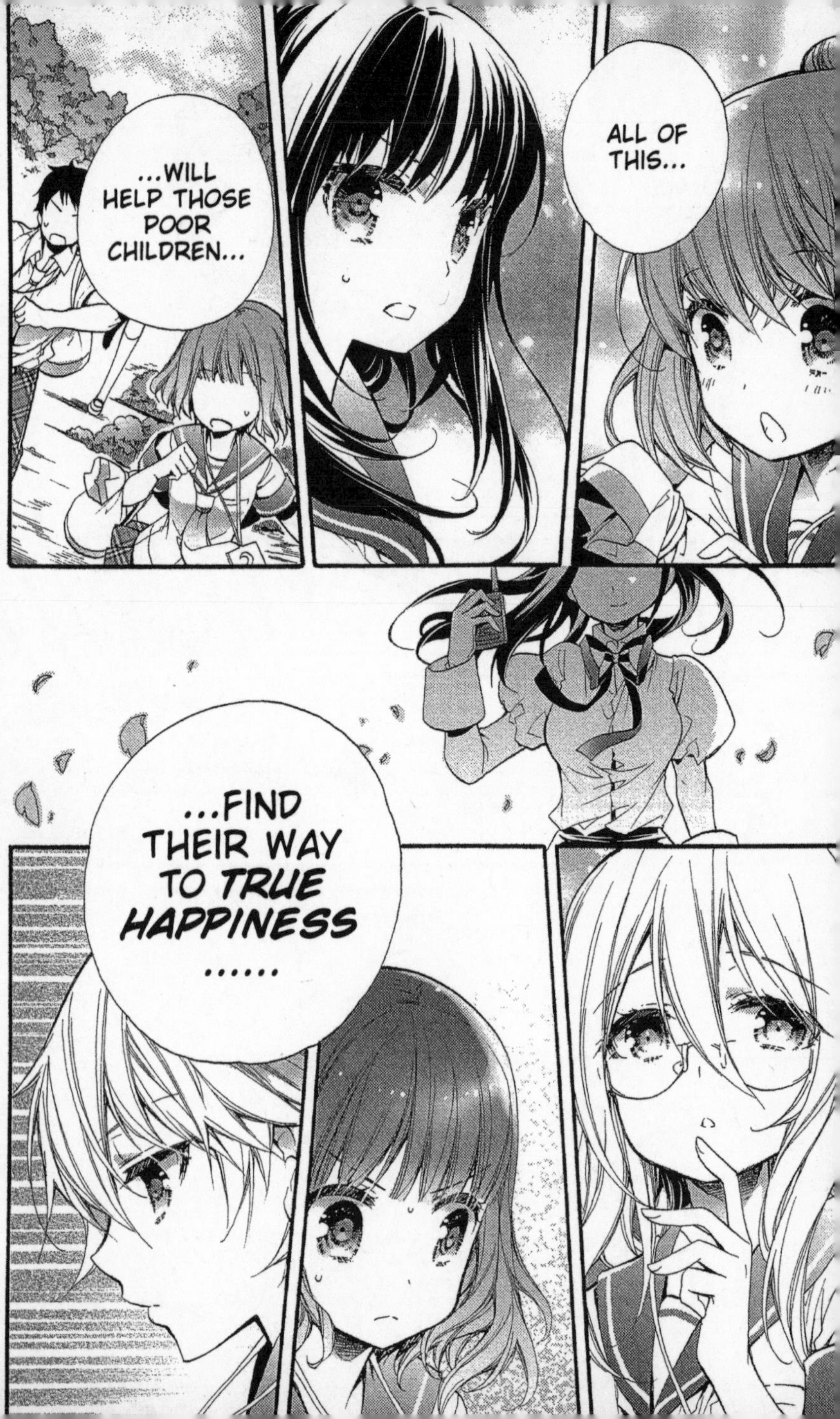
ALL OF THIS...
...WILL HELP THOSE POOR CHILDREN...
...FIND THEIR WAY TO *TRUE HAPPINESS* ......

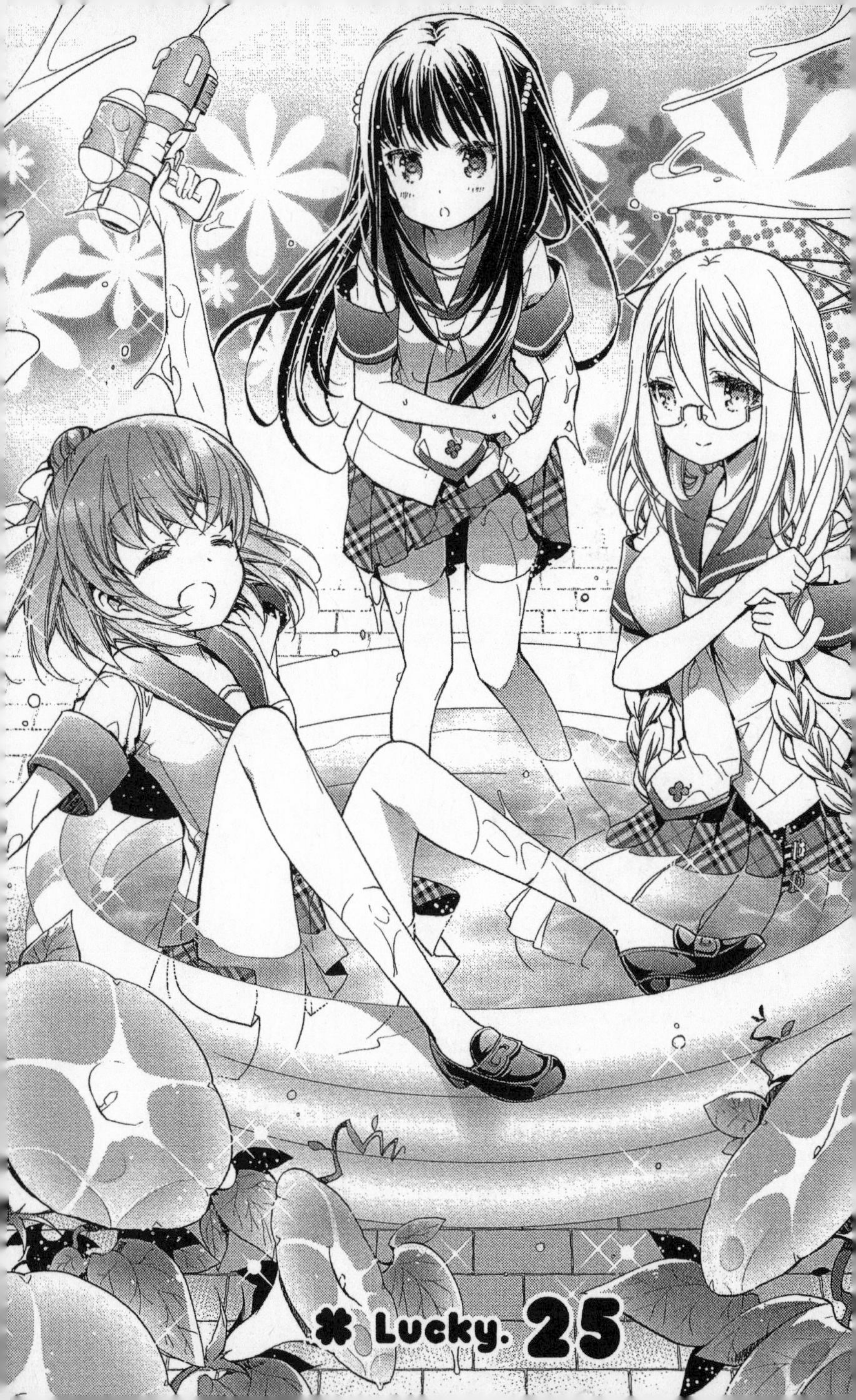
✱ Lucky. 25

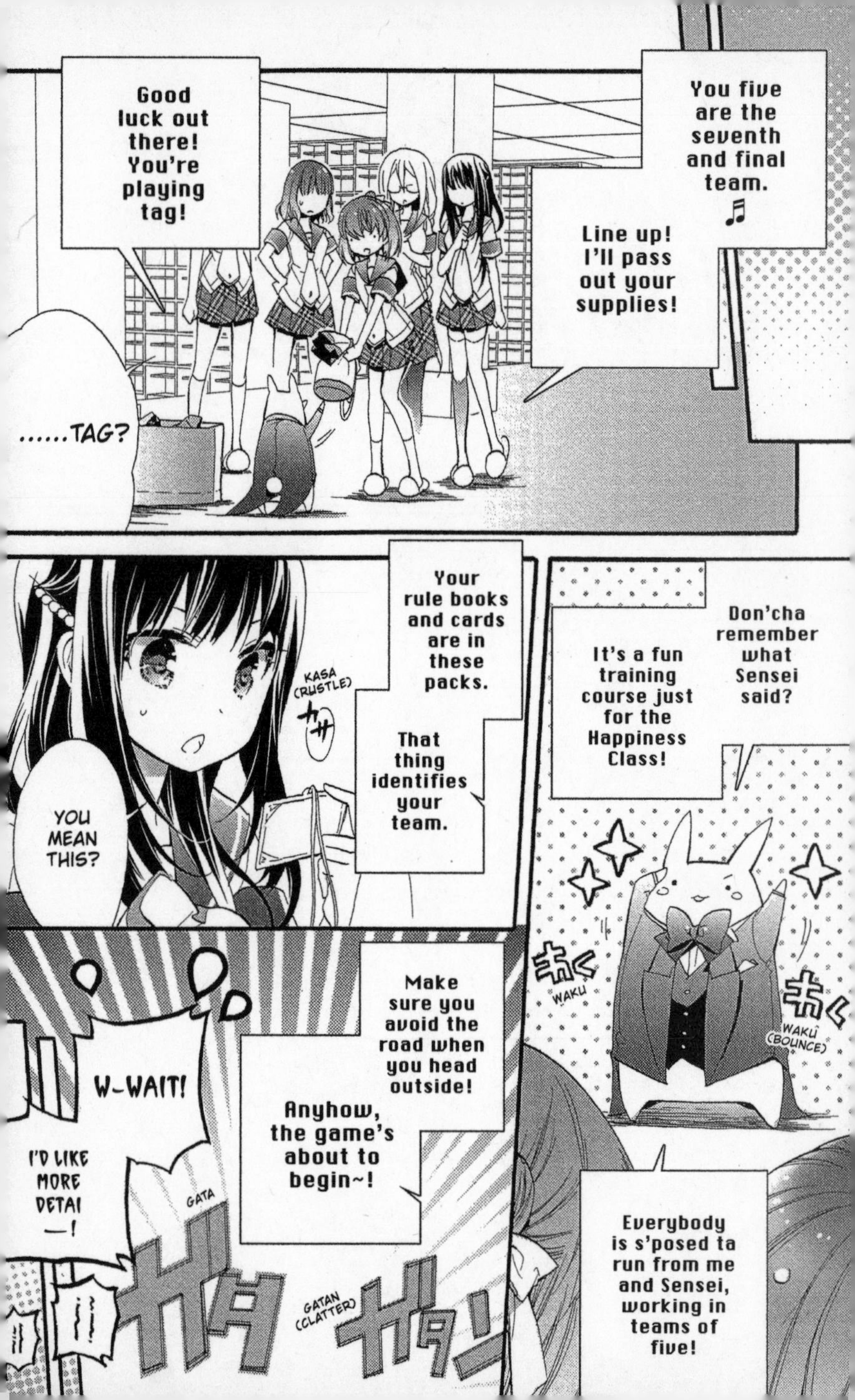
You five are the seventh and final team. ♬
Line up! I'll pass out your supplies!
Good luck out there! You're playing tag!
......TAG?
Don'cha remember what Sensei said?
It's a fun training course just for the Happiness Class!
WAKU
WAKU (BOUNCE)
Everybody is s'posed ta run from me and Sensei, working in teams of five!
Your rule books and cards are in these packs.
KASA (RUSTLE)
YOU MEAN THIS?
That thing identifies your team.
Make sure you avoid the road when you head outside!
Anyhow, the game's about to begin~!
W-WAIT!
I'D LIKE MORE DETAI—!
GATA
GATAN (CLATTER)

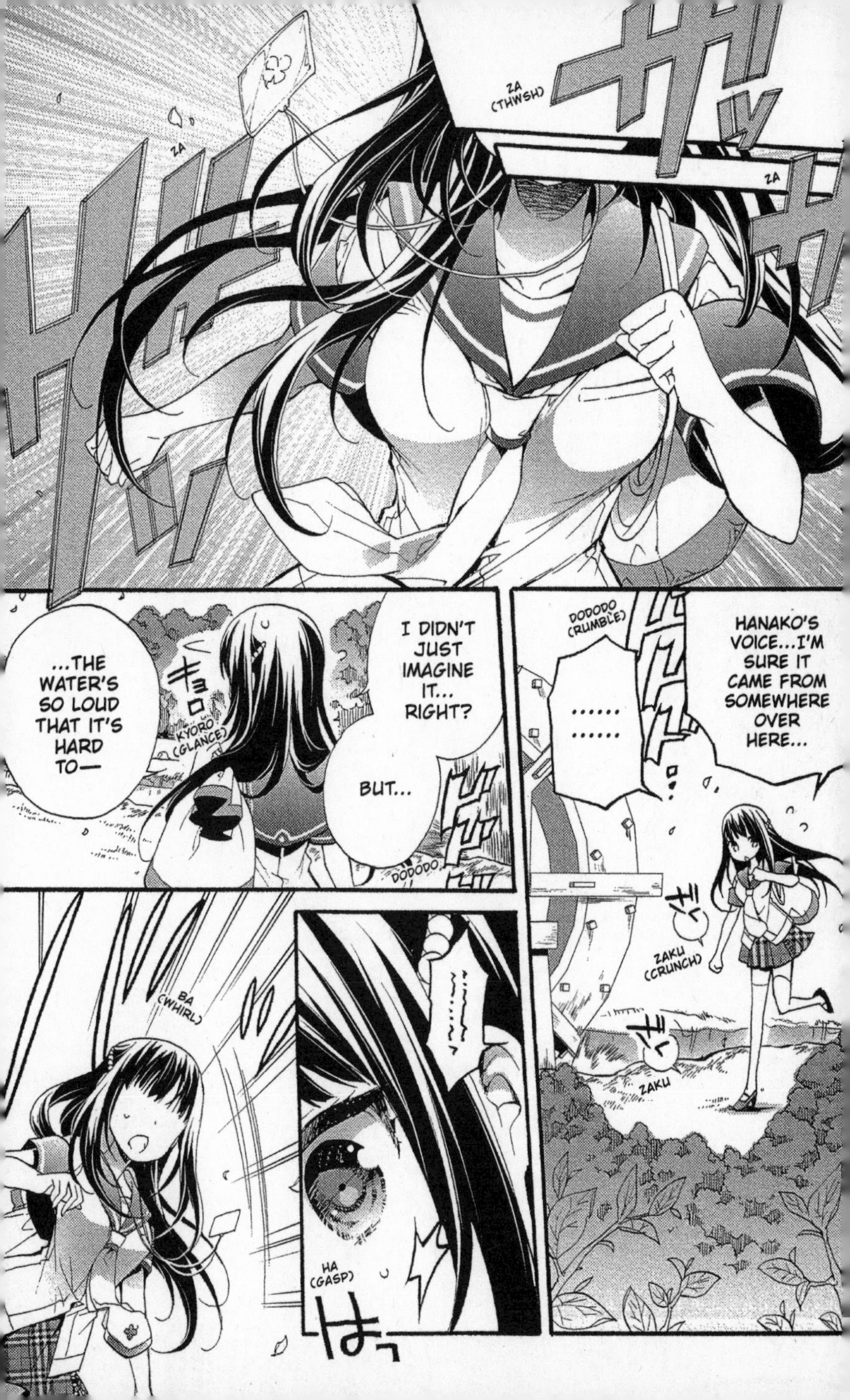
ZA (THWSH)
ZA
ZA
DODODO (RUMBLE)
HANAKO'S VOICE...I'M SURE IT CAME FROM SOMEWHERE OVER HERE...
......
......
ZAKU (CRUNCH)
ZAKU
I DIDN'T JUST IMAGINE IT... RIGHT?
BUT...
DODODO
...THE WATER'S SO LOUD THAT IT'S HARD TO—
KYORO (GLANCE)
HA (GASP)
BA (WHIRL)

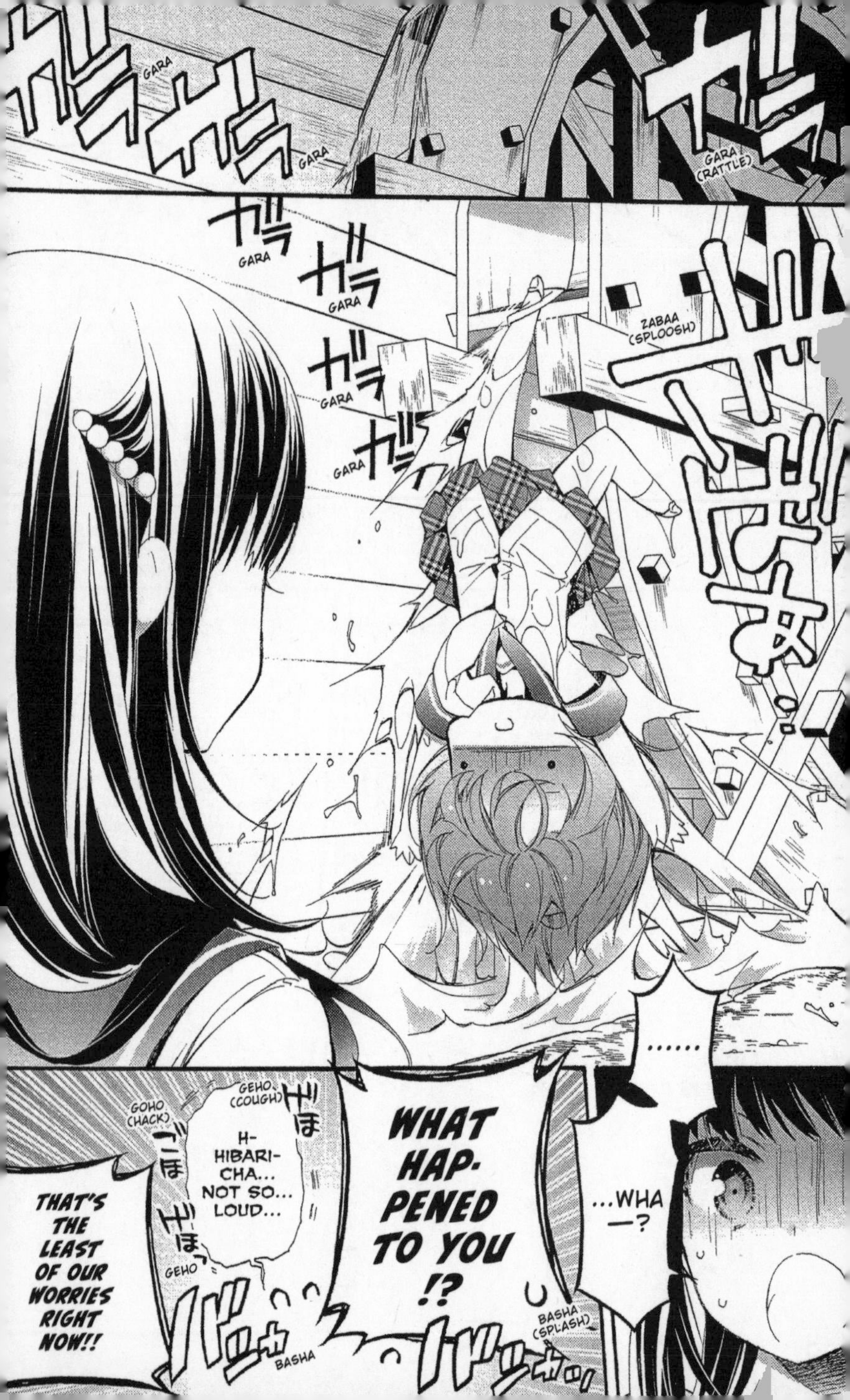
GARA (RATTLE)
GARA
GARA
ZABAA (SPLOOSH)
GARA
GARA
GARA
GARA
......
...WHA—?
BASHA (SPLASH)
WHAT HAP-PENED TO YOU!?
BASHA
GEHO (COUGH)
H-HIBARI-CHA... NOT SO... LOUD...
GOHO (HACK)
GEHO
THAT'S THE LEAST OF OUR WORRIES RIGHT NOW!!

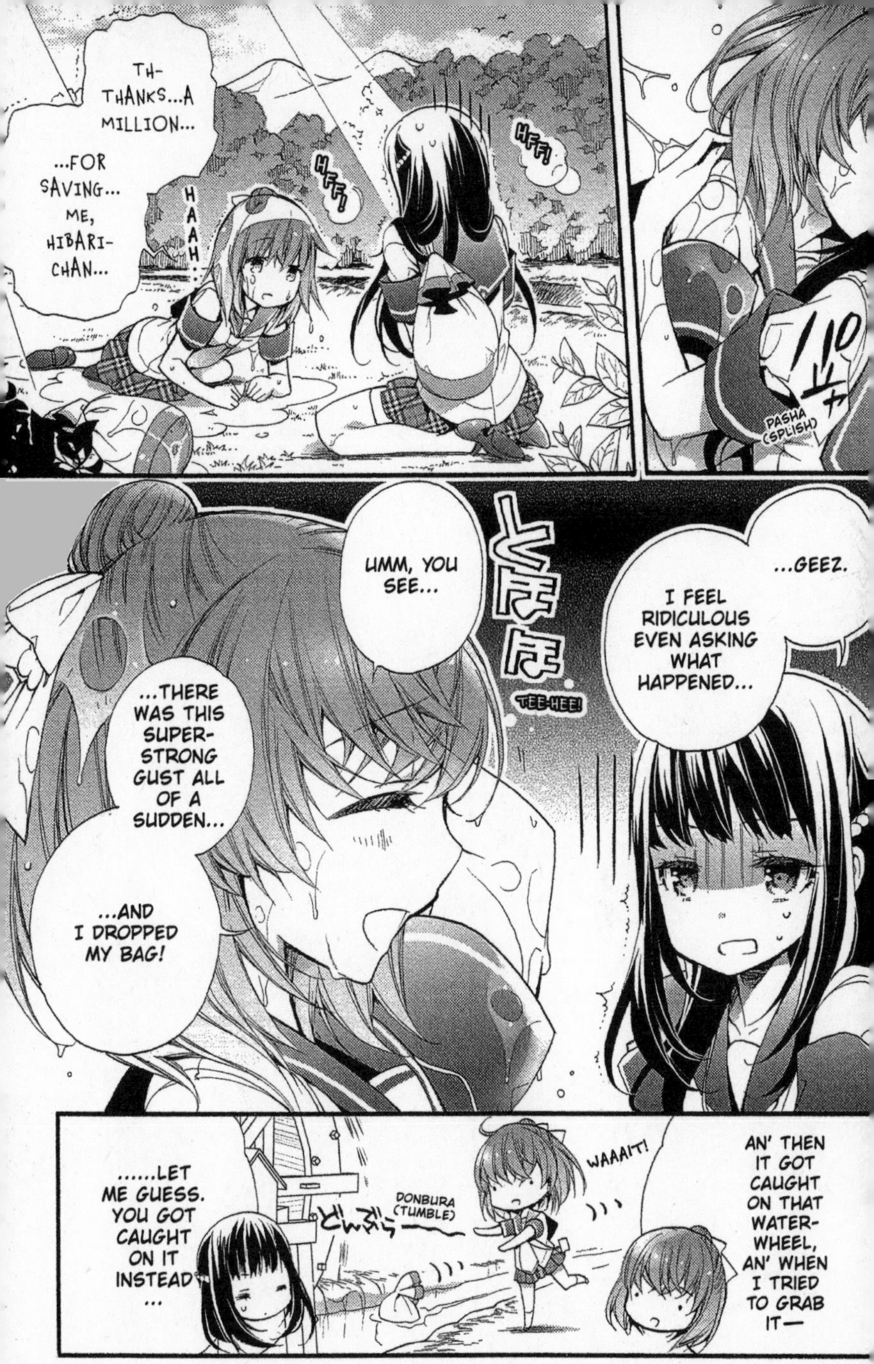
パシャ
PASHA (SPLISH)
HFF!
HFF!
TH- THANKS...A MILLION...
...FOR SAVING... ME, HIBARI-CHAN...
HAAH
...GEEZ.
I FEEL RIDICULOUS EVEN ASKING WHAT HAPPENED...
とほほ
TEE-HEE!
UMM, YOU SEE...
...THERE WAS THIS SUPER-STRONG GUST ALL OF A SUDDEN...
...AND I DROPPED MY BAG!
AN' THEN IT GOT CAUGHT ON THAT WATER-WHEEL, AN' WHEN I TRIED TO GRAB IT—
WAAAIT!
どんぶらーー
DONBURA (TUMBLE)
......LET ME GUESS. YOU GOT CAUGHT ON IT INSTEAD...

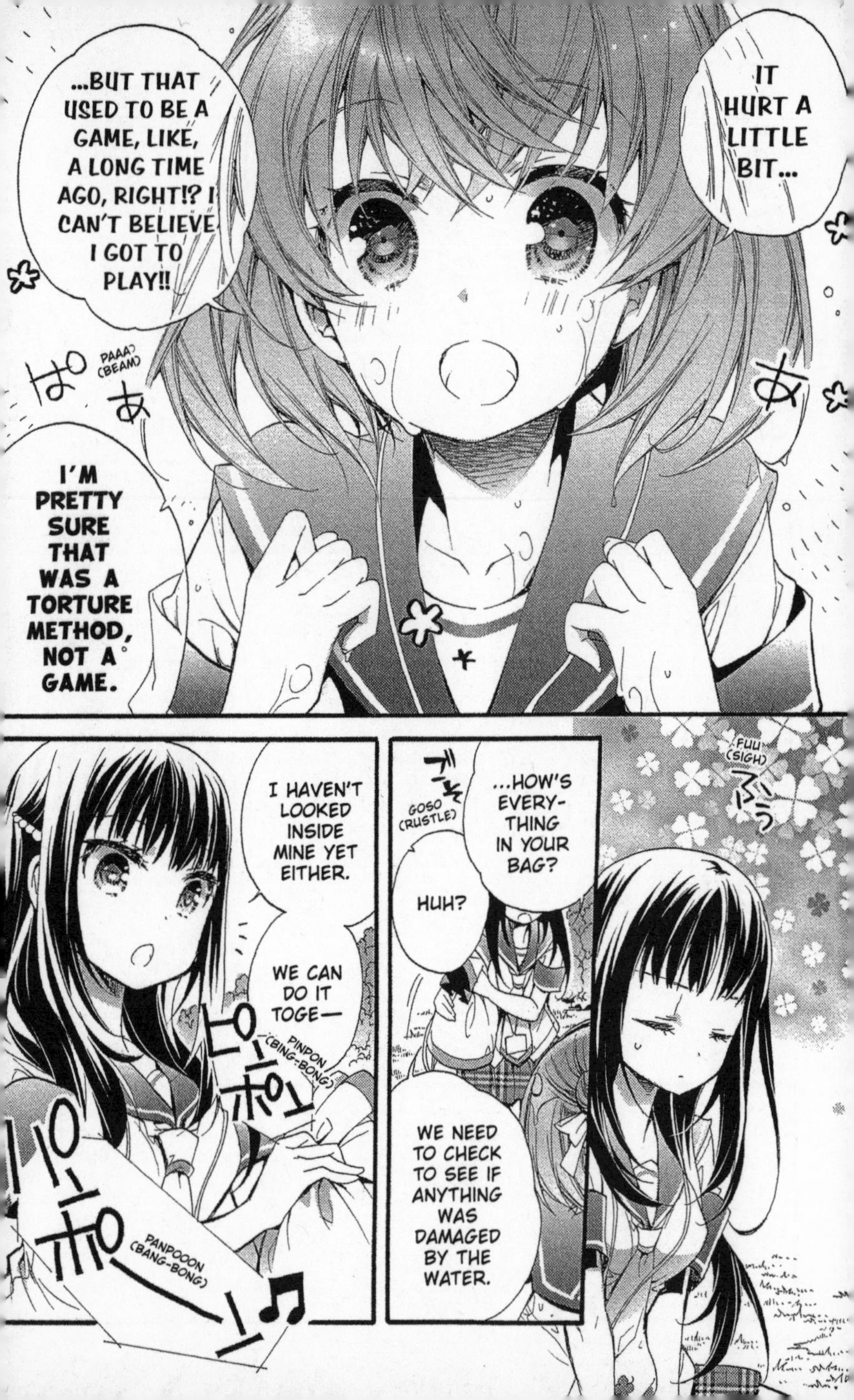
IT HURT A LITTLE BIT...
...BUT THAT USED TO BE A GAME, LIKE, A LONG TIME AGO, RIGHT!? I CAN'T BELIEVE I GOT TO PLAY!!
ぱあ
PAAA (BEAM)
あ
I'M PRETTY SURE THAT WAS A TORTURE METHOD, NOT A GAME.
ふぅ
FUU (SIGH)
...HOW'S EVERYTHING IN YOUR BAG?
ごそ
GOSO (RUSTLE)
HUH?
WE NEED TO CHECK TO SEE IF ANYTHING WAS DAMAGED BY THE WATER.
I HAVEN'T LOOKED INSIDE MINE YET EITHER.
WE CAN DO IT TOGE—
ピンポン
PINPON (BING-BONG)
パンポーン♪
PANPOOON (BANG-BONG)

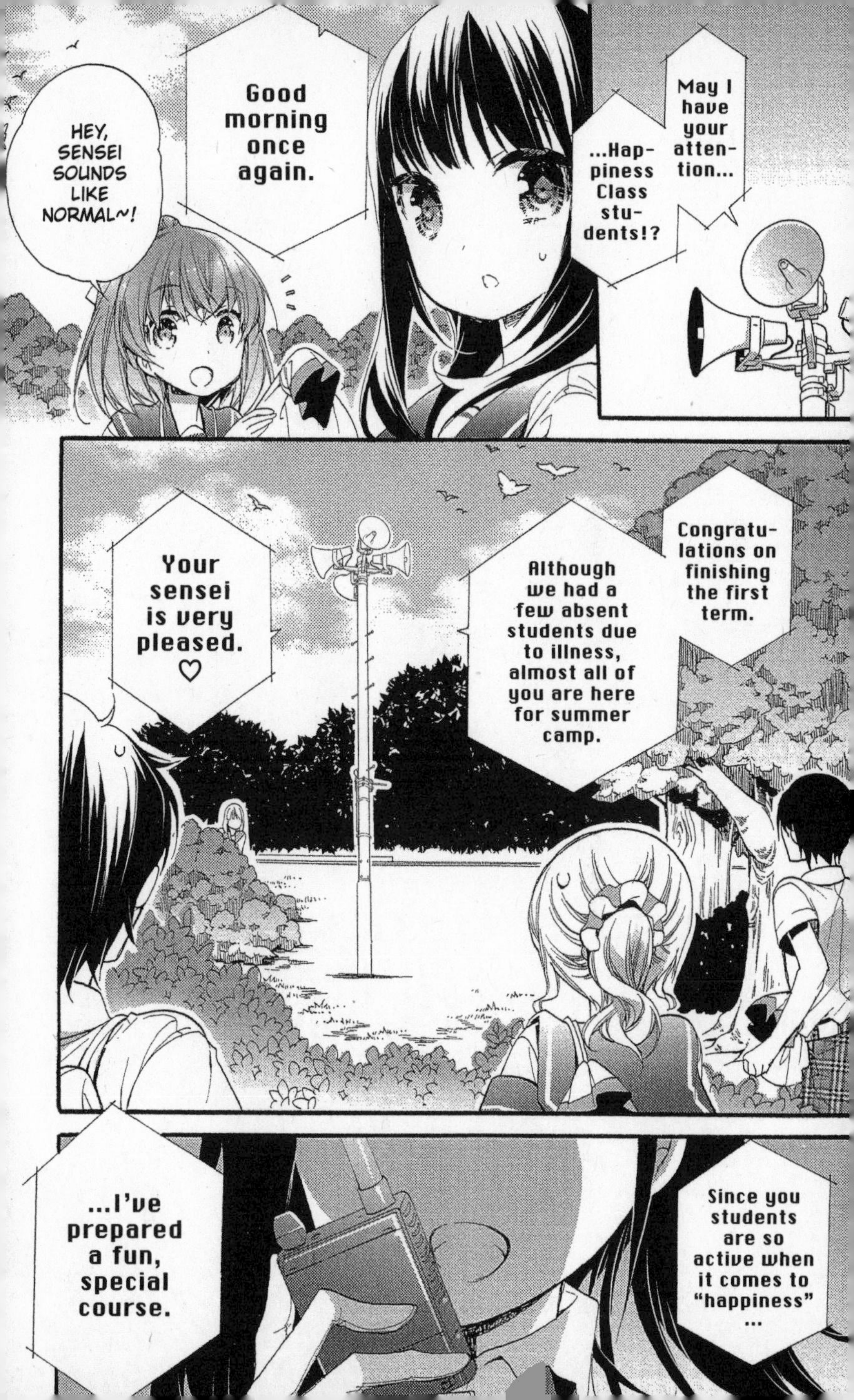
May I have your attention...
...Hap-piness Class students!?
Good morning once again.
HEY, SENSEI SOUNDS LIKE NORMAL~!
Congratulations on finishing the first term.
Although we had a few absent students due to illness, almost all of you are here for summer camp.
Your sensei is very pleased. ♡
Since you students are so active when it comes to "happiness"...
...I've prepared a fun, special course.

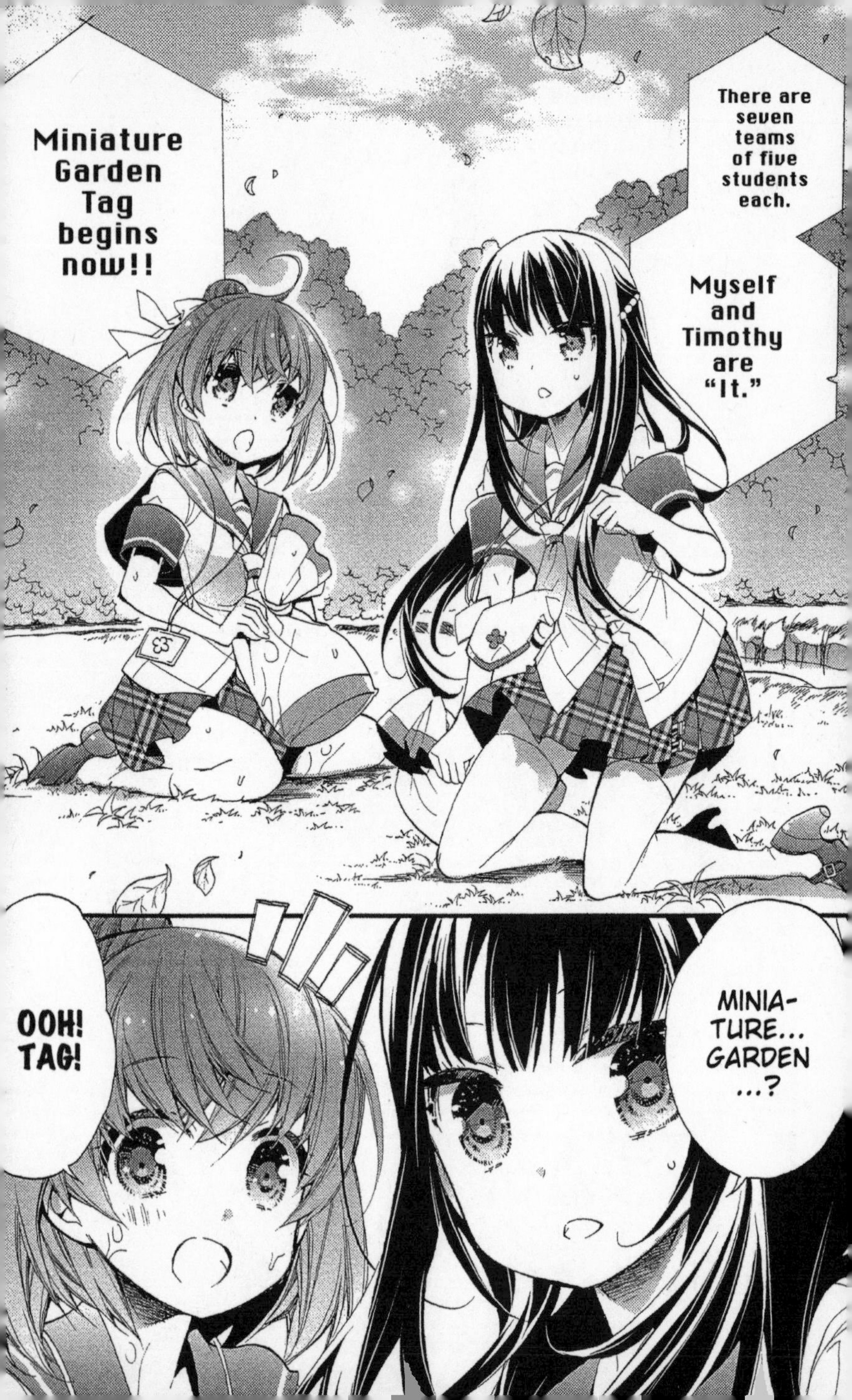
There are seven teams of five students each.
Myself and Timothy are "It."
Miniature Garden Tag begins now!!
MINIA-TURE... GARDEN ...?
OOH! TAG!

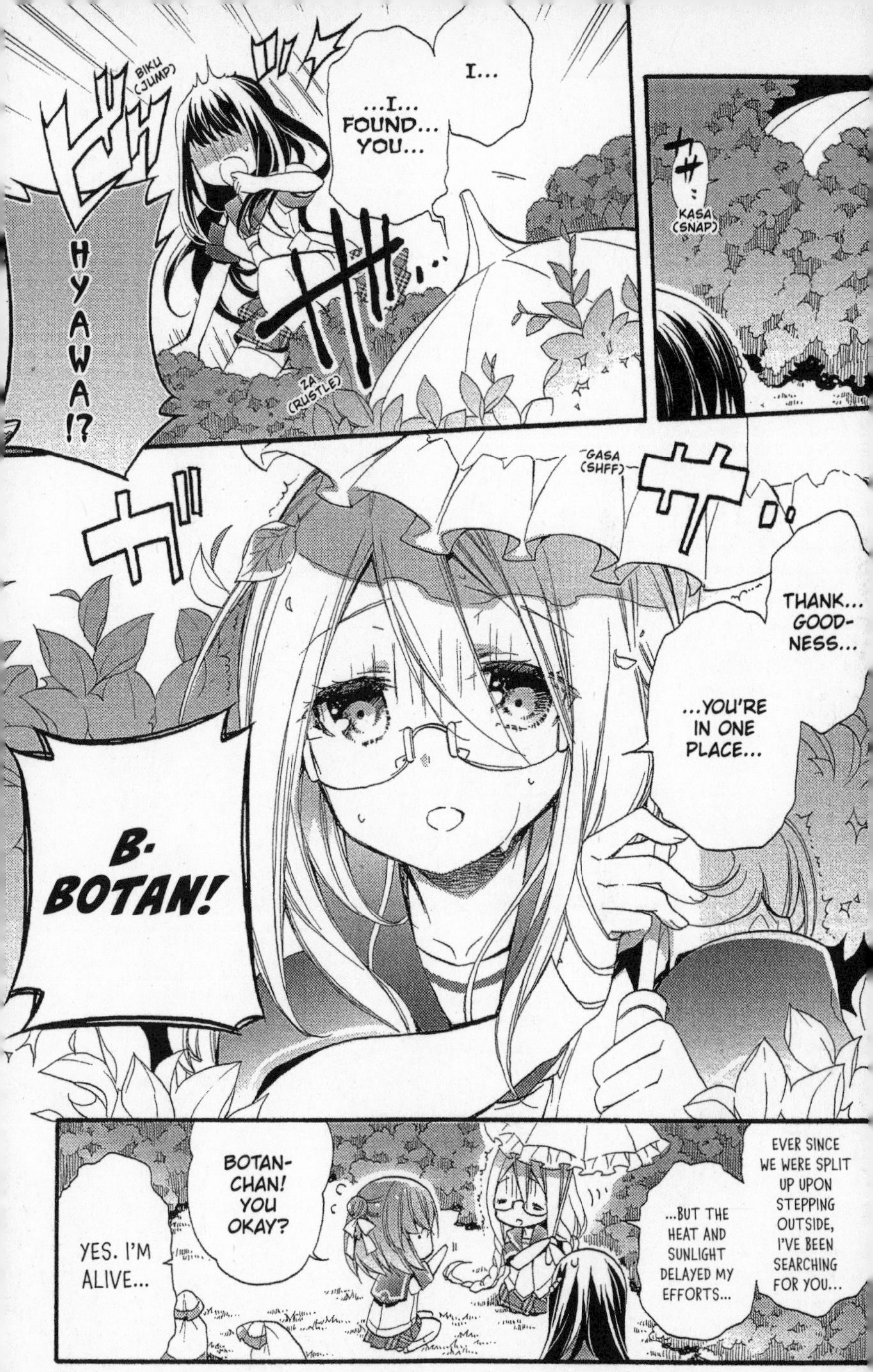
KASA (SNAP)
I...
...I... FOUND... YOU...
BIKU (JUMP)
HYAWA!?
ZA (RUSTLE)
GASA (SHFF)
THANK... GOODNESS...
...YOU'RE IN ONE PLACE...
B-BOTAN!
EVER SINCE WE WERE SPLIT UP UPON STEPPING OUTSIDE, I'VE BEEN SEARCHING FOR YOU...
...BUT THE HEAT AND SUNLIGHT DELAYED MY EFFORTS...
BOTAN-CHAN! YOU OKAY?
YES. I'M ALIVE...

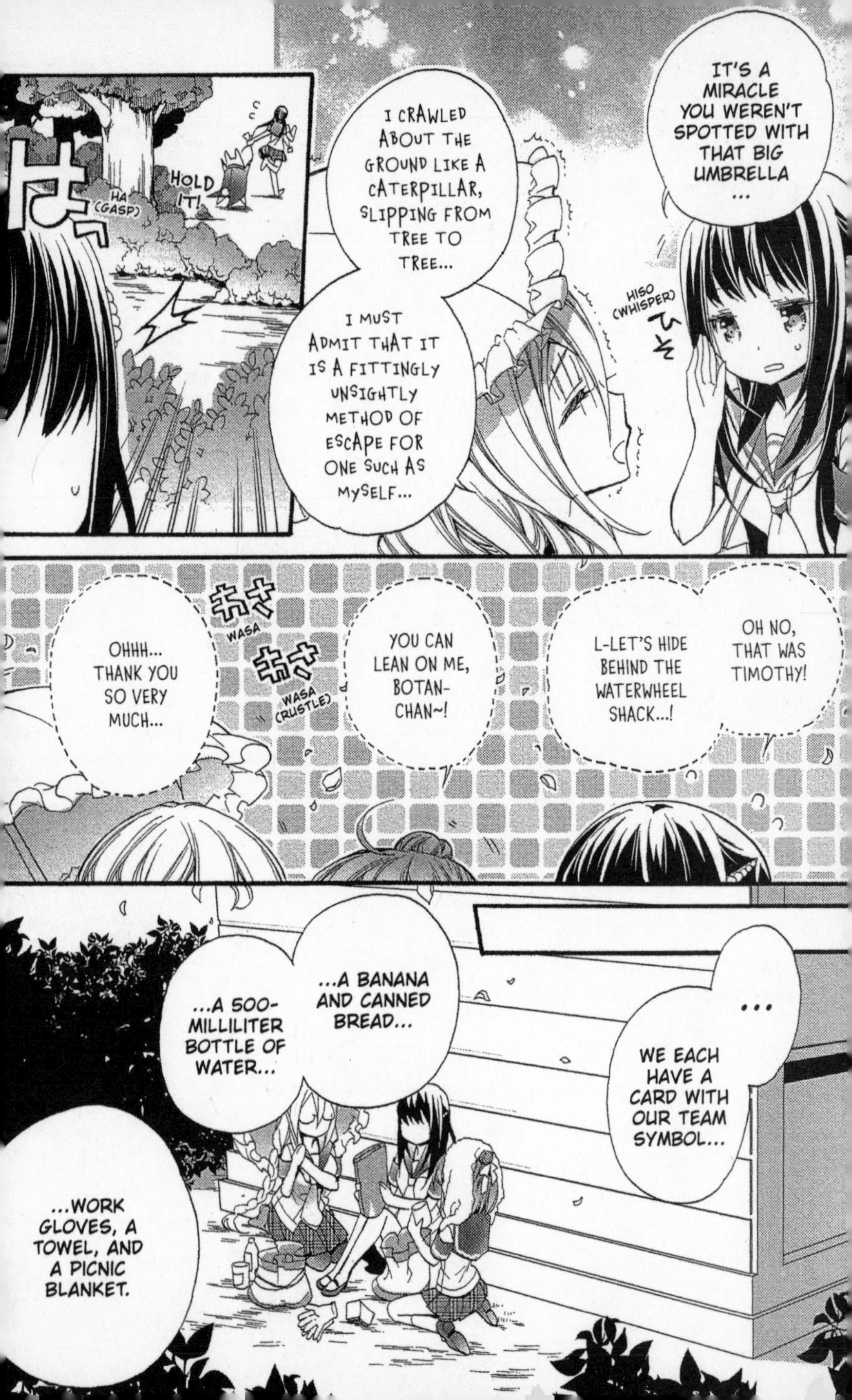
IT'S A MIRACLE YOU WEREN'T SPOTTED WITH THAT BIG UMBRELLA ...
HISO (WHISPER)
I CRAWLED ABOUT THE GROUND LIKE A CATERPILLAR, SLIPPING FROM TREE TO TREE...
I MUST ADMIT THAT IT IS A FITTINGLY UNSIGHTLY METHOD OF ESCAPE FOR ONE SUCH AS MYSELF...
HOLD IT!
HA (GASP)
OH NO, THAT WAS TIMOTHY!
L-LET'S HIDE BEHIND THE WATERWHEEL SHACK...!
YOU CAN LEAN ON ME, BOTAN-CHAN~!
WASA
WASA (RUSTLE)
OHHH... THANK YOU SO VERY MUCH...
...
WE EACH HAVE A CARD WITH OUR TEAM SYMBOL...
...A BANANA AND CANNED BREAD...
...A 500-MILLILITER BOTTLE OF WATER...
...WORK GLOVES, A TOWEL, AND A PICNIC BLANKET.

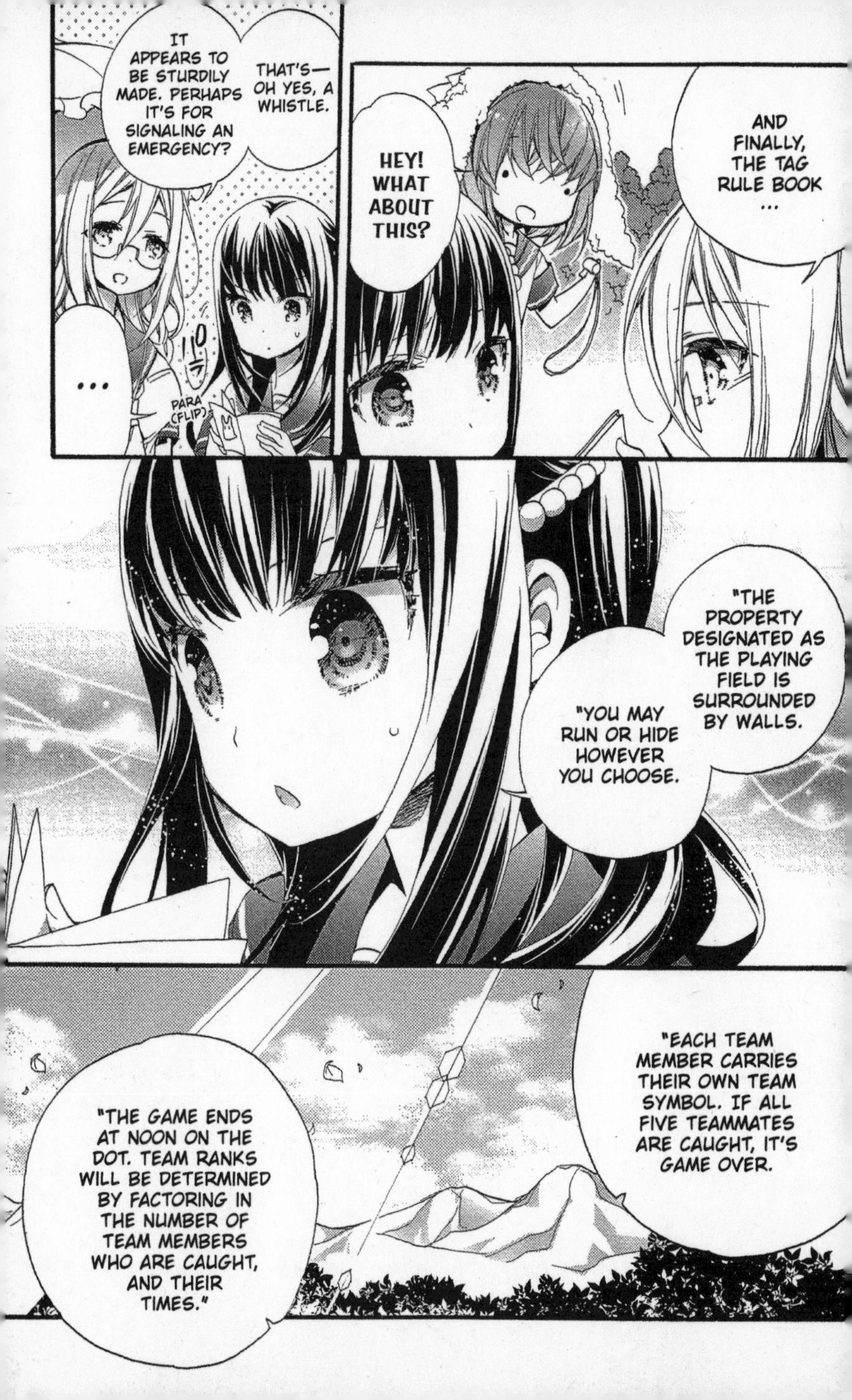
AND FINALLY, THE TAG RULE BOOK ...
HEY! WHAT ABOUT THIS?
THAT'S— OH YES, A WHISTLE.
IT APPEARS TO BE STURDILY MADE. PERHAPS IT'S FOR SIGNALING AN EMERGENCY?
...
PARA (FLIP)
"THE PROPERTY DESIGNATED AS THE PLAYING FIELD IS SURROUNDED BY WALLS.
"YOU MAY RUN OR HIDE HOWEVER YOU CHOOSE.
"EACH TEAM MEMBER CARRIES THEIR OWN TEAM SYMBOL. IF ALL FIVE TEAMMATES ARE CAUGHT, IT'S GAME OVER.
"THE GAME ENDS AT NOON ON THE DOT. TEAM RANKS WILL BE DETERMINED BY FACTORING IN THE NUMBER OF TEAM MEMBERS WHO ARE CAUGHT, AND THEIR TIMES."

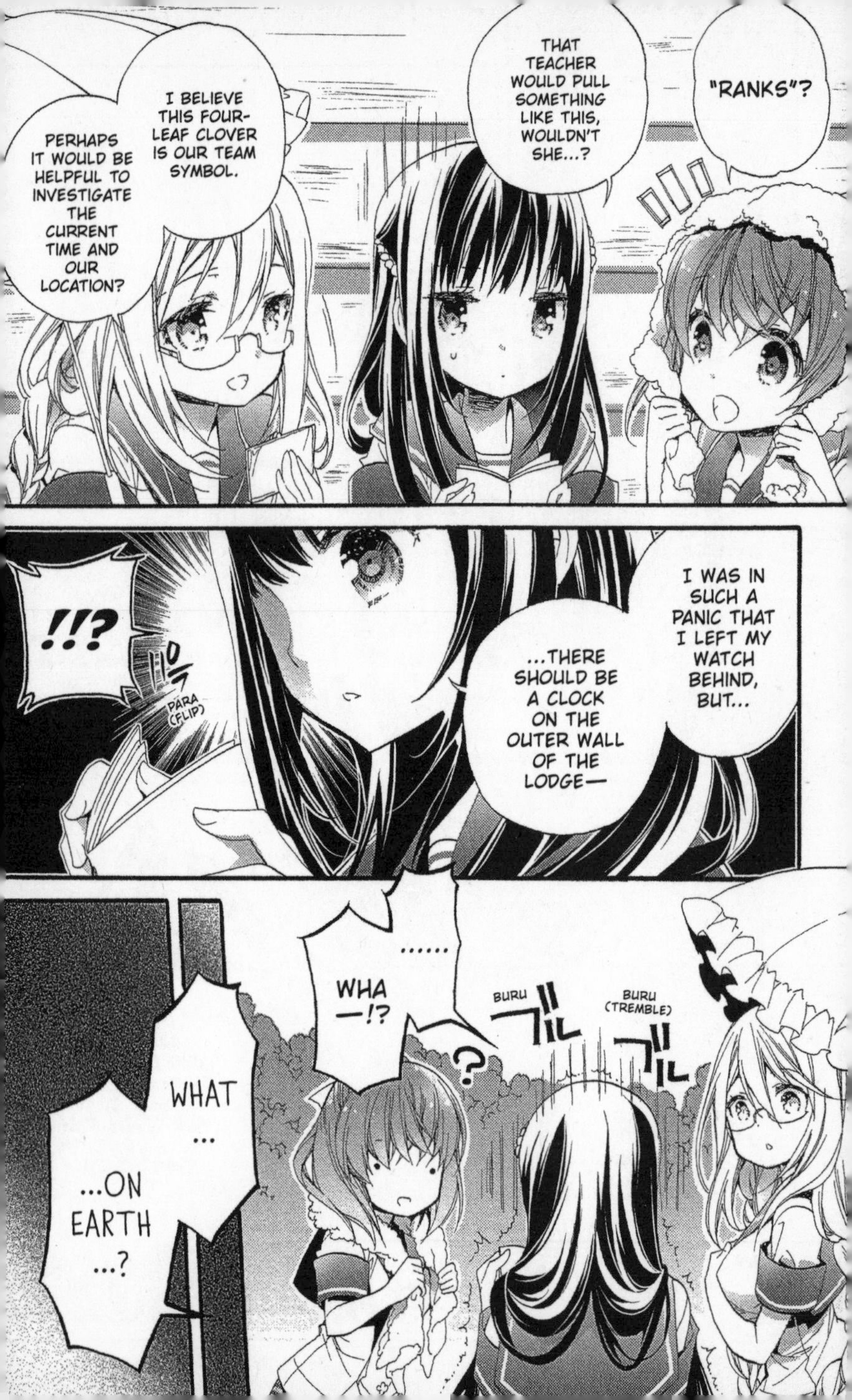
"RANKS"?
THAT TEACHER WOULD PULL SOMETHING LIKE THIS, WOULDN'T SHE...?
I BELIEVE THIS FOUR-LEAF CLOVER IS OUR TEAM SYMBOL.
PERHAPS IT WOULD BE HELPFUL TO INVESTIGATE THE CURRENT TIME AND OUR LOCATION?
I WAS IN SUCH A PANIC THAT I LEFT MY WATCH BEHIND, BUT...
...THERE SHOULD BE A CLOCK ON THE OUTER WALL OF THE LODGE—
PARA (FLIP)
!!?
BURU (TREMBLE)
BURU
......
WHA—!?
?
WHAT ... ...ON EARTH ...?

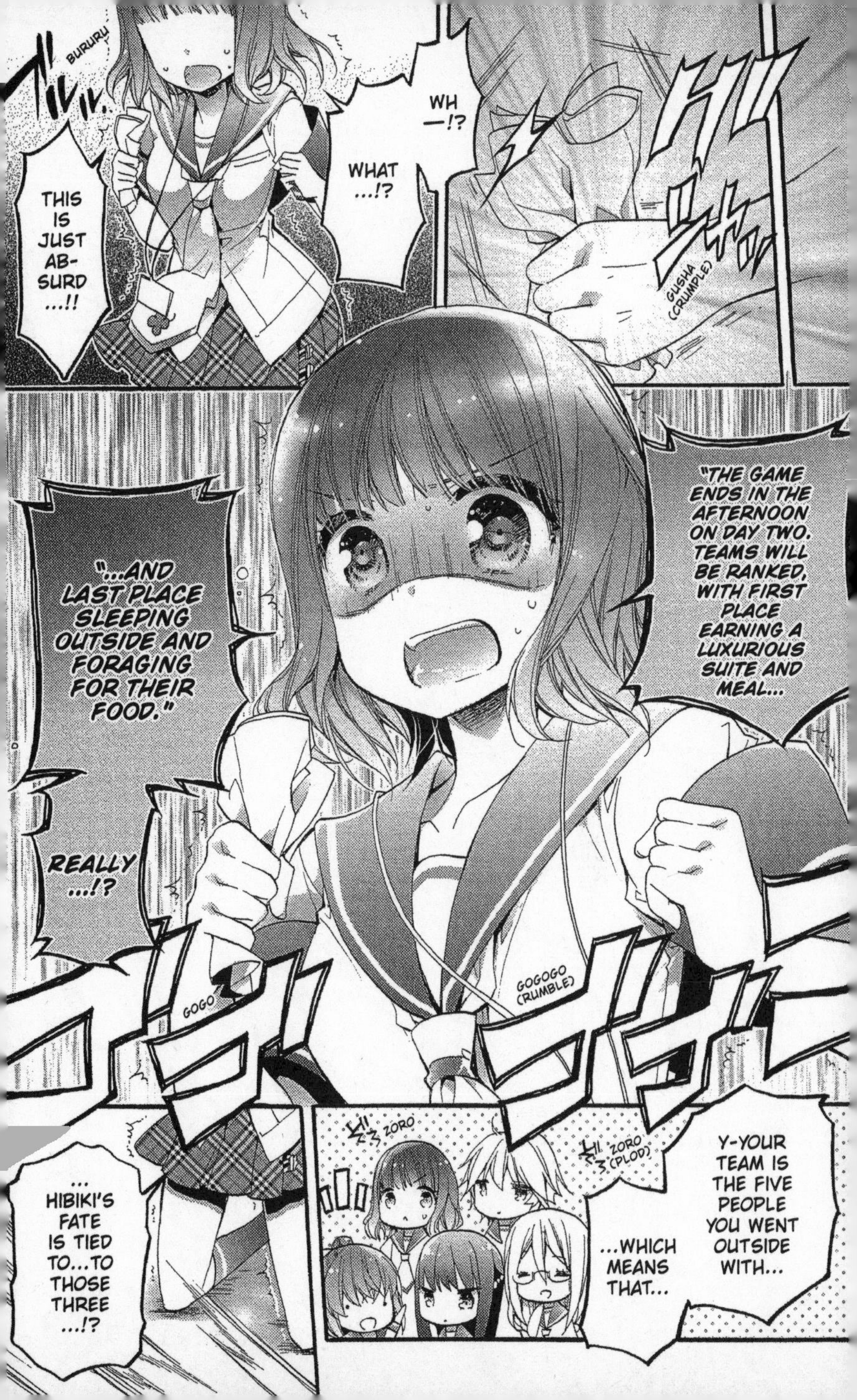
GUSHA (CRUMPLE)
WH—!?
WHAT ...!?
BURURU
THIS IS JUST AB-SURD ...!!
"THE GAME ENDS IN THE AFTERNOON ON DAY TWO. TEAMS WILL BE RANKED, WITH FIRST PLACE EARNING A LUXURIOUS SUITE AND MEAL...
"...AND LAST PLACE SLEEPING OUTSIDE AND FORAGING FOR THEIR FOOD."
REALLY ...!?
GOGOGO (RUMBLE)
GOGO
Y-YOUR TEAM IS THE FIVE PEOPLE YOU WENT OUTSIDE WITH...
...WHICH MEANS THAT...
ZORO (PLOD)
ZORO
... HIBIKI'S FATE IS TIED TO...TO THOSE THREE ...!?

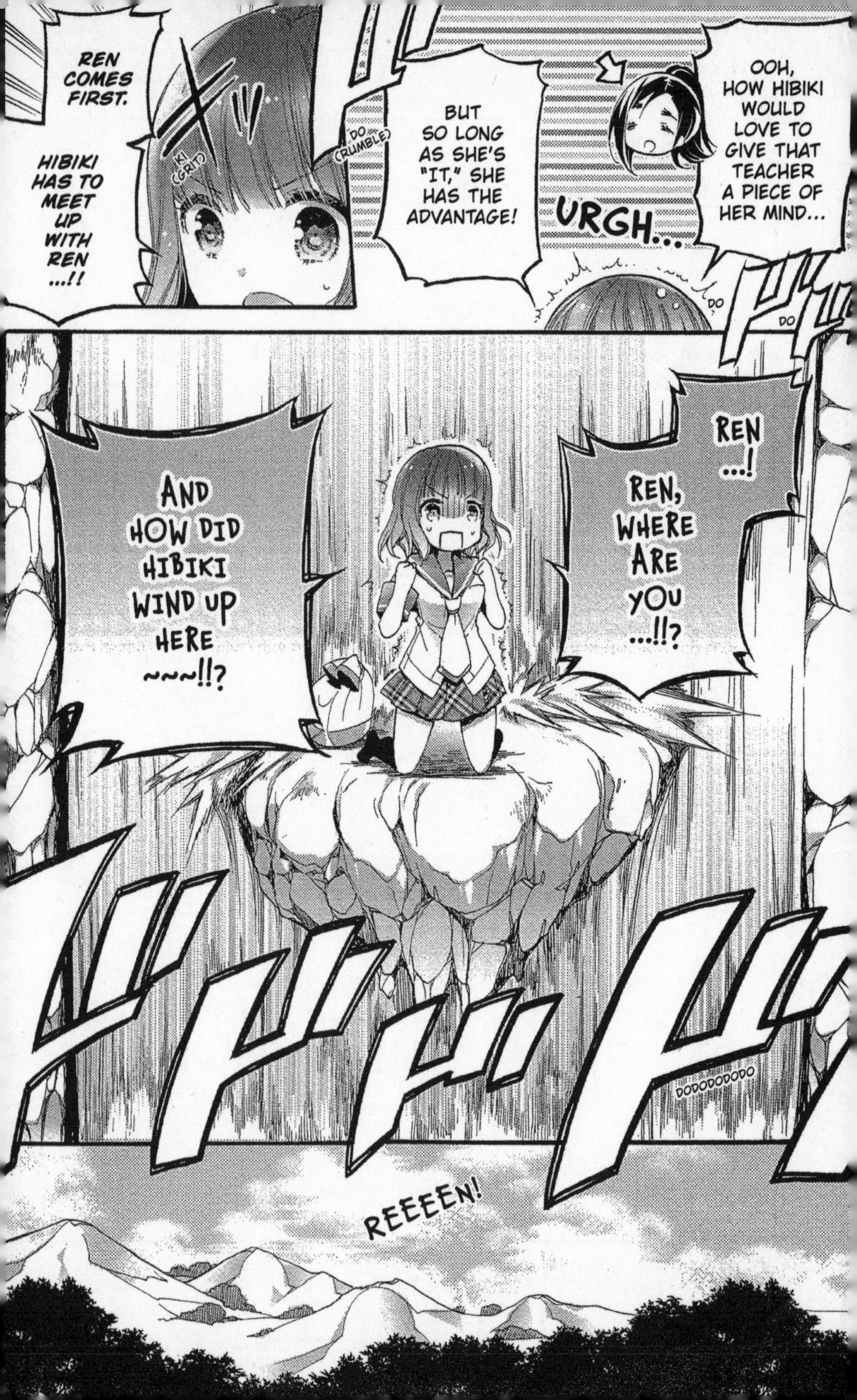
OOH, HOW HIBIKI WOULD LOVE TO GIVE THAT TEACHER A PIECE OF HER MIND...
URGH...
DO
DO
BUT SO LONG AS SHE'S "IT," SHE HAS THE ADVANTAGE!
DO (RUMBLE)
KI (GRIT)
REN COMES FIRST.
HIBIKI HAS TO MEET UP WITH REN ...!!
REN ...!
REN, WHERE ARE YOU ...!!?
AND HOW DID HIBIKI WIND UP HERE ~~~!!?
DODODODODO
REEEEN!

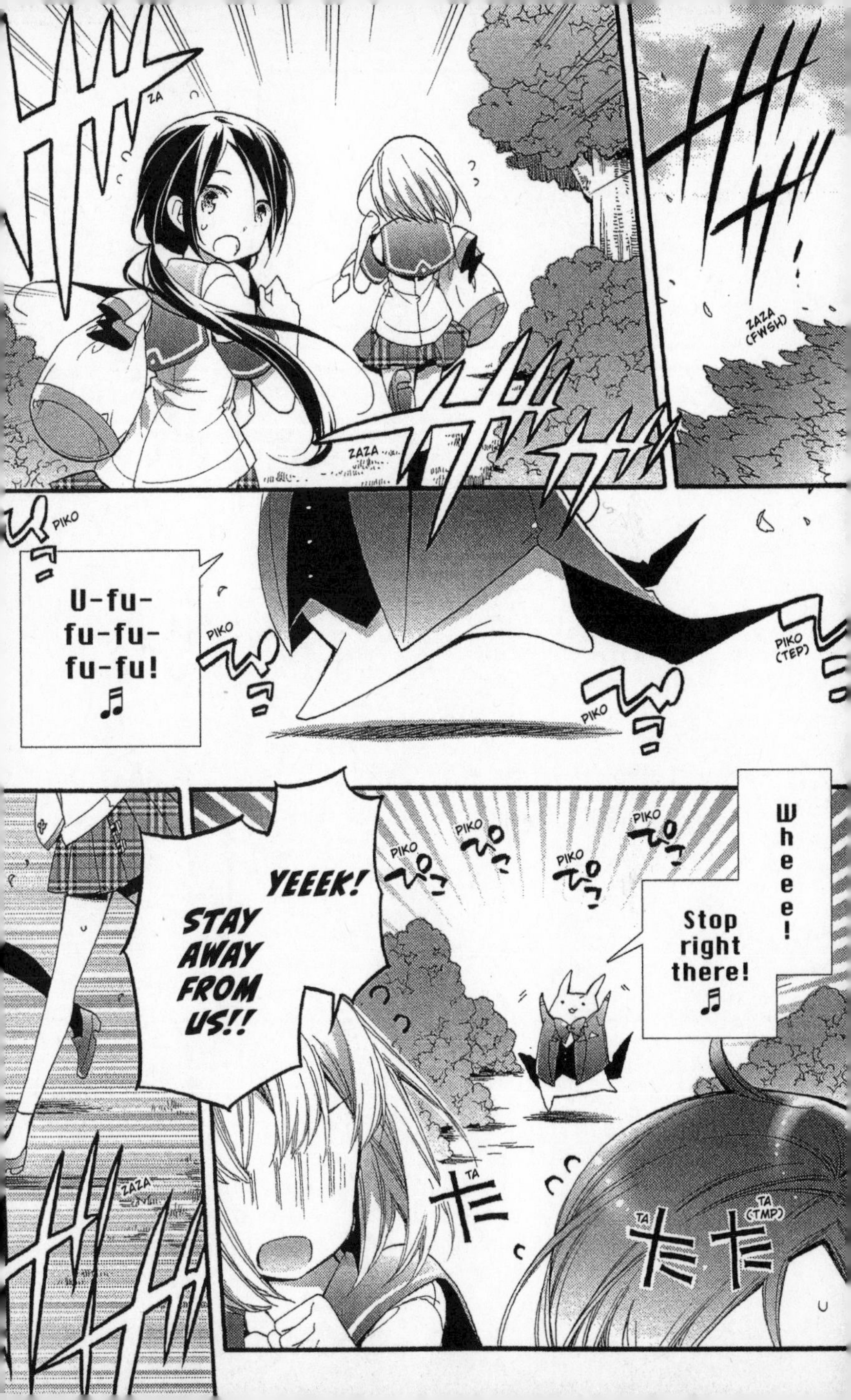
ZAZA (FWSH)
ZA
ZAZA
PIKO (TEP)
PIKO
PIKO
U-fu-fu-fu-fu-fu-fu! ♫
PIKO
Wheeee!
PIKO
PIKO
Stop right there! ♫
PIKO
PIKO
YEEEK!
STAY AWAY FROM US!!
TA (TMP)
TA
TA
ZAZA

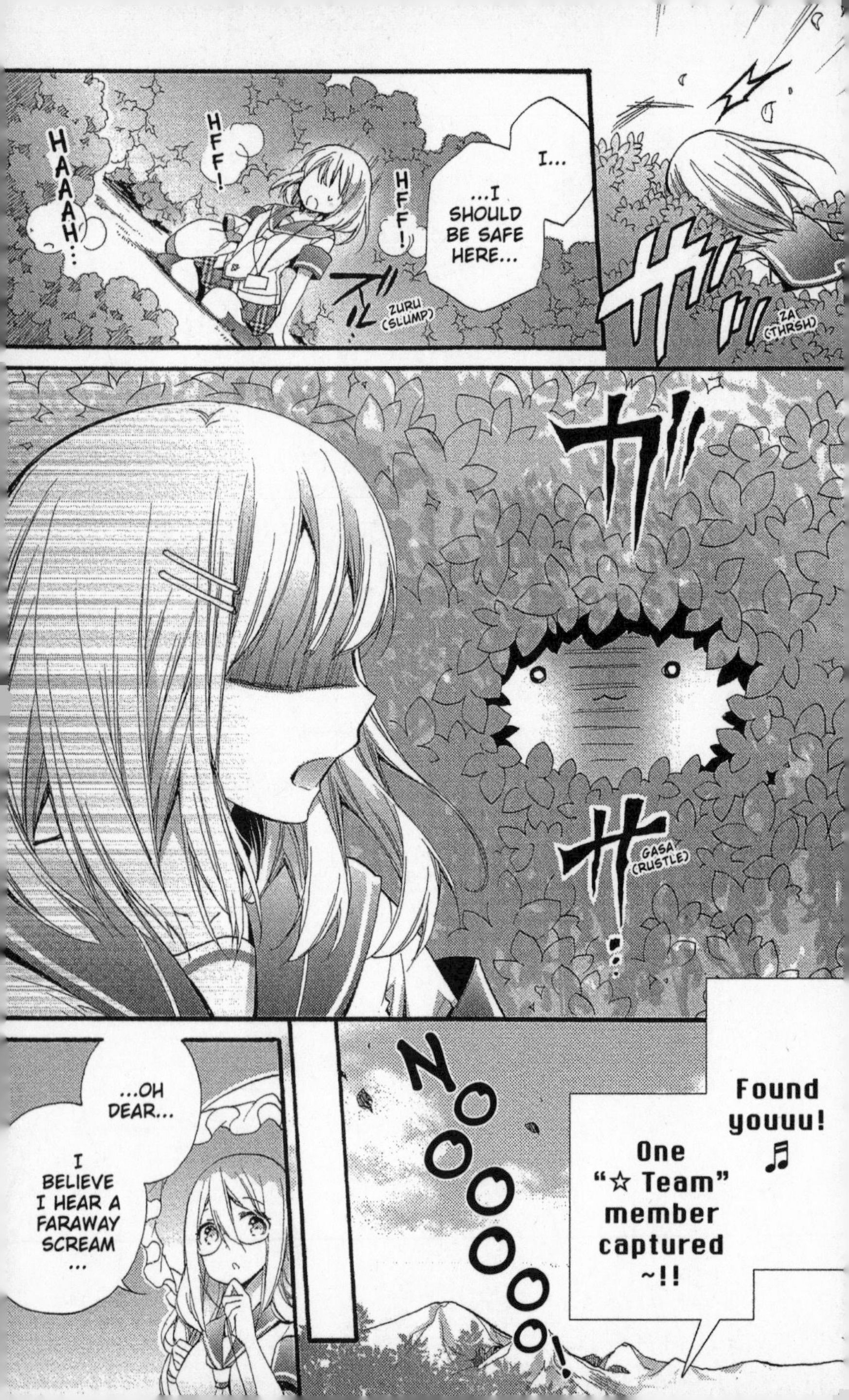
ZA (THRSH)
I...
...I SHOULD BE SAFE HERE...
HFF!
HFF!
HAAAH...
ZURU (SLUMP)
GASA (RUSTLE)
Found youuu! ♬
One "☆ Team" member captured ~!!
NOOOOOO!
...OH DEAR...
I BELIEVE I HEAR A FARAWAY SCREAM ...

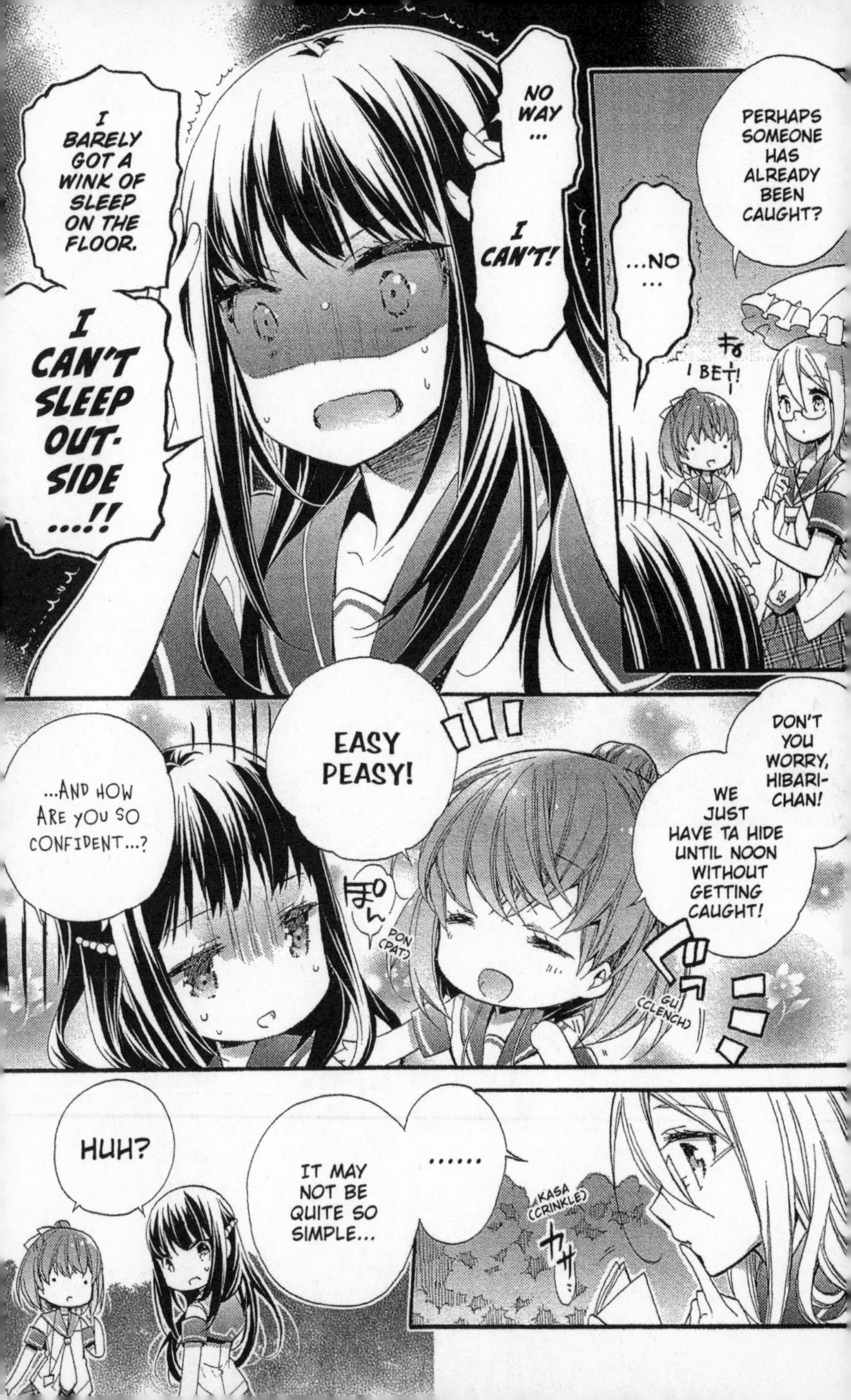
PERHAPS SOMEONE HAS ALREADY BEEN CAUGHT?
...NO ...
I BET!
NO WAY ...
I CAN'T!
I BARELY GOT A WINK OF SLEEP ON THE FLOOR.
I CAN'T SLEEP OUT-SIDE ...!!
DON'T YOU WORRY, HIBARI-CHAN!
WE JUST HAVE TA HIDE UNTIL NOON WITHOUT GETTING CAUGHT!
GU (CLENCH)
EASY PEASY!
PON (PAT)
...AND HOW ARE YOU SO CONFIDENT...?
KASA (CRINKLE)
......
IT MAY NOT BE QUITE SO SIMPLE...
HUH?

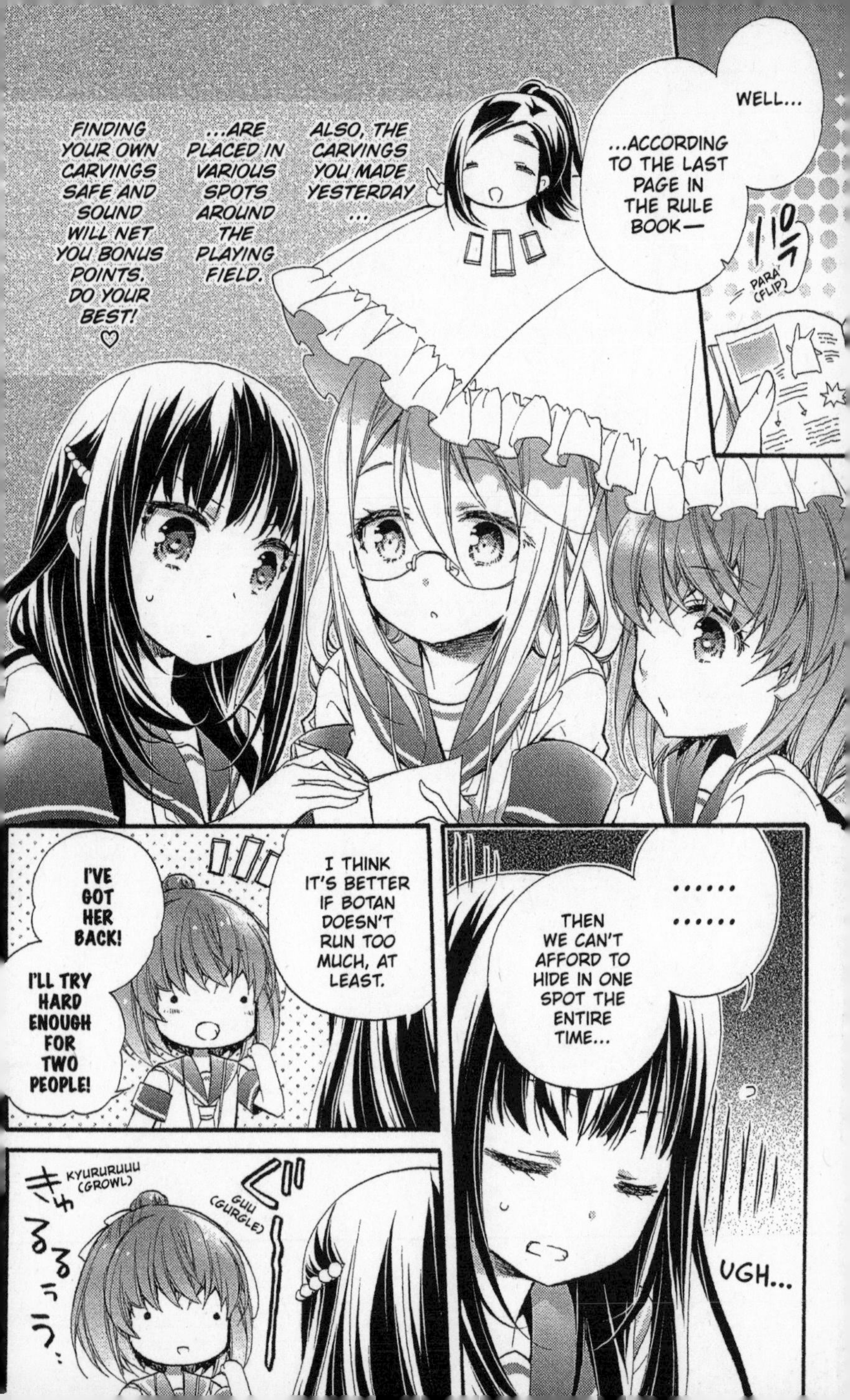
WELL...
...ACCORDING TO THE LAST PAGE IN THE RULE BOOK—
PARA (FLIP)
ALSO, THE CARVINGS YOU MADE YESTERDAY...
...ARE PLACED IN VARIOUS SPOTS AROUND THE PLAYING FIELD.
FINDING YOUR OWN CARVINGS SAFE AND SOUND WILL NET YOU BONUS POINTS. DO YOUR BEST! ♡
......
......
THEN WE CAN'T AFFORD TO HIDE IN ONE SPOT THE ENTIRE TIME...
UGH...
I THINK IT'S BETTER IF BOTAN DOESN'T RUN TOO MUCH, AT LEAST.
I'VE GOT HER BACK!
I'LL TRY HARD ENOUGH FOR TWO PEOPLE!
GUU (GURGLE)
KYURURUUU (GROWL)

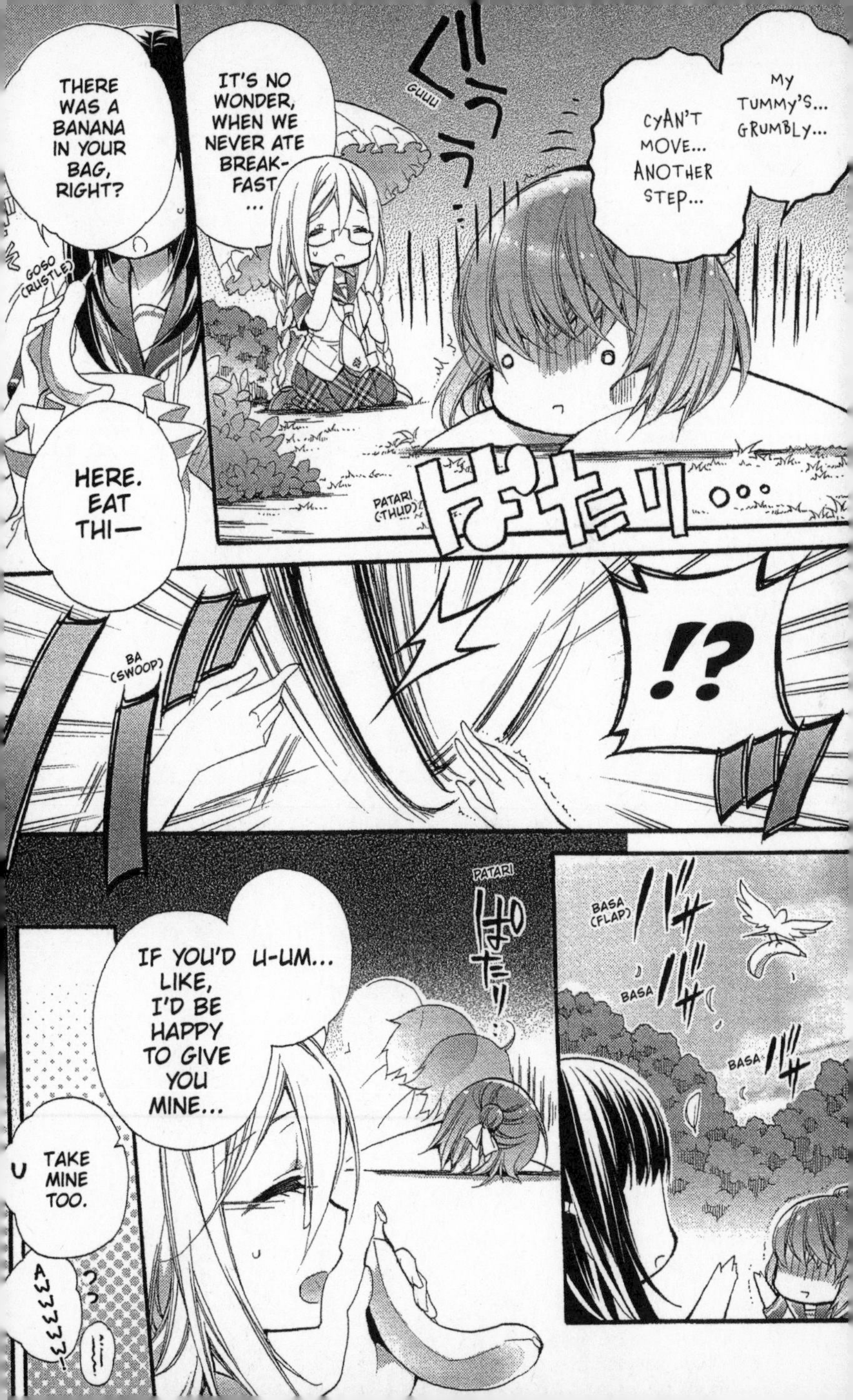
MY TUMMY'S... GRUMBLY...
CYAN'T MOVE... ANOTHER STEP...
GUUU
IT'S NO WONDER, WHEN WE NEVER ATE BREAKFAST...
PATARI (THUD)
THERE WAS A BANANA IN YOUR BAG, RIGHT?
GOSO (RUSTLE)
HERE. EAT THI—
!?
BA (SWOOP)
BASA (FLAP)
BASA
BASA
PATARI
U-UM...
IF YOU'D LIKE, I'D BE HAPPY TO GIVE YOU MINE...
U
TAKE MINE TOO.
AWWWWW!

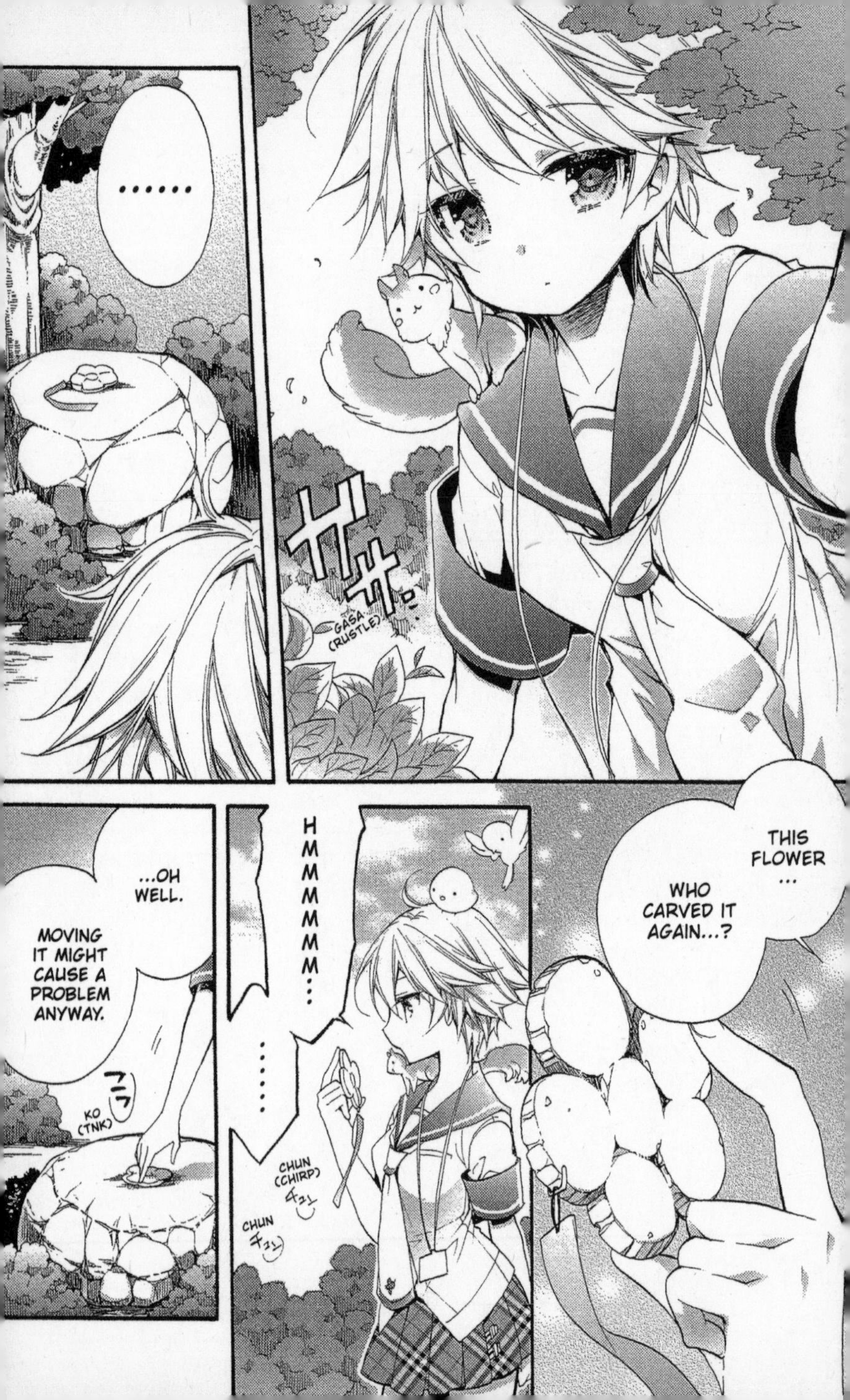
GASA (RUSTLE)
......
THIS FLOWER ...
WHO CARVED IT AGAIN...?
HMMMMMM...
......
CHUN (CHIRP)
CHUN
...OH WELL.
MOVING IT MIGHT CAUSE A PROBLEM ANYWAY.
KO (TNK)

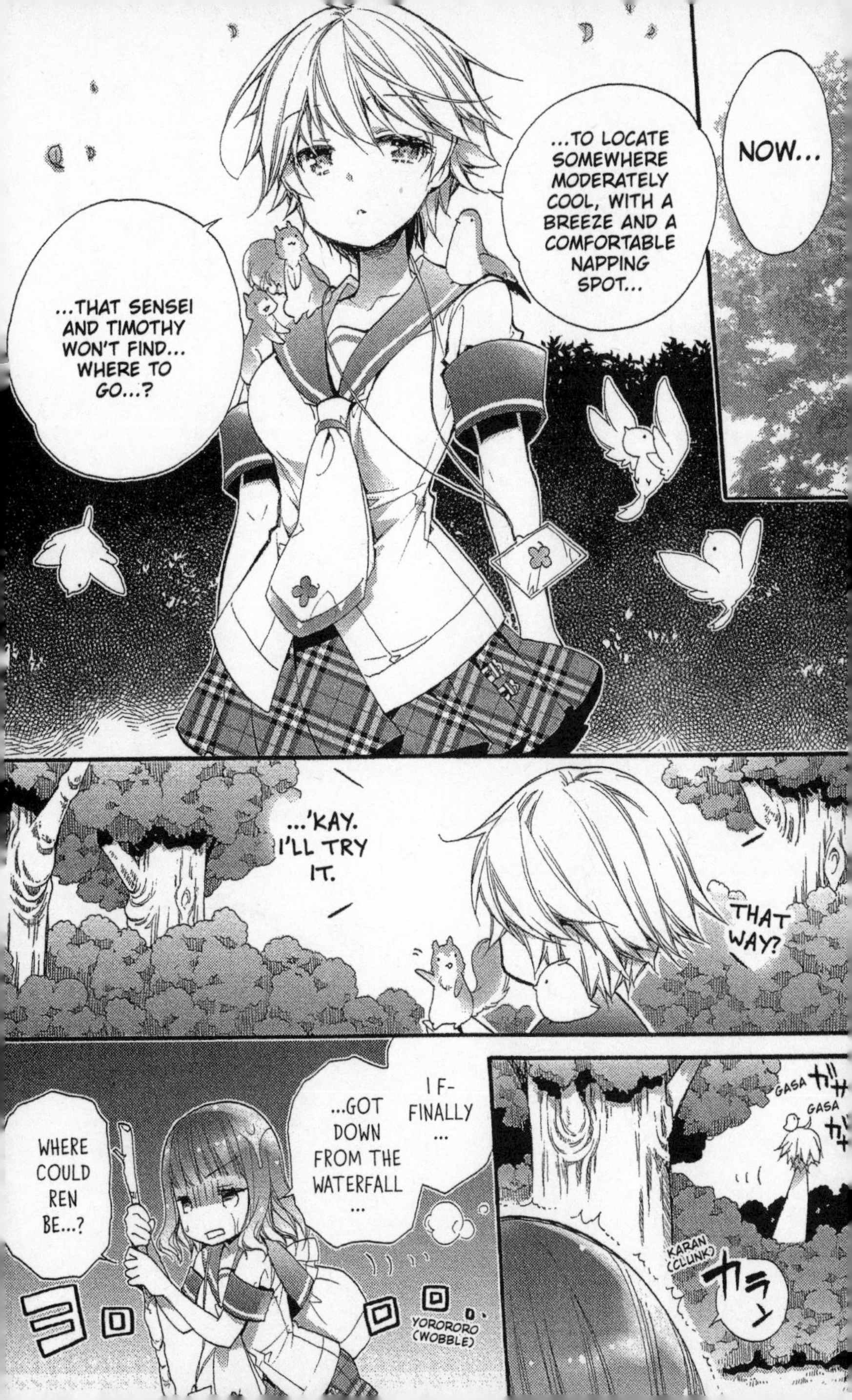
NOW...
...TO LOCATE SOMEWHERE MODERATELY COOL, WITH A BREEZE AND A COMFORTABLE NAPPING SPOT...
...THAT SENSEI AND TIMOTHY WON'T FIND... WHERE TO GO...?
THAT WAY?
...'KAY. I'LL TRY IT.
GASA
GASA
KARAN (CLUNK)
I F-FINALLY...
...GOT DOWN FROM THE WATERFALL...
WHERE COULD REN BE...?
YOROROROR (WOBBLE)

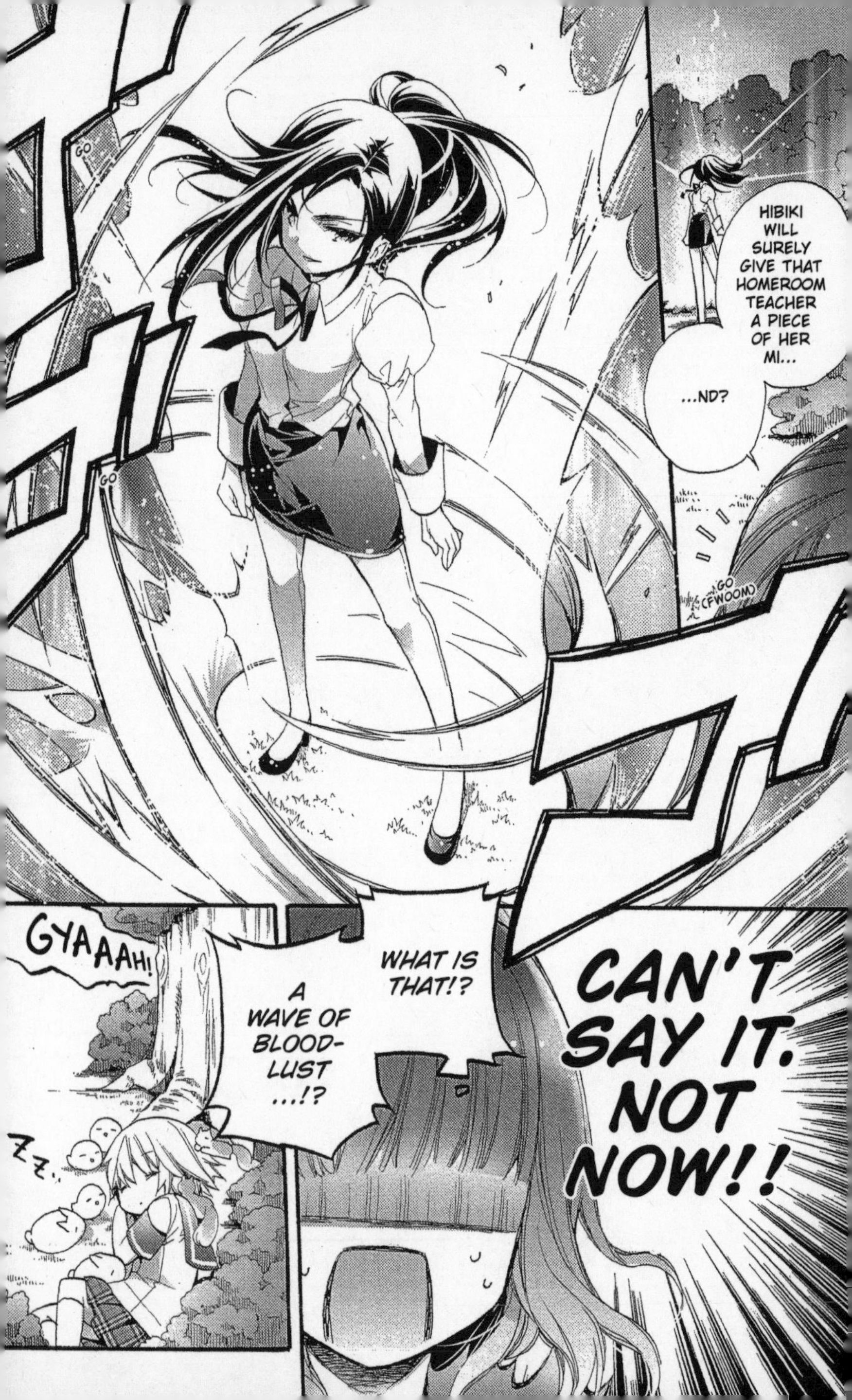
HIBIKI WILL SURELY GIVE THAT HOMEROOM TEACHER A PIECE OF HER MI...
...ND?
GO (FWOOM)
GO
GO
CAN'T SAY IT. NOT NOW!!
WHAT IS THAT!?
A WAVE OF BLOOD-LUST...!?
GYAAAH!
Z Z

Anne Happy

unhappy go lucky!

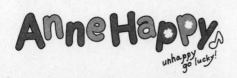

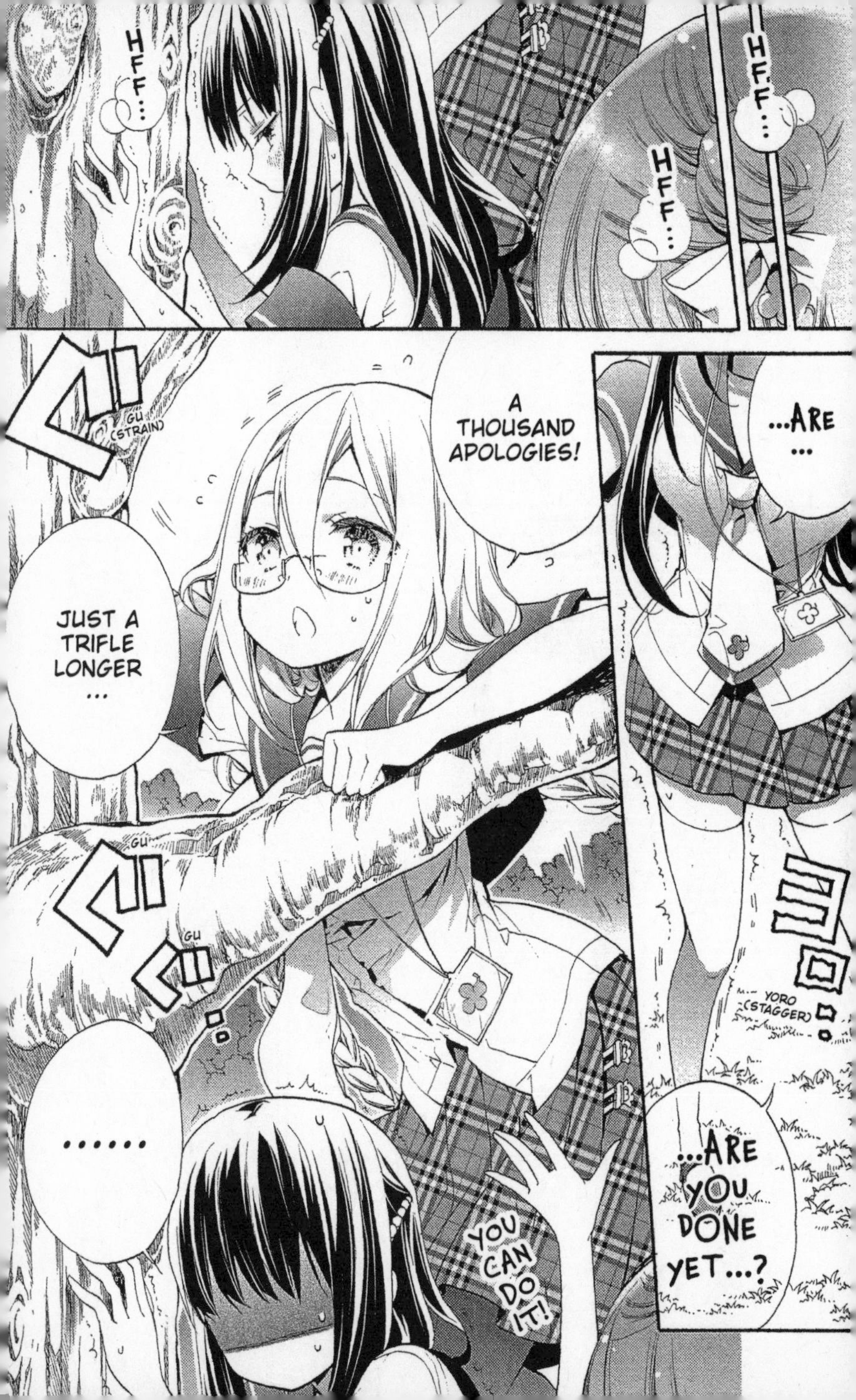
HFF...
HFF...
HFF...
...ARE ...
YORO (STAGGER)
...ARE YOU DONE YET...?
A THOUSAND APOLOGIES!
GU (STRAIN)
JUST A TRIFLE LONGER ...
GU
GU
......
YOU CAN DO IT!

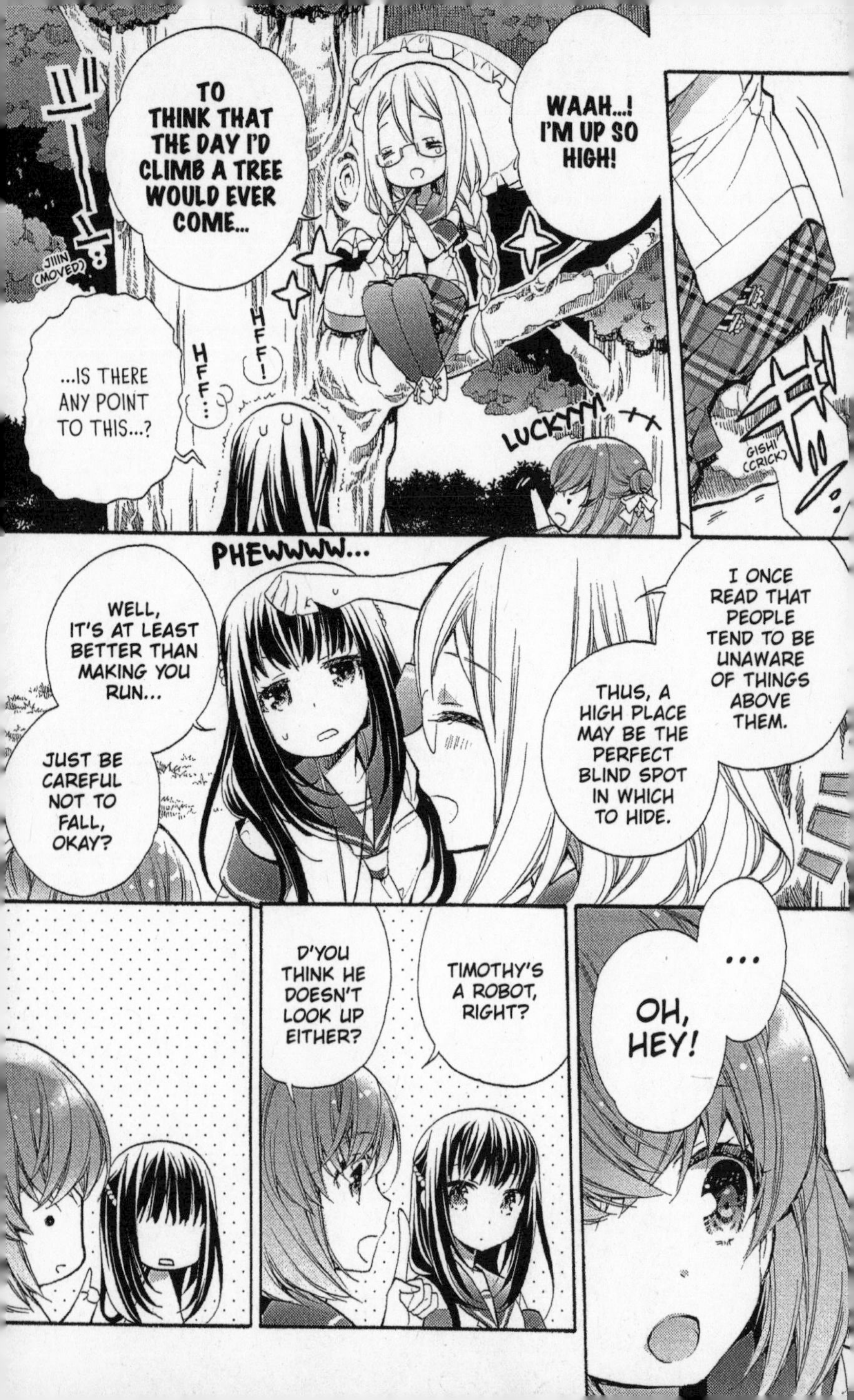
GISHI (CRICK)
WAAH...! I'M UP SO HIGH!
TO THINK THAT THE DAY I'D CLIMB A TREE WOULD EVER COME...
JIIN (MOVED)
LUCKYYY!
HFF!
HFF...
...IS THERE ANY POINT TO THIS...?
PHEWWWW...
I ONCE READ THAT PEOPLE TEND TO BE UNAWARE OF THINGS ABOVE THEM.
THUS, A HIGH PLACE MAY BE THE PERFECT BLIND SPOT IN WHICH TO HIDE.
WELL, IT'S AT LEAST BETTER THAN MAKING YOU RUN...
JUST BE CAREFUL NOT TO FALL, OKAY?
...
OH, HEY!
TIMOTHY'S A ROBOT, RIGHT?
D'YOU THINK HE DOESN'T LOOK UP EITHER?

✤ Lucky. 26

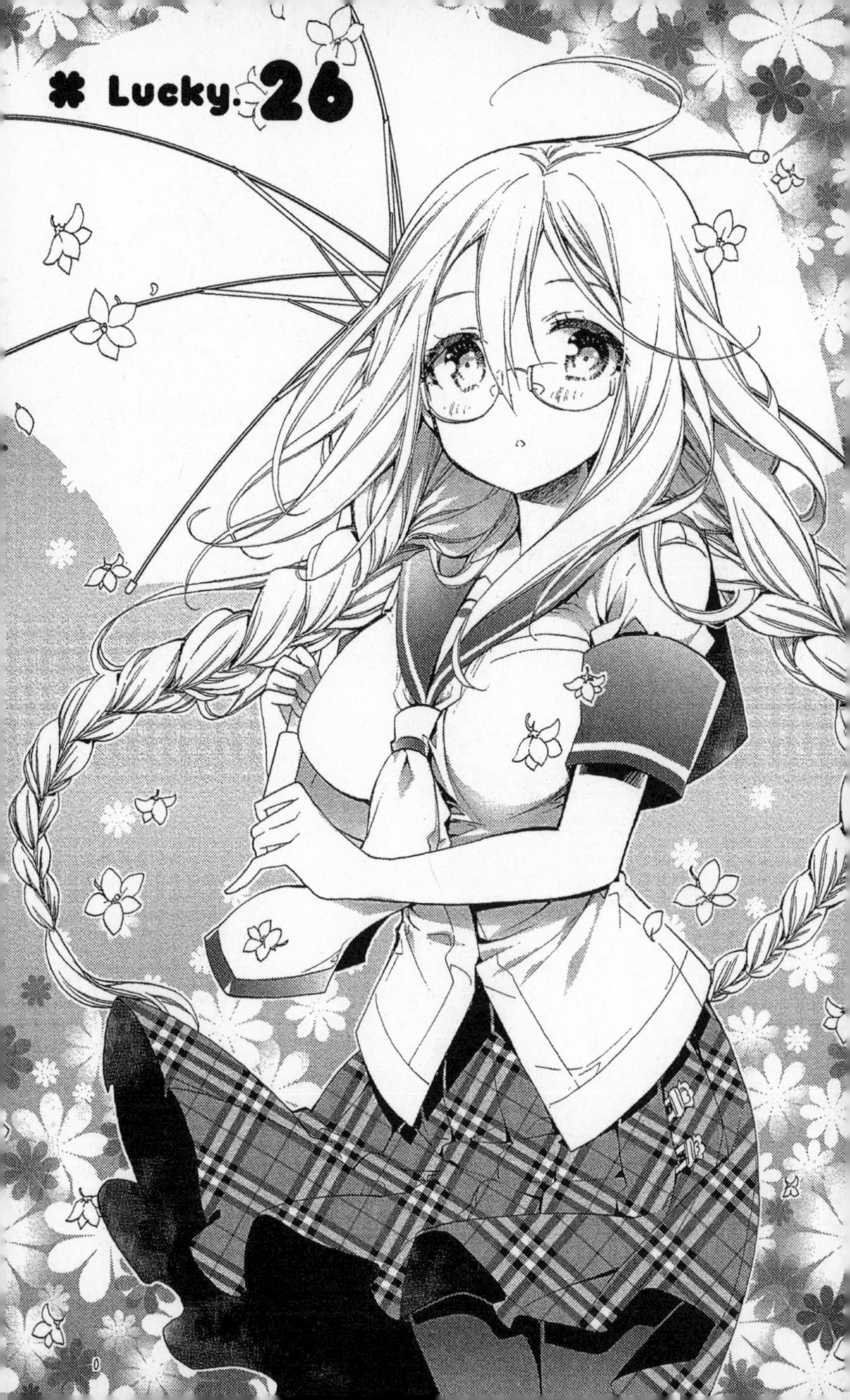

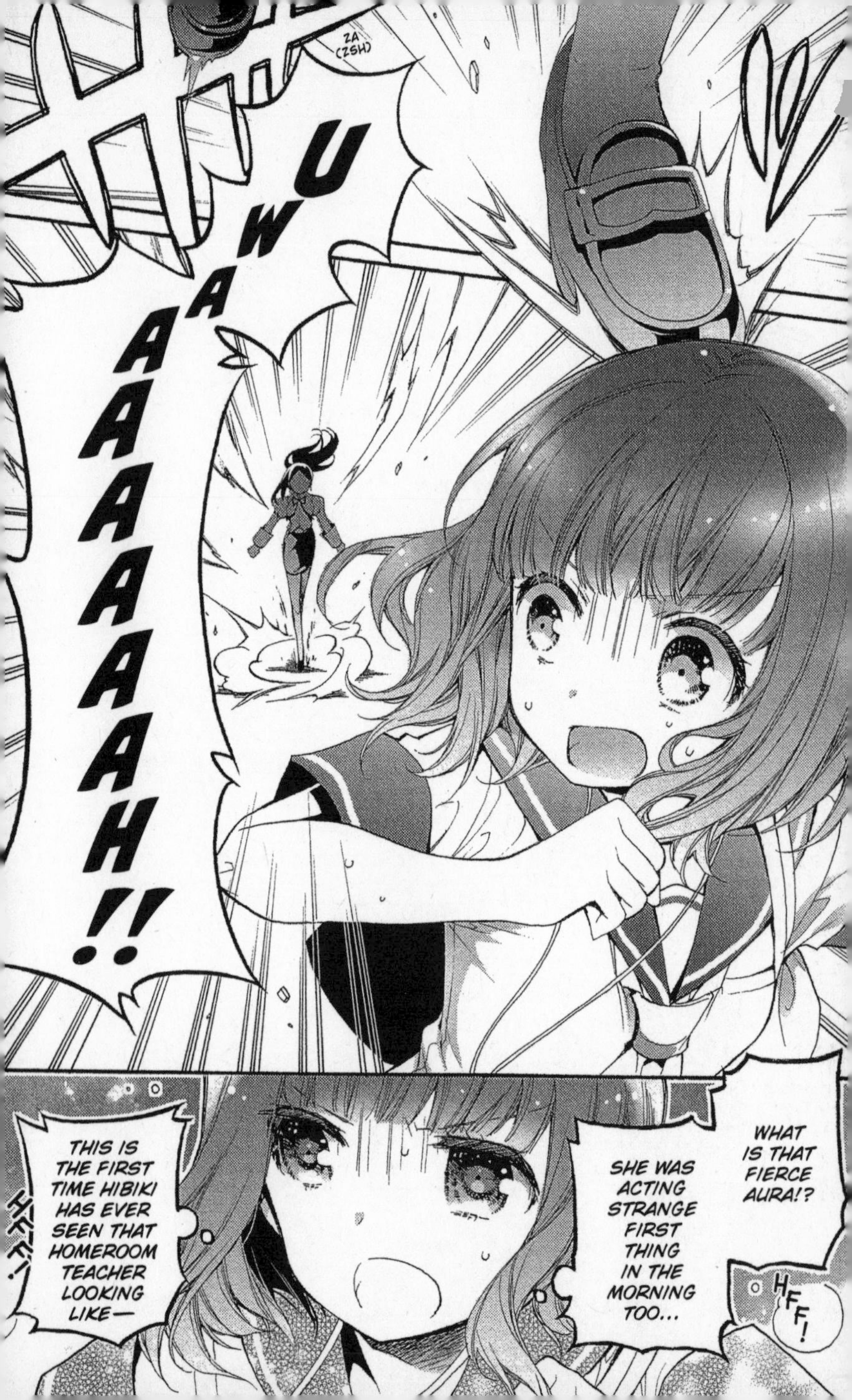
ZA (ZSH)
UWAAAAAAAH!!
WHAT IS THAT FIERCE AURA!?
HFF!
SHE WAS ACTING STRANGE FIRST THING IN THE MORNING TOO...
THIS IS THE FIRST TIME HIBIKI HAS EVER SEEN THAT HOMEROOM TEACHER LOOKING LIKE—

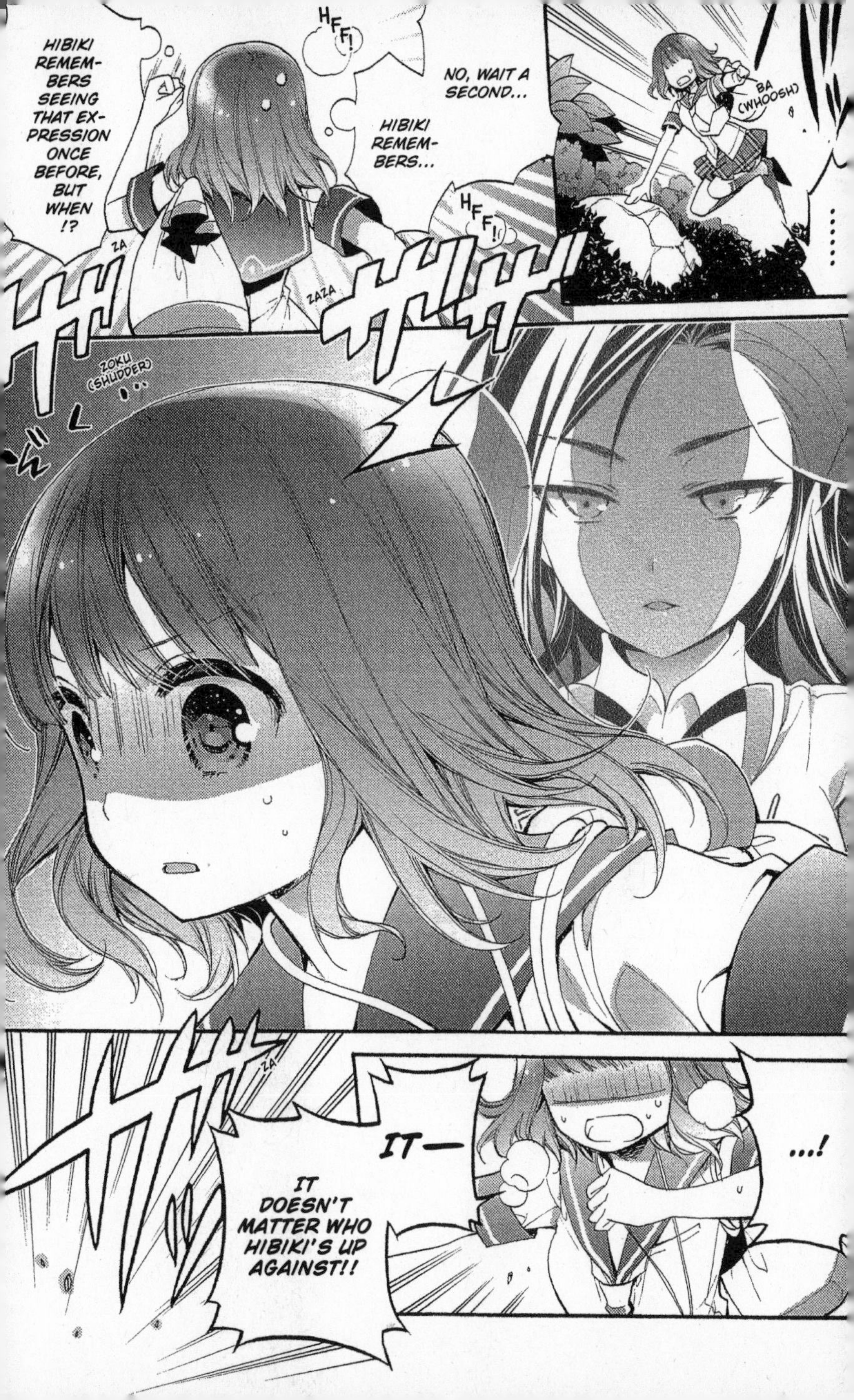
BA (WHOOSH)
......
HFF!
NO, WAIT A SECOND...
HIBIKI REMEMBERS...
HIBIKI REMEMBERS SEEING THAT EXPRESSION ONCE BEFORE, BUT WHEN!?
HFF!
ZA
ZAZA
ZOKU (SHUDDER)
...!
IT—
IT DOESN'T MATTER WHO HIBIKI'S UP AGAINST!!
ZA

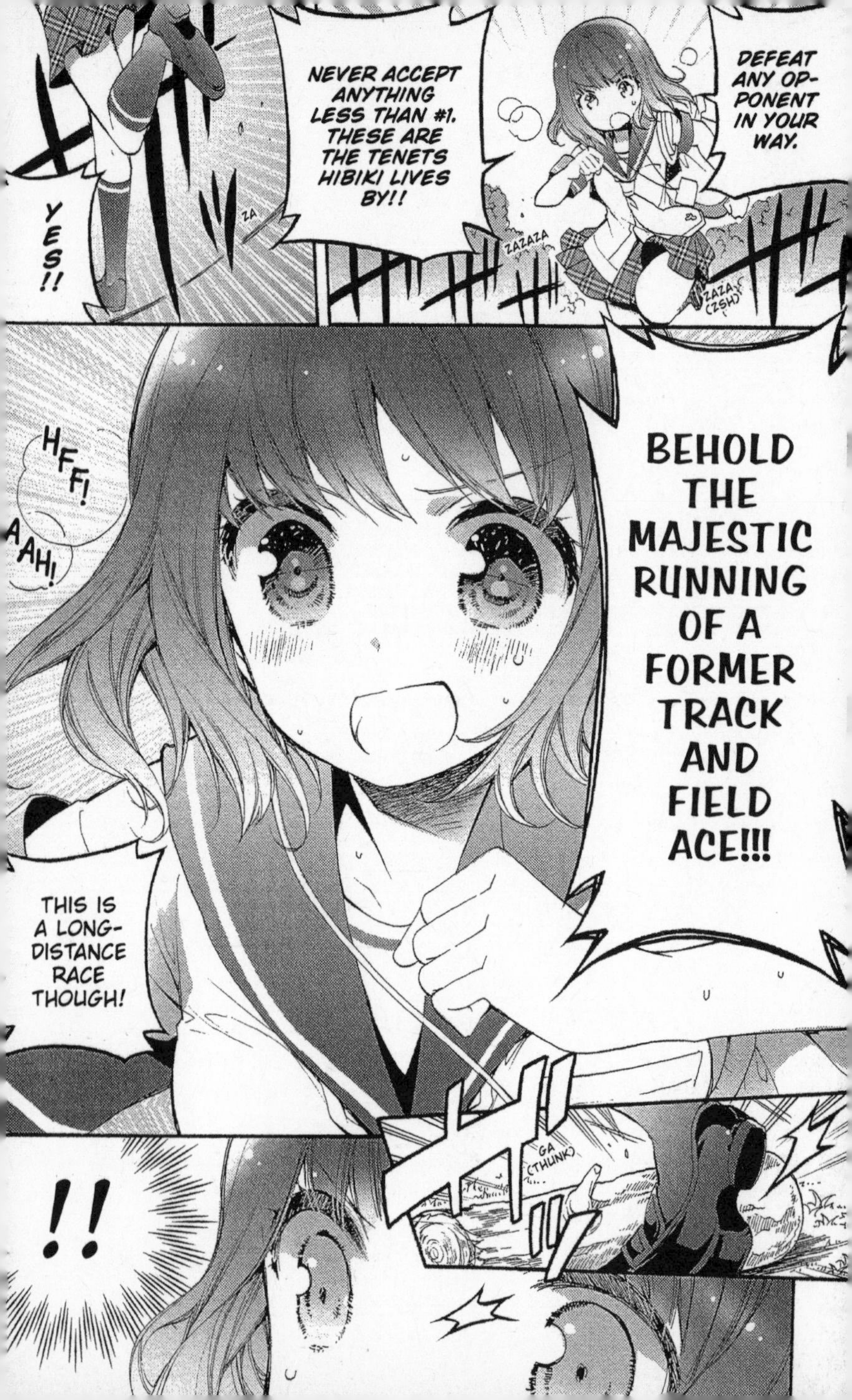
DEFEAT ANY OP-PONENT IN YOUR WAY.
ZAZAZA
ZAZA (ZSH)
NEVER ACCEPT ANYTHING LESS THAN #1. THESE ARE THE TENETS HIBIKI LIVES BY!!
ZA
YES!!
BEHOLD THE MAJESTIC RUNNING OF A FORMER TRACK AND FIELD ACE!!!
HFF!
AAAH!
THIS IS A LONG-DISTANCE RACE THOUGH!
GA (THUNK)
!!

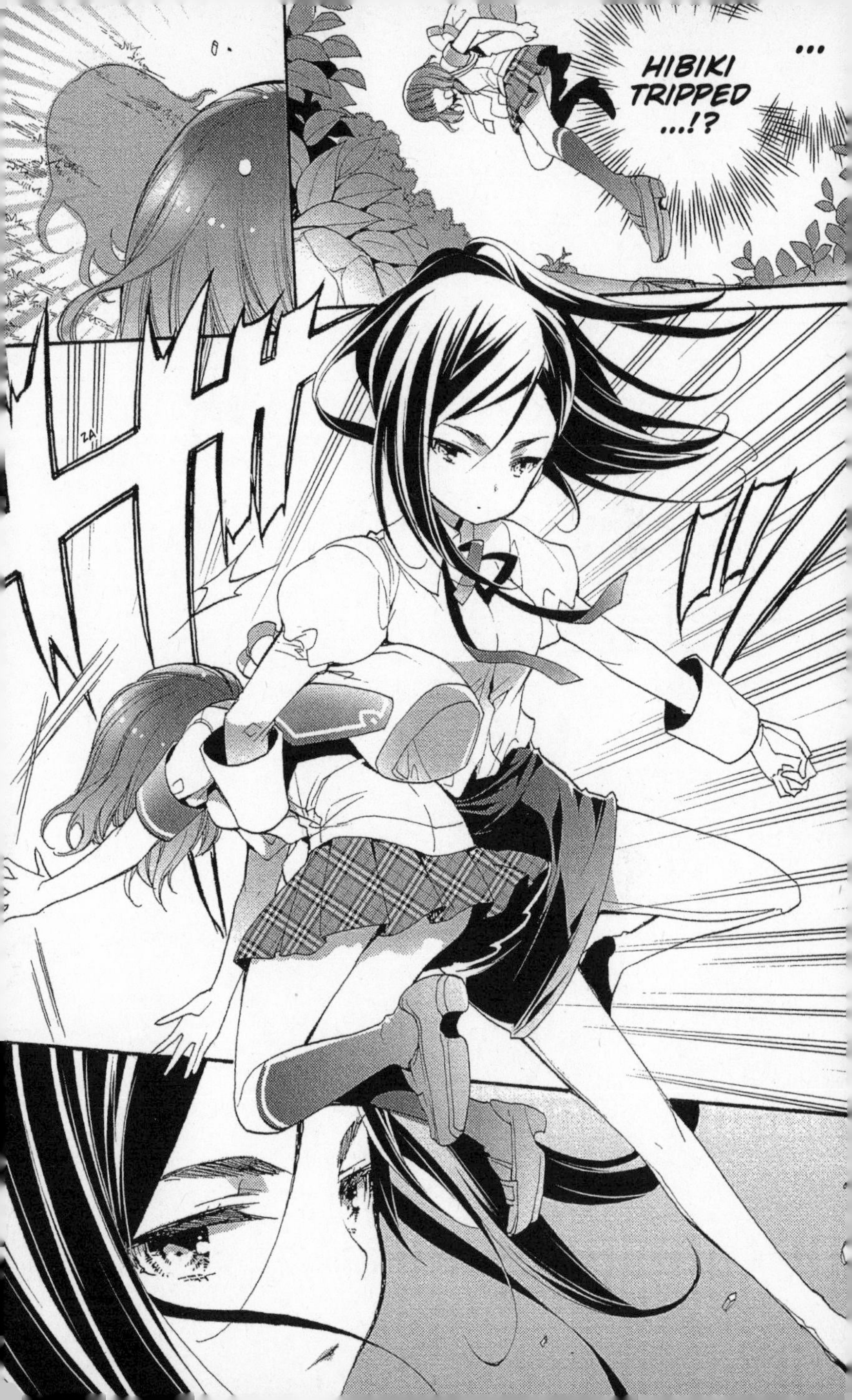
...
HIBIKI TRIPPED ...!?
ZA

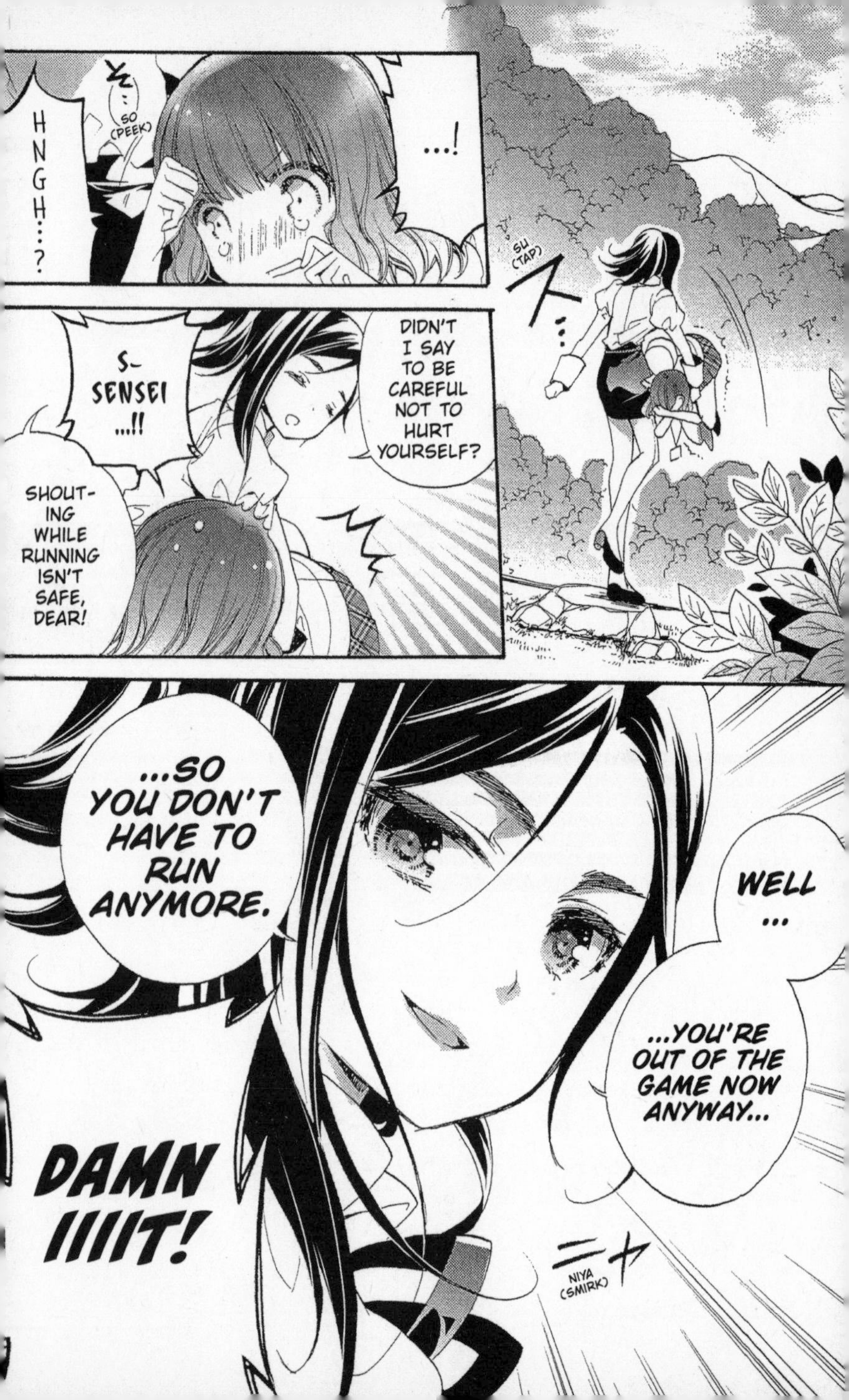
SU (TAP)
...!
SO (PEEK)
HNGH...?
DIDN'T I SAY TO BE CAREFUL NOT TO HURT YOURSELF?
S-SENSEI ...!!
SHOUTING WHILE RUNNING ISN'T SAFE, DEAR!
WELL ...
...YOU'RE OUT OF THE GAME NOW ANYWAY...
...SO YOU DON'T HAVE TO RUN ANYMORE.
NIYA (SMIRK)
DAMN IIIIT!

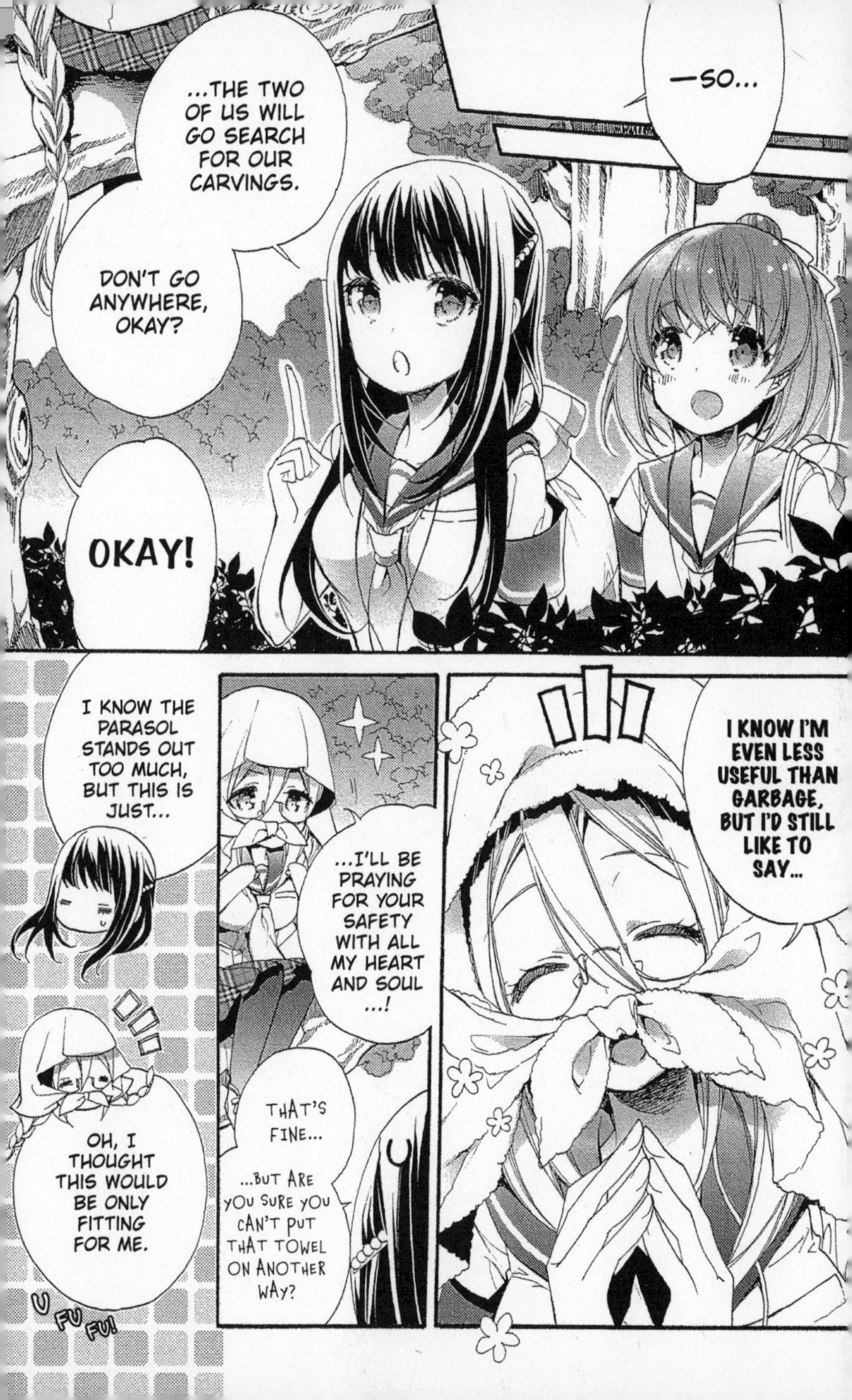
—SO...
...THE TWO OF US WILL GO SEARCH FOR OUR CARVINGS.
DON'T GO ANYWHERE, OKAY?
OKAY!
I KNOW I'M EVEN LESS USEFUL THAN GARBAGE, BUT I'D STILL LIKE TO SAY...
...I'LL BE PRAYING FOR YOUR SAFETY WITH ALL MY HEART AND SOUL ...!
THAT'S FINE...
...BUT ARE YOU SURE YOU CAN'T PUT THAT TOWEL ON ANOTHER WAY?
I KNOW THE PARASOL STANDS OUT TOO MUCH, BUT THIS IS JUST...
OH, I THOUGHT THIS WOULD BE ONLY FITTING FOR ME.
UFUFU!

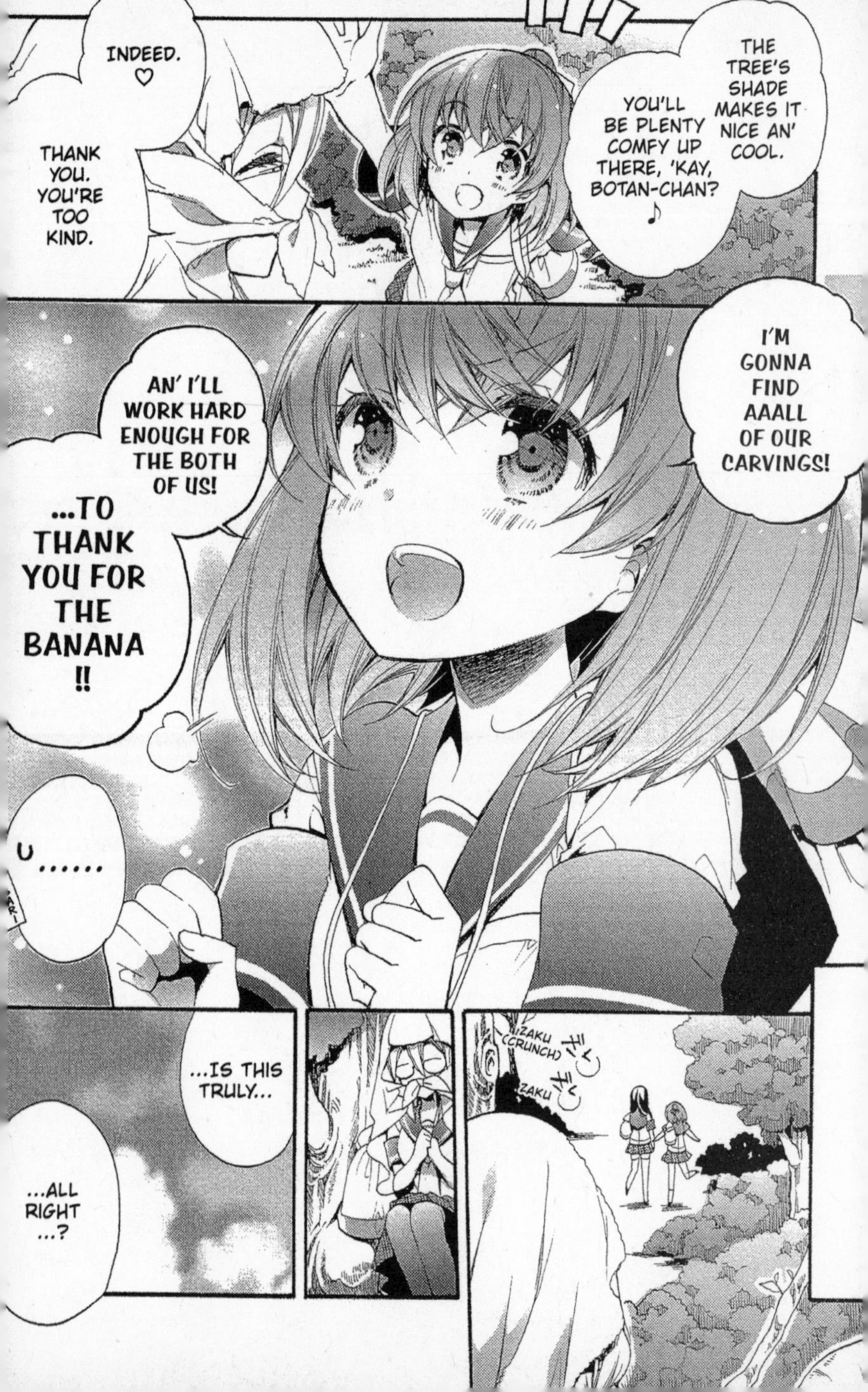
THE TREE'S SHADE MAKES IT NICE AN' COOL.
YOU'LL BE PLENTY COMFY UP THERE, 'KAY, BOTAN-CHAN? ♪
INDEED. ♡
THANK YOU. YOU'RE TOO KIND.
I'M GONNA FIND AAALL OF OUR CARVINGS!
AN' I'LL WORK HARD ENOUGH FOR THE BOTH OF US!
...TO THANK YOU FOR THE BANANA!!
U......
ZAKU (CRUNCH)
ZAKU
...IS THIS TRULY...
...ALL RIGHT ...?

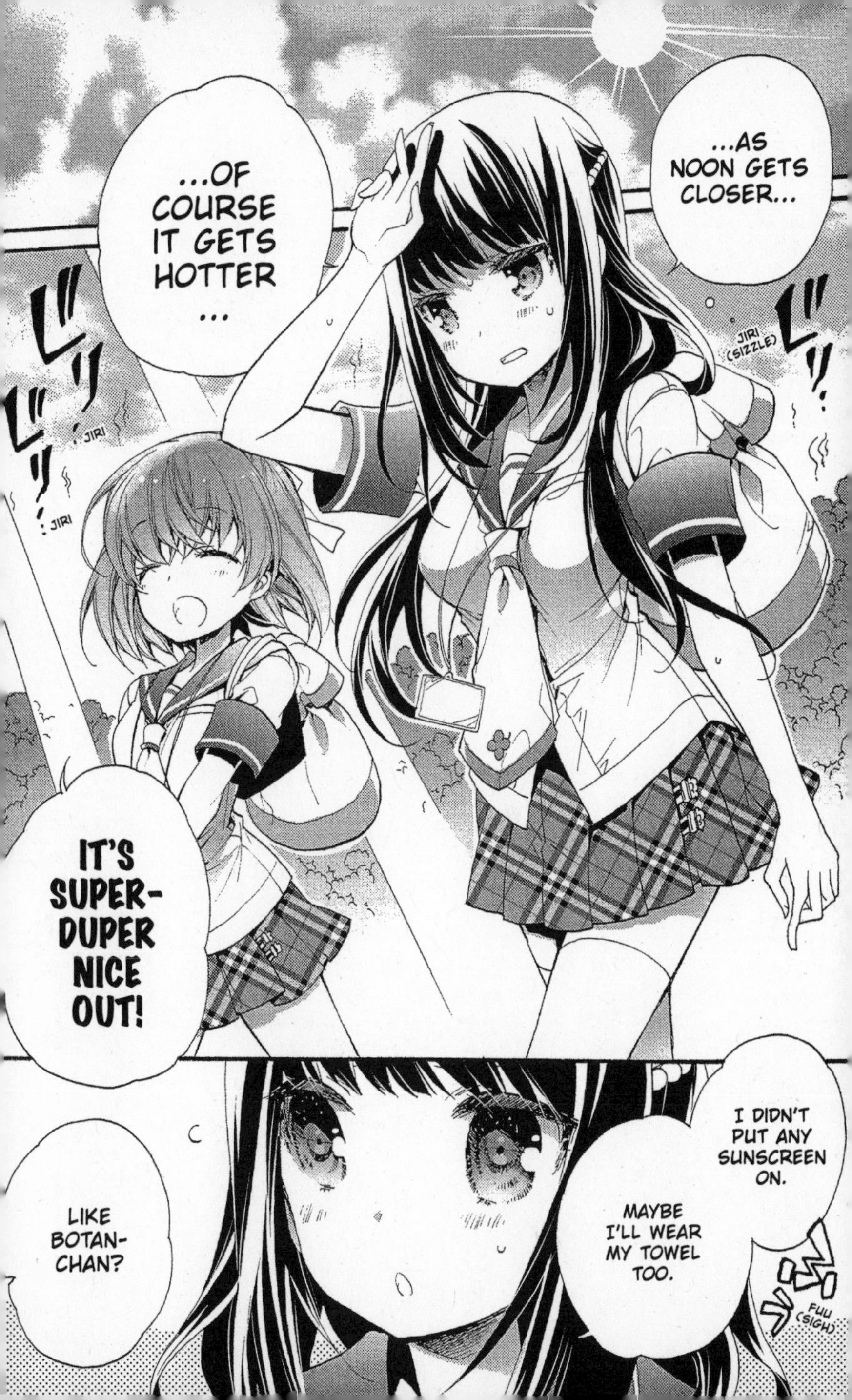
...AS NOON GETS CLOSER...
JIRI (SIZZLE)
...OF COURSE IT GETS HOTTER ...
JIRI
JIRI
IT'S SUPER-DUPER NICE OUT!
I DIDN'T PUT ANY SUNSCREEN ON.
MAYBE I'LL WEAR MY TOWEL TOO.
FUU (SIGH)
LIKE BOTAN-CHAN?

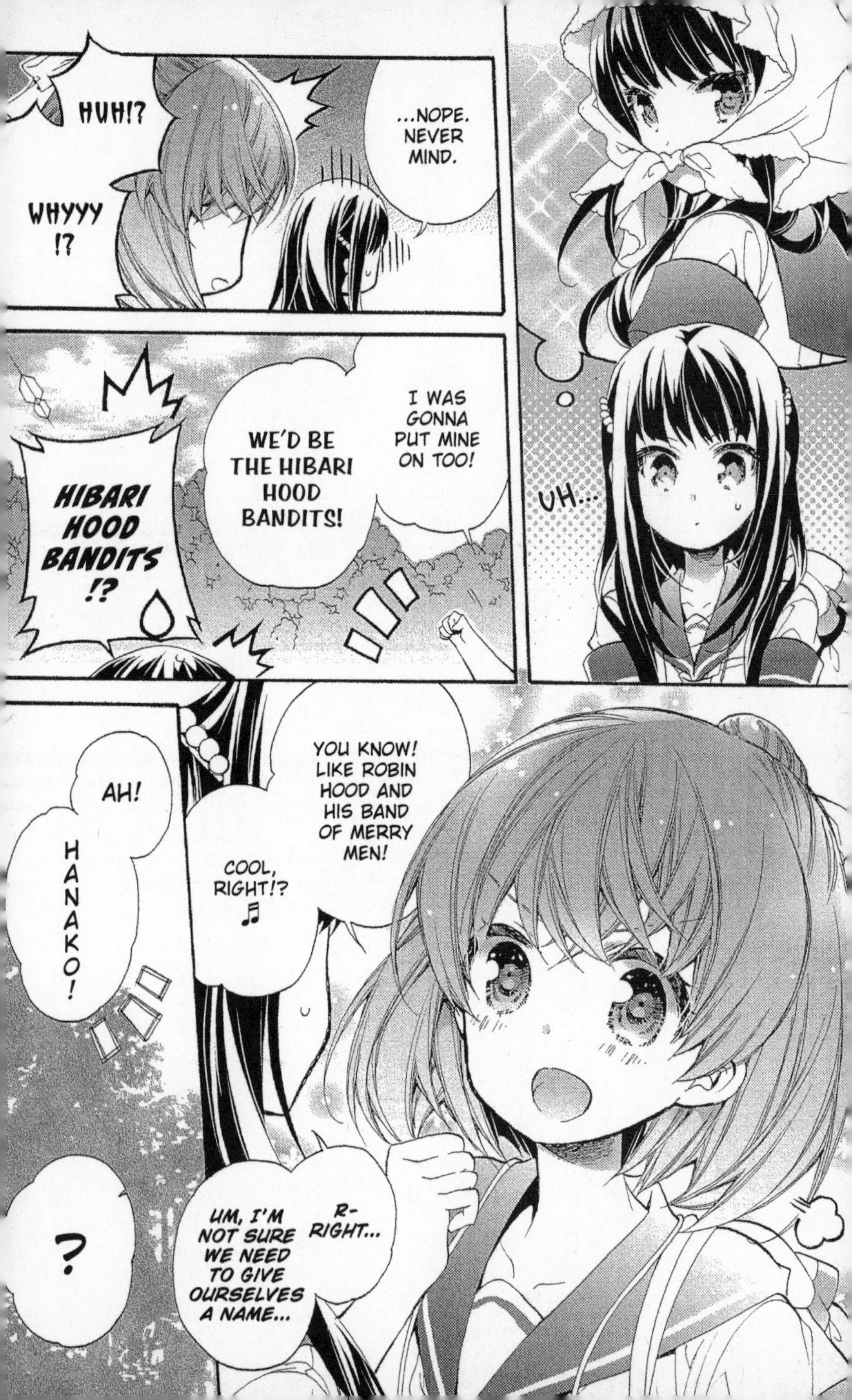
UH...
...NOPE. NEVER MIND.
HUH!?
WHYYY!?
I WAS GONNA PUT MINE ON TOO!
WE'D BE THE HIBARI HOOD BANDITS!
HIBARI HOOD BANDITS!?
YOU KNOW! LIKE ROBIN HOOD AND HIS BAND OF MERRY MEN!
COOL, RIGHT!? ♫
AH!
HANAKO!
R-RIGHT...
UM, I'M NOT SURE WE NEED TO GIVE OURSELVES A NAME...
?

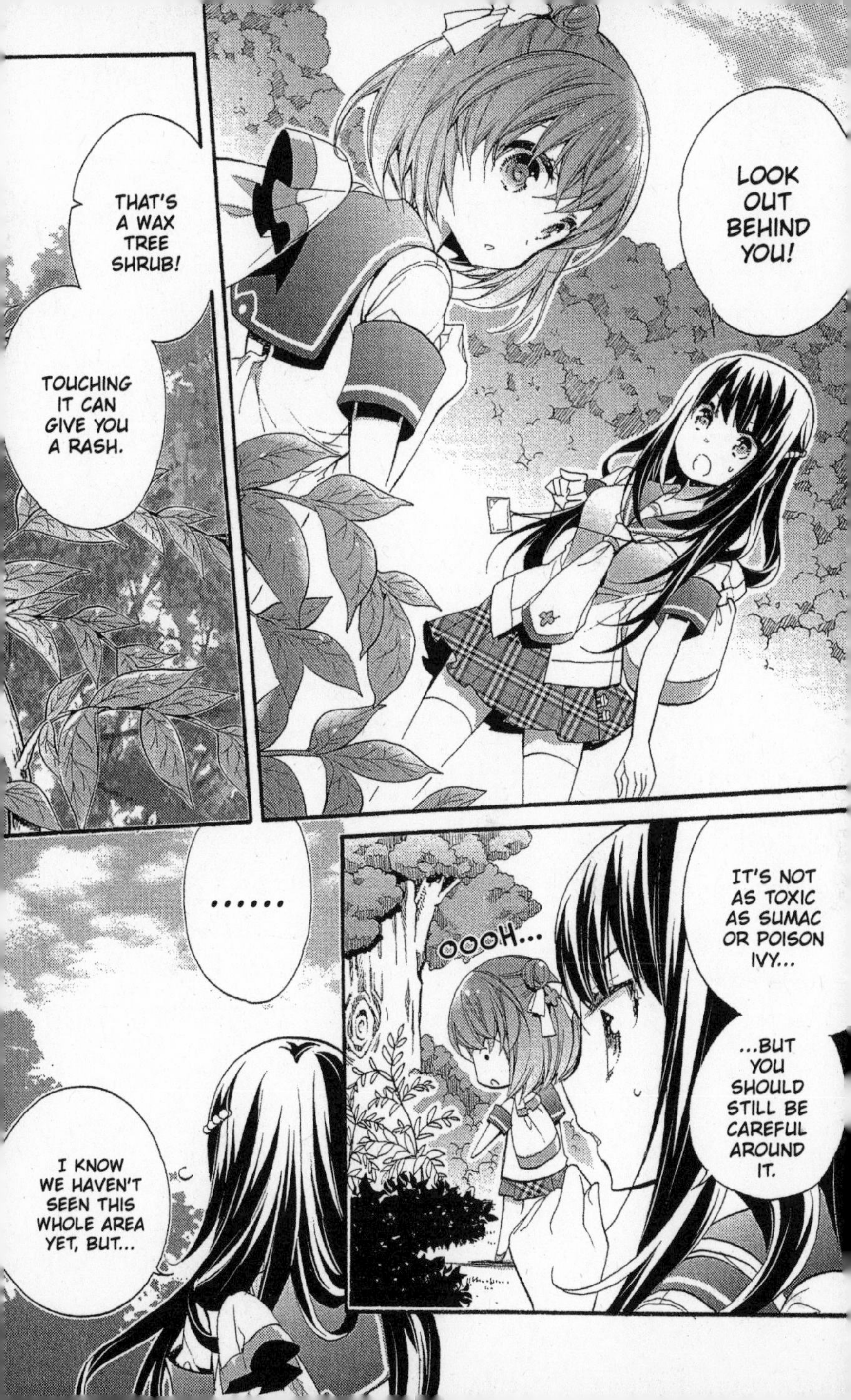
LOOK OUT BEHIND YOU!
THAT'S A WAX TREE SHRUB!
TOUCHING IT CAN GIVE YOU A RASH.
IT'S NOT AS TOXIC AS SUMAC OR POISON IVY...
OOOH...
...BUT YOU SHOULD STILL BE CAREFUL AROUND IT.
......
I KNOW WE HAVEN'T SEEN THIS WHOLE AREA YET, BUT...

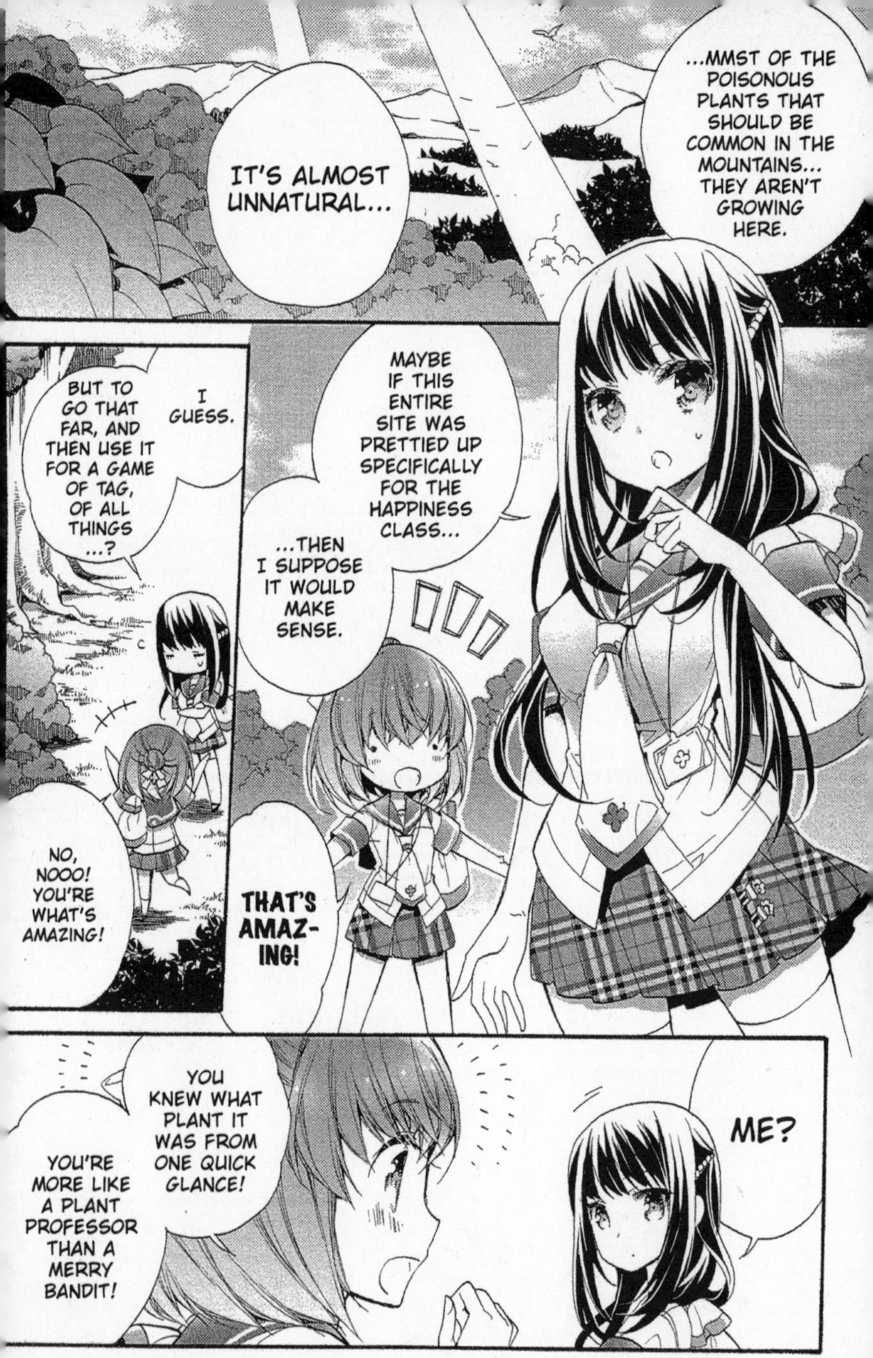
...MMST OF THE POISONOUS PLANTS THAT SHOULD BE COMMON IN THE MOUNTAINS... THEY AREN'T GROWING HERE.
IT'S ALMOST UNNATURAL...
MAYBE IF THIS ENTIRE SITE WAS PRETTIED UP SPECIFICALLY FOR THE HAPPINESS CLASS...
...THEN I SUPPOSE IT WOULD MAKE SENSE.
THAT'S AMAZ-ING!
I GUESS.
BUT TO GO THAT FAR, AND THEN USE IT FOR A GAME OF TAG, OF ALL THINGS ...?
NO, NOOO! YOU'RE WHAT'S AMAZING!
ME?
YOU KNEW WHAT PLANT IT WAS FROM ONE QUICK GLANCE!
YOU'RE MORE LIKE A PLANT PROFESSOR THAN A MERRY BANDIT!

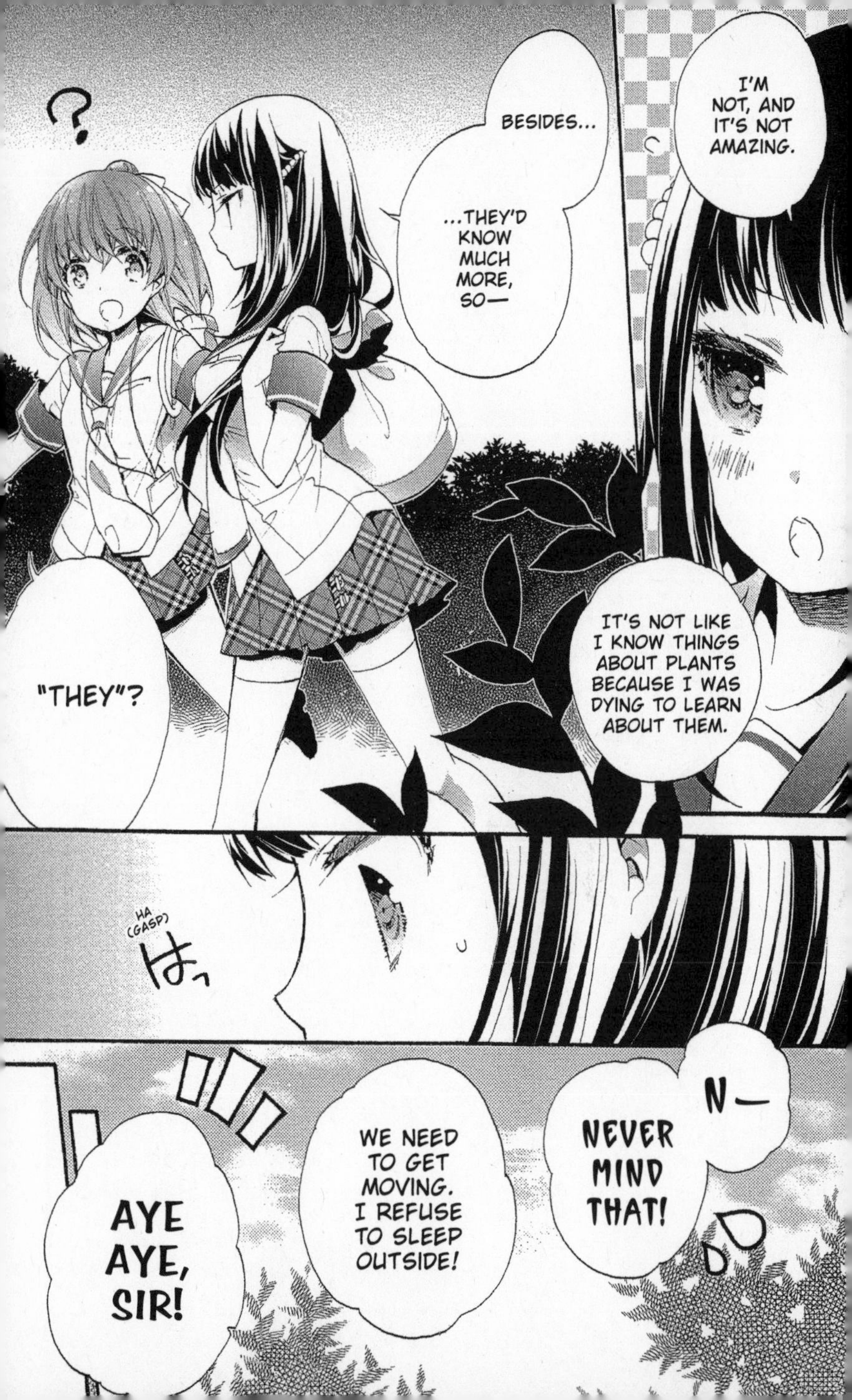
I'M NOT, AND IT'S NOT AMAZING.
IT'S NOT LIKE I KNOW THINGS ABOUT PLANTS BECAUSE I WAS DYING TO LEARN ABOUT THEM.
BESIDES...
...THEY'D KNOW MUCH MORE, SO—
?
"THEY"?
HA (GASP)
はっ
N—
NEVER MIND THAT!
WE NEED TO GET MOVING. I REFUSE TO SLEEP OUTSIDE!
AYE AYE, SIR!

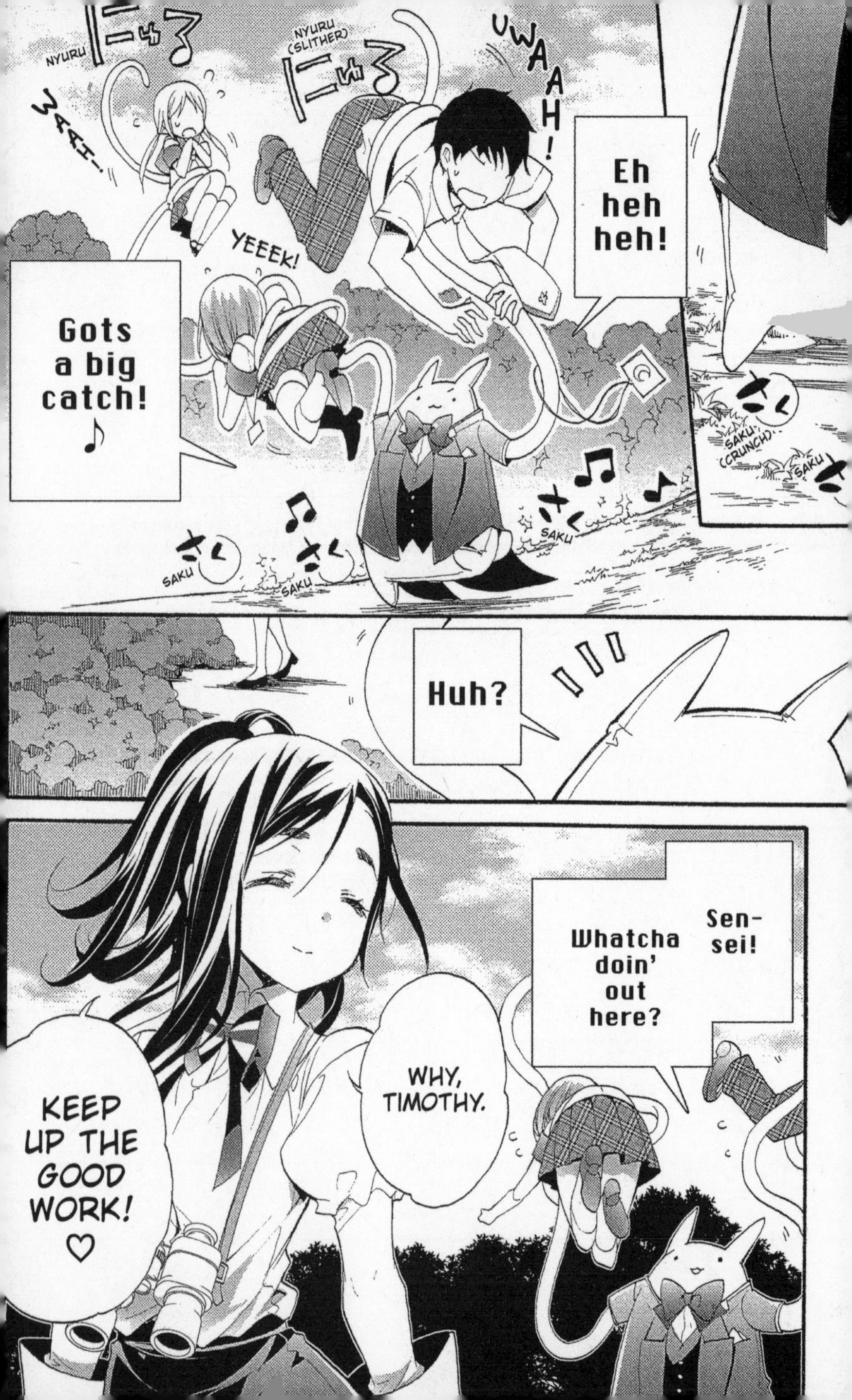
SAKU (CRUNCH)
SAKU
UWAAAH!
にゅる
NYURU (SLITHER)
にゅる
NYURU
WAAAI--
Eh heh heh!
YEEEK!
Gots a big catch! ♪
SAKU
SAKU
SAKU
SAKU
Huh?
Sen-sei! Whatcha doin' out here?
WHY, TIMOTHY.
KEEP UP THE GOOD WORK! ♡

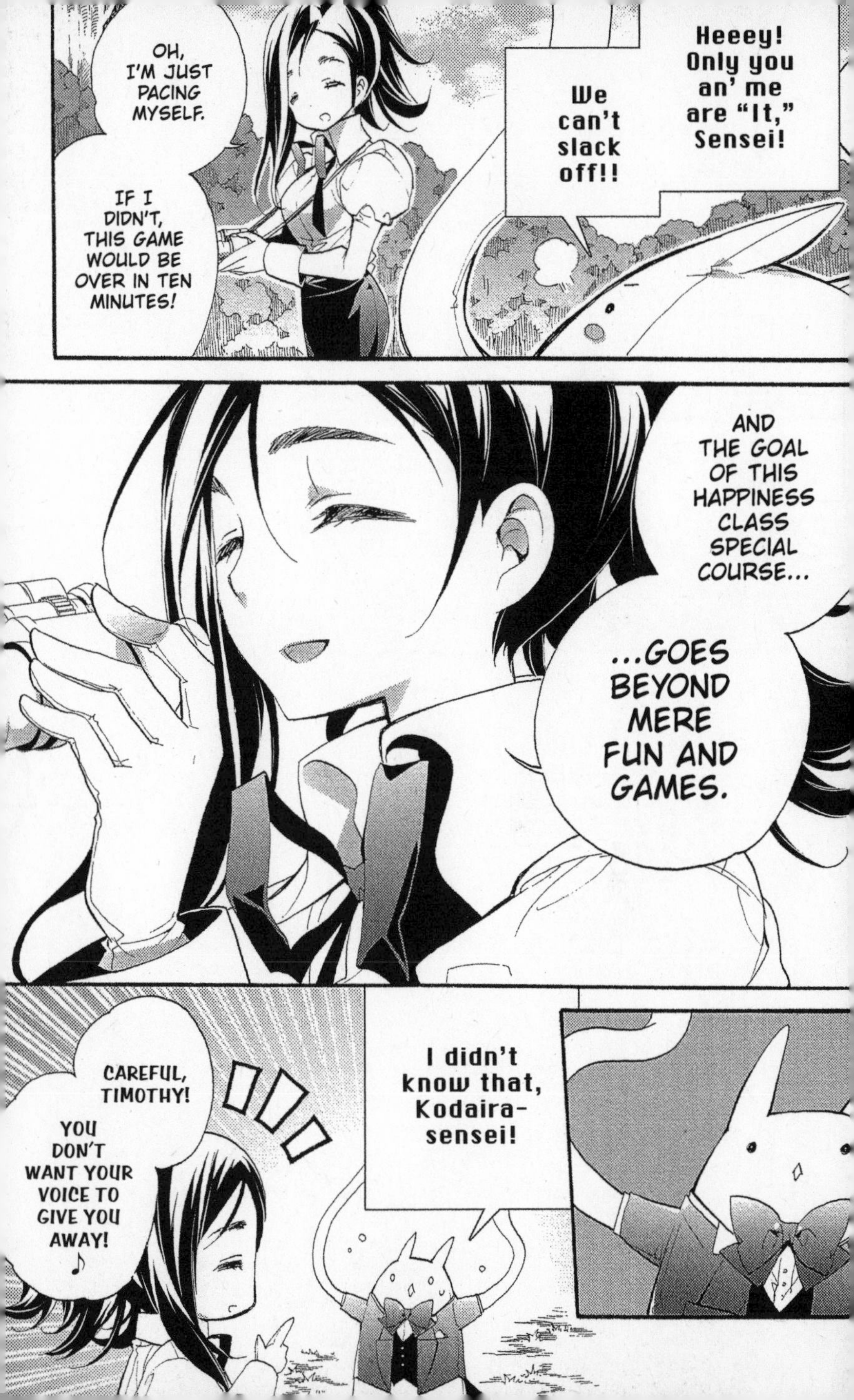
Heeey! Only you an' me are "It," Sensei!
We can't slack off!!
OH, I'M JUST PACING MYSELF.
IF I DIDN'T, THIS GAME WOULD BE OVER IN TEN MINUTES!
AND THE GOAL OF THIS HAPPINESS CLASS SPECIAL COURSE...
...GOES BEYOND MERE FUN AND GAMES.
I didn't know that, Kodaira-sensei!
CAREFUL, TIMOTHY!
YOU DON'T WANT YOUR VOICE TO GIVE YOU AWAY! ♪

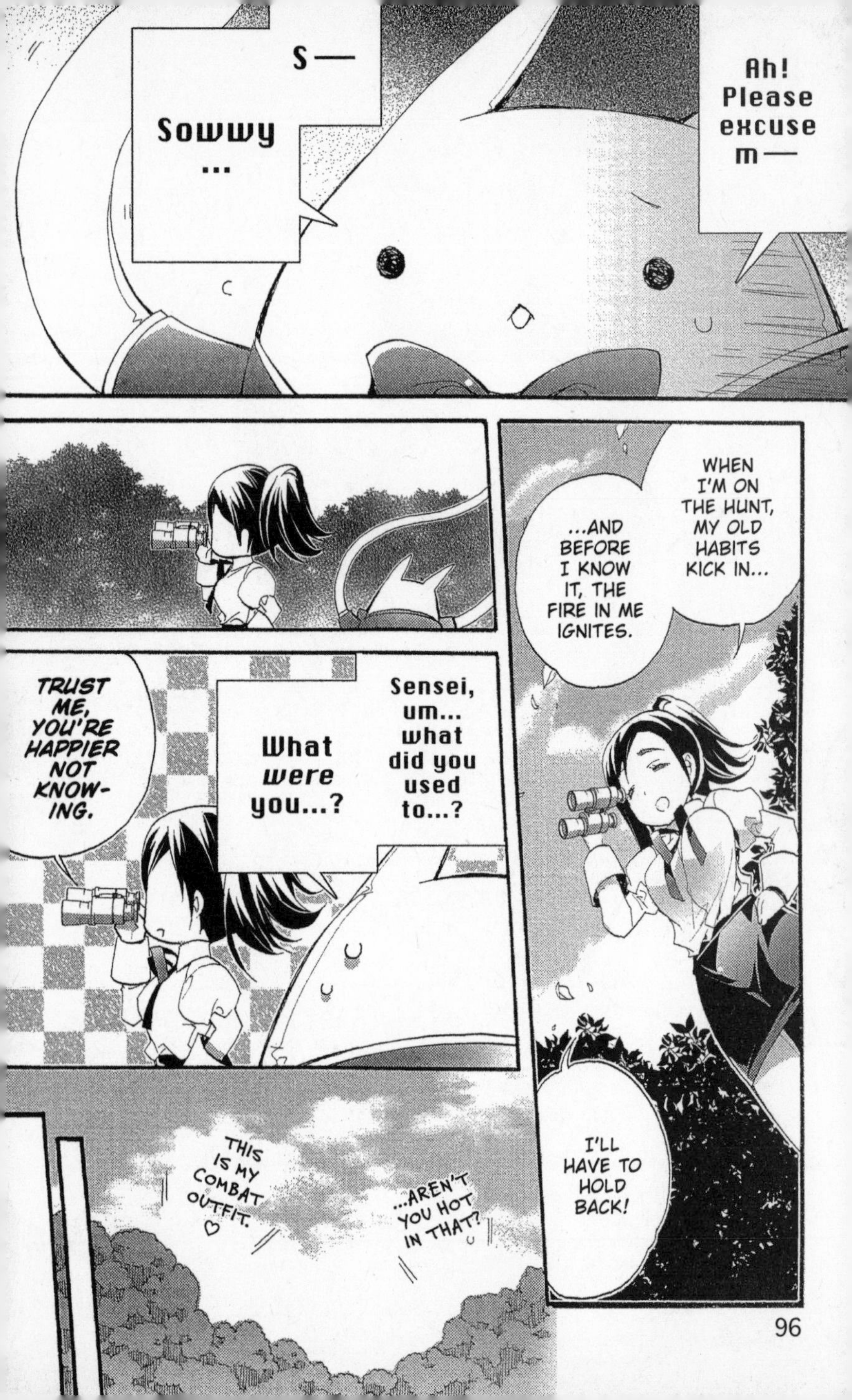
Ah! Please excuse m—
S— Sowwy...
WHEN I'M ON THE HUNT, MY OLD HABITS KICK IN...
...AND BEFORE I KNOW IT, THE FIRE IN ME IGNITES.
I'LL HAVE TO HOLD BACK!
Sensei, um... what did you used to...?
What were you...?
TRUST ME, YOU'RE HAPPIER NOT KNOW-ING.
...AREN'T YOU HOT IN THAT?
THIS IS MY COMBAT OUTFIT. ♡

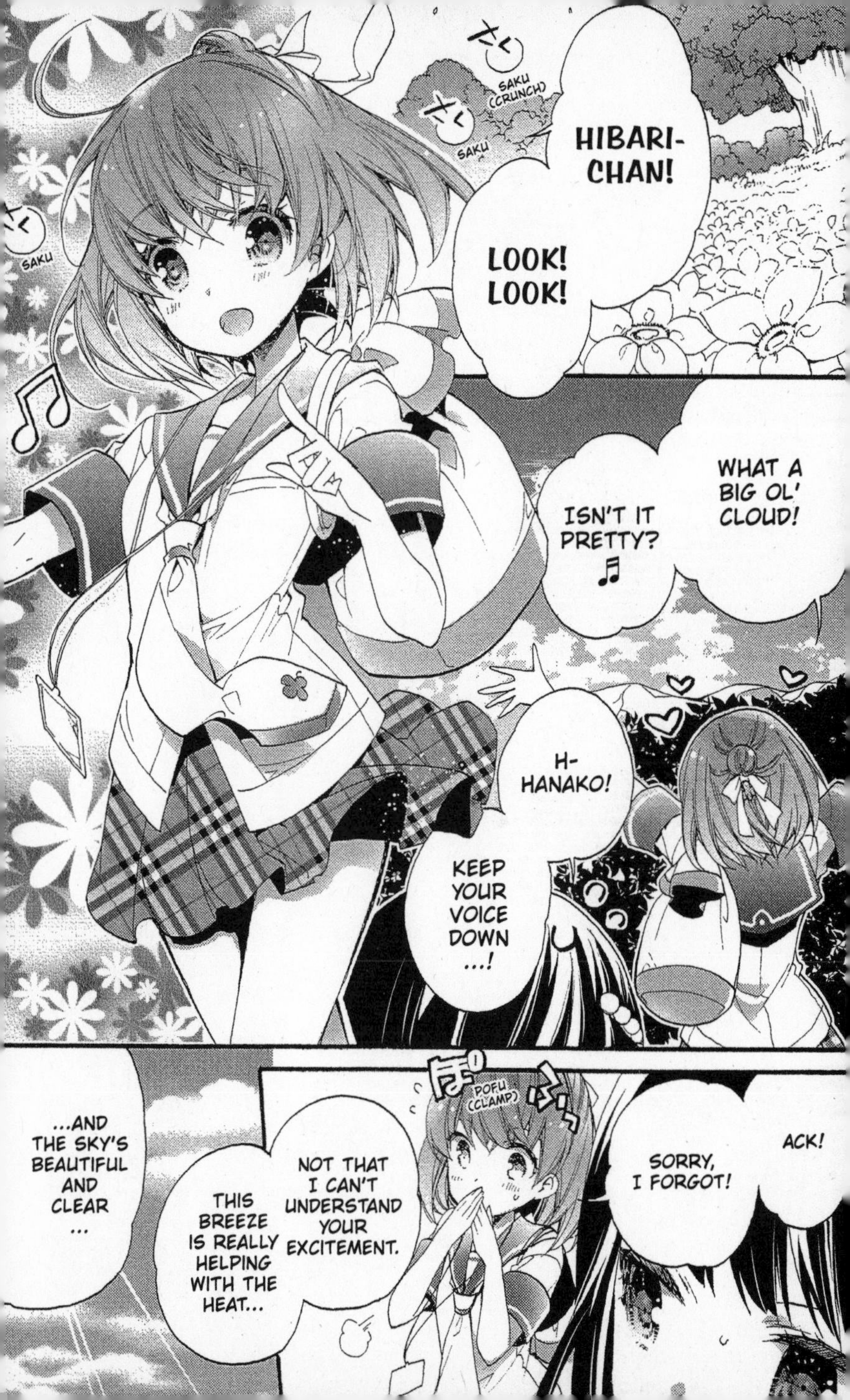
SAKU (CRUNCH)
SAKU
HIBARI-CHAN!
LOOK! LOOK!
WHAT A BIG OL' CLOUD!
ISN'T IT PRETTY? ♫
H-HANAKO!
KEEP YOUR VOICE DOWN ...!
SAKU
POFU (CLAMP)
ACK!
SORRY, I FORGOT!
NOT THAT I CAN'T UNDERSTAND YOUR EXCITEMENT.
THIS BREEZE IS REALLY HELPING WITH THE HEAT...
...AND THE SKY'S BEAUTIFUL AND CLEAR ...

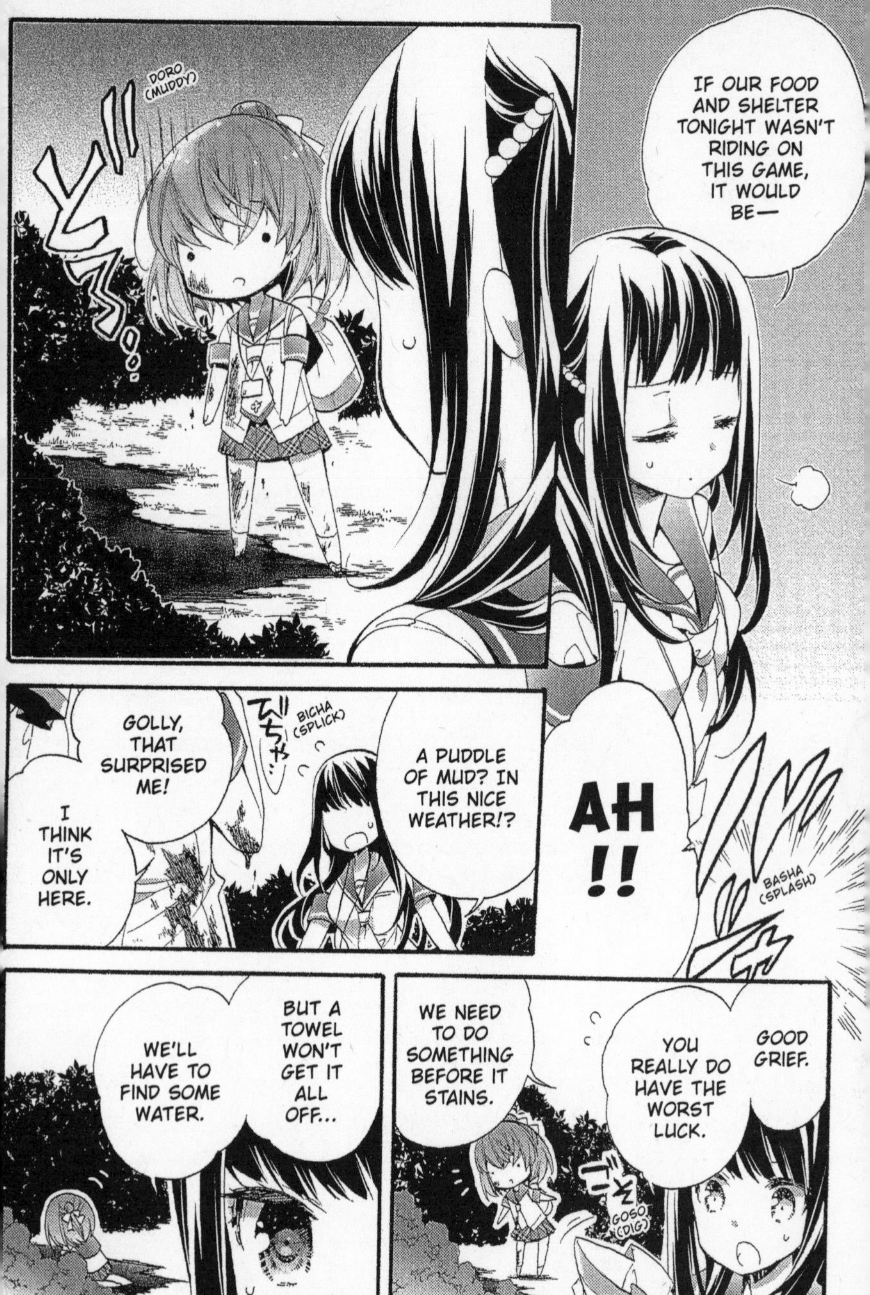
IF OUR FOOD AND SHELTER TONIGHT WASN'T RIDING ON THIS GAME, IT WOULD BE—
DORO (MUDDY)
AH!!
BASHA (SPLASH)
A PUDDLE OF MUD? IN THIS NICE WEATHER!?
BICHA (SPLICK)
GOLLY, THAT SURPRISED ME!
I THINK IT'S ONLY HERE.
GOOD GRIEF.
YOU REALLY DO HAVE THE WORST LUCK.
GOSO (DIG)
WE NEED TO DO SOMETHING BEFORE IT STAINS.
BUT A TOWEL WON'T GET IT ALL OFF...
WE'LL HAVE TO FIND SOME WATER.

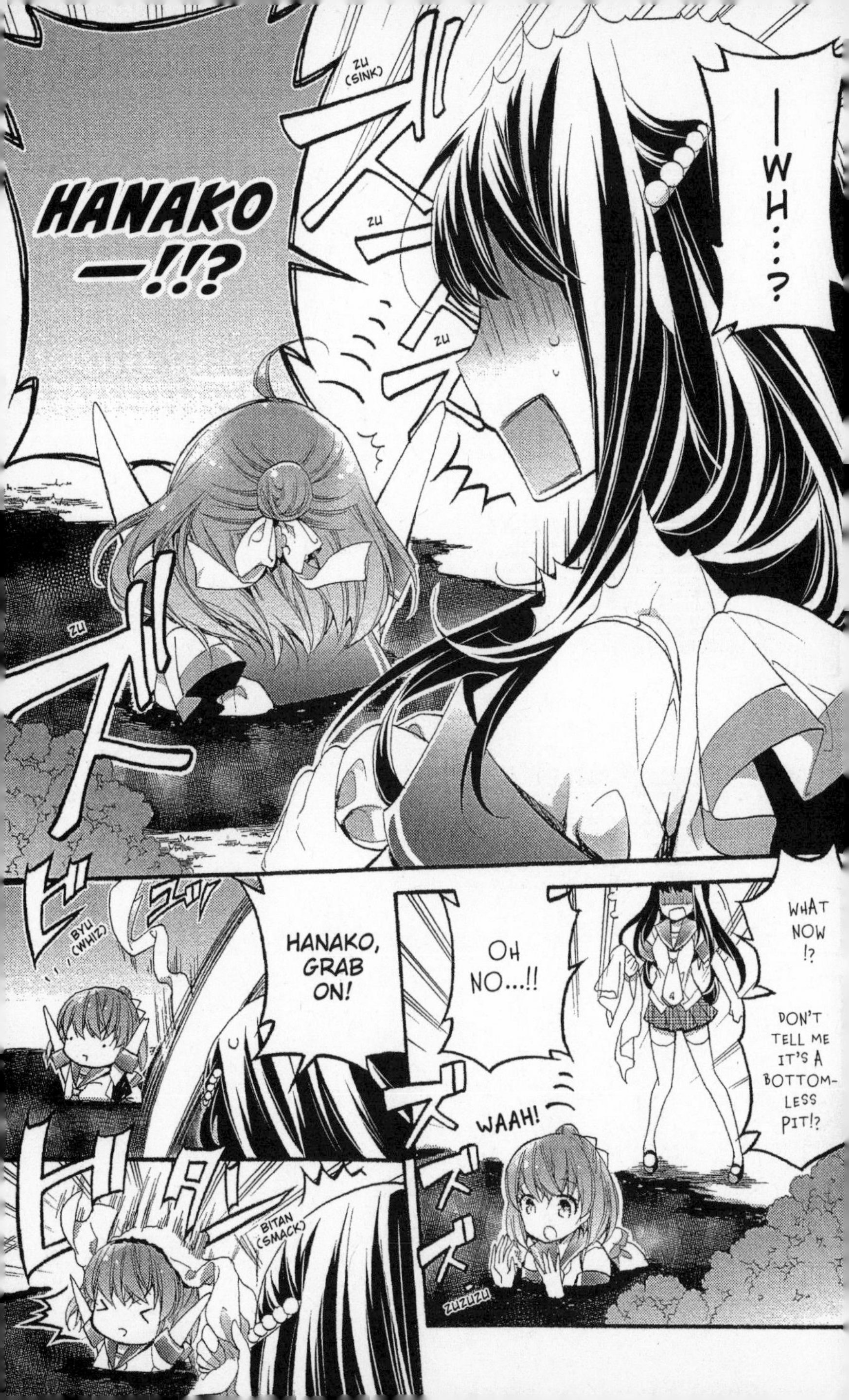
—WH...?
ZU (SINK)
HANAKO—!!?
ZU
ZU
ZU
WHAT NOW!?
DON'T TELL ME IT'S A BOTTOMLESS PIT!?
OH NO...!!
WAAH!
ZUZUZU
HANAKO, GRAB ON!
BYU (WHIZ)
BITAN (SMACK)

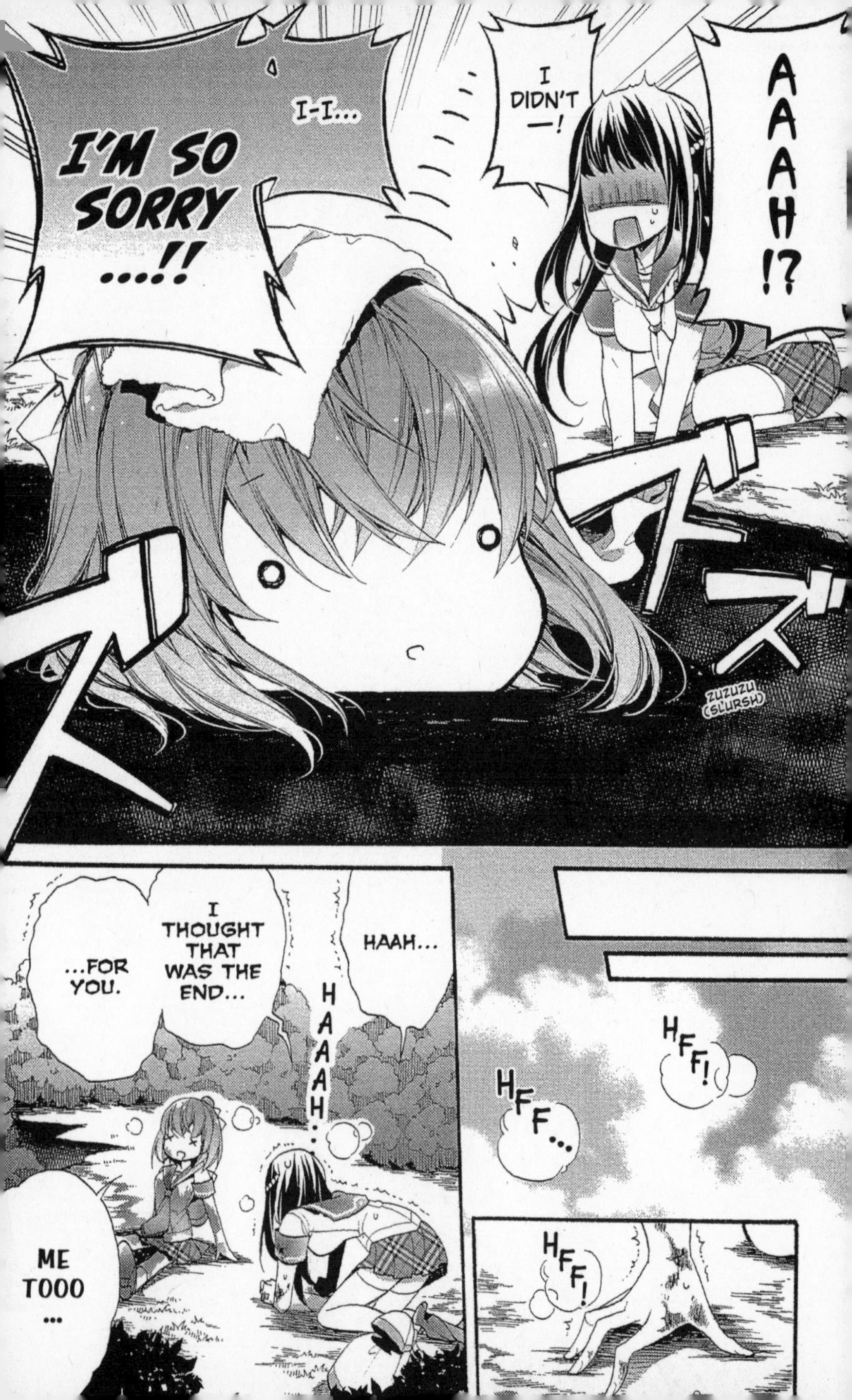
AAAAH!?
I DIDN'T —!
I-I...
I'M SO SORRY ....!!
ZUZUZU (SLURSH)
HFF!
HFF...
HFF!
HAAH...
HAAAAH...
I THOUGHT THAT WAS THE END...
...FOR YOU.
ME TOOO ...

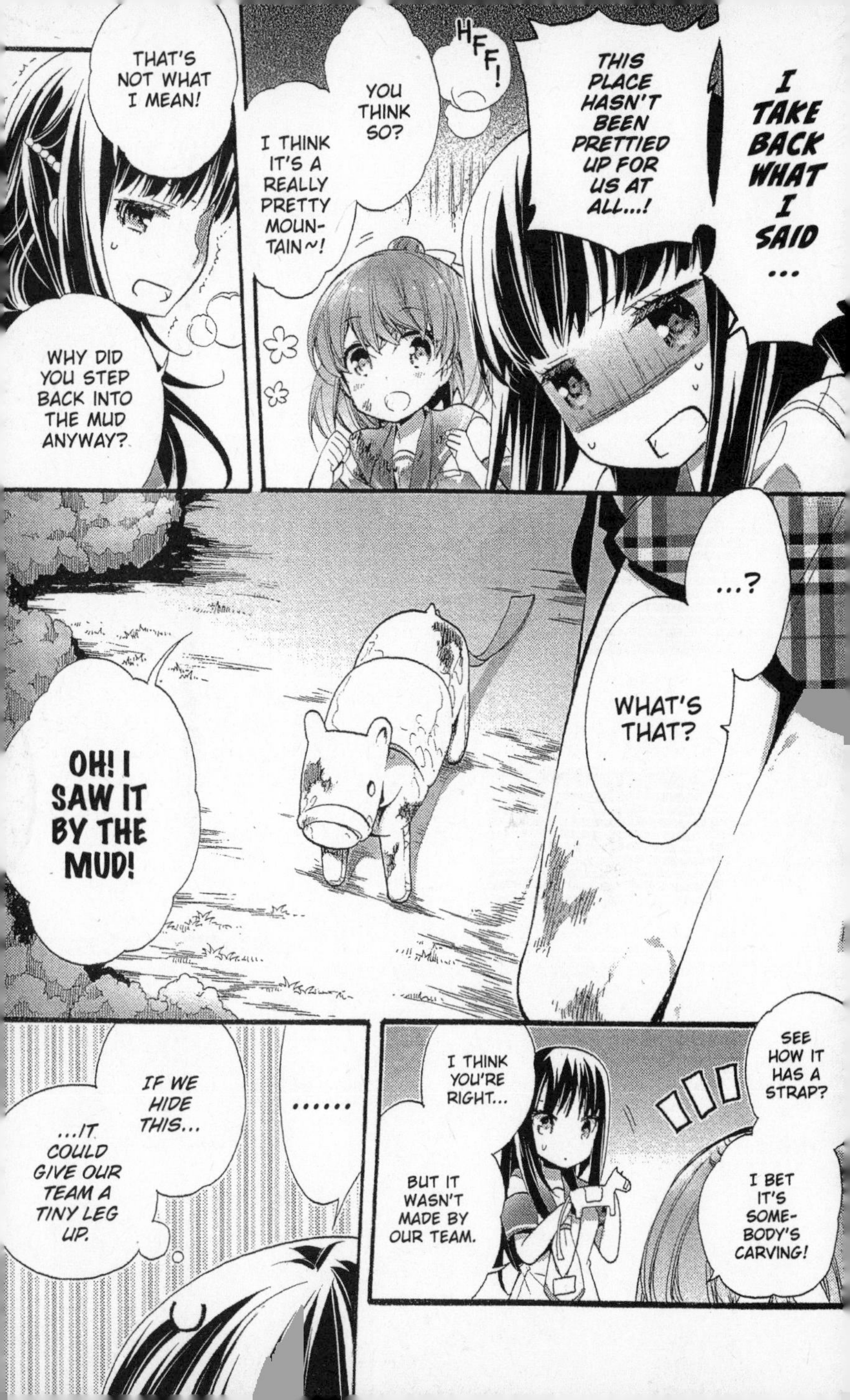
I TAKE BACK WHAT I SAID...
THIS PLACE HASN'T BEEN PRETTIED UP FOR US AT ALL...!
HFF!
YOU THINK SO?
I THINK IT'S A REALLY PRETTY MOUN-TAIN~!
THAT'S NOT WHAT I MEAN!
WHY DID YOU STEP BACK INTO THE MUD ANYWAY?
...?
WHAT'S THAT?
OH! I SAW IT BY THE MUD!
SEE HOW IT HAS A STRAP?
I BET IT'S SOME-BODY'S CARVING!
I THINK YOU'RE RIGHT...
BUT IT WASN'T MADE BY OUR TEAM.
......
IF WE HIDE THIS...
...IT COULD GIVE OUR TEAM A TINY LEG UP.

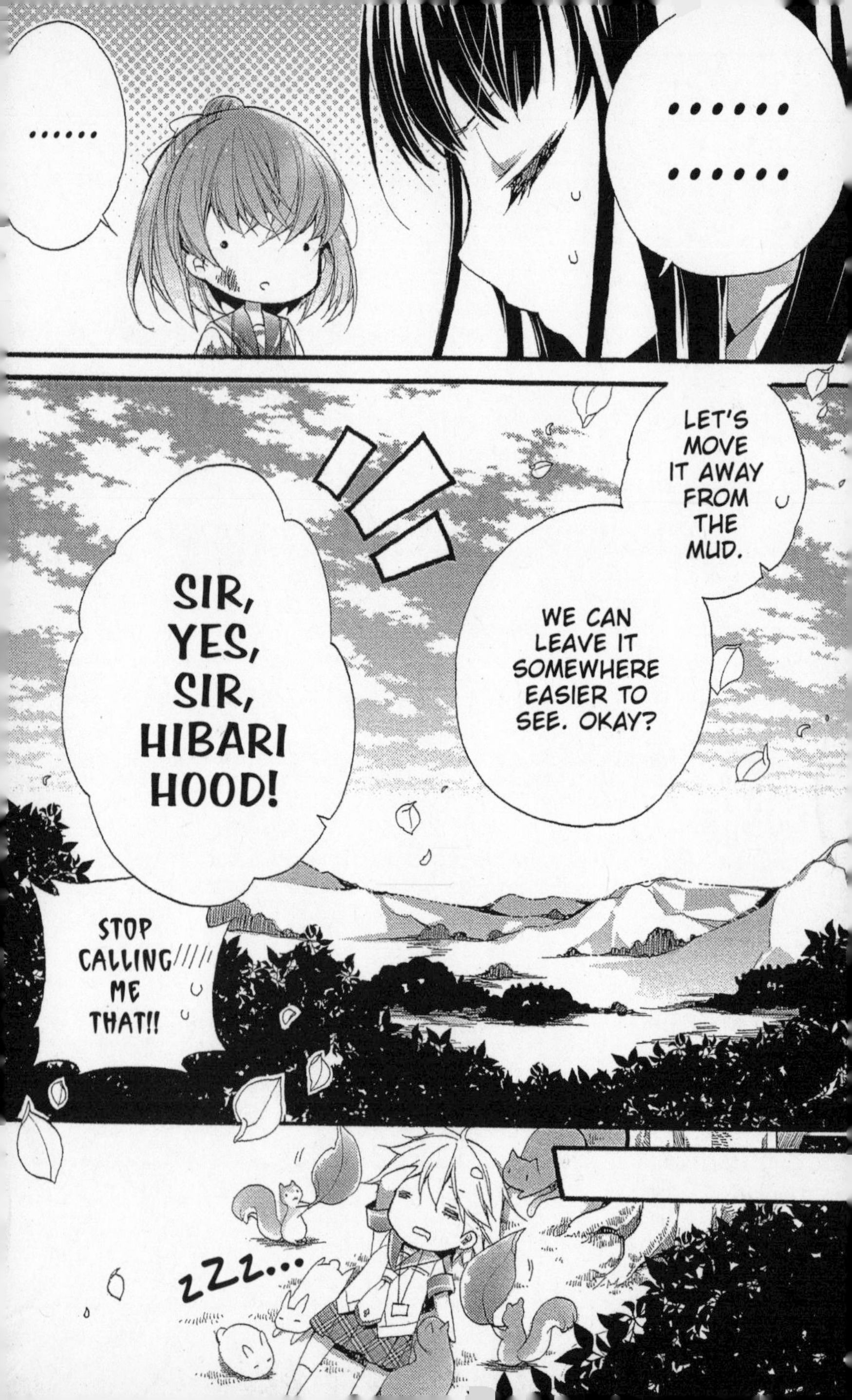
....
......
LET'S MOVE IT AWAY FROM THE MUD.
WE CAN LEAVE IT SOMEWHERE EASIER TO SEE. OKAY?
SIR, YES, SIR, HIBARI HOOD!
STOP CALLING ME THAT!!
zZZ...

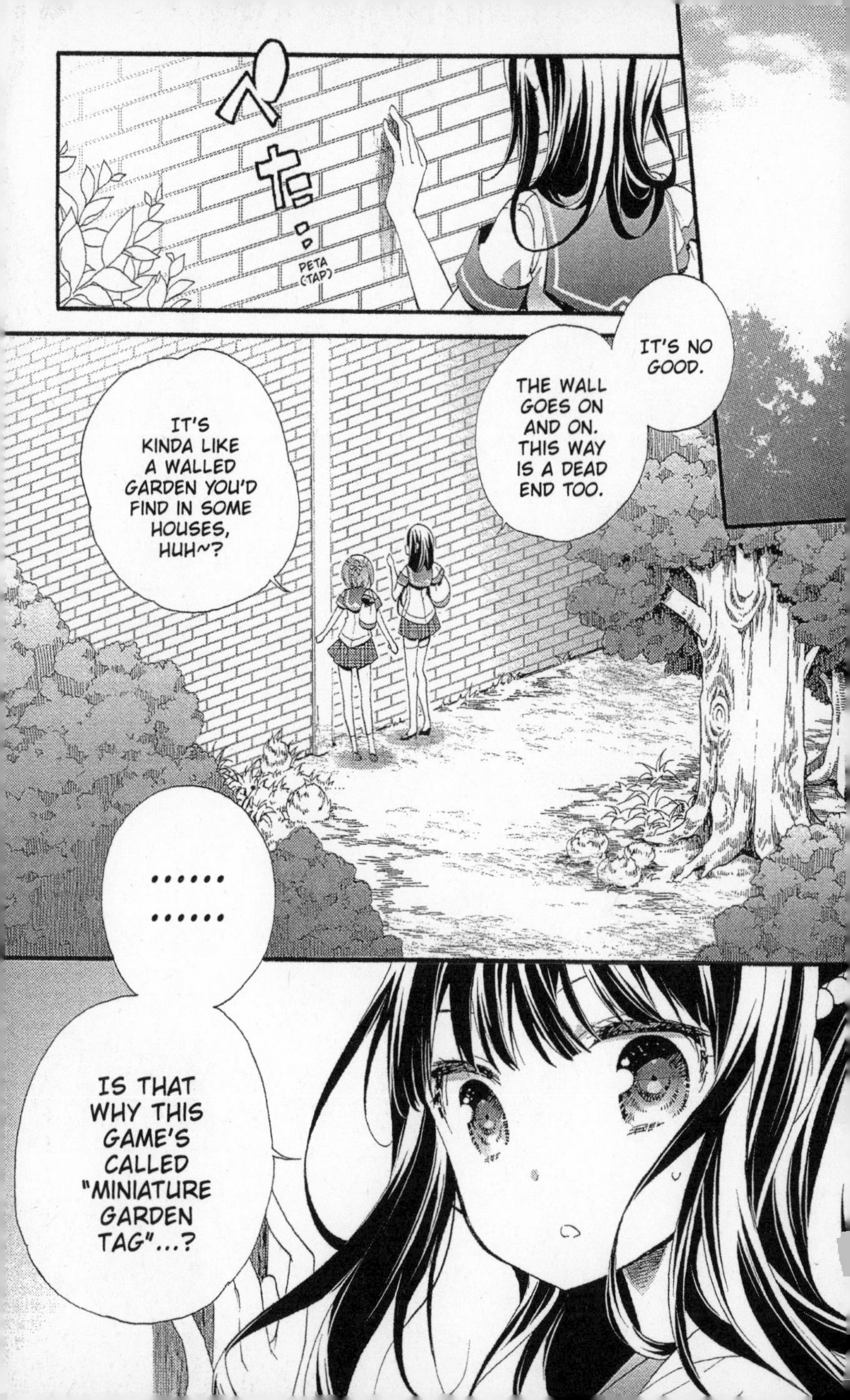
PETA (TAP)
IT'S NO GOOD.
THE WALL GOES ON AND ON. THIS WAY IS A DEAD END TOO.
IT'S KINDA LIKE A WALLED GARDEN YOU'D FIND IN SOME HOUSES, HUH~?
....
IS THAT WHY THIS GAME'S CALLED "MINIATURE GARDEN TAG"...?

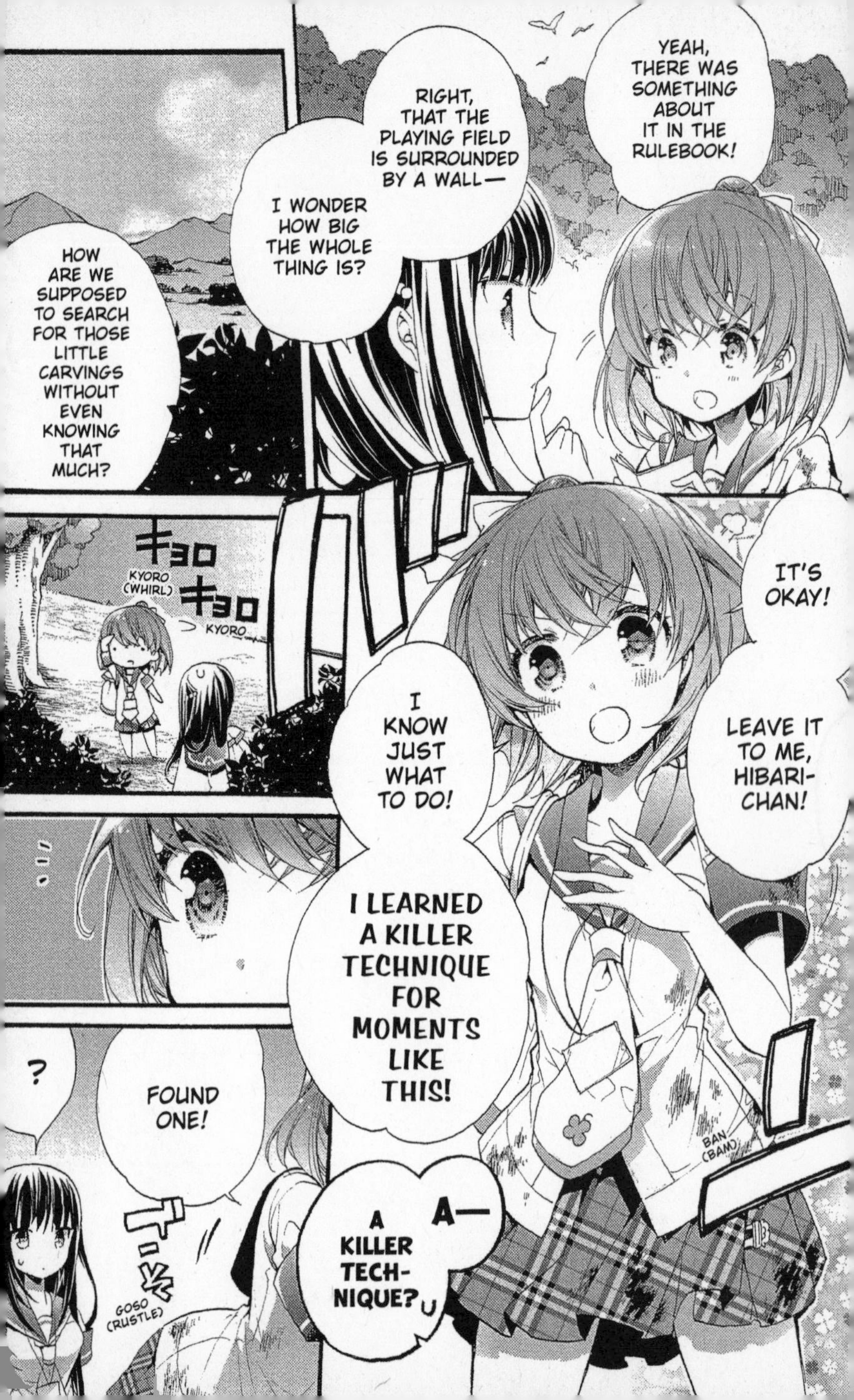
YEAH, THERE WAS SOMETHING ABOUT IT IN THE RULEBOOK!
RIGHT, THAT THE PLAYING FIELD IS SURROUNDED BY A WALL—
I WONDER HOW BIG THE WHOLE THING IS?
HOW ARE WE SUPPOSED TO SEARCH FOR THOSE LITTLE CARVINGS WITHOUT EVEN KNOWING THAT MUCH?
IT'S OKAY!
LEAVE IT TO ME, HIBARI-CHAN!
I KNOW JUST WHAT TO DO!
I LEARNED A KILLER TECHNIQUE FOR MOMENTS LIKE THIS!
BAN (BAM)
A—
A KILLER TECH-NIQUE?
キョロ
KYORO (WHIRL)
キョロ
KYORO
...
?
FOUND ONE!
ゴソ
GOSO (RUSTLE)

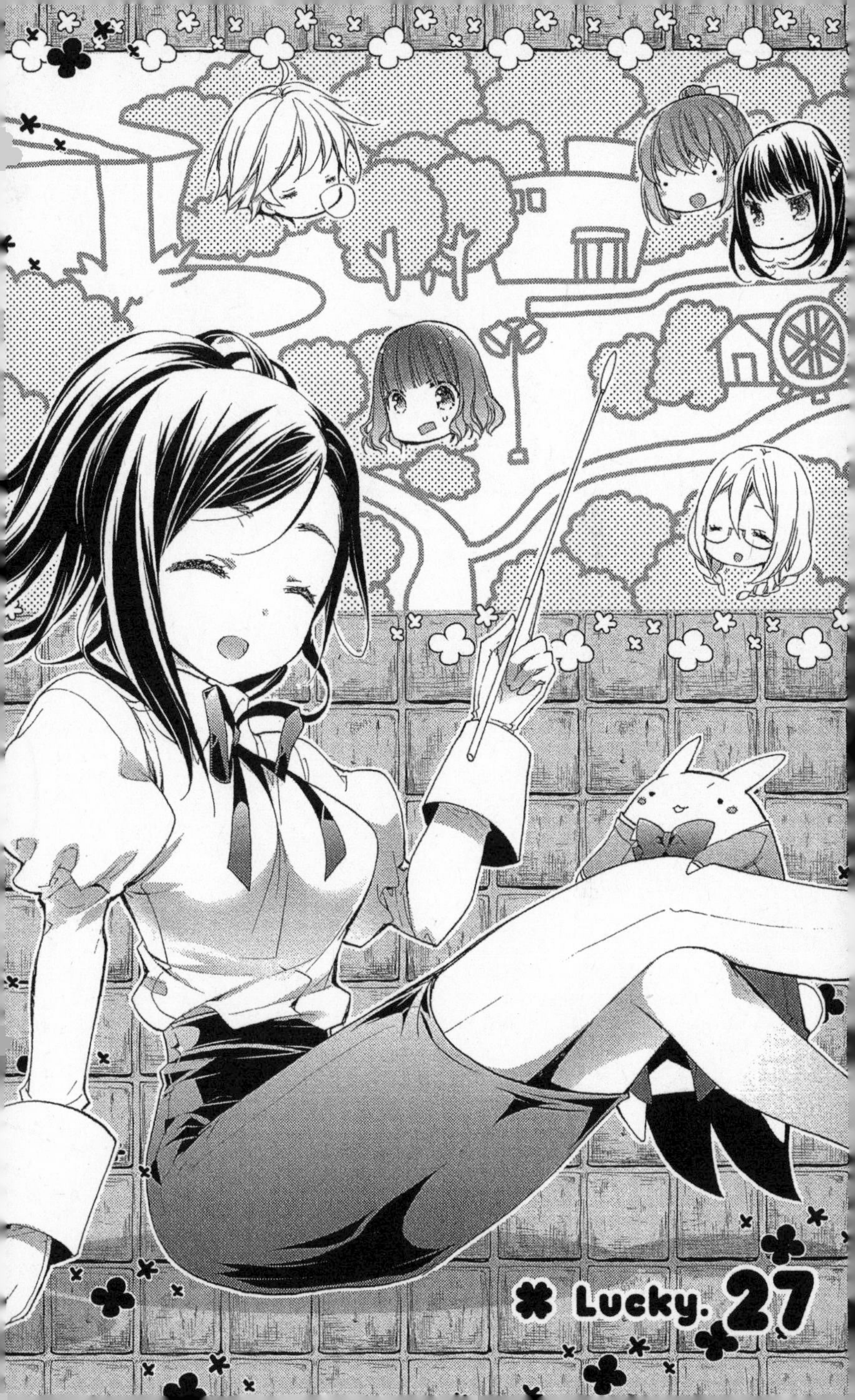
Lucky. 27

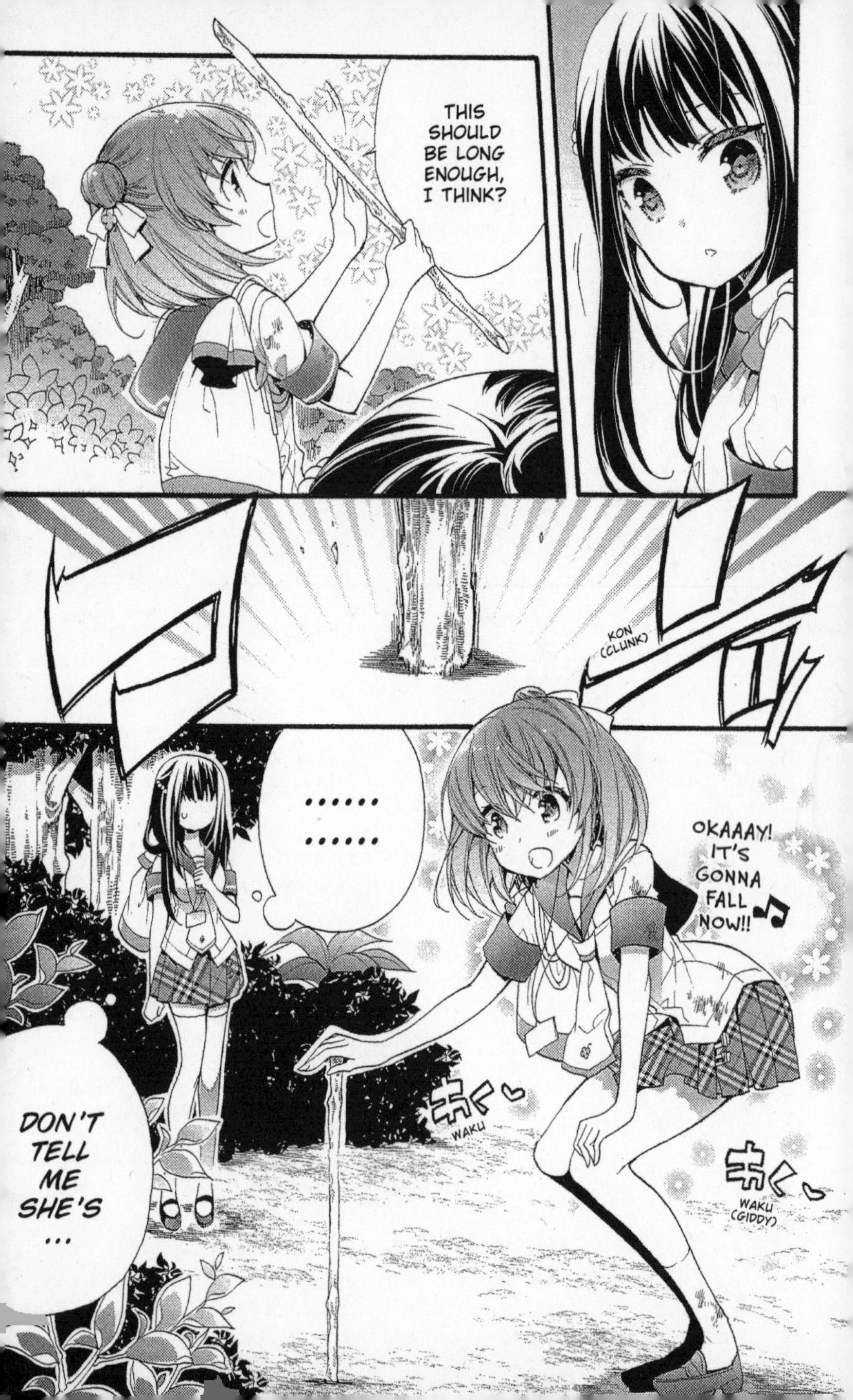

THIS SHOULD BE LONG ENOUGH, I THINK?
KON (CLUNK)
OKAAAY! IT'S GONNA FALL NOW!! ♪
WAKU (GIDDY)
WAKU
....
DON'T TELL ME SHE'S ...

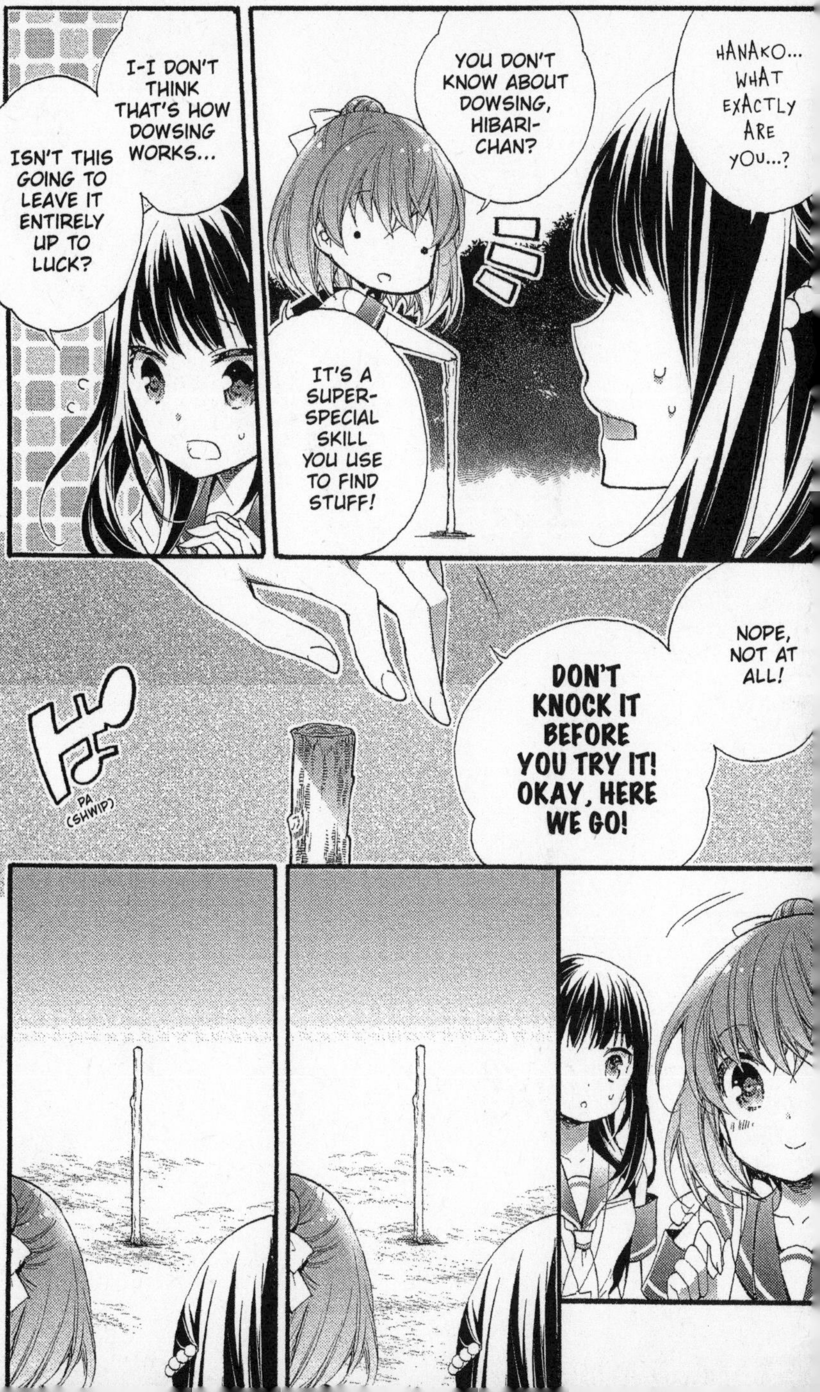
HANAKO... WHAT EXACTLY ARE YOU...?
YOU DON'T KNOW ABOUT DOWSING, HIBARI-CHAN?
IT'S A SUPER-SPECIAL SKILL YOU USE TO FIND STUFF!
I-I DON'T THINK THAT'S HOW DOWSING WORKS...
ISN'T THIS GOING TO LEAVE IT ENTIRELY UP TO LUCK?
NOPE, NOT AT ALL!
DON'T KNOCK IT BEFORE YOU TRY IT! OKAY, HERE WE GO!
PA (SHWIP)

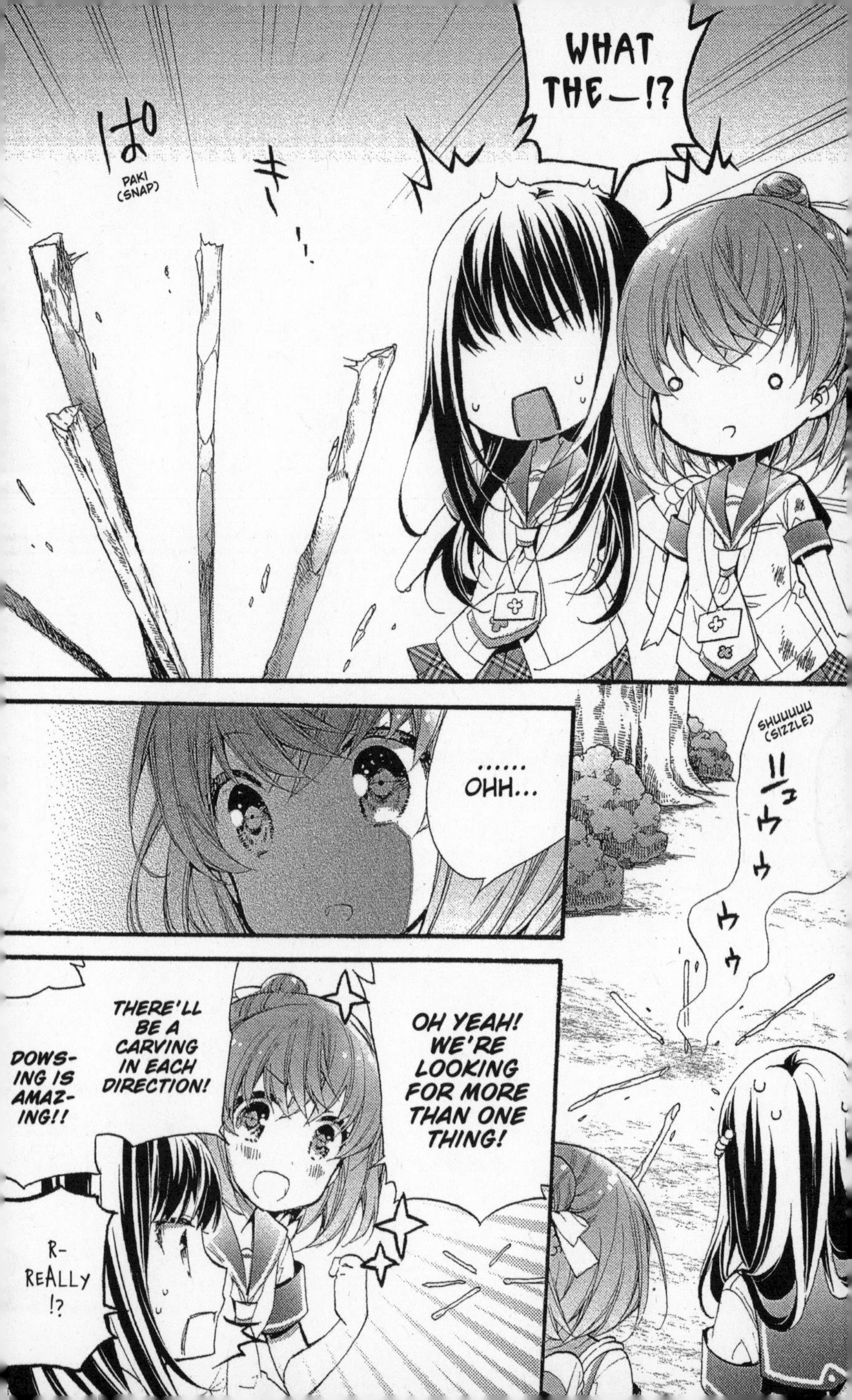
WHAT THE—!?
ぱき
PAKI (SNAP)
......OHH...
シュウゥゥゥ
SHUUUUU (SIZZLE)
OH YEAH! WE'RE LOOKING FOR MORE THAN ONE THING!
THERE'LL BE A CARVING IN EACH DIRECTION!
DOWS-ING IS AMAZ-ING!!
R-REALLY!?

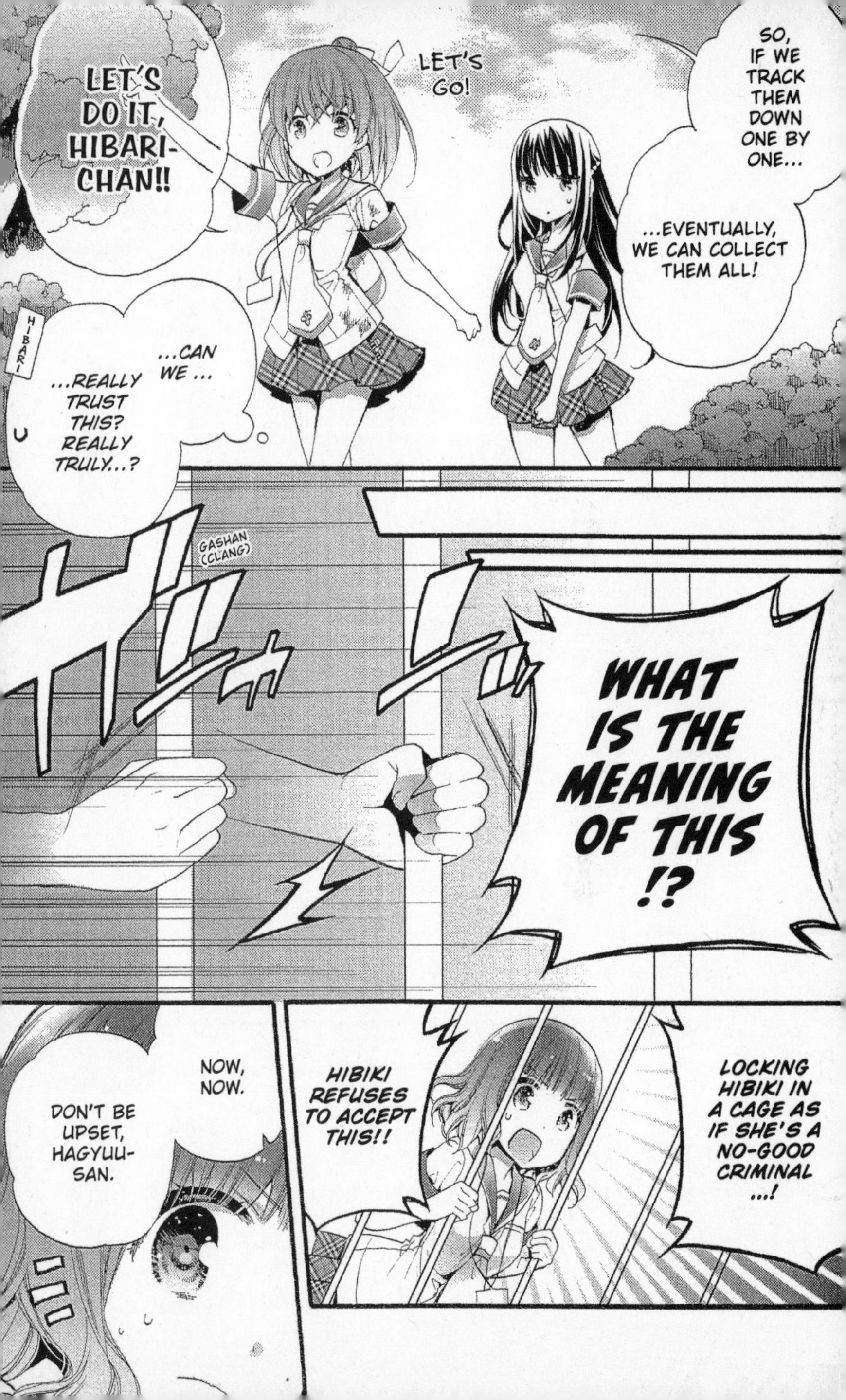

SO, IF WE TRACK THEM DOWN ONE BY ONE...
...EVENTUALLY, WE CAN COLLECT THEM ALL!
LET'S GO!
LET'S DO IT, HIBARI-CHAN!!
HIBARI
...CAN WE ...
...REALLY TRUST THIS? REALLY TRULY...?
GASHAN (CLANG)
WHAT IS THE MEANING OF THIS !?
LOCKING HIBIKI IN A CAGE AS IF SHE'S A NO-GOOD CRIMINAL ...!
HIBIKI REFUSES TO ACCEPT THIS!!
NOW, NOW.
DON'T BE UPSET, HAGYUU-SAN.

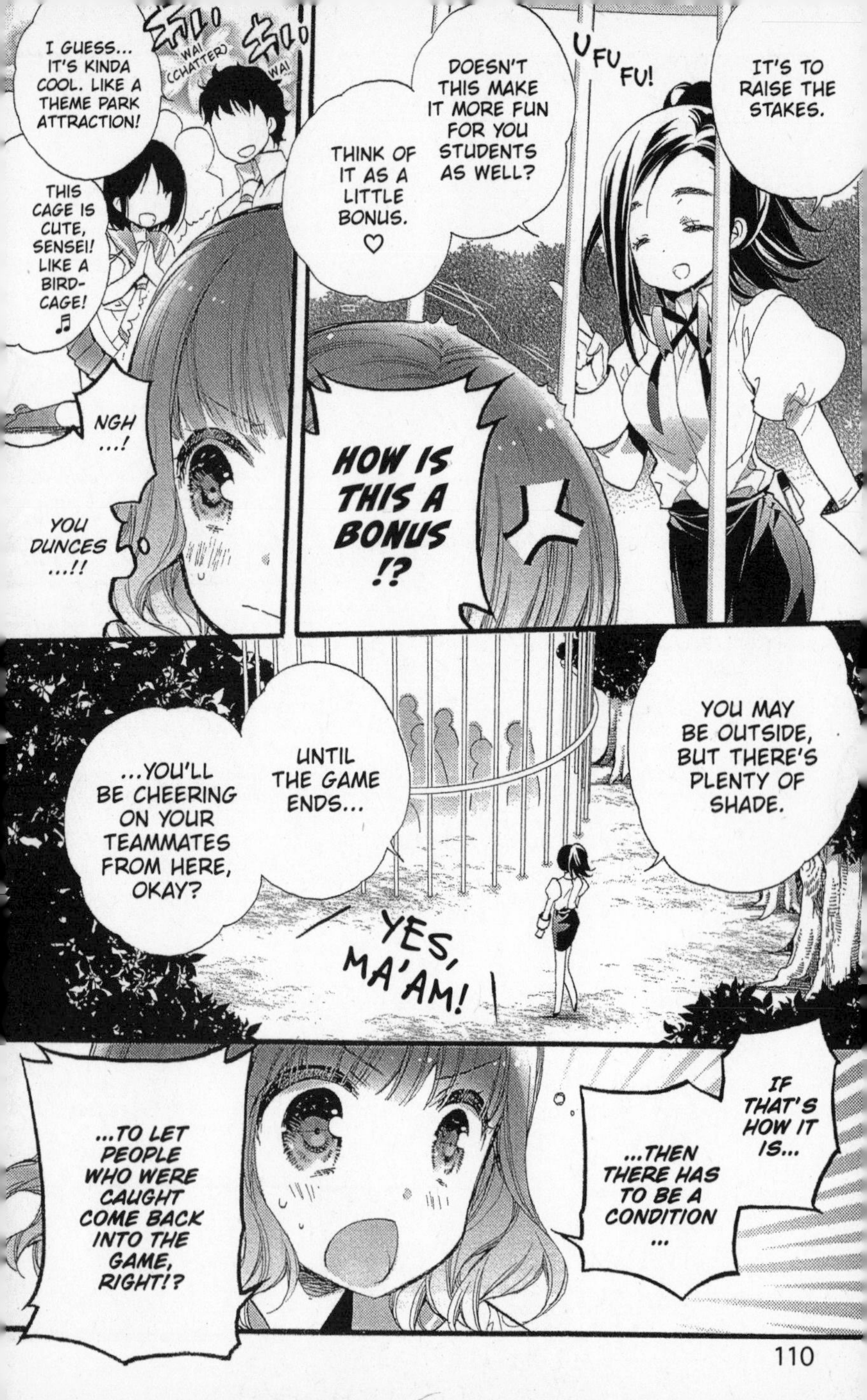
UFUFUFU!
IT'S TO RAISE THE STAKES.
DOESN'T THIS MAKE IT MORE FUN FOR YOU STUDENTS AS WELL?
THINK OF IT AS A LITTLE BONUS. ♡
HOW IS THIS A BONUS!?
WAI
WAI (CHATTER)
I GUESS... IT'S KINDA COOL. LIKE A THEME PARK ATTRACTION!
THIS CAGE IS CUTE, SENSEI! LIKE A BIRD-CAGE! ♬
NGH ...!
YOU DUNCES ...!!
YOU MAY BE OUTSIDE, BUT THERE'S PLENTY OF SHADE.
UNTIL THE GAME ENDS...
...YOU'LL BE CHEERING ON YOUR TEAMMATES FROM HERE, OKAY?
YES, MA'AM!
IF THAT'S HOW IT IS...
...THEN THERE HAS TO BE A CONDITION ...
...TO LET PEOPLE WHO WERE CAUGHT COME BACK INTO THE GAME, RIGHT!?

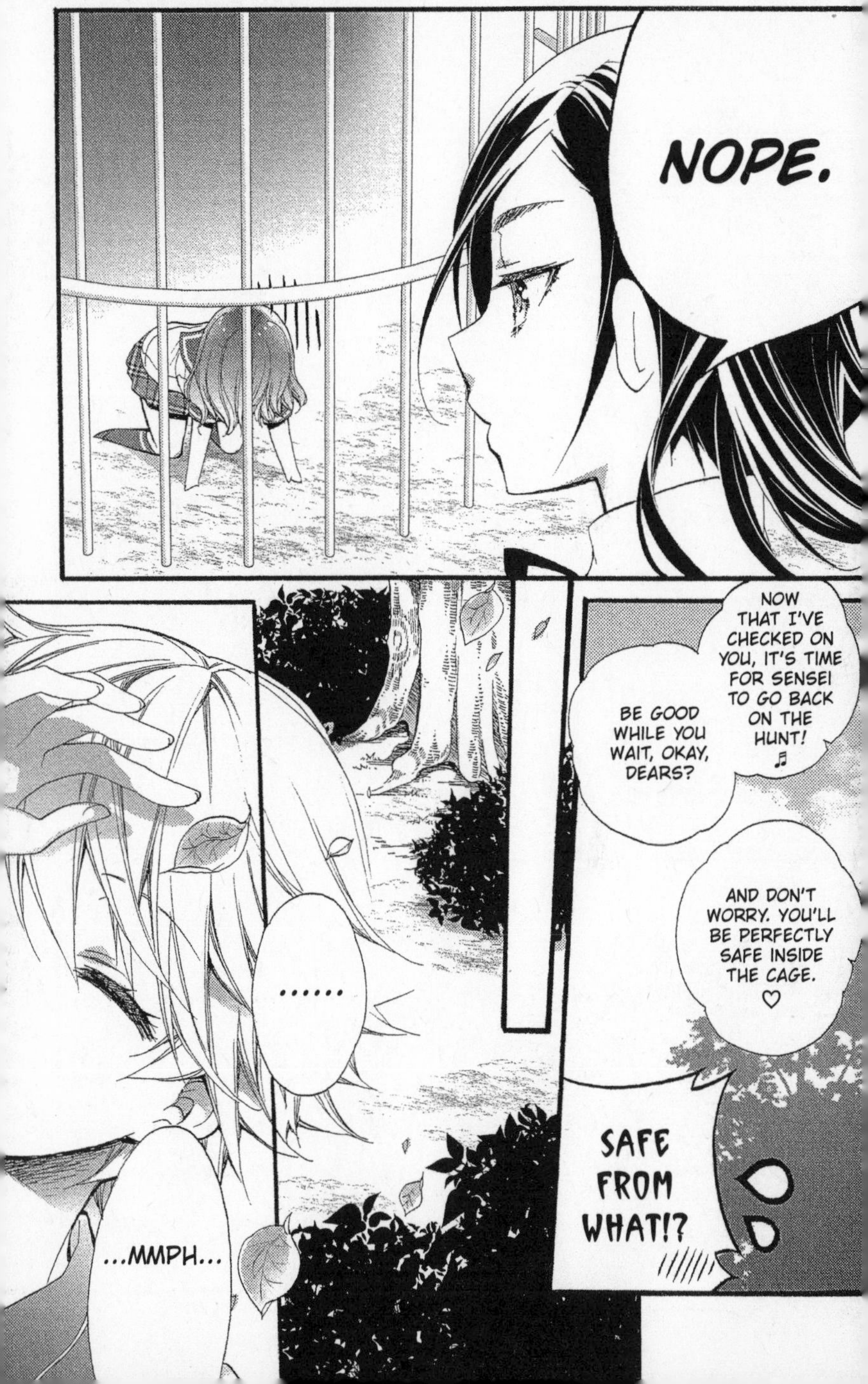
NOPE.
NOW THAT I'VE CHECKED ON YOU, IT'S TIME FOR SENSEI TO GO BACK ON THE HUNT! ♫
BE GOOD WHILE YOU WAIT, OKAY, DEARS?
AND DON'T WORRY. YOU'LL BE PERFECTLY SAFE INSIDE THE CAGE. ♡
SAFE FROM WHAT!?
......
...MMPH...

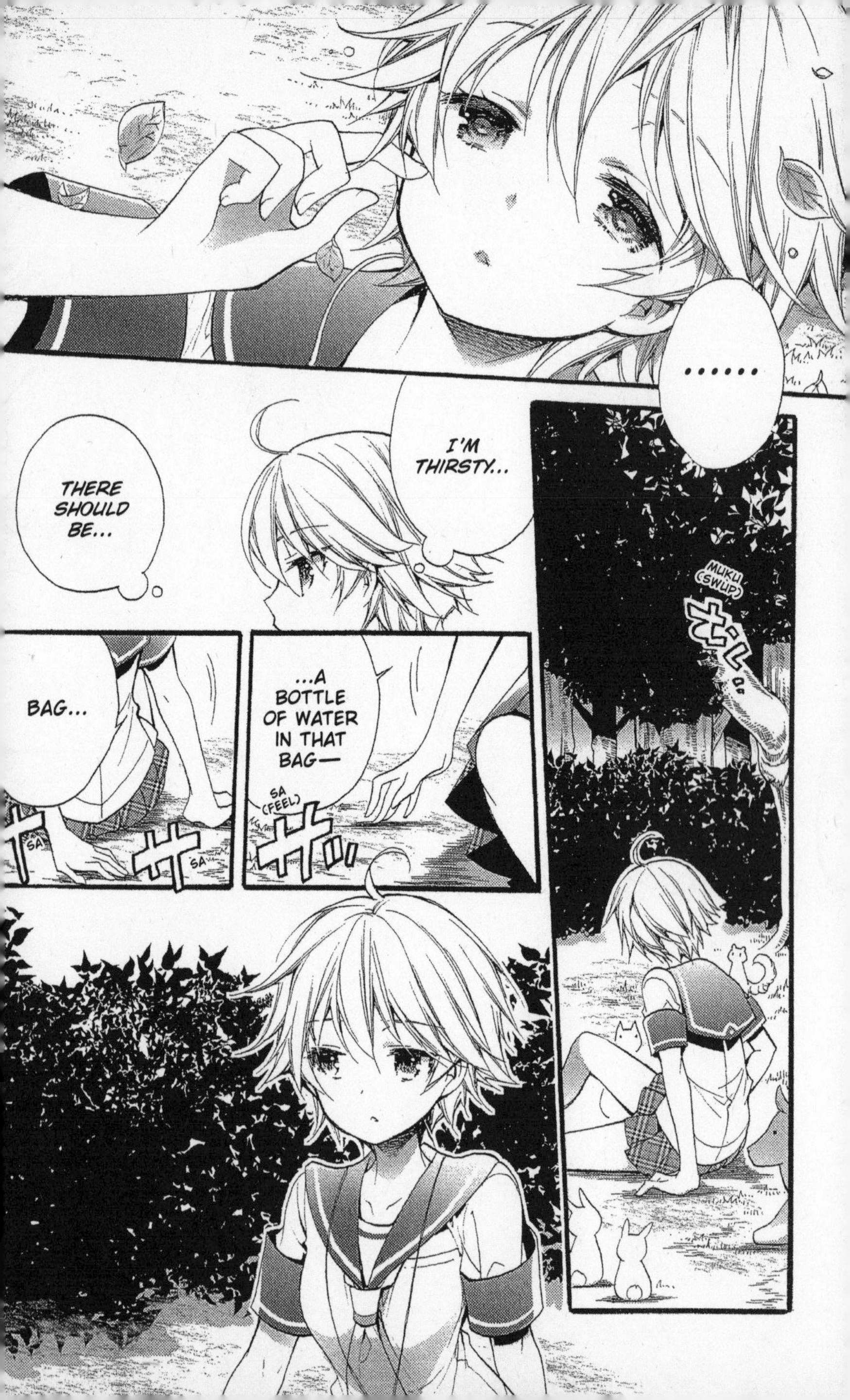
......
MUKU (SWLIP)
I'M THIRSTY...
THERE SHOULD BE...
...A BOTTLE OF WATER IN THAT BAG—
SA (FEEL)
BAG...
SA
SA

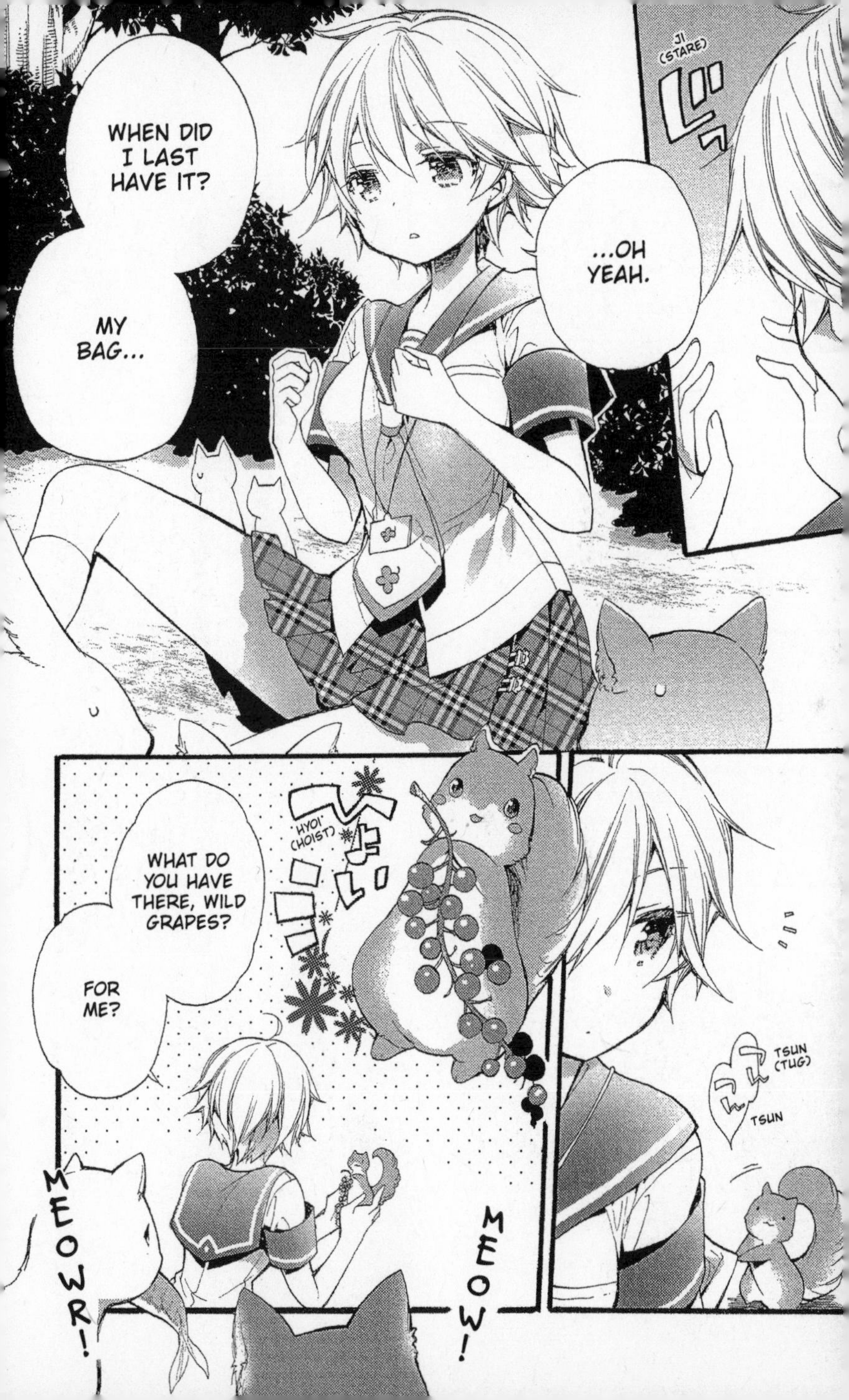
JI (STARE)
WHEN DID I LAST HAVE IT?
MY BAG...
...OH YEAH.
TSUN (TUG)
TSUN
HYOI (HOIST)
WHAT DO YOU HAVE THERE, WILD GRAPES?
FOR ME?
MEOW!
MEOWR!

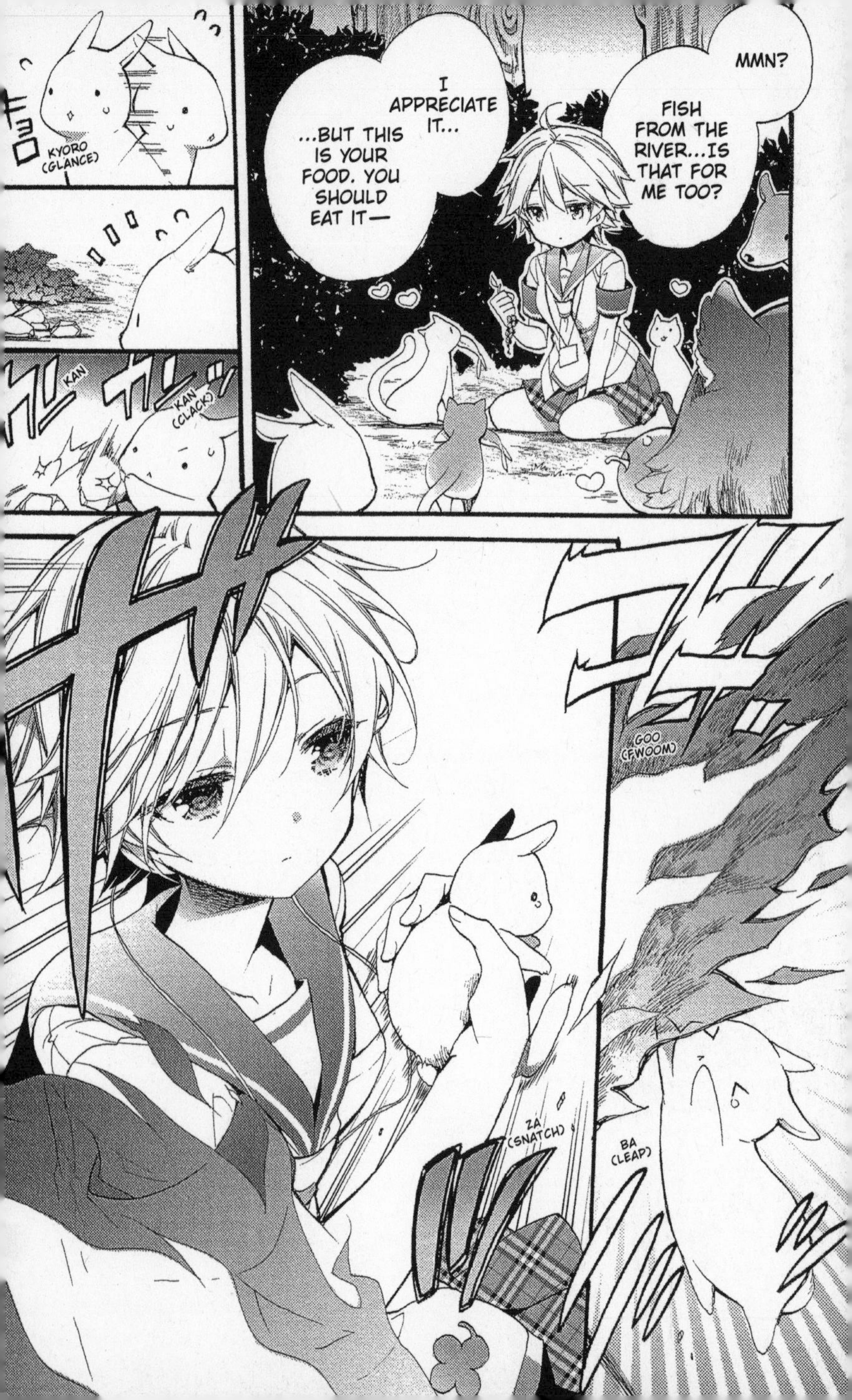
MMN?
FISH FROM THE RIVER...IS THAT FOR ME TOO?
I APPRECIATE IT...
...BUT THIS IS YOUR FOOD. YOU SHOULD EAT IT—
KYORO (GLANCE)
KAN
KAN (CLACK)
GOO (FWOOM)
BA (LEAP)
ZA (SNATCH)

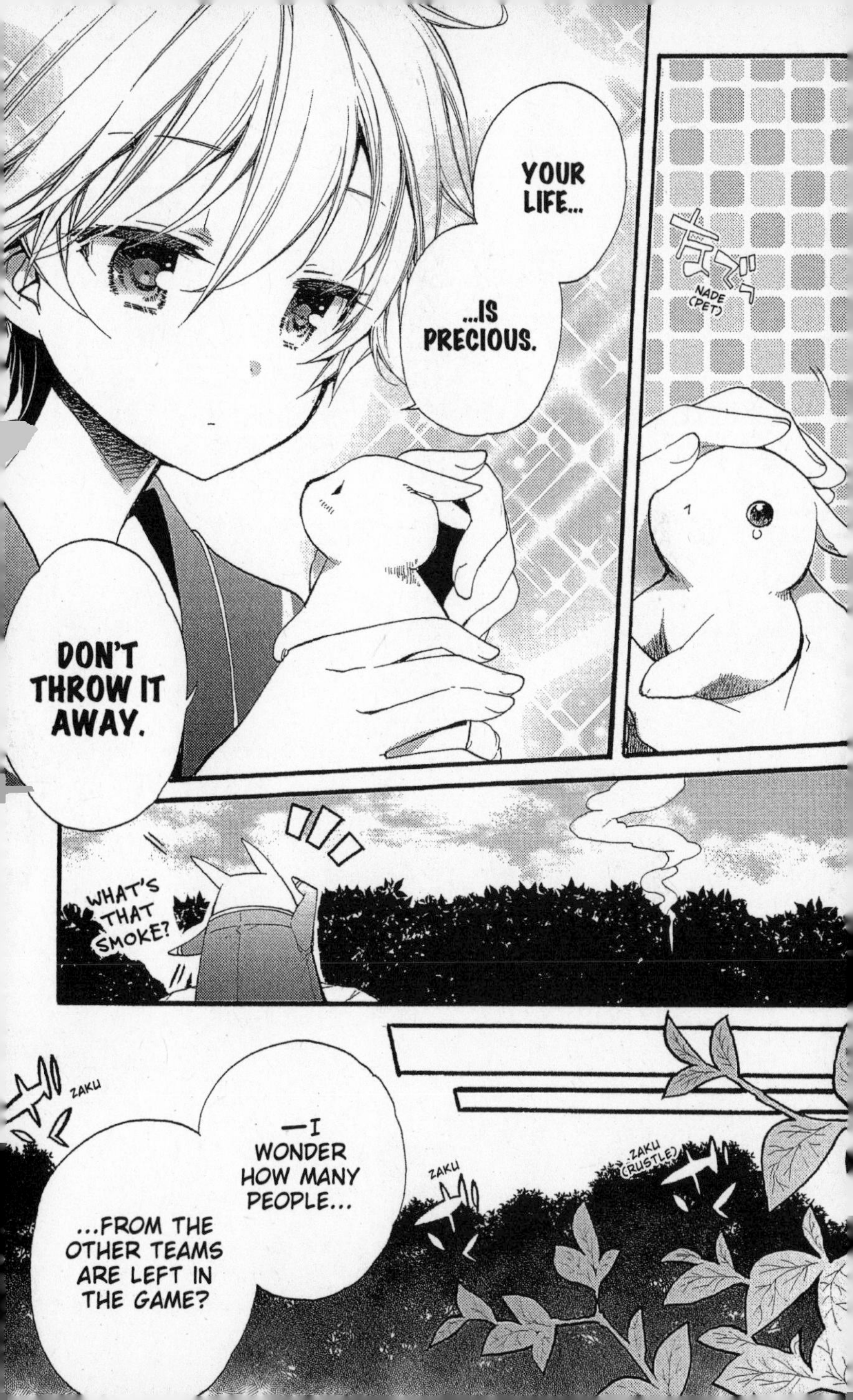
NADE (PET)
YOUR LIFE...
...IS PRECIOUS.
DON'T THROW IT AWAY.
WHAT'S THAT SMOKE?
ZAKU (RUSTLE)
ZAKU
—I WONDER HOW MANY PEOPLE...
...FROM THE OTHER TEAMS ARE LEFT IN THE GAME?
ZAKU

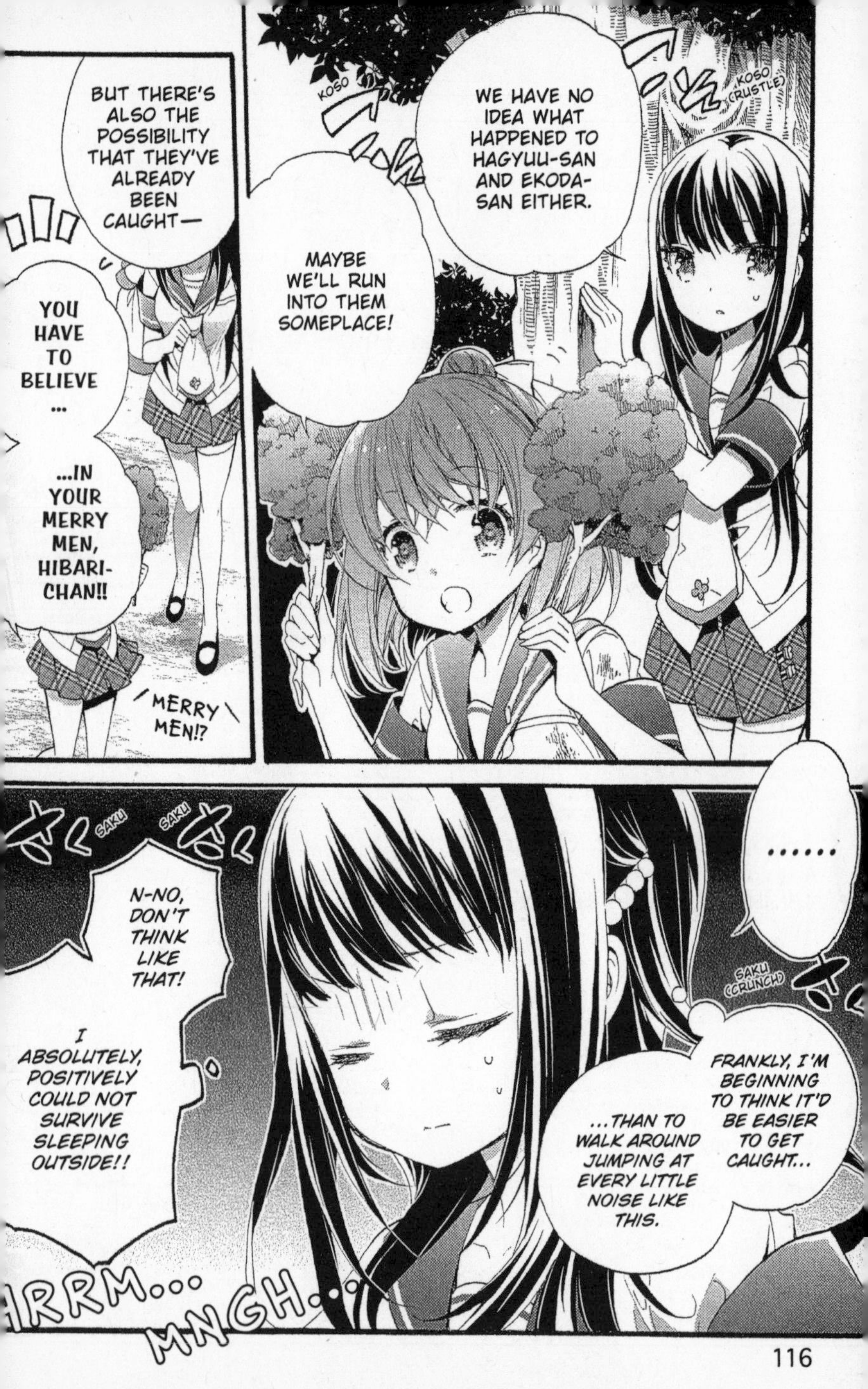

KOSO (RUSTLE)
WE HAVE NO IDEA WHAT HAPPENED TO HAGYUU-SAN AND EKODA-SAN EITHER.
KOSO
MAYBE WE'LL RUN INTO THEM SOMEPLACE!
BUT THERE'S ALSO THE POSSIBILITY THAT THEY'VE ALREADY BEEN CAUGHT—
YOU HAVE TO BELIEVE ...
...IN YOUR MERRY MEN, HIBARI-CHAN!!
MERRY MEN!?
......
SAKU (CRUNCH)
FRANKLY, I'M BEGINNING TO THINK IT'D BE EASIER TO GET CAUGHT...
...THAN TO WALK AROUND JUMPING AT EVERY LITTLE NOISE LIKE THIS.
SAKU
SAKU
N-NO, DON'T THINK LIKE THAT!
I ABSOLUTELY, POSITIVELY COULD NOT SURVIVE SLEEPING OUTSIDE!!
MNGH...
RRM...

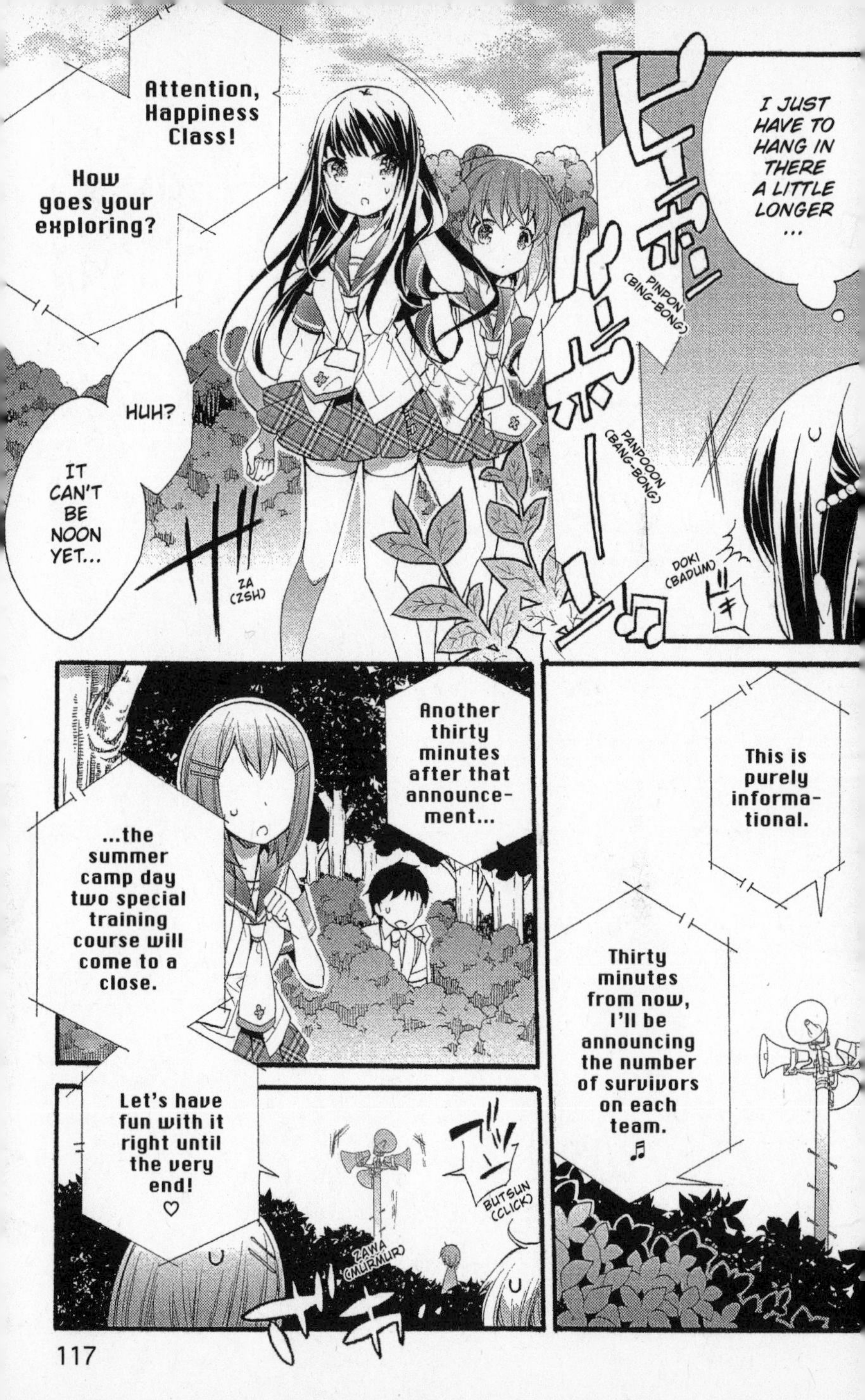
I JUST HAVE TO HANG IN THERE A LITTLE LONGER...
PINPON (BING-BONG)
PANPOOON (BANG-BONG)
DOKI (BADUM)
Attention, Happiness Class!
How goes your exploring?
HUH?
IT CAN'T BE NOON YET...
ZA (ZSH)
This is purely informational.
Thirty minutes from now, I'll be announcing the number of survivors on each team. ♬
Another thirty minutes after that announcement...
...the summer camp day two special training course will come to a close.
Let's have fun with it right until the very end! ♡
BUTSUN (CLICK)
ZAWA (MURMUR)

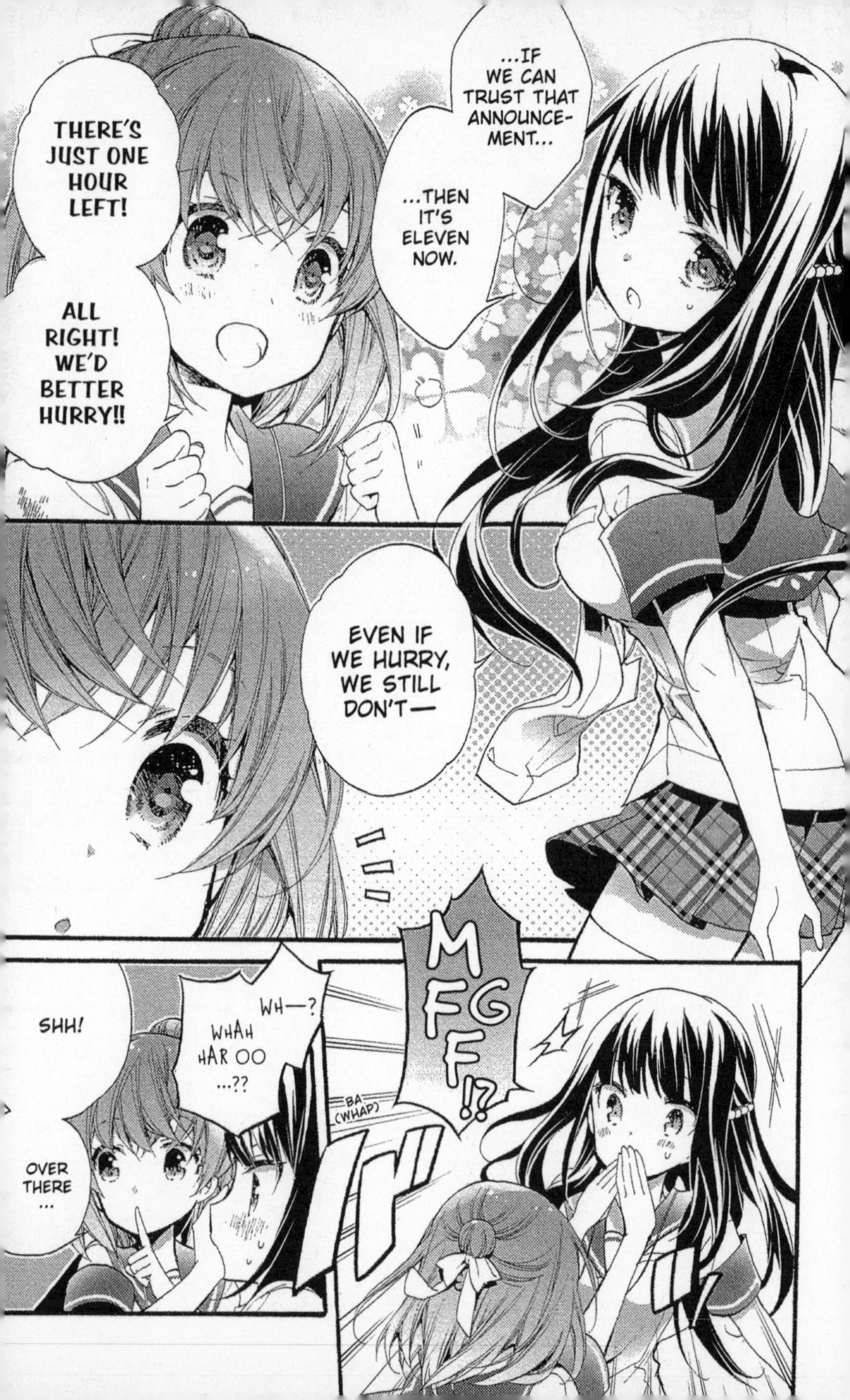
...IF WE CAN TRUST THAT ANNOUNCEMENT...
...THEN IT'S ELEVEN NOW.
THERE'S JUST ONE HOUR LEFT!
ALL RIGHT! WE'D BETTER HURRY!!
EVEN IF WE HURRY, WE STILL DON'T—
MFGF!?
BA (WHAP)
WH—?
WHAH HAR OO ...??
SHH!
OVER THERE ...

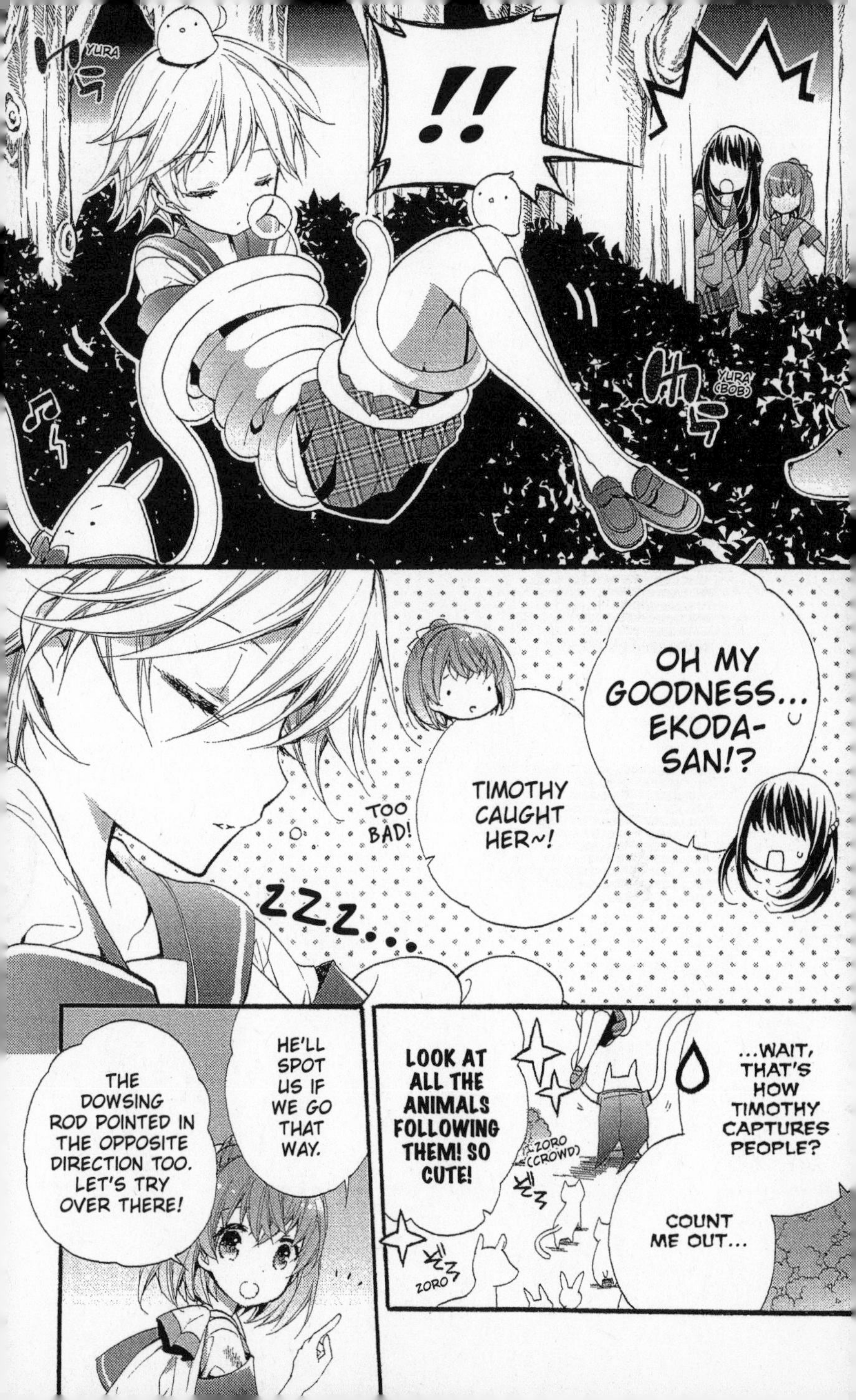
YURA (BOB)
!!
YURA
OH MY GOODNESS... EKODA-SAN!?
TIMOTHY CAUGHT HER~!
TOO BAD!
ZZZ...
...WAIT, THAT'S HOW TIMOTHY CAPTURES PEOPLE?
COUNT ME OUT...
LOOK AT ALL THE ANIMALS FOLLOWING THEM! SO CUTE!
ZORO (CROWD)
ZORO
HE'LL SPOT US IF WE GO THAT WAY.
THE DOWSING ROD POINTED IN THE OPPOSITE DIRECTION TOO. LET'S TRY OVER THERE!

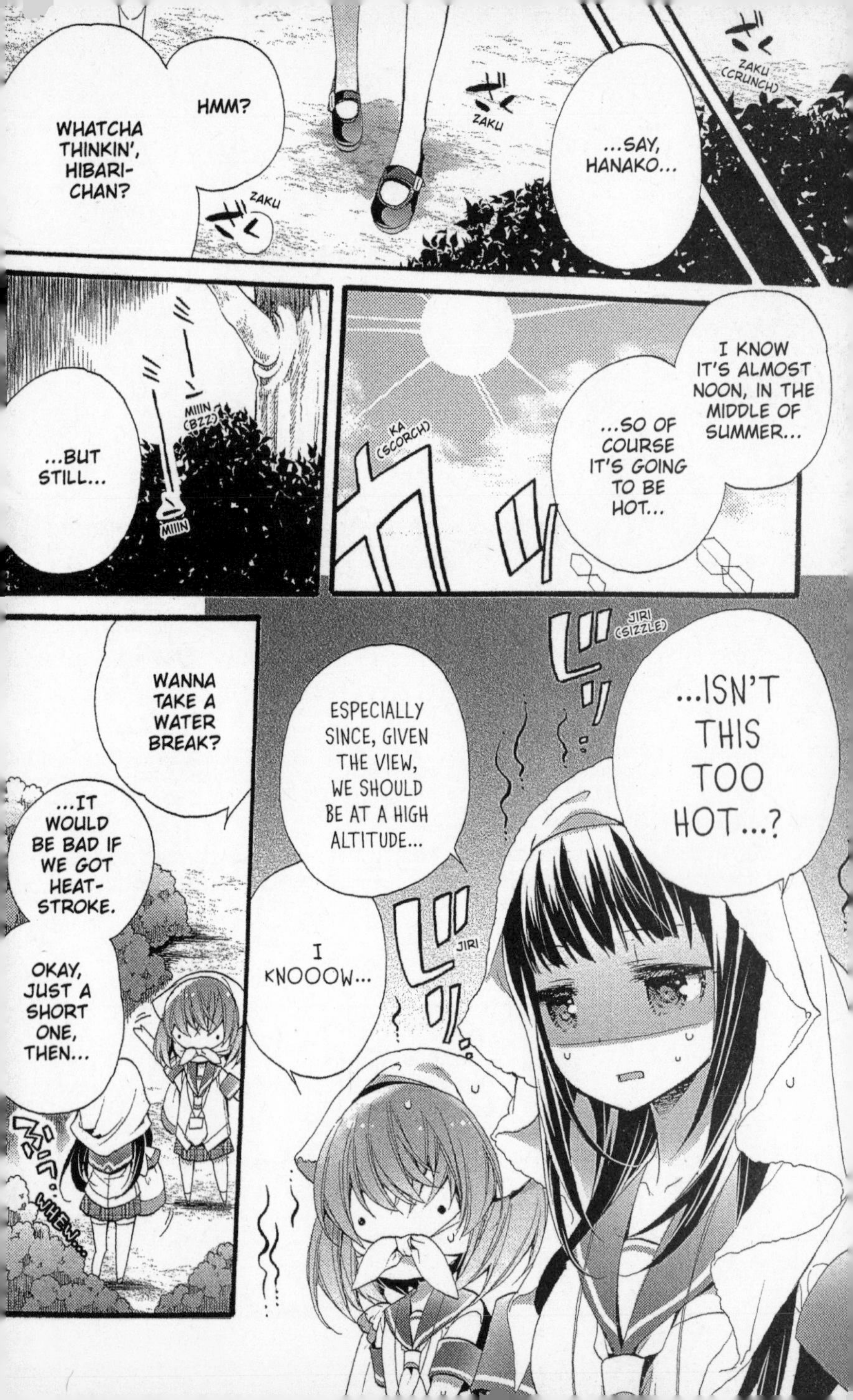
ZAKU (CRUNCH)
...SAY, HANAKO...
ZAKU
HMM?
WHATCHA THINKIN', HIBARI-CHAN?
ZAKU
I KNOW IT'S ALMOST NOON, IN THE MIDDLE OF SUMMER...
...SO OF COURSE IT'S GOING TO BE HOT...
KA (SCORCH)
MIIN (BZZ)
MIIN
...BUT STILL...
JIRI (SIZZLE)
...ISN'T THIS TOO HOT...?
ESPECIALLY SINCE, GIVEN THE VIEW, WE SHOULD BE AT A HIGH ALTITUDE...
JIRI
I KNOOOW...
WANNA TAKE A WATER BREAK?
...IT WOULD BE BAD IF WE GOT HEAT-STROKE.
OKAY, JUST A SHORT ONE, THEN...
WHEW...

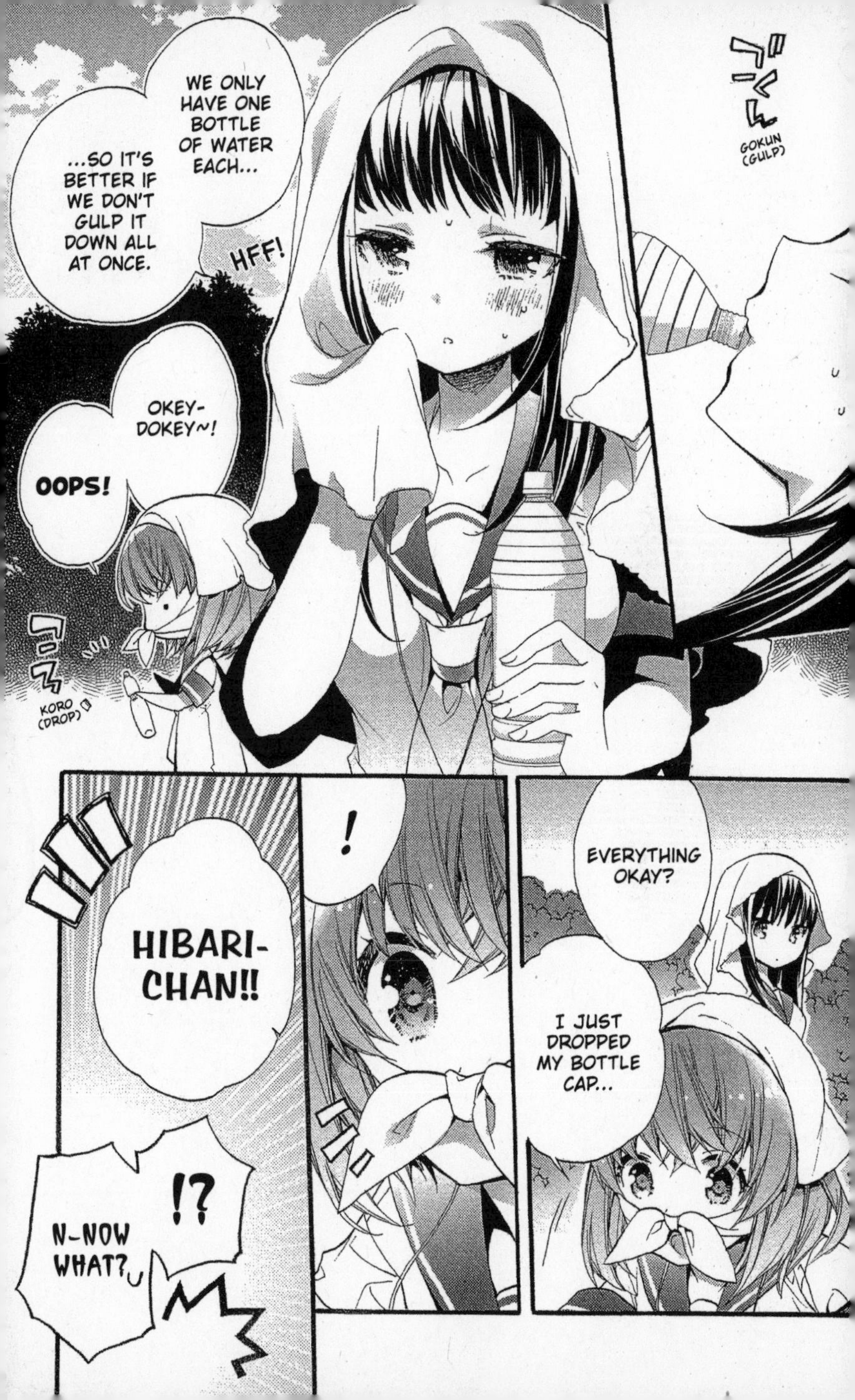
GOKUN (GULP)
WE ONLY HAVE ONE BOTTLE OF WATER EACH...
...SO IT'S BETTER IF WE DON'T GULP IT DOWN ALL AT ONCE.
HFF!
OKEY-DOKEY~!
OOPS!
KORO (DROP)
EVERYTHING OKAY?
I JUST DROPPED MY BOTTLE CAP...
!
HIBARI-CHAN!!
!?
N-NOW WHAT?

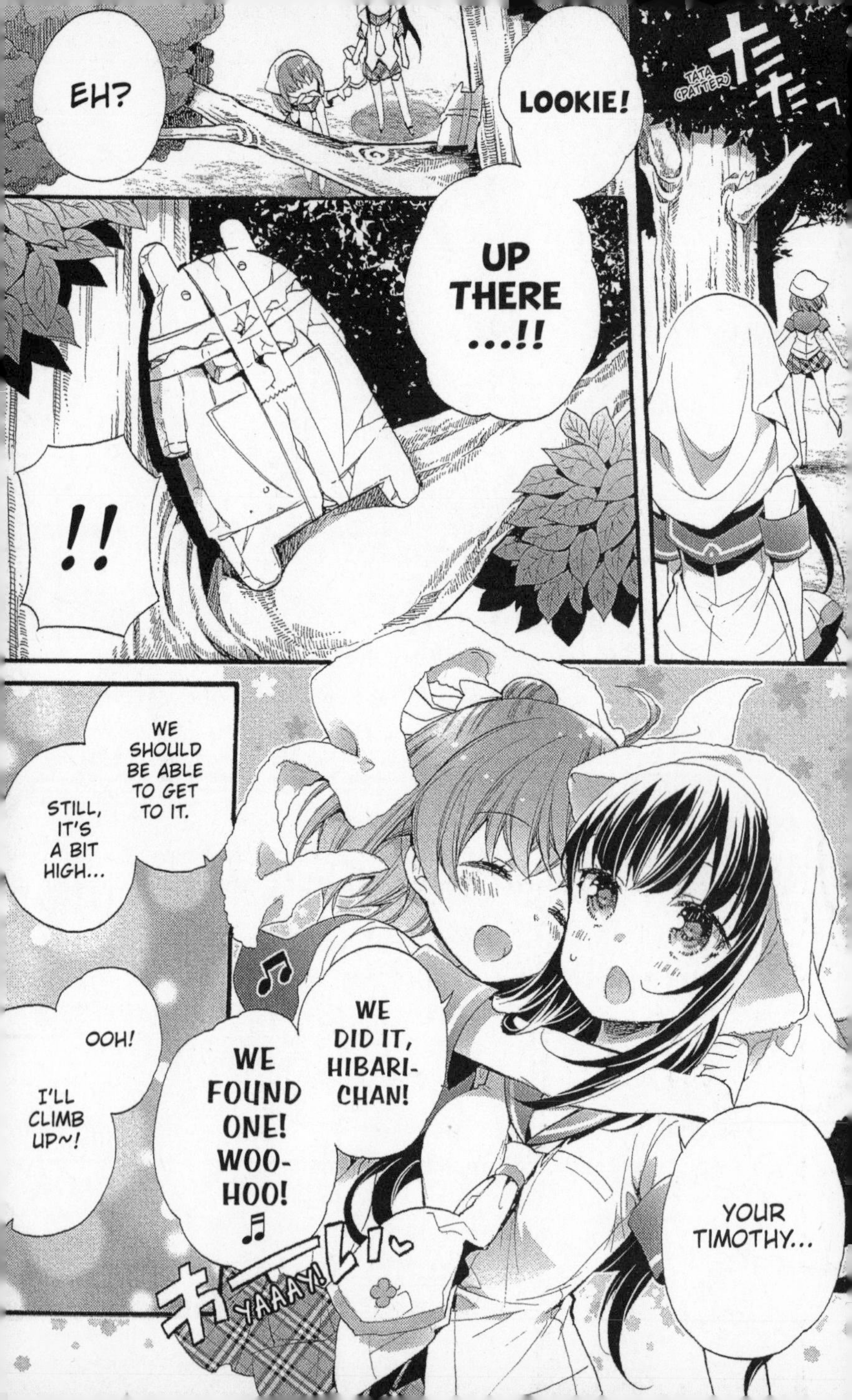
TATA (PATTER)
LOOKIE!
EH?
UP THERE ...!!
!!
WE DID IT, HIBARI-CHAN!
WE FOUND ONE! WOO-HOO! ♫
YAAAY!
YOUR TIMOTHY...
STILL, IT'S A BIT HIGH...
WE SHOULD BE ABLE TO GET TO IT.
OOH!
I'LL CLIMB UP~!

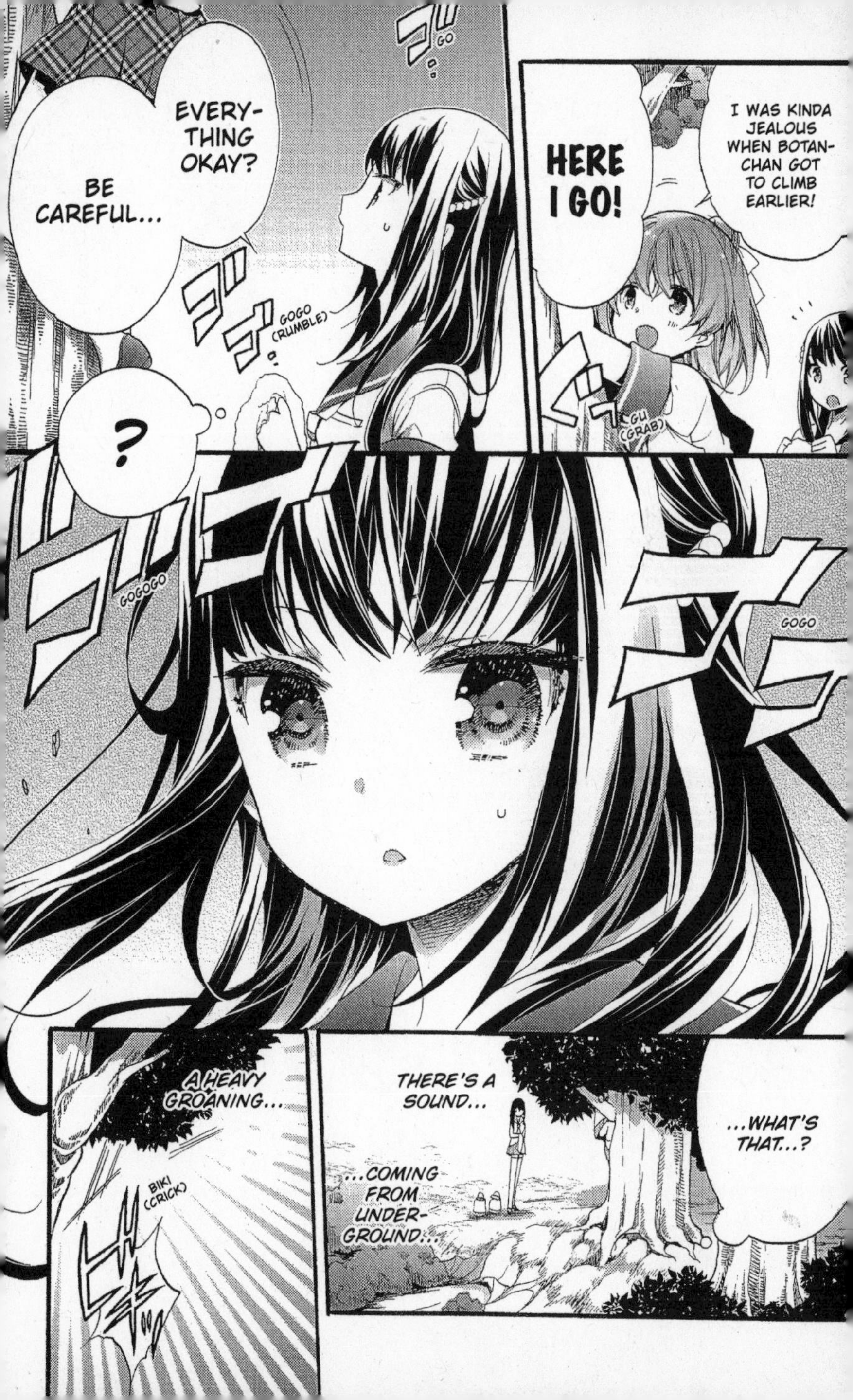

I WAS KINDA JEALOUS WHEN BOTAN-CHAN GOT TO CLIMB EARLIER!
HERE I GO!
GU (GRAB)
GO
EVERY-THING OKAY?
BE CAREFUL...
GOGO (RUMBLE)
?
GOGO
GOGOGO
...WHAT'S THAT...?
THERE'S A SOUND...
...COMING FROM UNDER-GROUND...
A HEAVY GROANING...
BIKI (CRICK)

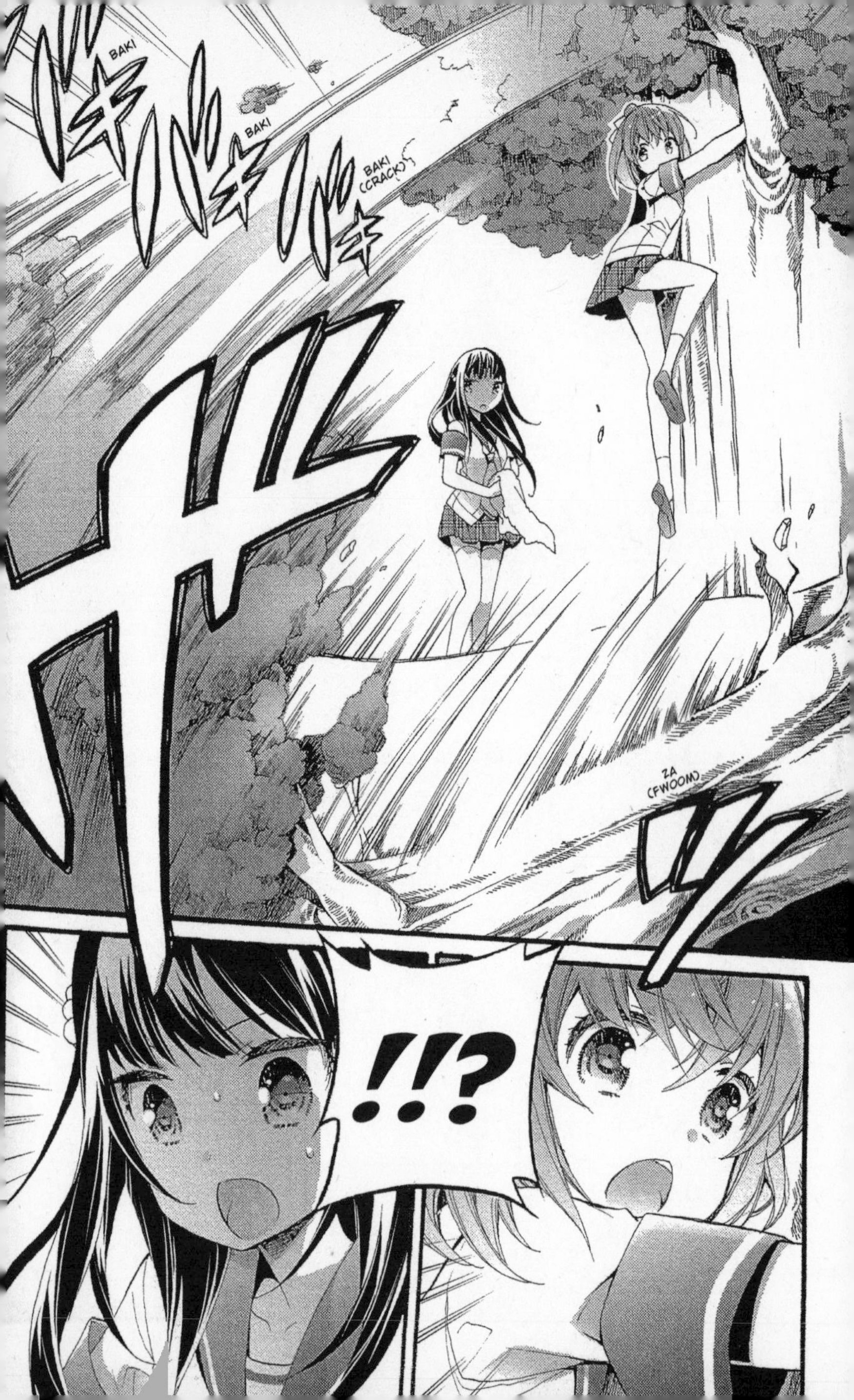
BAKI
BAKI
BAKI (CRACK)
ZA (FWOOM)
!!?

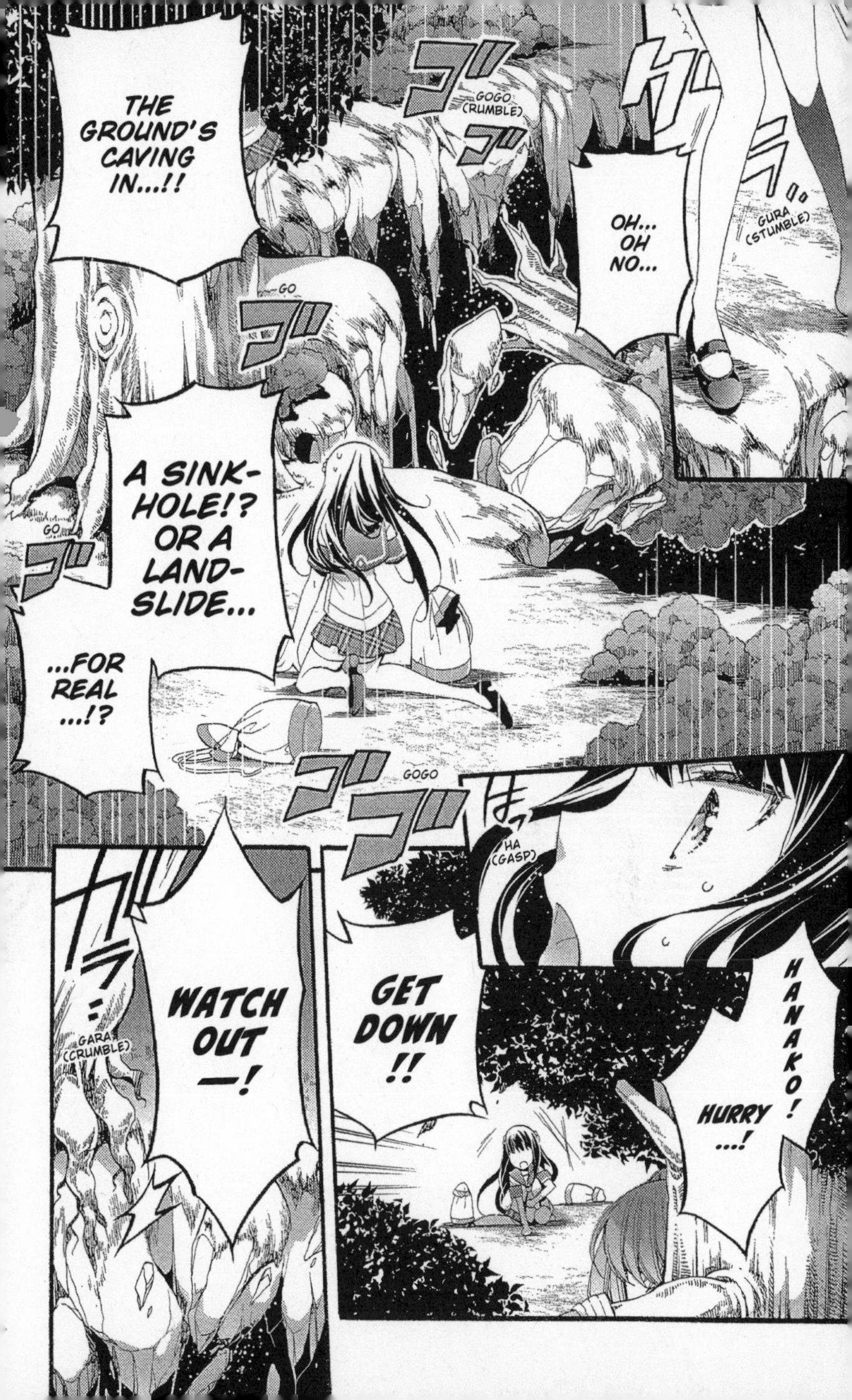
GURA (STUMBLE)
OH... OH NO...
GOGO (RUMBLE)
THE GROUND'S CAVING IN...!!
GO
A SINK-HOLE!? OR A LAND-SLIDE...
GO
...FOR REAL ...!?
GOGO
HA (GASP)
HANAKO!
HURRY ...!
GET DOWN !!
WATCH OUT —!
GARA (CRUMBLE)

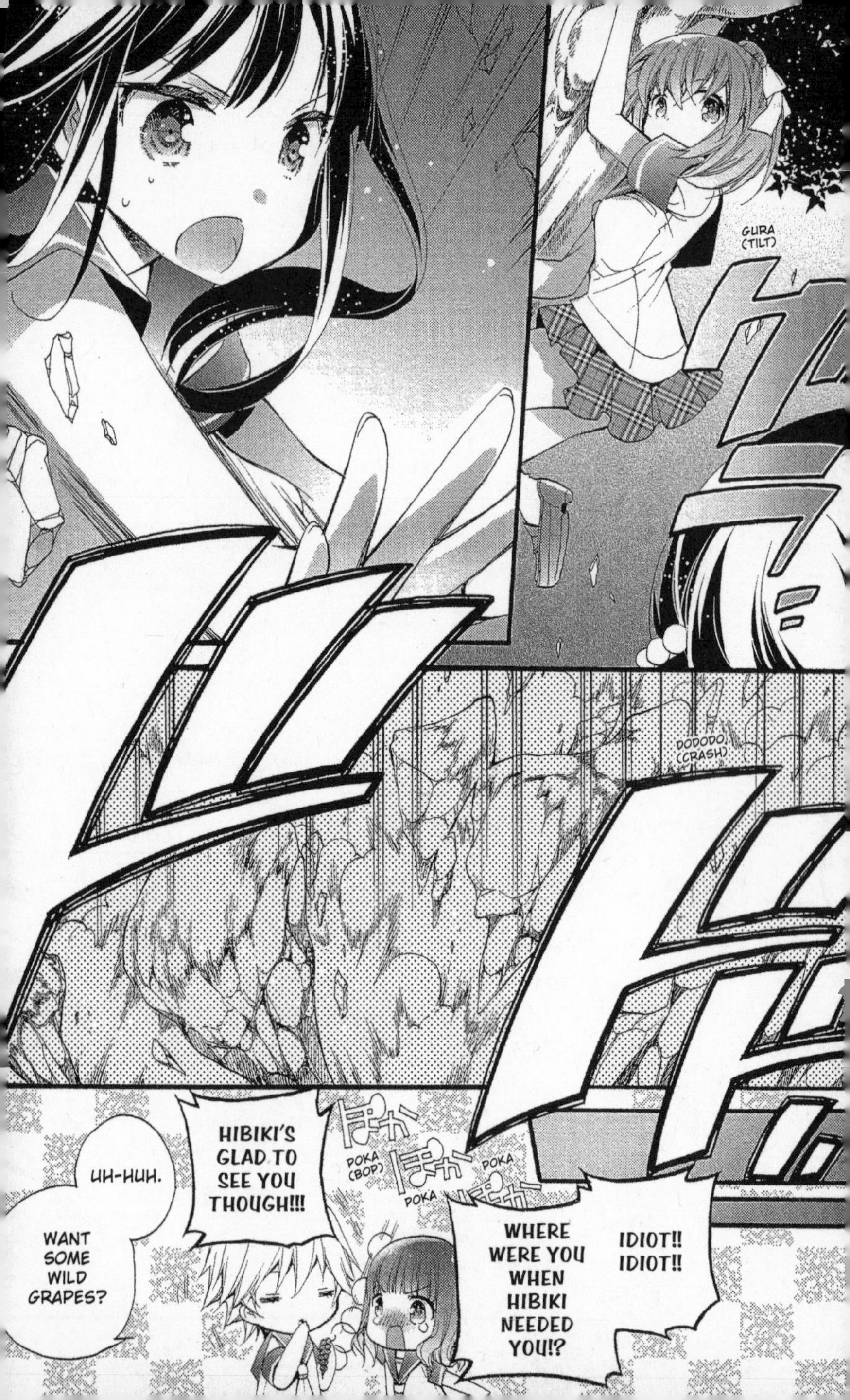
GURA (TILT)
DODODO (CRASH)
IDIOT!! IDIOT!!
WHERE WERE YOU WHEN HIBIKI NEEDED YOU!?
POKA
POKA
POKA (BOP)
HIBIKI'S GLAD TO SEE YOU THOUGH!!!
UH-HUH.
WANT SOME WILD GRAPES?

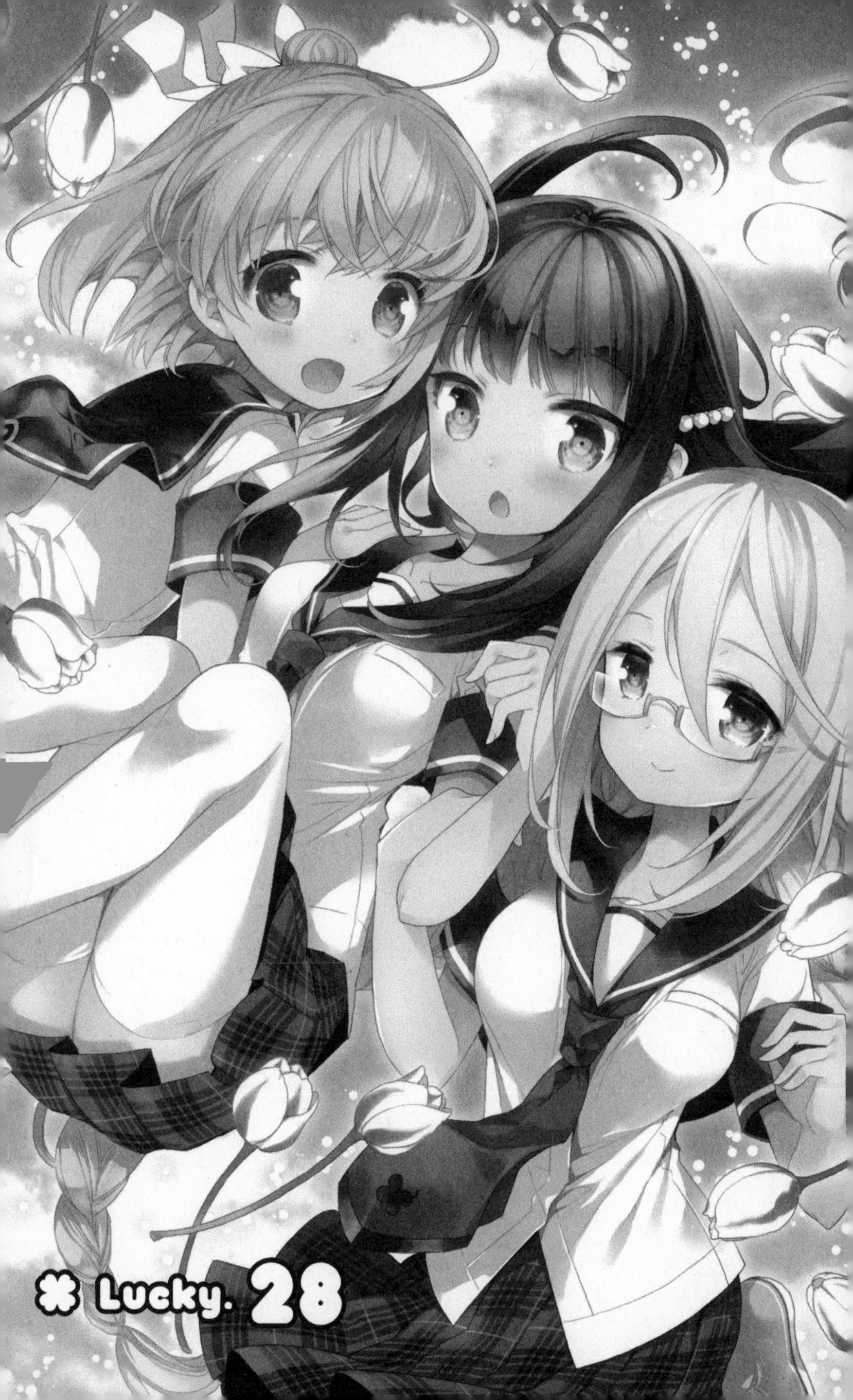
Lucky. 28

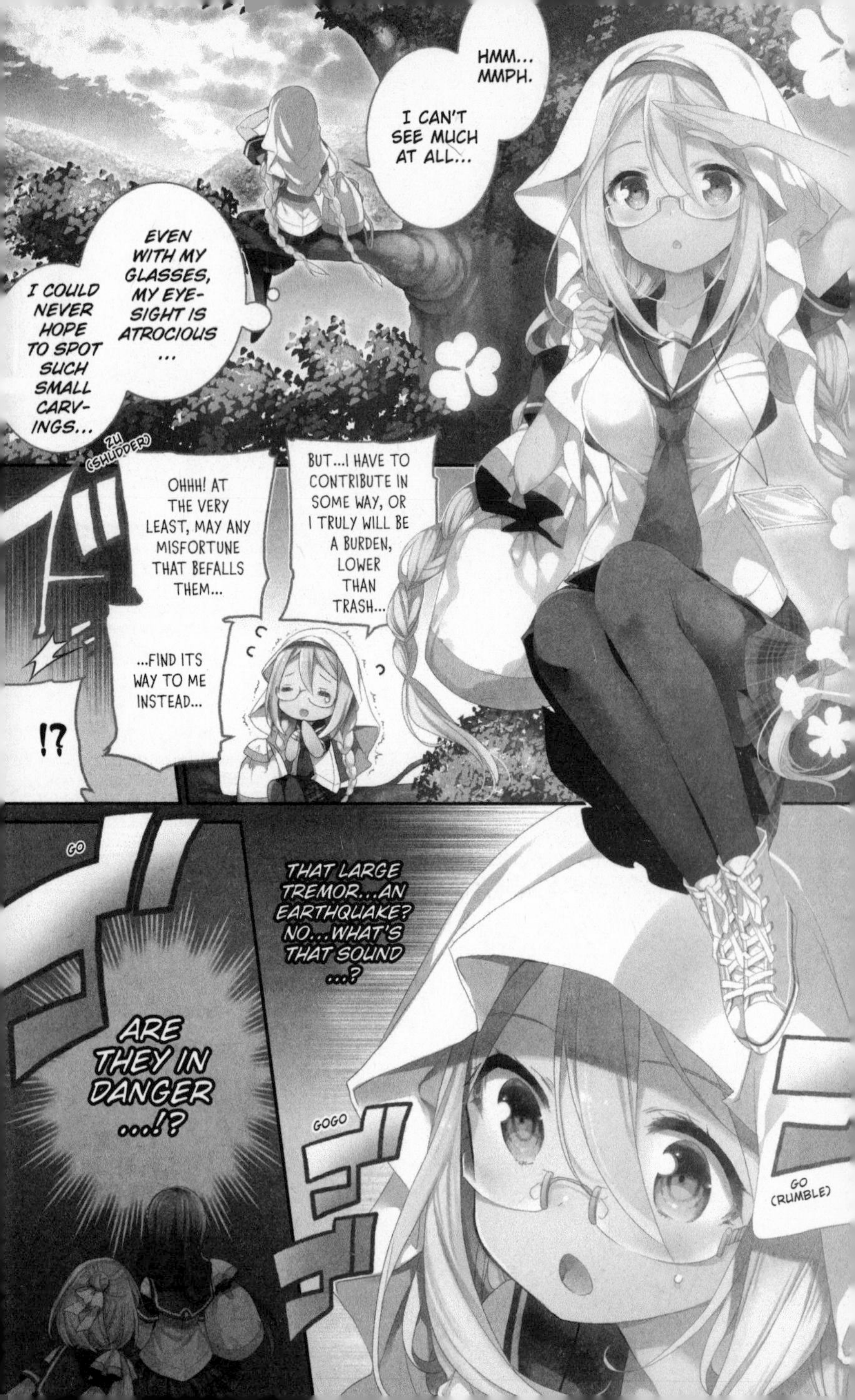
HMM... MMPH.
I CAN'T SEE MUCH AT ALL...
EVEN WITH MY GLASSES, MY EYE-SIGHT IS ATROCIOUS...
I COULD NEVER HOPE TO SPOT SUCH SMALL CARV-INGS...
BUT...I HAVE TO CONTRIBUTE IN SOME WAY, OR I TRULY WILL BE A BURDEN, LOWER THAN TRASH...
OHHH! AT THE VERY LEAST, MAY ANY MISFORTUNE THAT BEFALLS THEM...
...FIND ITS WAY TO ME INSTEAD...
ZU (SHUDDER)
!?
GO (RUMBLE)
THAT LARGE TREMOR...AN EARTHQUAKE? NO...WHAT'S THAT SOUND...?
GOGO
GO
ARE THEY IN DANGER...!?

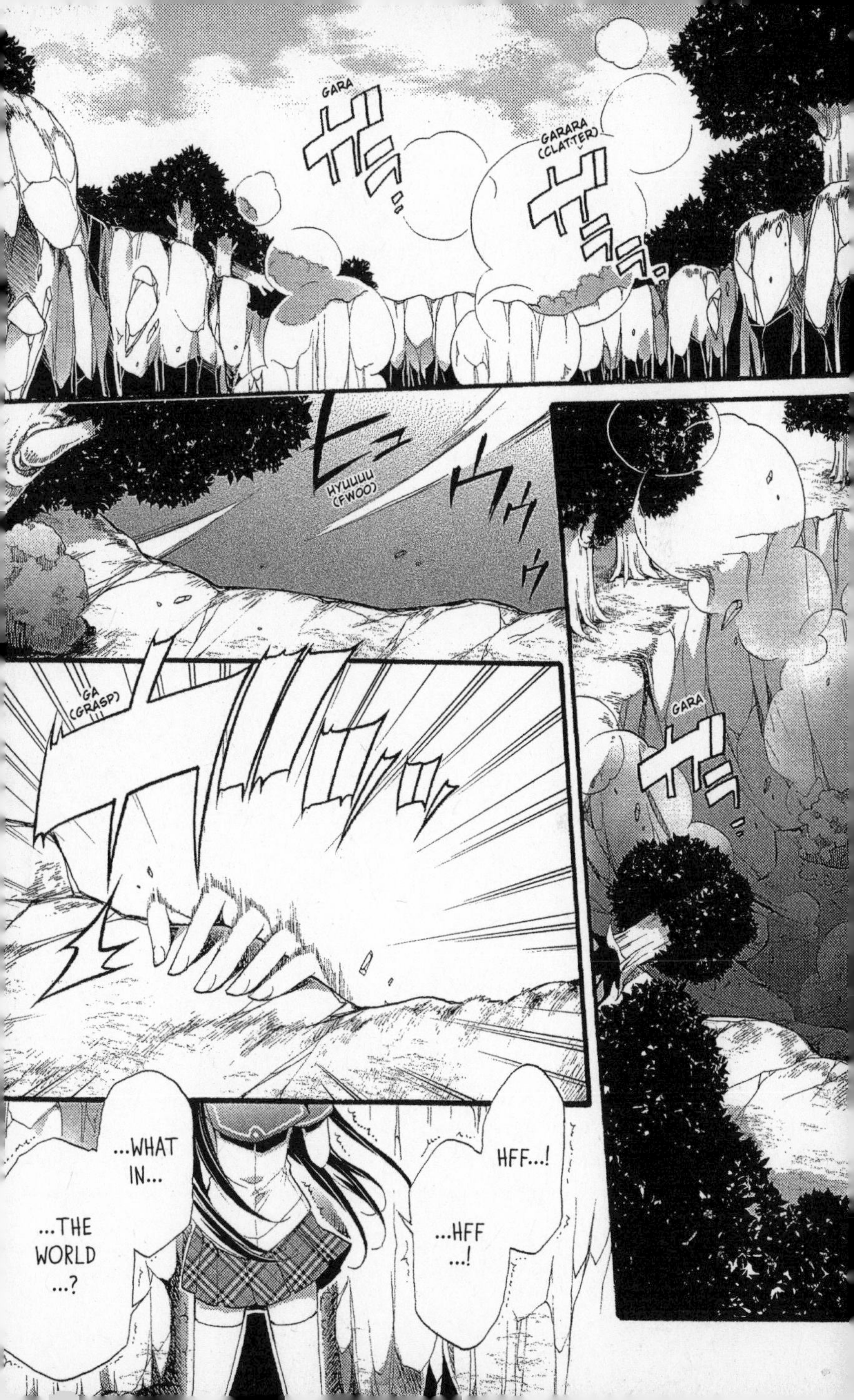
GARARA (CLATTER)
GARA
GARA
HYUUUU (FWOO)
GA (GRASP)
HFF...!
...HFF ...!
...WHAT IN...
...THE WORLD ...?

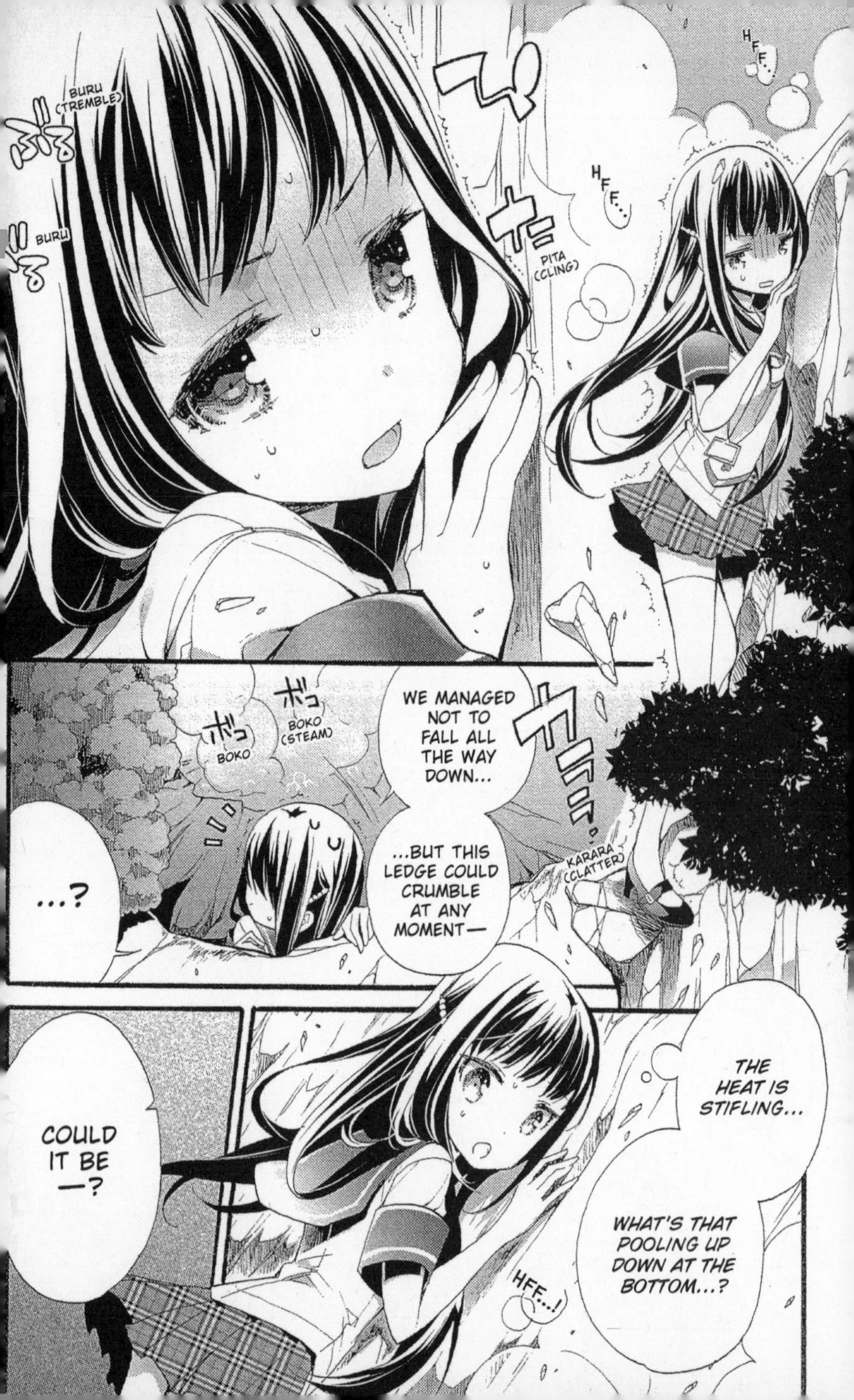
HFF...
HFF...
PITA (CLING)
ぶる
BURU (TREMBLE)
ぶる
BURU
WE MANAGED NOT TO FALL ALL THE WAY DOWN...
...BUT THIS LEDGE COULD CRUMBLE AT ANY MOMENT—
KARARA (CLATTER)
ボコ
BOKO (STEAM)
ボコ
BOKO
...?
THE HEAT IS STIFLING...
WHAT'S THAT POOLING UP DOWN AT THE BOTTOM...?
HFF...!
COULD IT BE—?

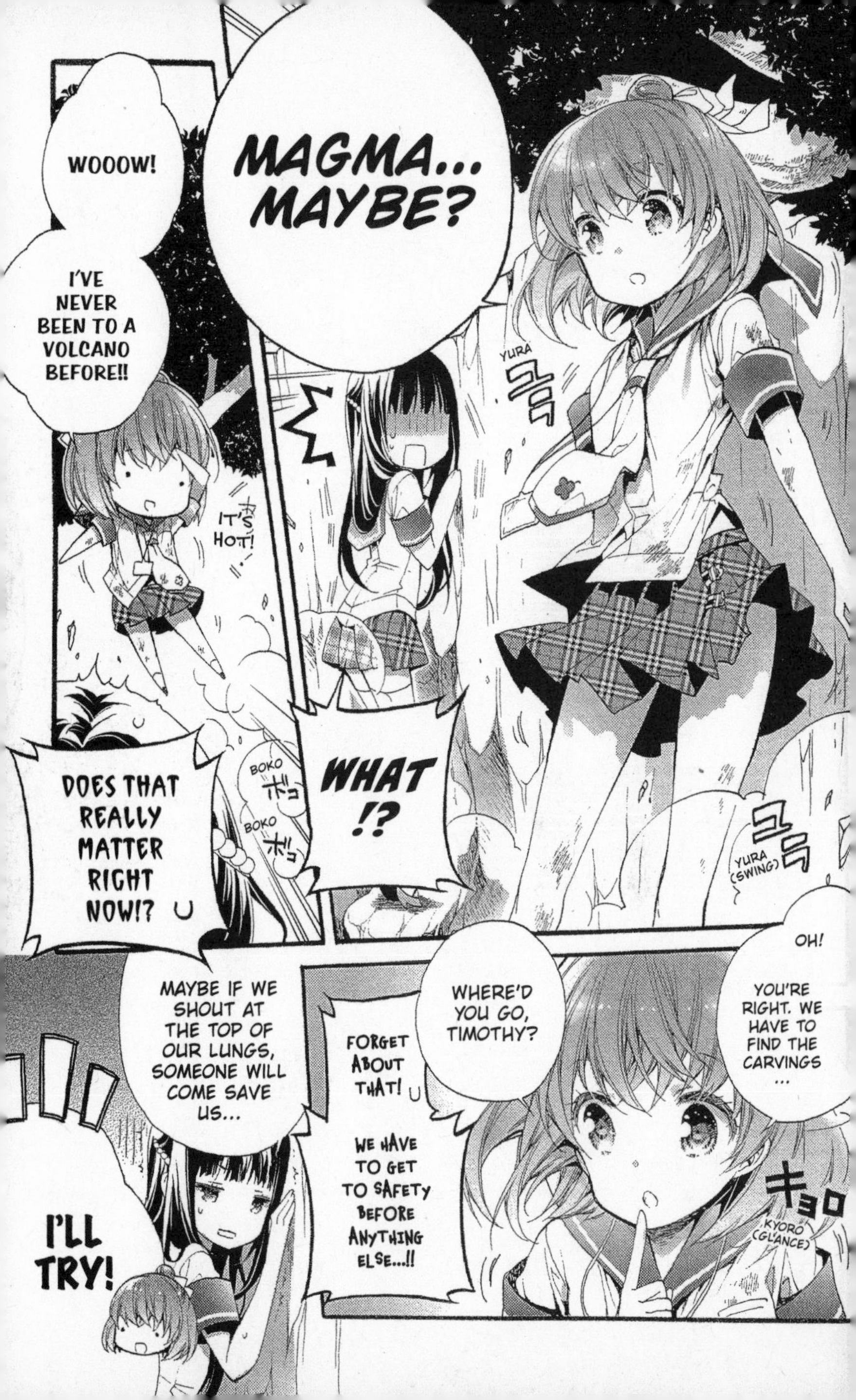
MAGMA... MAYBE?
YURA
ユラ
ユラ
YURA (SWING)
WHAT!?
WOOOW!
I'VE NEVER BEEN TO A VOLCANO BEFORE!!
IT'S HOT!
BOKO
ボコ
BOKO
ボコ
DOES THAT REALLY MATTER RIGHT NOW!?
OH!
YOU'RE RIGHT. WE HAVE TO FIND THE CARVINGS...
WHERE'D YOU GO, TIMOTHY?
キョロ
KYORO (GLANCE)
FORGET ABOUT THAT!
WE HAVE TO GET TO SAFETY BEFORE ANYTHING ELSE...!!
MAYBE IF WE SHOUT AT THE TOP OF OUR LUNGS, SOMEONE WILL COME SAVE US...
I'LL TRY!

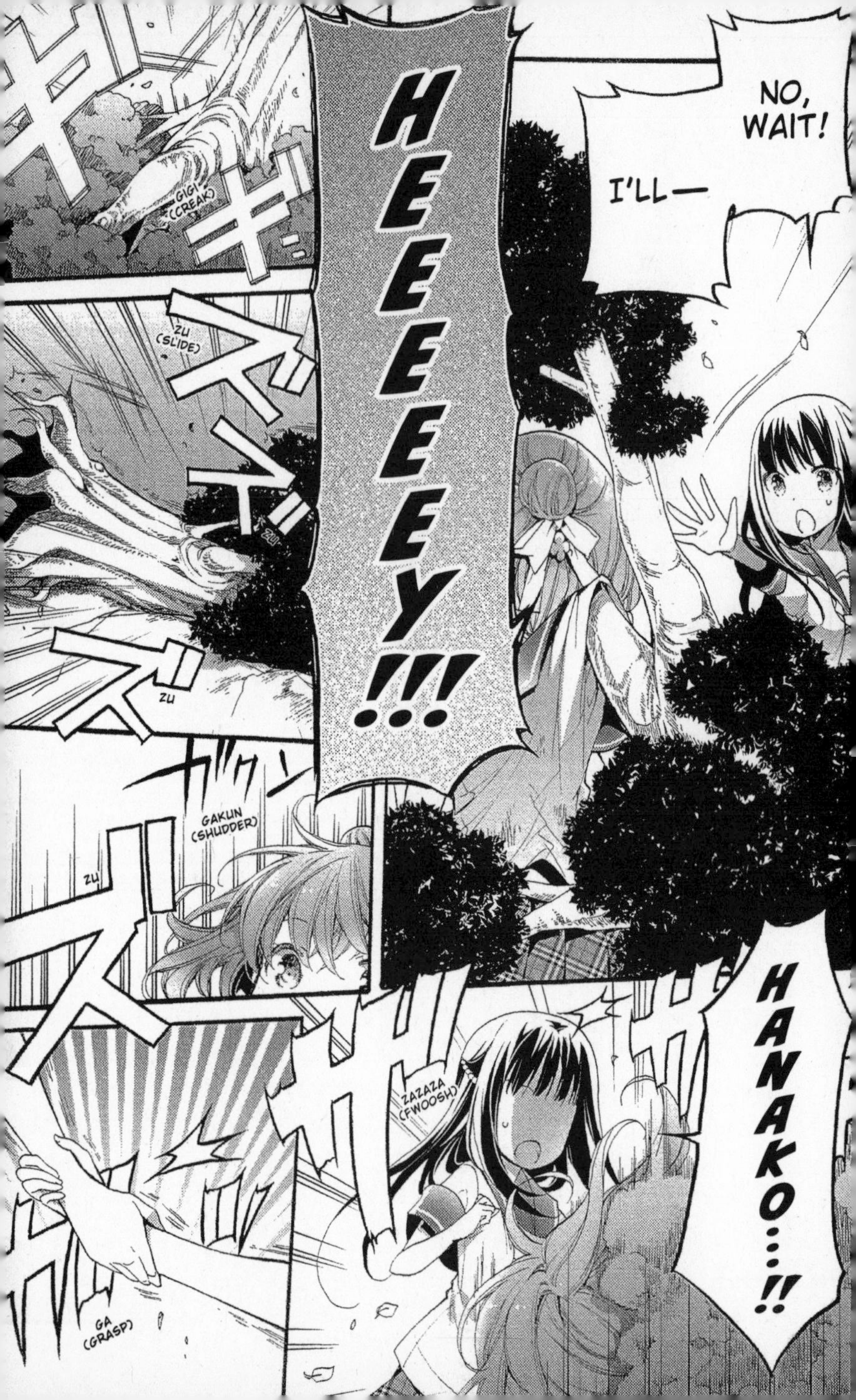
NO, WAIT!
I'LL—
HEEEEEY!!!
GIGI (CREAK)
ZU (SLIDE)
ZU
ZU
GAKUN (SHUDDER)
ZU
HANAKO...!!
ZAZAZA (FWOOSH)
GA (GRASP)

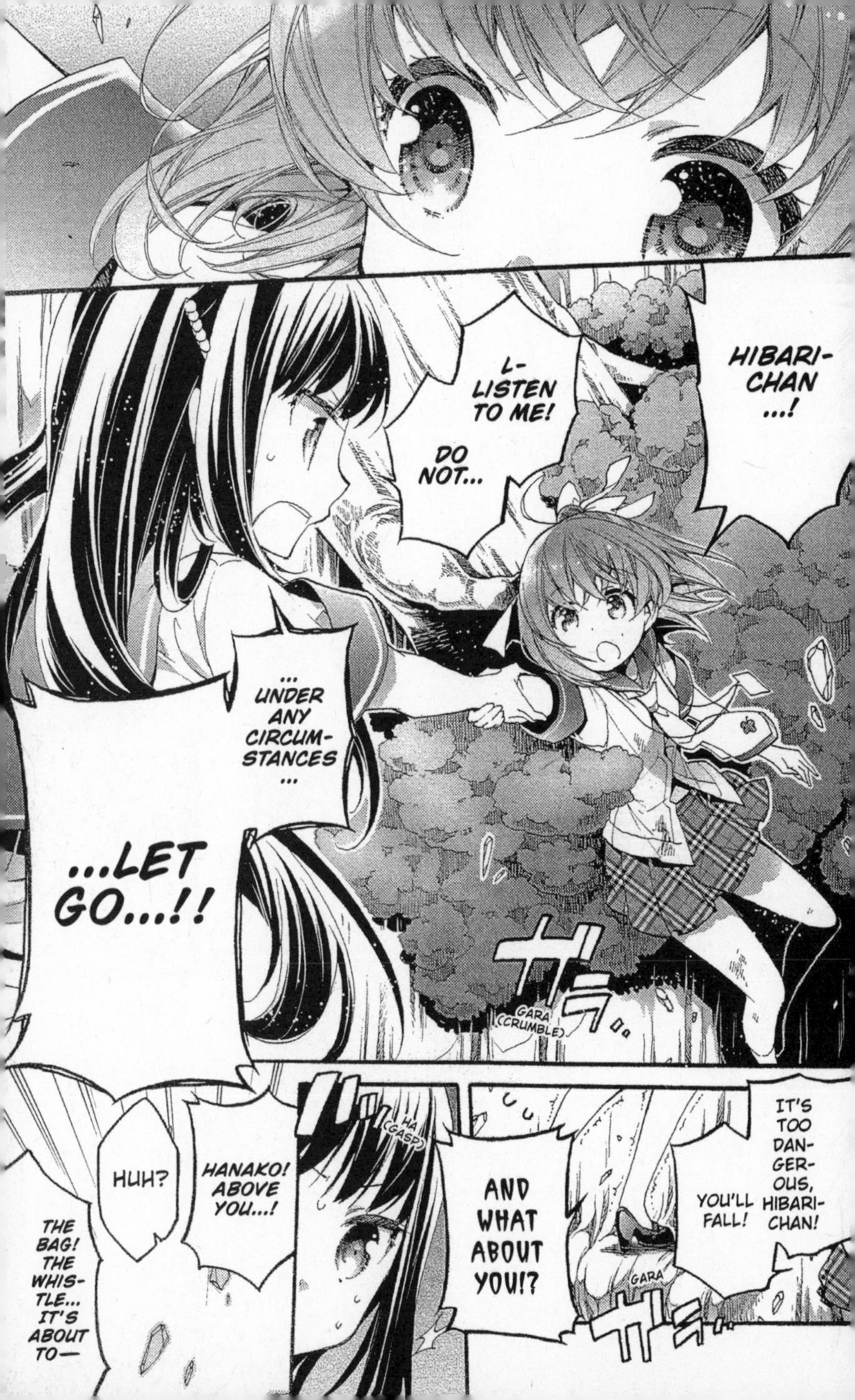
HIBARI-CHAN ...!
L-LISTEN TO ME!
DO NOT...
... UNDER ANY CIRCUMSTANCES ...
...LET GO...!!
GARA (CRUMBLE)
IT'S TOO DANGEROUS, HIBARI-CHAN!
YOU'LL FALL!
GARA
HA (GASP)
AND WHAT ABOUT YOU!?
HANAKO! ABOVE YOU...!
HUH?
THE BAG! THE WHISTLE... IT'S ABOUT TO—

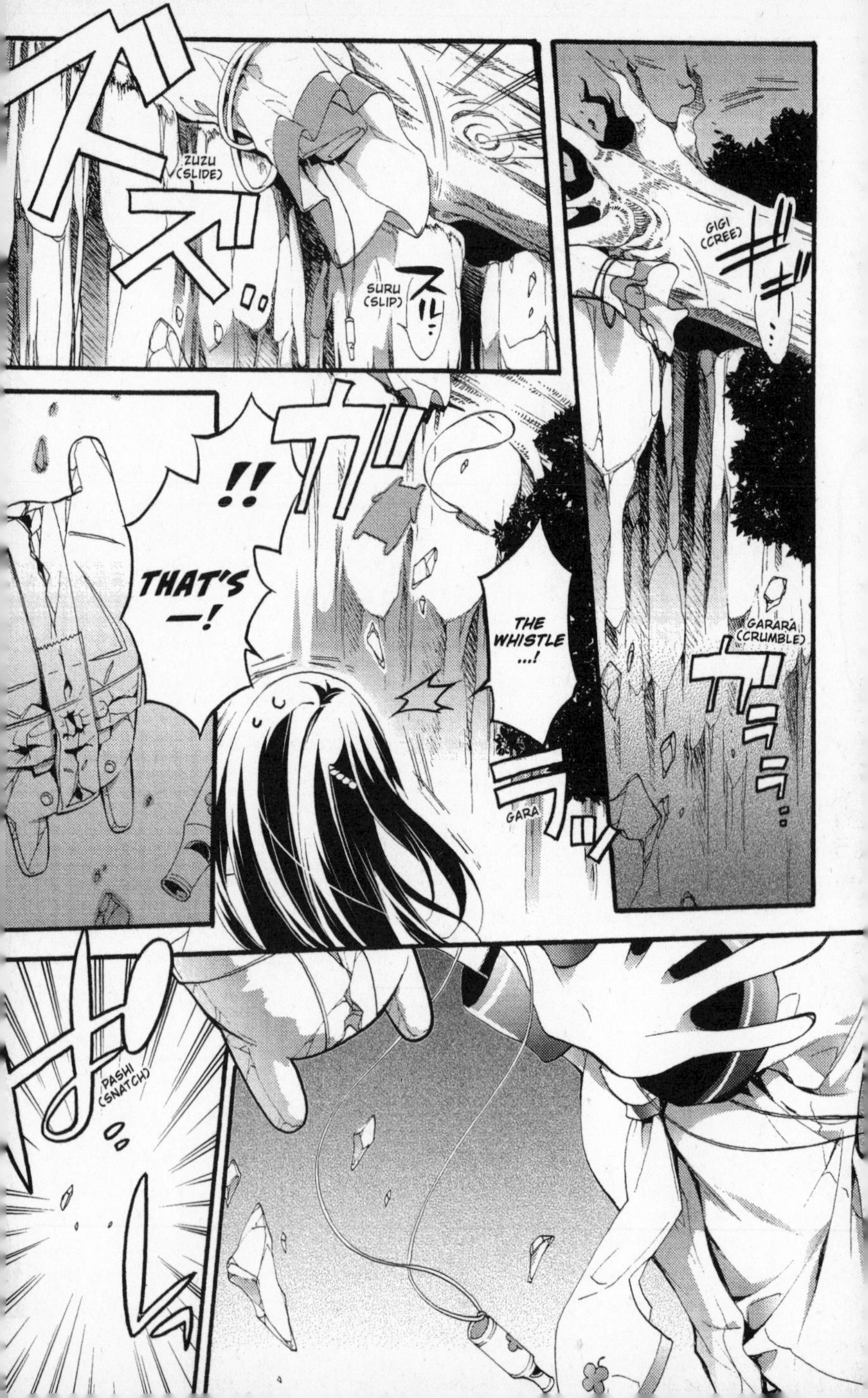

GIGI (CREE)
ZUZU (SLIDE)
SURU (SLIP)
GARARA (CRUMBLE)
!!
THAT'S —!
THE WHISTLE ...!
GARA
PASHI (SNATCH)

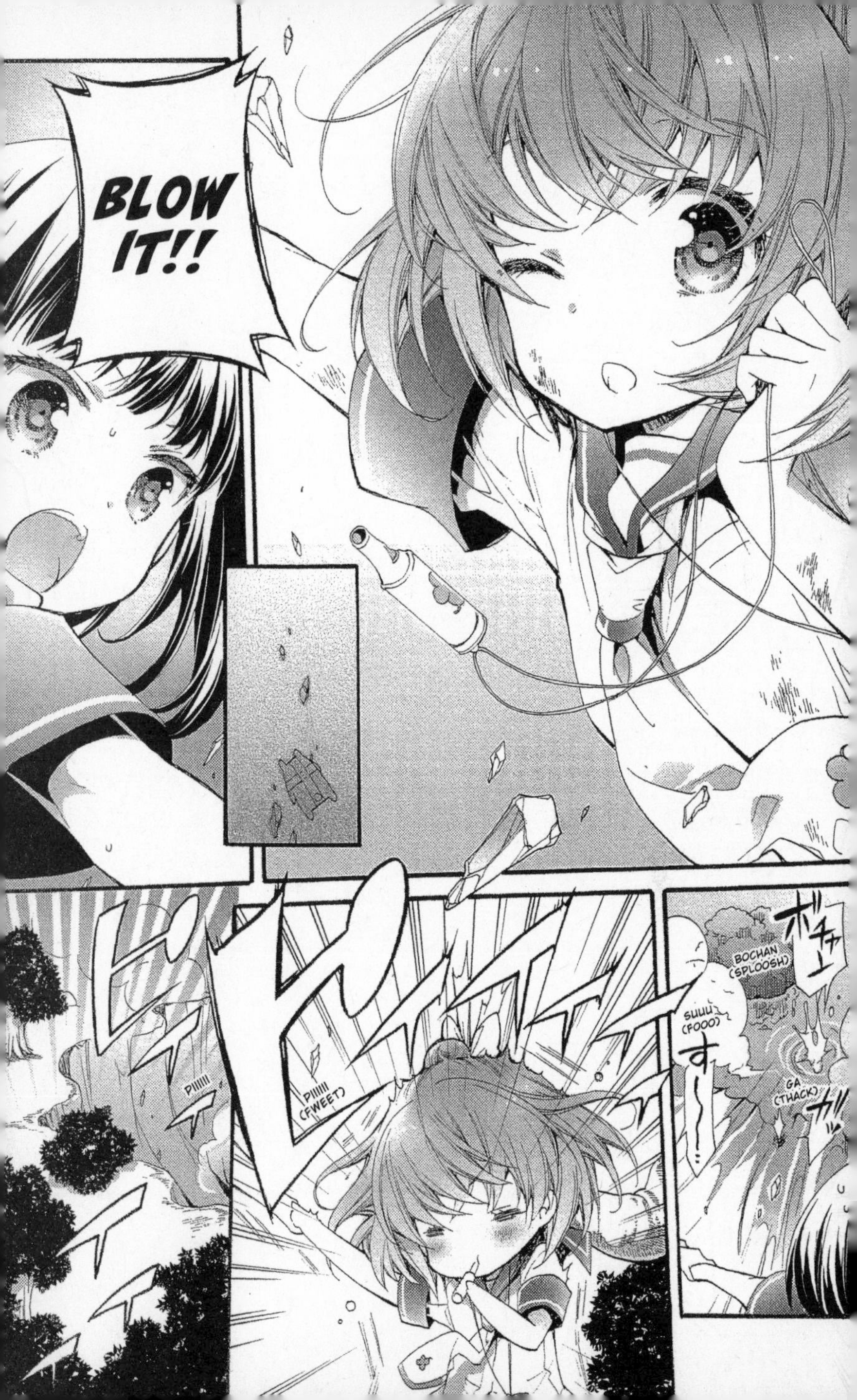
BLOW IT!!
ボチャン
BOCHAN (SPLOOSH)
す～…
SUUU (FOOO)
ガッ
GA (THACK)
PIIIIII (FWEET)
PIIIIII

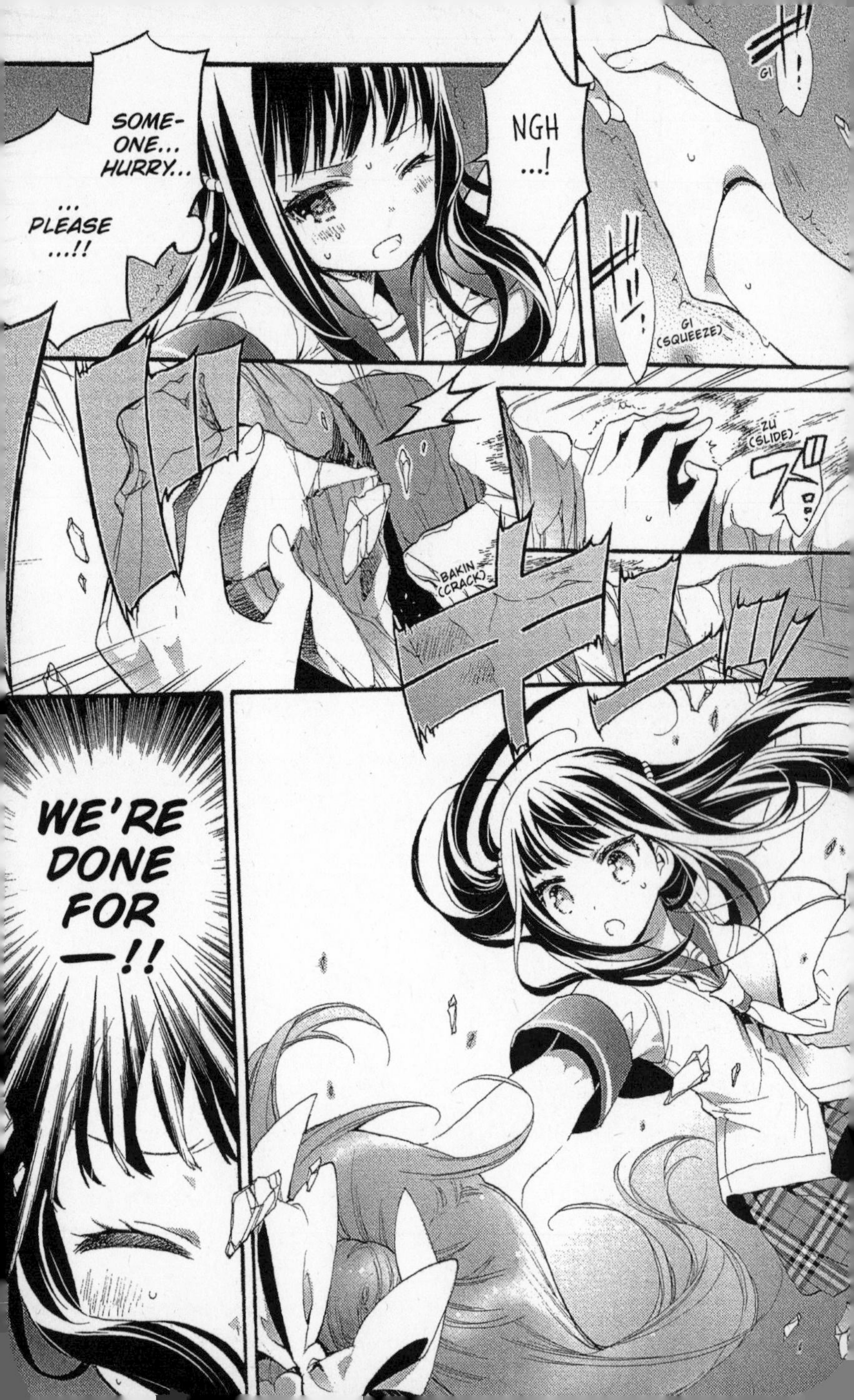
GI
NGH ...!
GI (SQUEEZE)
SOME-ONE... HURRY...
... PLEASE ...!!
ZU (SLIDE)
BAKIN (CRACK)
WE'RE DONE FOR —!!

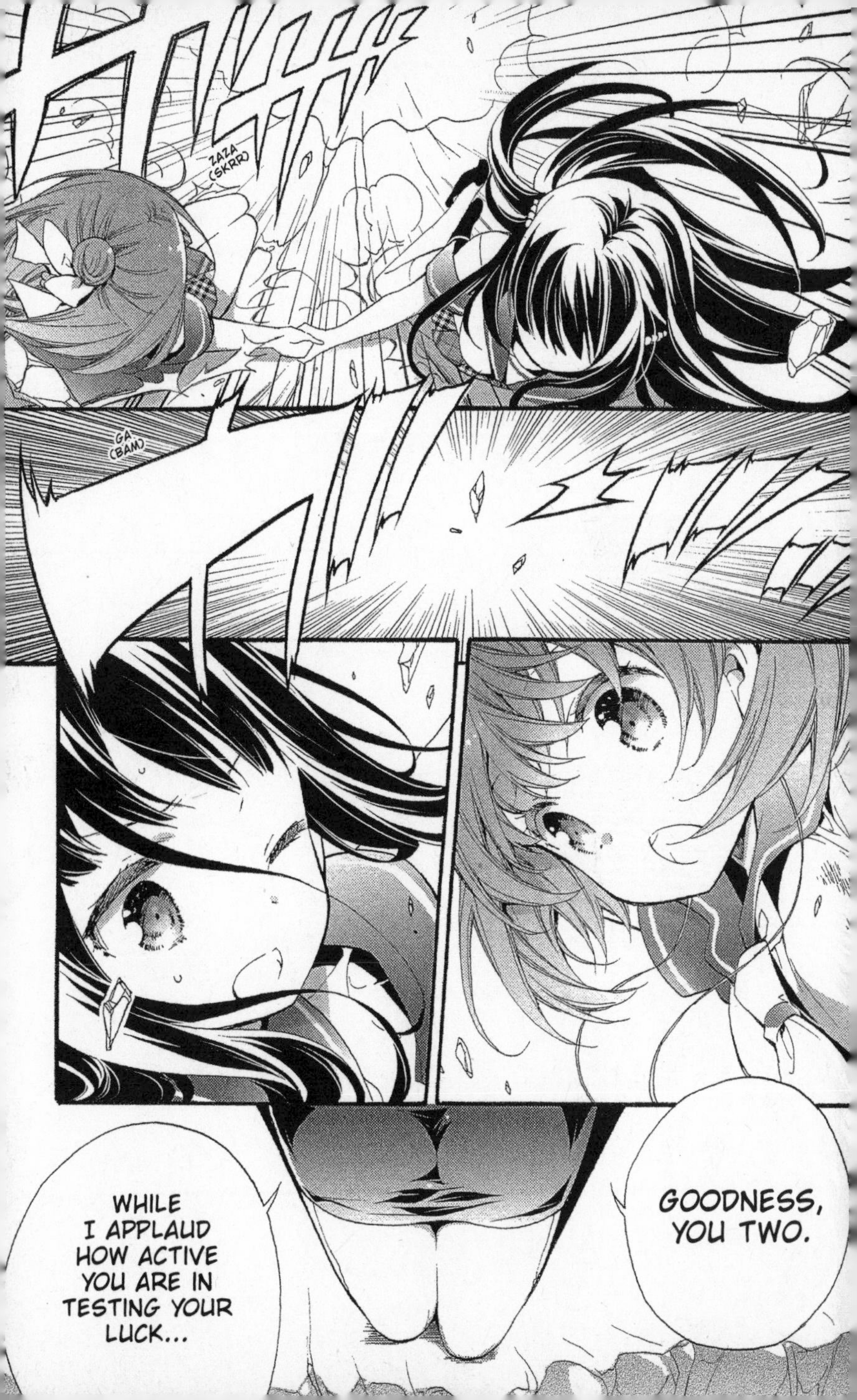
ZAZA (SKRR)
GA (BAM)
GOODNESS, YOU TWO.
WHILE I APPLAUD HOW ACTIVE YOU ARE IN TESTING YOUR LUCK...

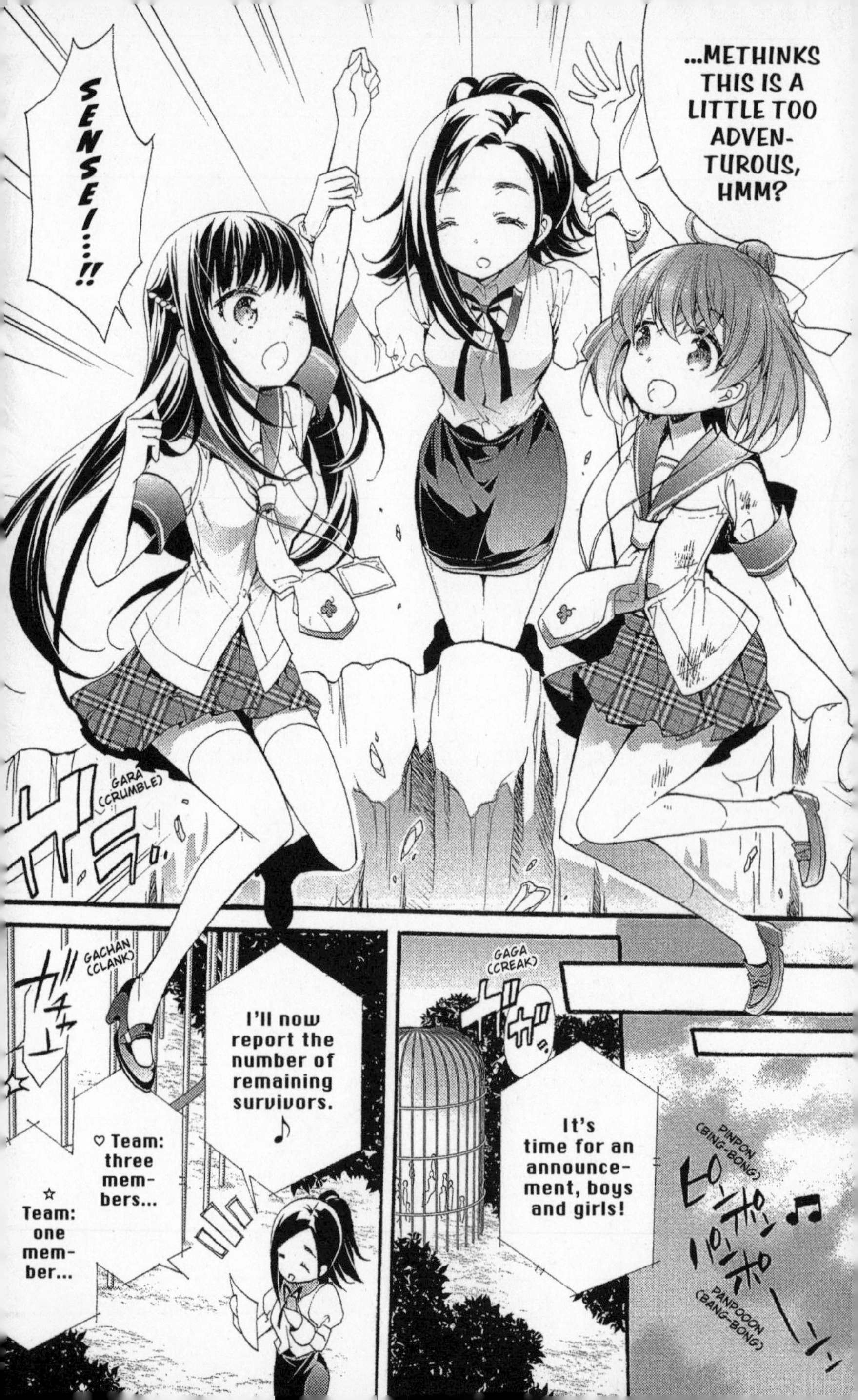
...METHINKS THIS IS A LITTLE TOO ADVENTUROUS, HMM?
SENSEI...!!
GARA (CRUMBLE)
PINPON (BING-BONG)
PANPOOON (BANG-BONG)
GAGA (CREAK)
It's time for an announcement, boys and girls!
GACHAN (CLANK)
I'll now report the number of remaining survivors. ♪
♡ Team: three members...
☆ Team: one member...

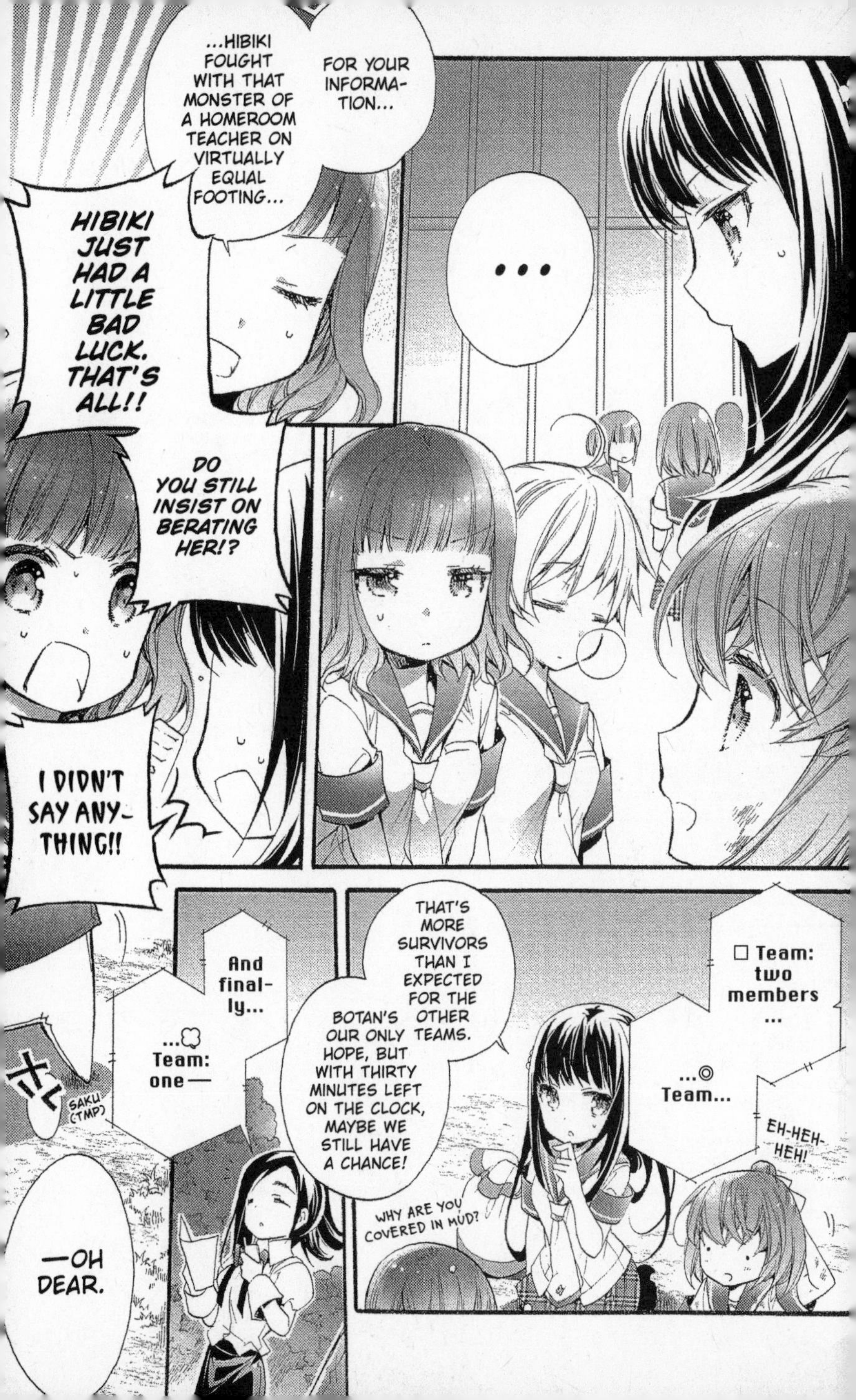
...
FOR YOUR INFORMATION...
...HIBIKI FOUGHT WITH THAT MONSTER OF A HOMEROOM TEACHER ON VIRTUALLY EQUAL FOOTING...
HIBIKI JUST HAD A LITTLE BAD LUCK. THAT'S ALL!!
DO YOU STILL INSIST ON BERATING HER!?
I DIDN'T SAY ANYTHING!!
□ Team: two members...
...◎ Team...
EH-HEH-HEH!
WHY ARE YOU COVERED IN MUD?
THAT'S MORE SURVIVORS THAN I EXPECTED FOR THE OTHER TEAMS.
BOTAN'S OUR ONLY HOPE, BUT WITH THIRTY MINUTES LEFT ON THE CLOCK, MAYBE WE STILL HAVE A CHANCE!
And finally...
...✿ Team: one—
SAKU (TMP)
—OH DEAR.

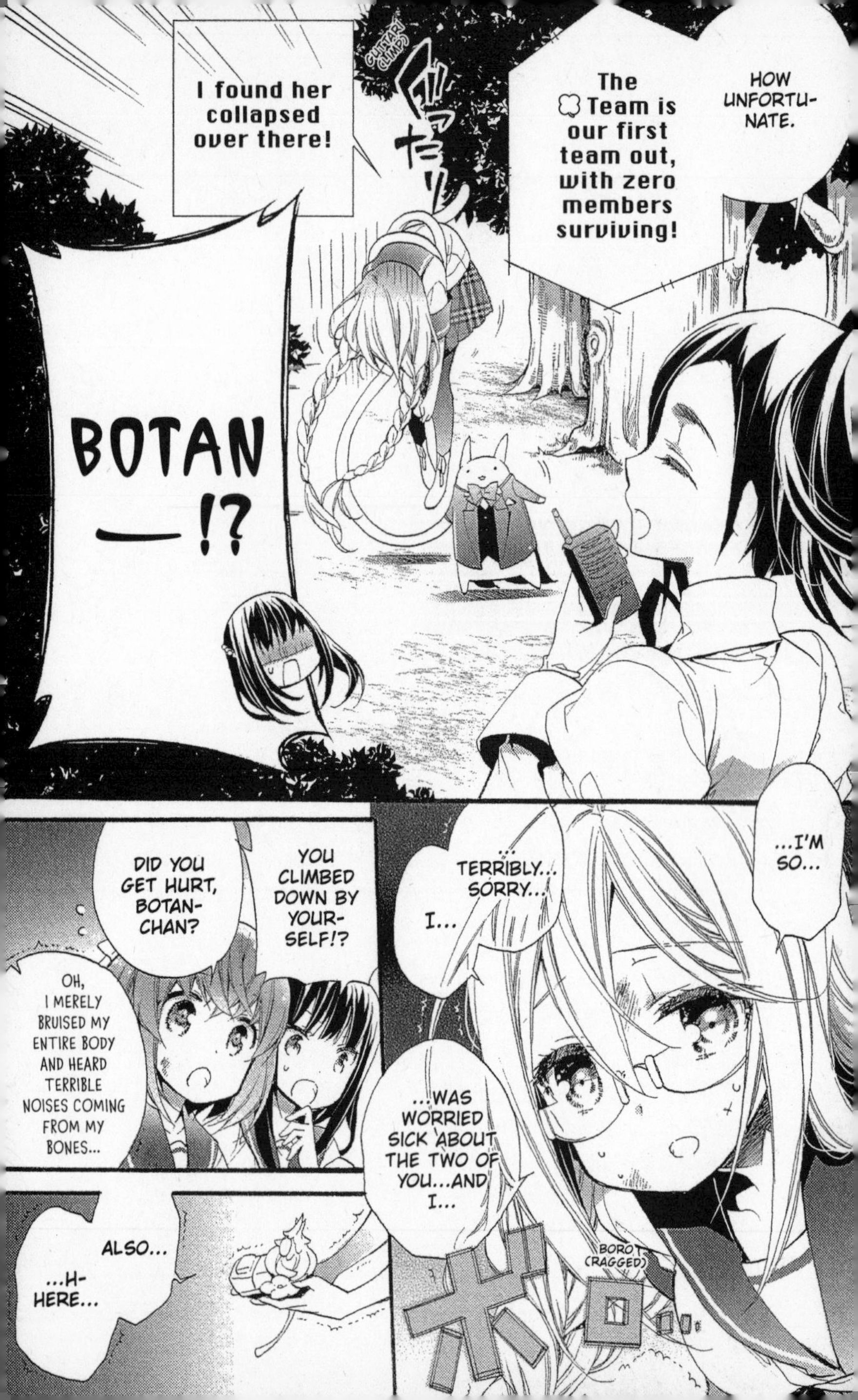
HOW UNFORTUNATE.
The ✿ Team is our first team out, with zero members surviving!
GUTTARI (LIMP)
I found her collapsed over there!
BOTAN—!?
...I'M SO...
...TERRIBLY... SORRY...
I...
...WAS WORRIED SICK ABOUT THE TWO OF YOU...AND I...
BORO (RAGGED)
YOU CLIMBED DOWN BY YOURSELF!?
DID YOU GET HURT, BOTAN-CHAN?
OH, I MERELY BRUISED MY ENTIRE BODY AND HEARD TERRIBLE NOISES COMING FROM MY BONES...
ALSO...
...H-HERE...

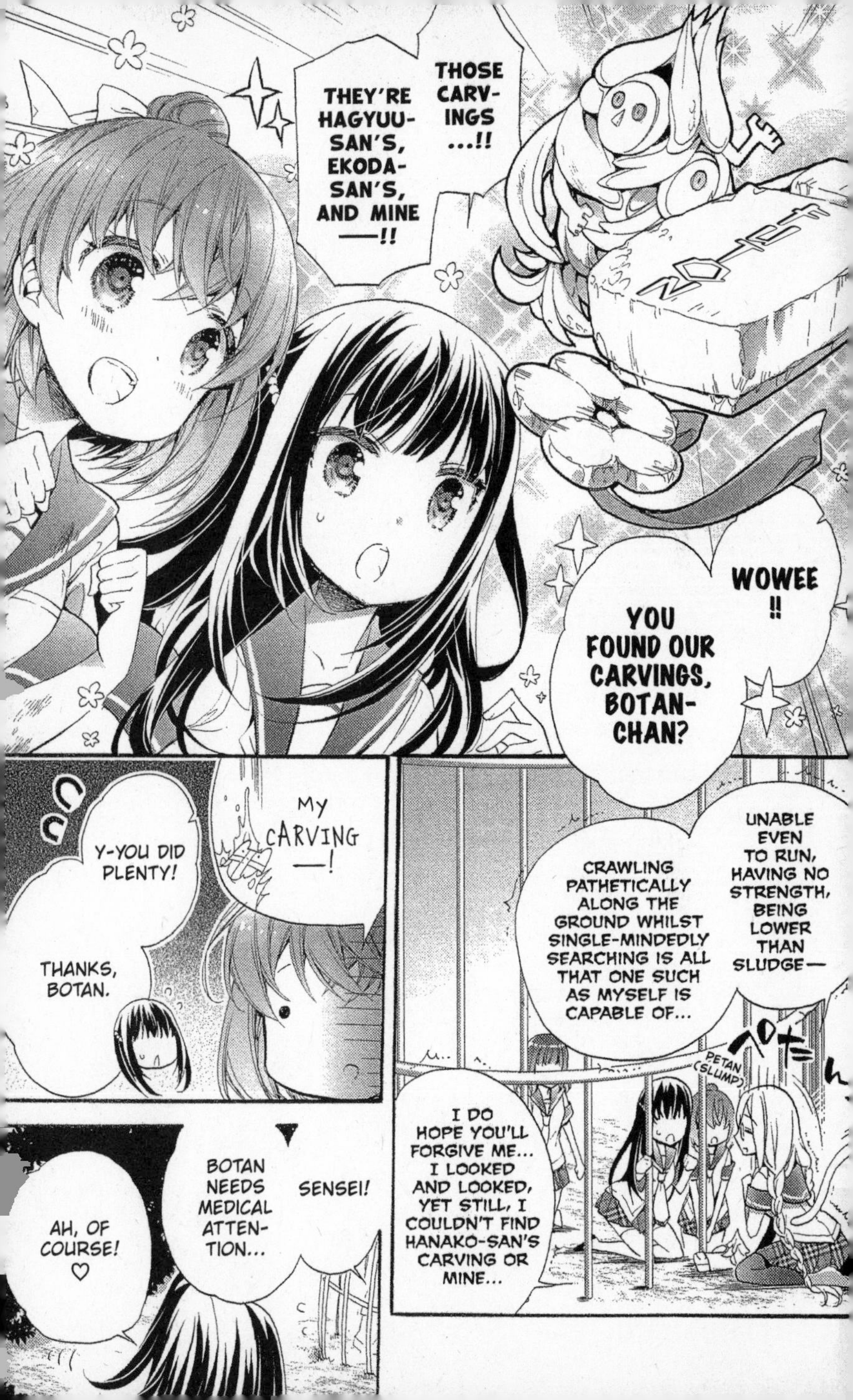
THOSE CARVINGS...!!
THEY'RE HAGYUU-SAN'S, EKODA-SAN'S, AND MINE—!!
WOWEE!!
YOU FOUND OUR CARVINGS, BOTAN-CHAN?
UNABLE EVEN TO RUN, HAVING NO STRENGTH, BEING LOWER THAN SLUDGE—
CRAWLING PATHETICALLY ALONG THE GROUND WHILST SINGLE-MINDEDLY SEARCHING IS ALL THAT ONE SUCH AS MYSELF IS CAPABLE OF...
PETAN (SLUMP)
I DO HOPE YOU'LL FORGIVE ME... I LOOKED AND LOOKED, YET STILL, I COULDN'T FIND HANAKO-SAN'S CARVING OR MINE...
MY CARVING—!
Y-YOU DID PLENTY!
THANKS, BOTAN.
SENSEI!
BOTAN NEEDS MEDICAL ATTENTION...
AH, OF COURSE! ♡

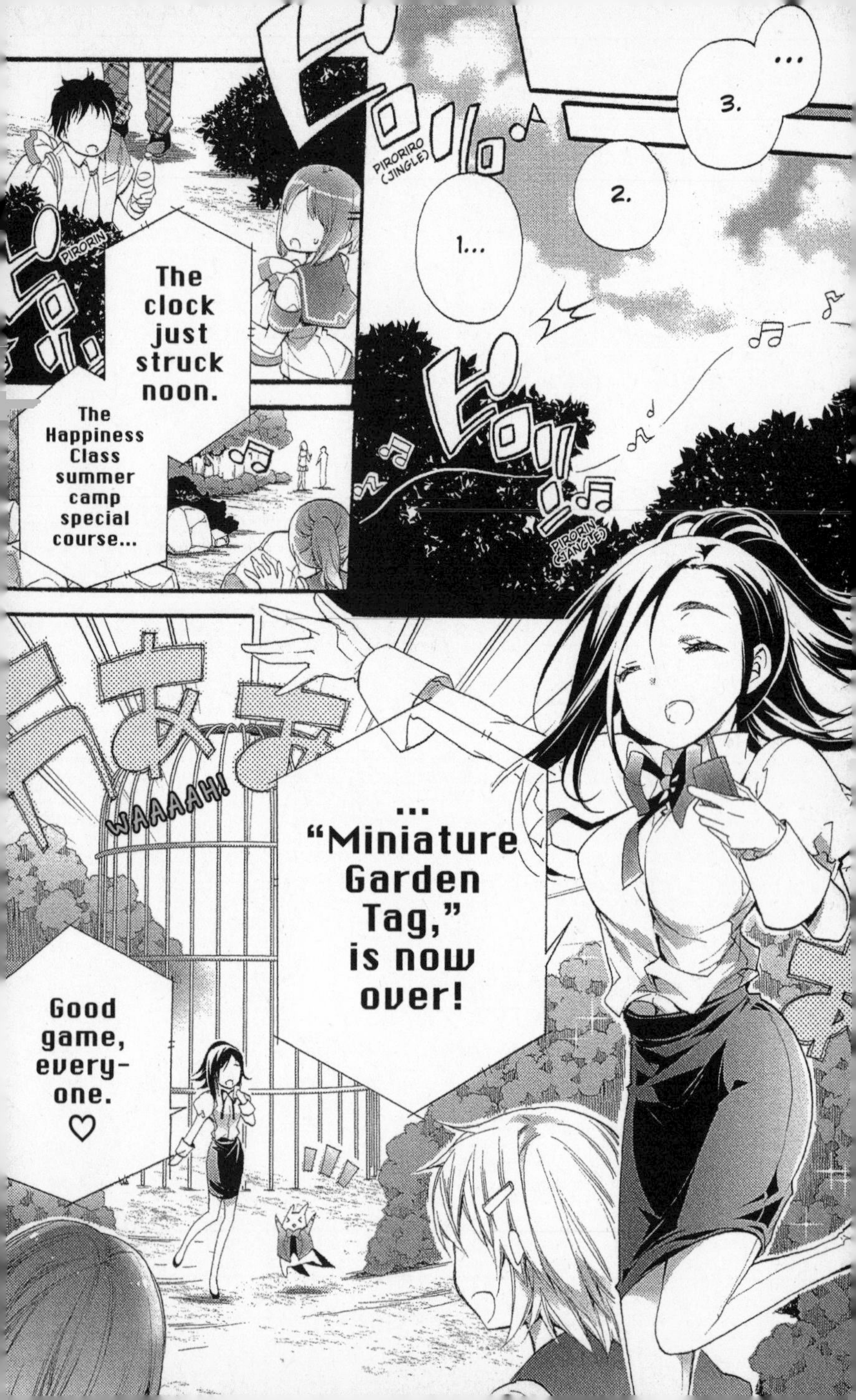
...
3.
2.
1...
PIRORIRO (JINGLE)
PIRORIN (JINGLE)
PIRORIN
The clock just struck noon.
The Happiness Class summer camp special course...
..."Miniature Garden Tag," is now over!
WAAAAH!
Good game, everyone. ♡

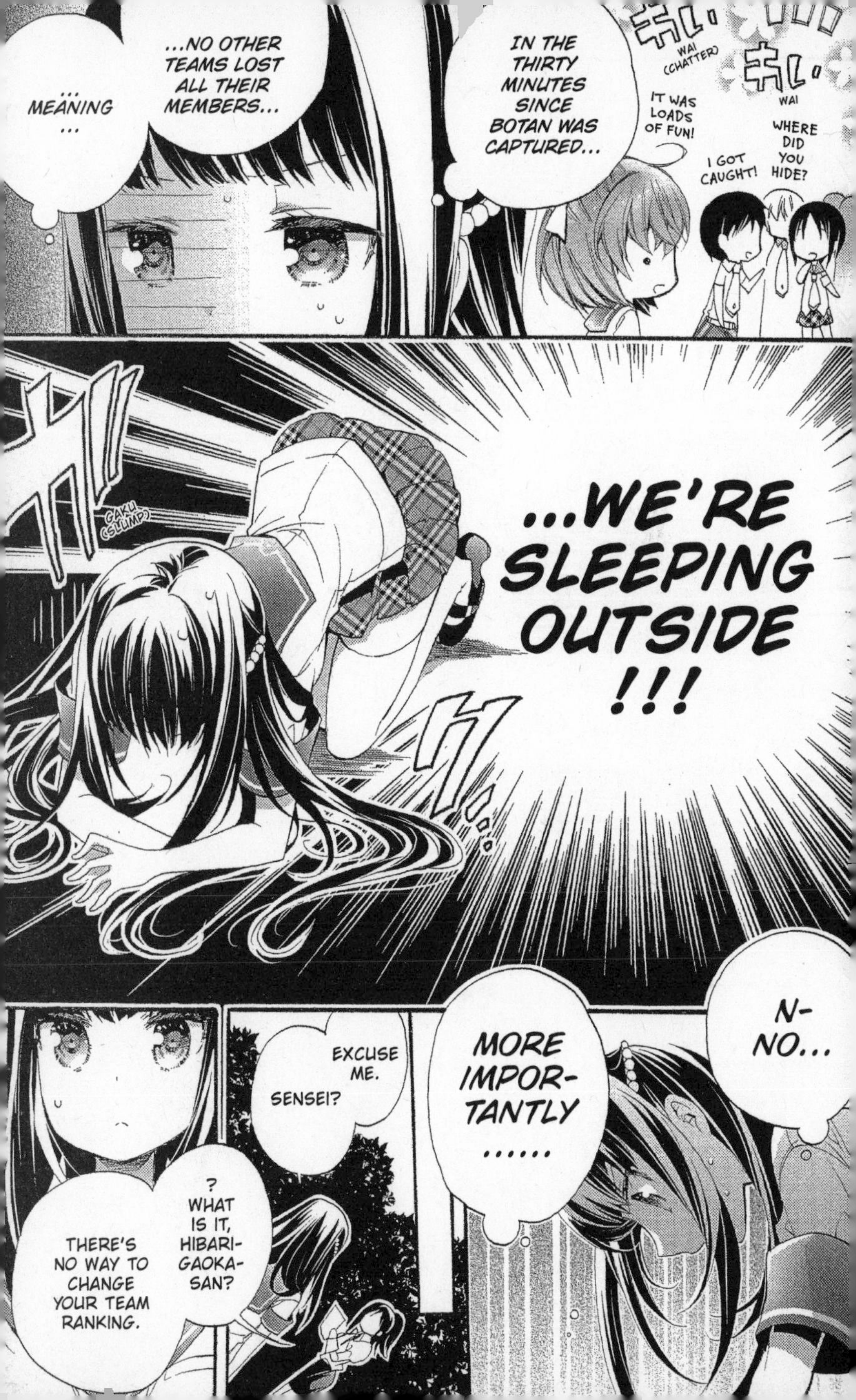
WAI (CHATTER)
WAI
IT WAS LOADS OF FUN!
WHERE DID YOU HIDE?
I GOT CAUGHT!
IN THE THIRTY MINUTES SINCE BOTAN WAS CAPTURED...
...NO OTHER TEAMS LOST ALL THEIR MEMBERS...
...MEANING...
GAKU (SLUMP)
...WE'RE SLEEPING OUTSIDE!!!
N-NO...
MORE IMPORTANTLY......
EXCUSE ME.
SENSEI?
? WHAT IS IT, HIBARIGAOKA-SAN?
THERE'S NO WAY TO CHANGE YOUR TEAM RANKING.

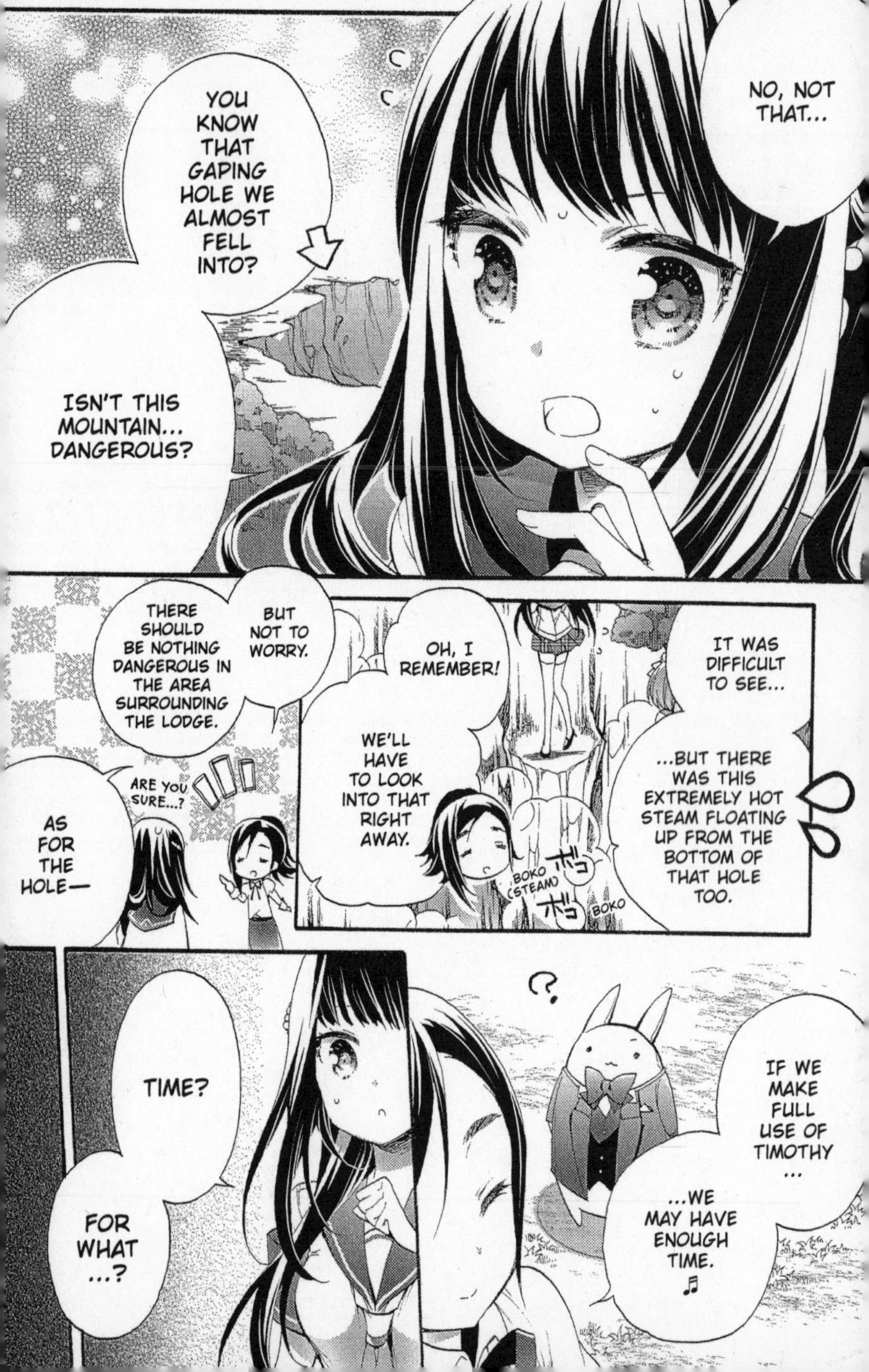
NO, NOT THAT...
YOU KNOW THAT GAPING HOLE WE ALMOST FELL INTO?
ISN'T THIS MOUNTAIN... DANGEROUS?
IT WAS DIFFICULT TO SEE...
...BUT THERE WAS THIS EXTREMELY HOT STEAM FLOATING UP FROM THE BOTTOM OF THAT HOLE TOO.
BOKO (STEAM)
BOKO
OH, I REMEMBER!
WE'LL HAVE TO LOOK INTO THAT RIGHT AWAY.
BUT NOT TO WORRY.
THERE SHOULD BE NOTHING DANGEROUS IN THE AREA SURROUNDING THE LODGE.
ARE YOU SURE...?
AS FOR THE HOLE—
IF WE MAKE FULL USE OF TIMOTHY...
...WE MAY HAVE ENOUGH TIME. ♬
TIME?
FOR WHAT...?

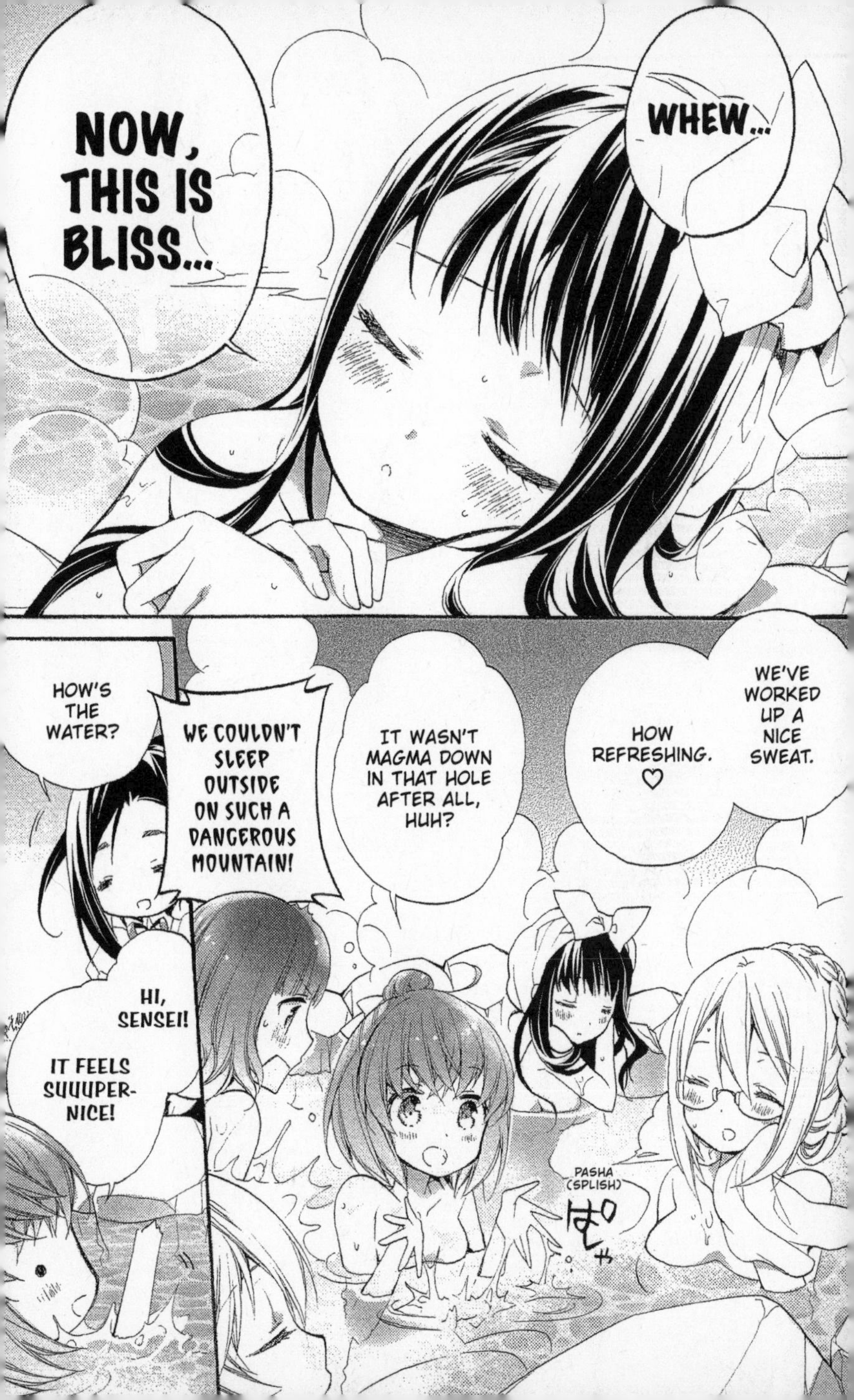
WHEW...
NOW, THIS IS BLISS...
WE'VE WORKED UP A NICE SWEAT.
HOW REFRESHING. ♡
IT WASN'T MAGMA DOWN IN THAT HOLE AFTER ALL, HUH?
WE COULDN'T SLEEP OUTSIDE ON SUCH A DANGEROUS MOUNTAIN!
HOW'S THE WATER?
PASHA (SPLISH)
HI, SENSEI!
IT FEELS SUUUPER-NICE!

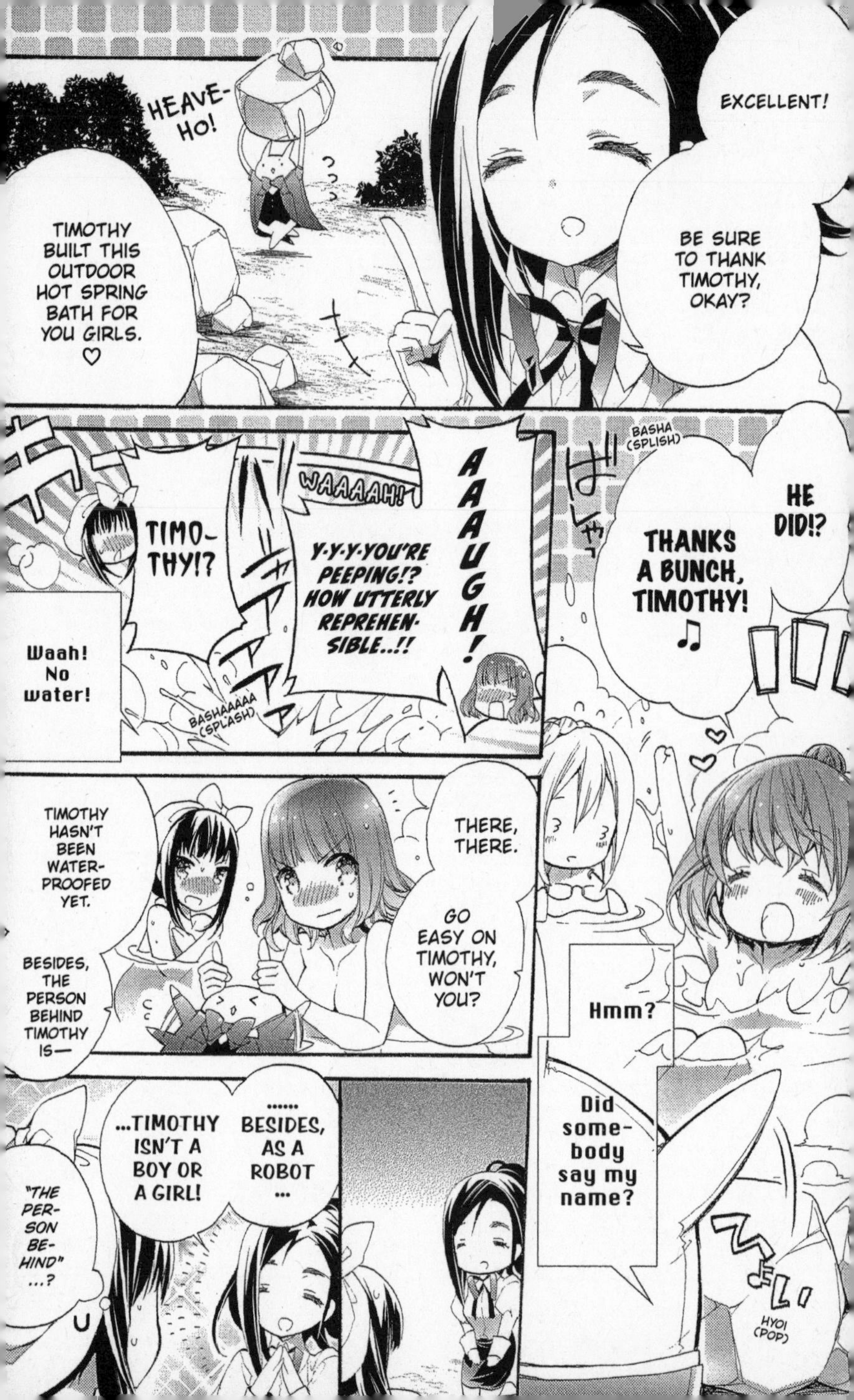
EXCELLENT!
HEAVE-HO!
BE SURE TO THANK TIMOTHY, OKAY?
TIMOTHY BUILT THIS OUTDOOR HOT SPRING BATH FOR YOU GIRLS. ♡
BASHA (SPLISH)
HE DID!?
THANKS A BUNCH, TIMOTHY! ♫
AAAAUGH!
WAAAAAH!
Y-Y-Y-YOU'RE PEEPING!? HOW UTTERLY REPREHEN-SIBLE..!!
TIMO-THY!?
BASHAAAAA (SPLASH)
Waah! No water!
Hmm?
THERE, THERE.
GO EASY ON TIMOTHY, WON'T YOU?
TIMOTHY HASN'T BEEN WATER-PROOFED YET.
BESIDES, THE PERSON BEHIND TIMOTHY IS—
Did some-body say my name?
HYOI (POP)
...... BESIDES, AS A ROBOT ...
...TIMOTHY ISN'T A BOY OR A GIRL!
"THE PER-SON BE-HIND" ...?

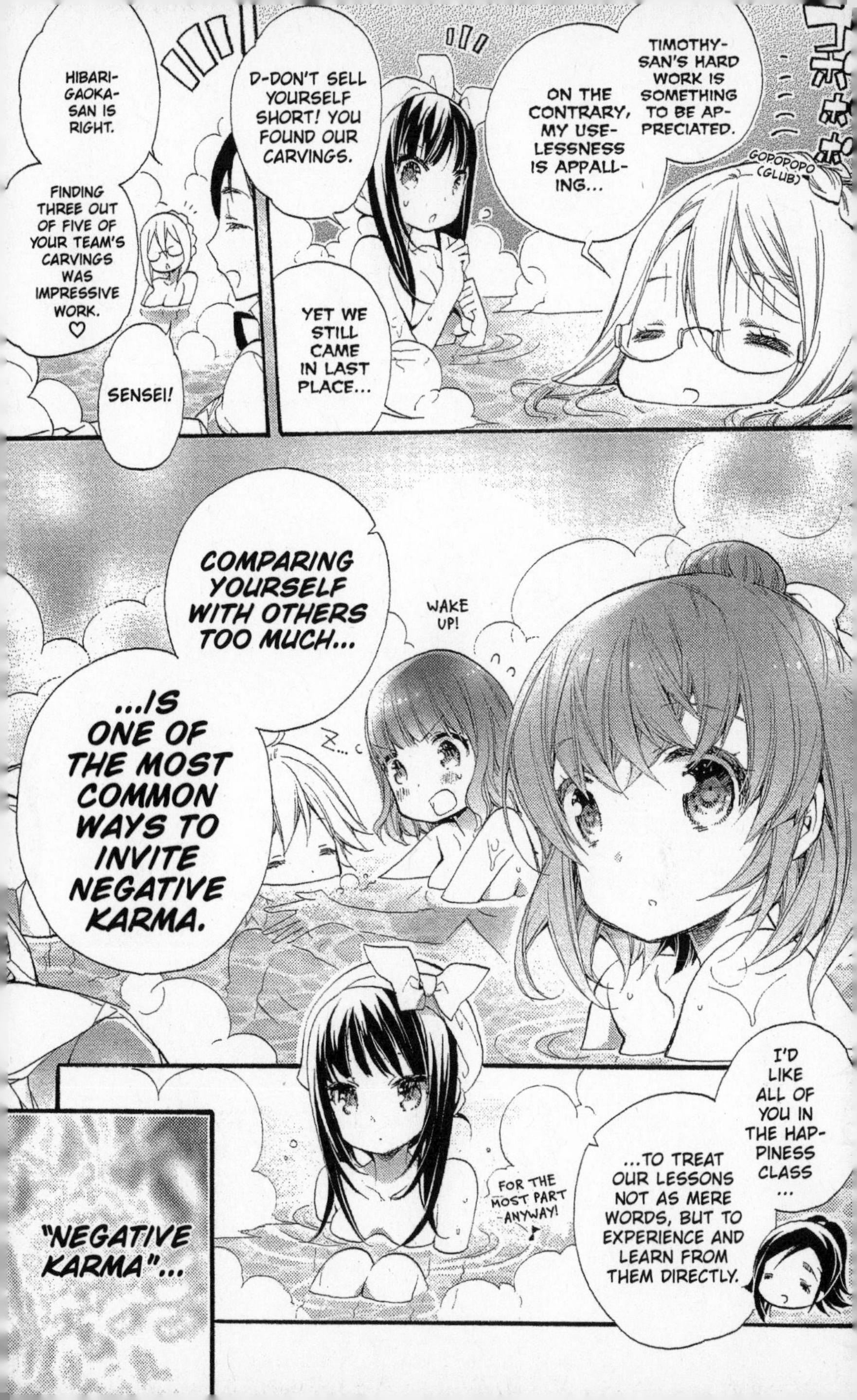
GOPOPOPO (GLUB)
TIMOTHY-SAN'S HARD WORK IS SOMETHING TO BE APPRECIATED.
ON THE CONTRARY, MY USELESSNESS IS APPALLING...
D-DON'T SELL YOURSELF SHORT! YOU FOUND OUR CARVINGS.
YET WE STILL CAME IN LAST PLACE...
HIBARIGAOKA-SAN IS RIGHT.
FINDING THREE OUT OF FIVE OF YOUR TEAM'S CARVINGS WAS IMPRESSIVE WORK. ♡
SENSEI!
COMPARING YOURSELF WITH OTHERS TOO MUCH...
...IS ONE OF THE MOST COMMON WAYS TO INVITE NEGATIVE KARMA.
WAKE UP!
Z...
I'D LIKE ALL OF YOU IN THE HAPPINESS CLASS...
...TO TREAT OUR LESSONS NOT AS MERE WORDS, BUT TO EXPERIENCE AND LEARN FROM THEM DIRECTLY.
FOR THE MOST PART ANYWAY! ♪
"NEGATIVE KARMA"...

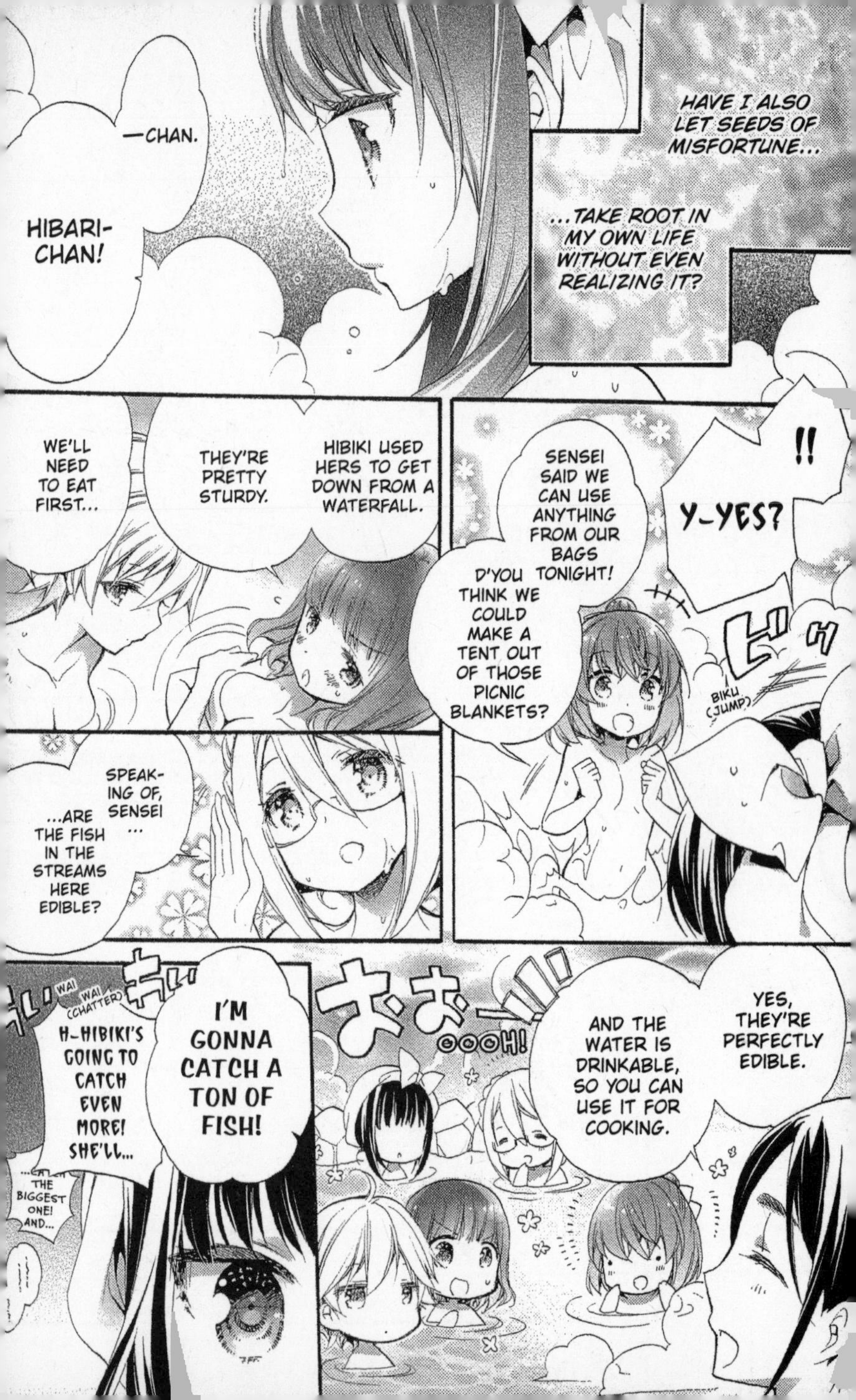
HAVE I ALSO LET SEEDS OF MISFORTUNE...
...TAKE ROOT IN MY OWN LIFE WITHOUT EVEN REALIZING IT?
—CHAN.
HIBARI-CHAN!
!!
Y-YES?
BIKU (JUMP)
SENSEI SAID WE CAN USE ANYTHING FROM OUR BAGS TONIGHT!
D'YOU THINK WE COULD MAKE A TENT OUT OF THOSE PICNIC BLANKETS?
HIBIKI USED HERS TO GET DOWN FROM A WATERFALL.
THEY'RE PRETTY STURDY.
WE'LL NEED TO EAT FIRST...
SPEAKING OF, SENSEI...
...ARE THE FISH IN THE STREAMS HERE EDIBLE?
YES, THEY'RE PERFECTLY EDIBLE.
AND THE WATER IS DRINKABLE, SO YOU CAN USE IT FOR COOKING.
OOOH!
I'M GONNA CATCH A TON OF FISH!
WAI WAI (CHATTER)
H-HIBIKI'S GOING TO CATCH EVEN MORE! SHE'LL...
THE BIGGEST ONE! AND...

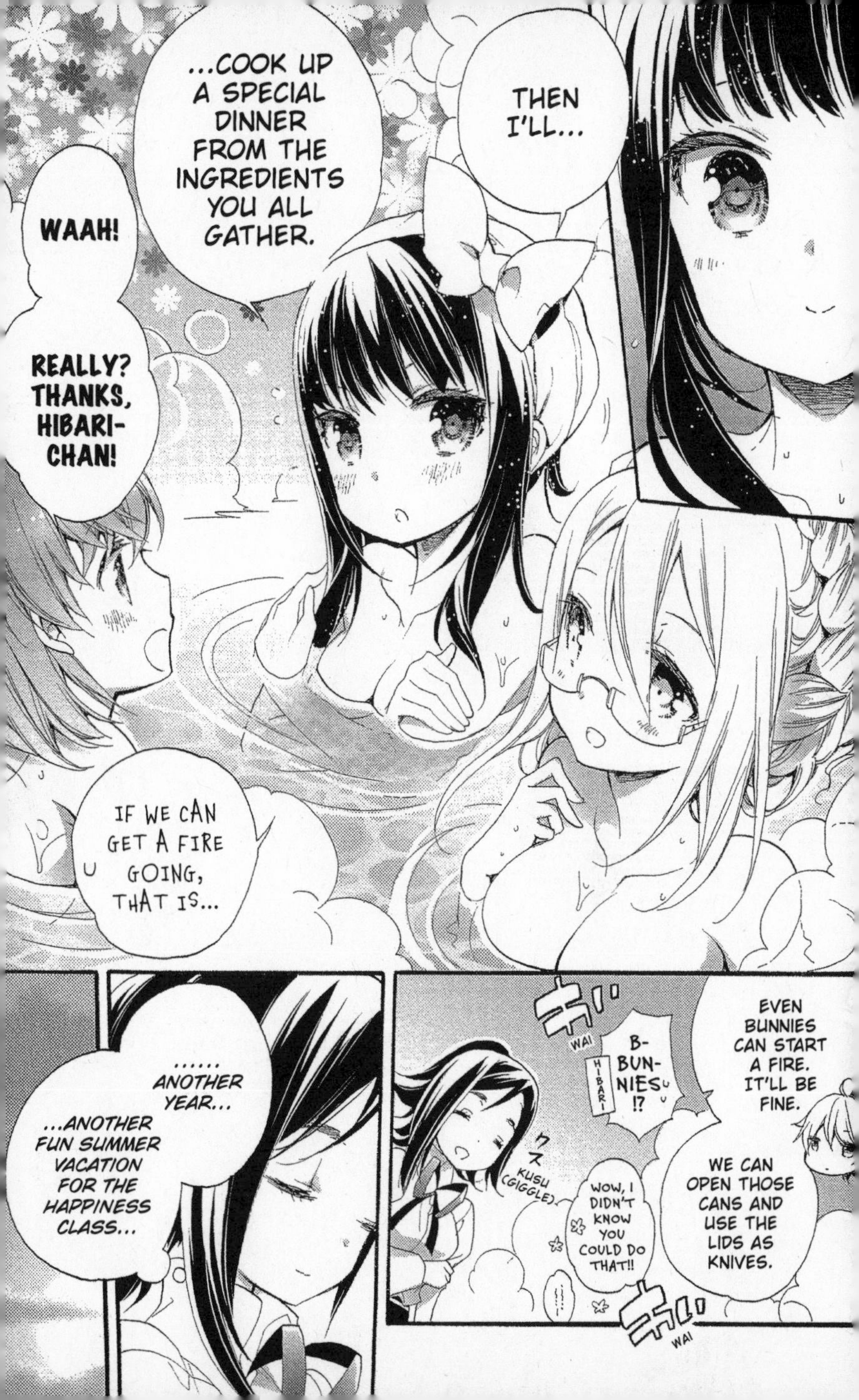
THEN I'LL...
...COOK UP A SPECIAL DINNER FROM THE INGREDIENTS YOU ALL GATHER.
WAAH!
REALLY? THANKS, HIBARI-CHAN!
IF WE CAN GET A FIRE GOING, THAT IS...
EVEN BUNNIES CAN START A FIRE. IT'LL BE FINE.
WE CAN OPEN THOSE CANS AND USE THE LIDS AS KNIVES.
WAI
B-BUNNIES!?
HIBARI
KUSU (GIGGLE)
WOW, I DIDN'T KNOW YOU COULD DO THAT!!
WAI
......ANOTHER YEAR...
...ANOTHER FUN SUMMER VACATION FOR THE HAPPINESS CLASS...

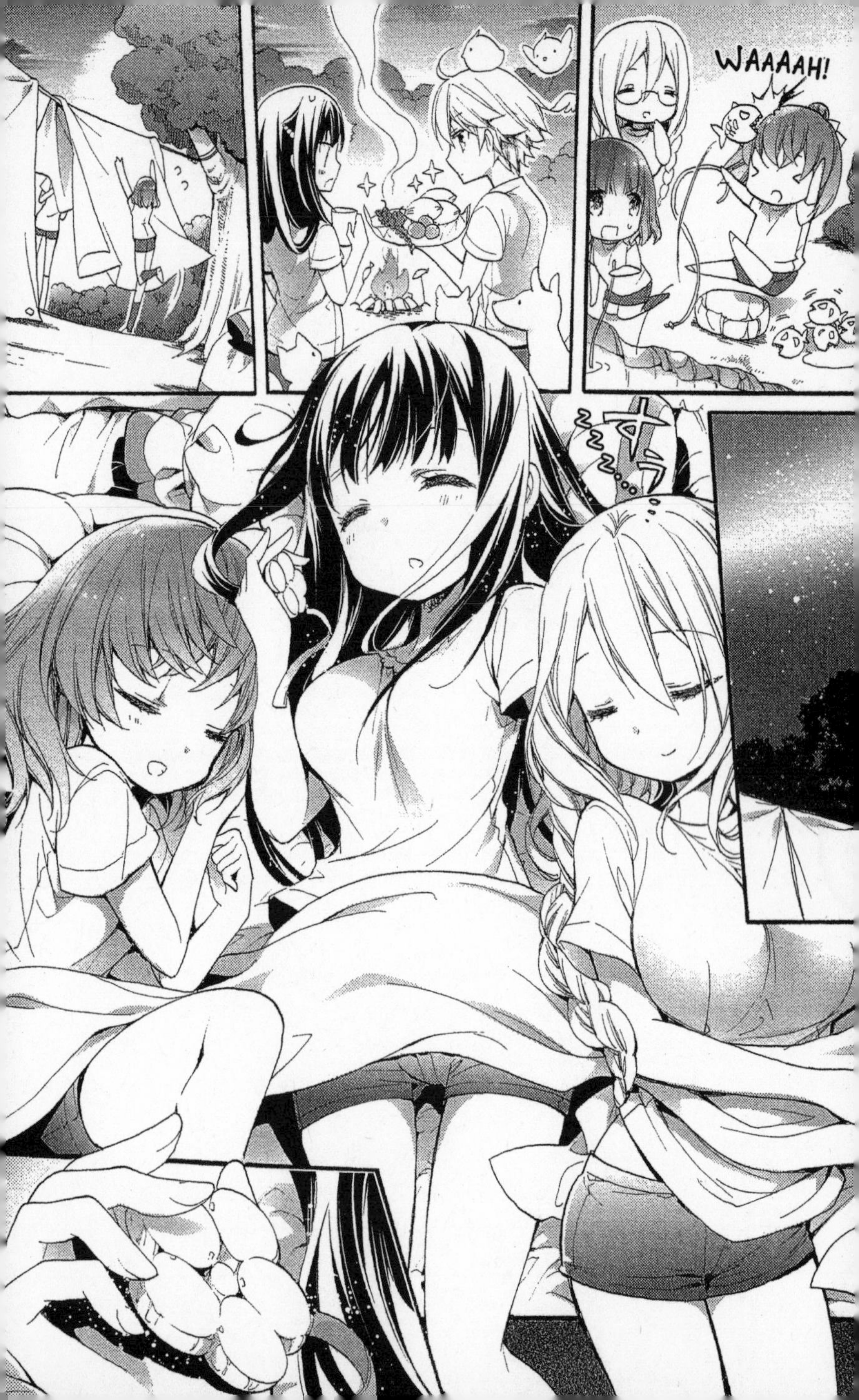
WAAAAH!
すう
zzz...

AnneHappy
unhappy go lucky!

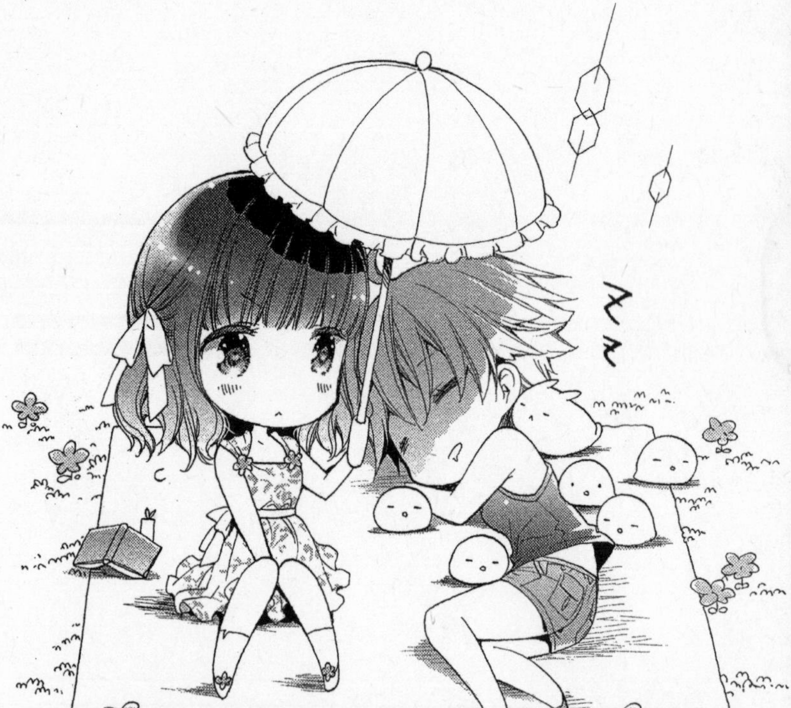
zz

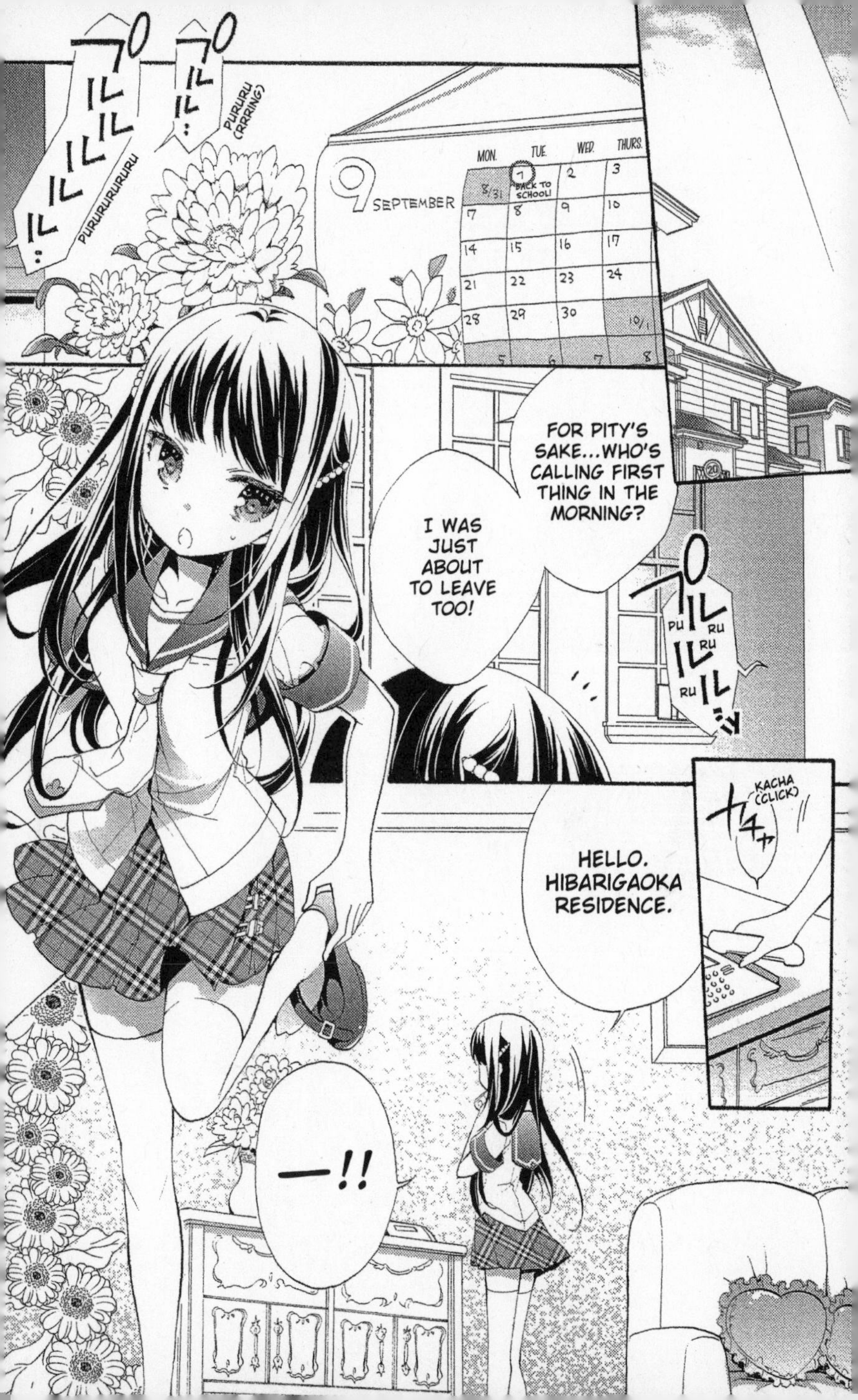

MON. TUE. WED. THURS.
8/31 1 2 3
BACK TO SCHOOL!
9 SEPTEMBER
7 8 9 10
14 15 16 17
21 22 23 24
28 29 30 10/1
5 6 7 8
プルル…
PURURU (RRRING)
プルルルルル…
PURURURURURU
プルルルッ
PU RU RU RU
FOR PITY'S SAKE...WHO'S CALLING FIRST THING IN THE MORNING?
I WAS JUST ABOUT TO LEAVE TOO!
...
カチャ
KACHA (CLICK)
HELLO. HIBARIGAOKA RESIDENCE.
—!!

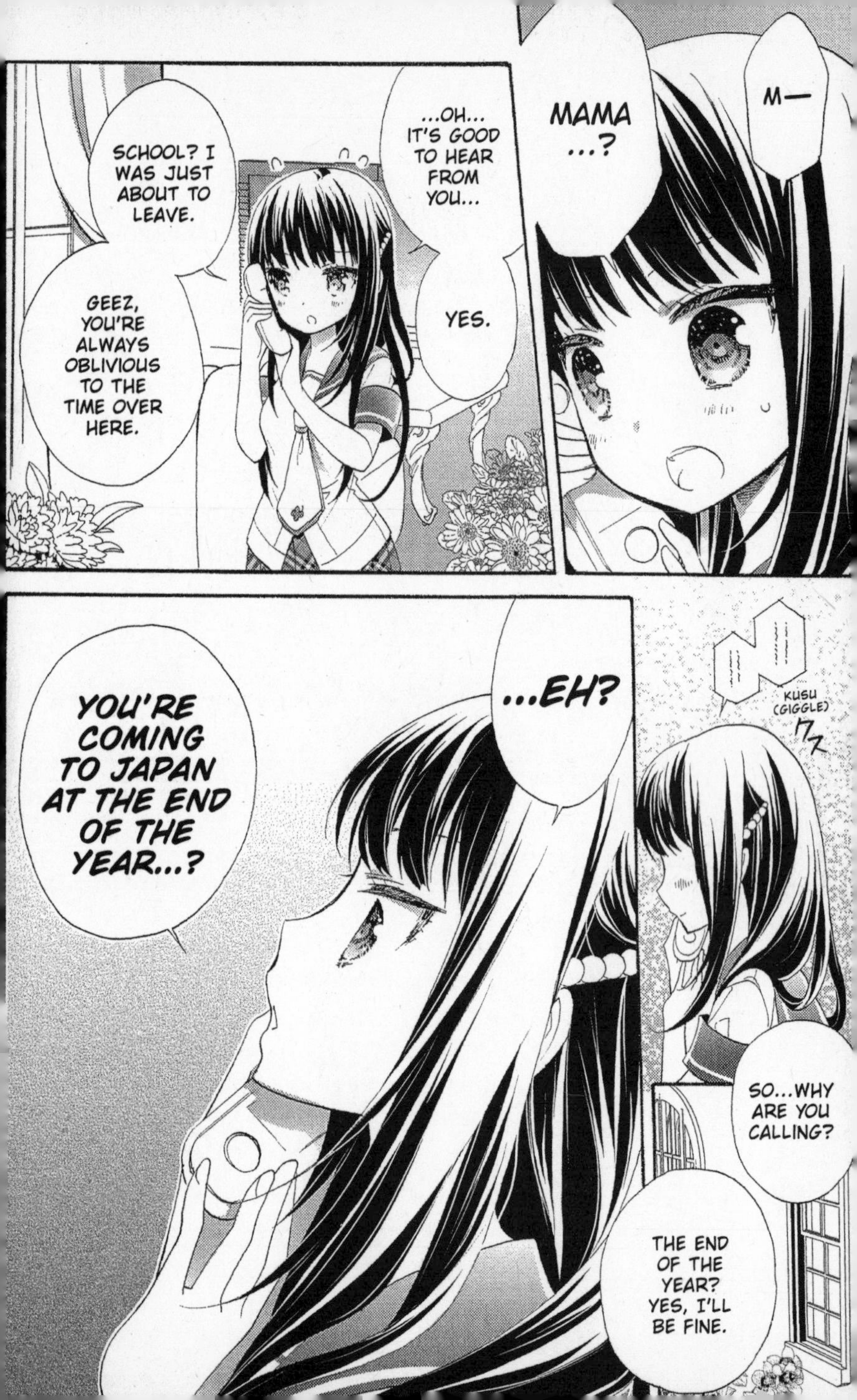
M—
MAMA ...?
...OH... IT'S GOOD TO HEAR FROM YOU...
YES.
SCHOOL? I WAS JUST ABOUT TO LEAVE.
GEEZ, YOU'RE ALWAYS OBLIVIOUS TO THE TIME OVER HERE.
......
KUSU (GIGGLE)
SO...WHY ARE YOU CALLING?
THE END OF THE YEAR? YES, I'LL BE FINE.
...EH?
YOU'RE COMING TO JAPAN AT THE END OF THE YEAR...?

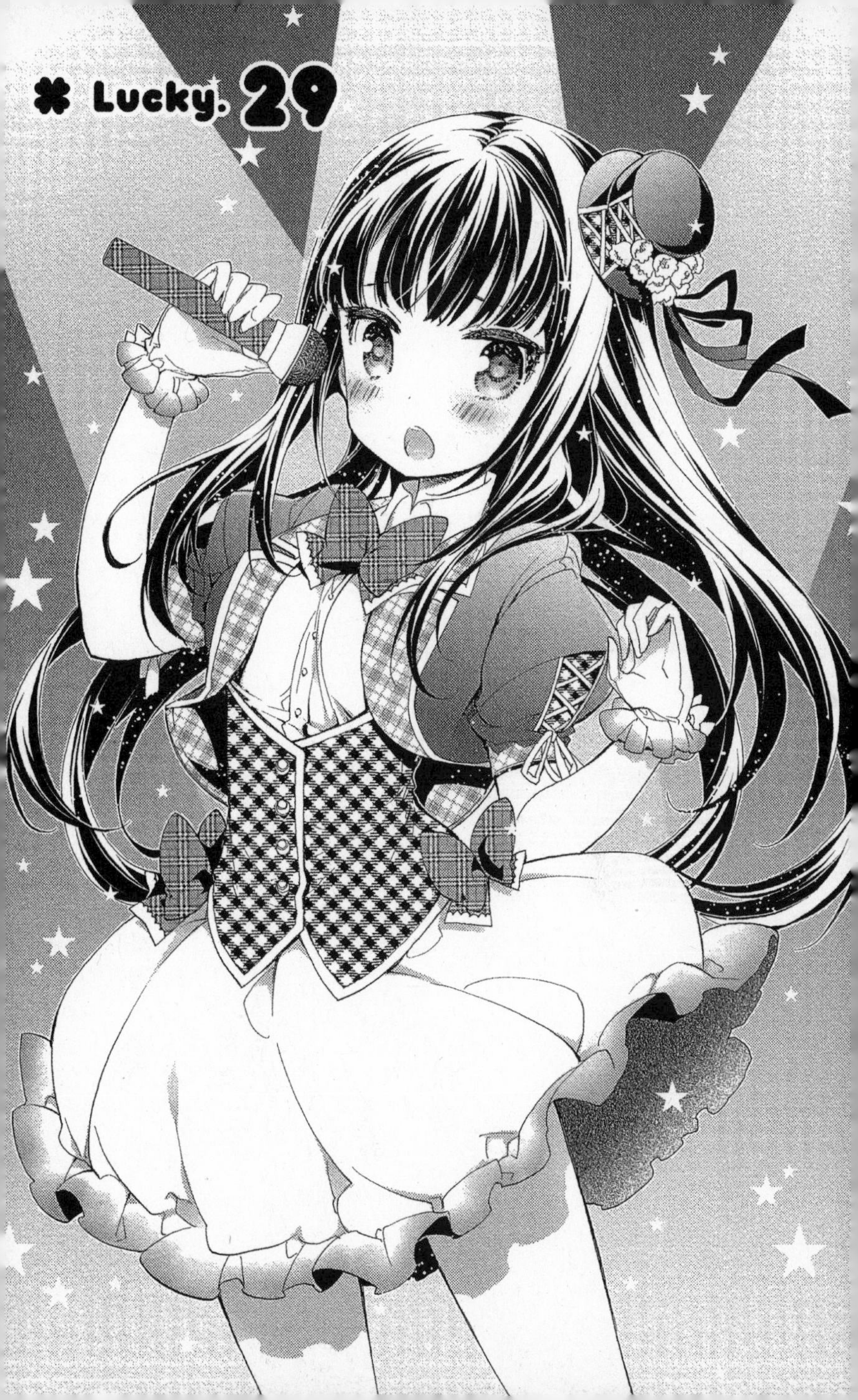
Lucky. 29

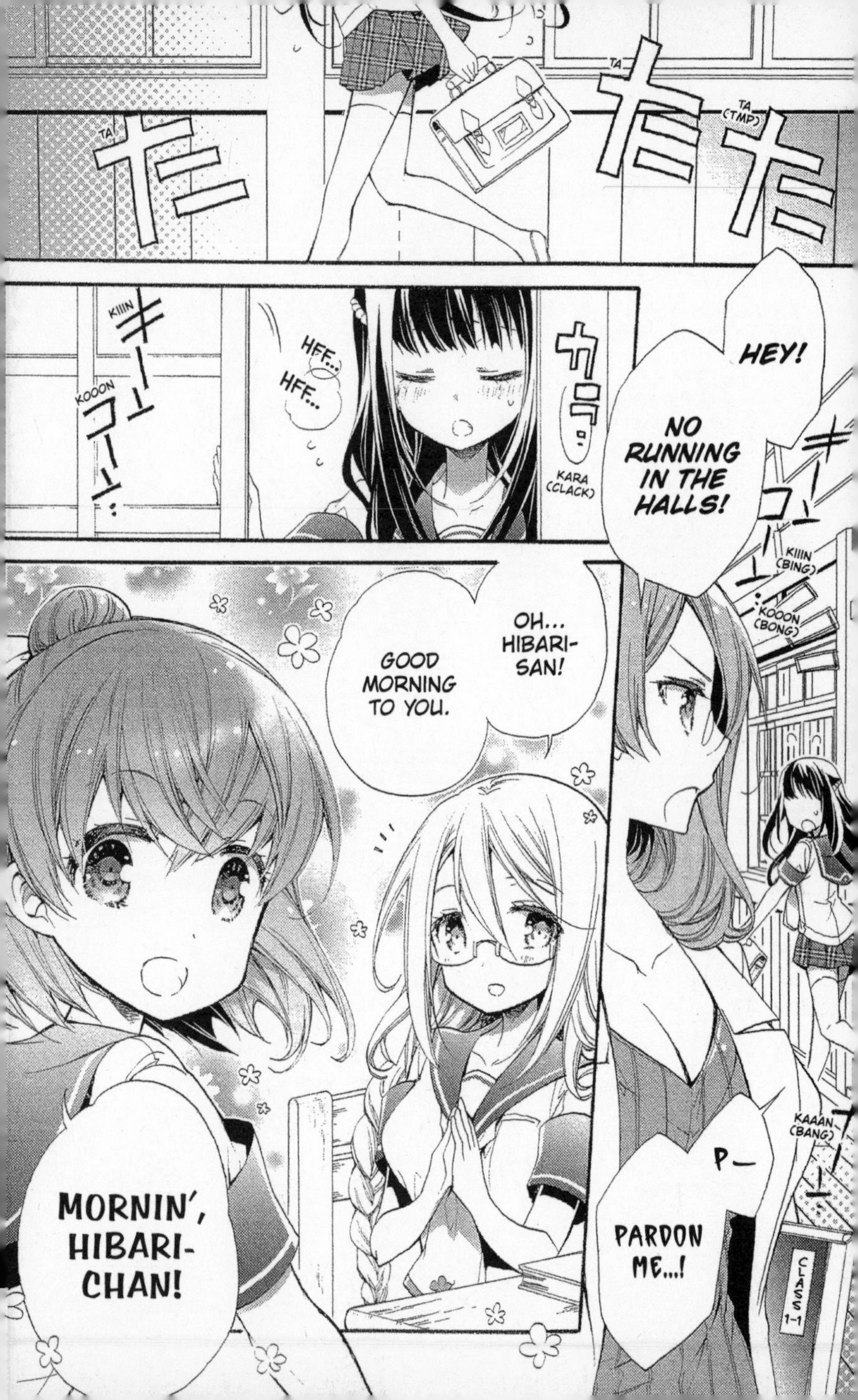
TA (TMP)
TA
TA
HEY!
NO RUNNING IN THE HALLS!
KIIN (BING)
KOOON (BONG)
KAAAN (BANG)
P—
PARDON ME...!
CLASS 1-1
KARA (CLACK)
HFF...
HFF...
KIIIN
KOOON
OH... HIBARI-SAN!
GOOD MORNING TO YOU.
MORNIN', HIBARI-CHAN!

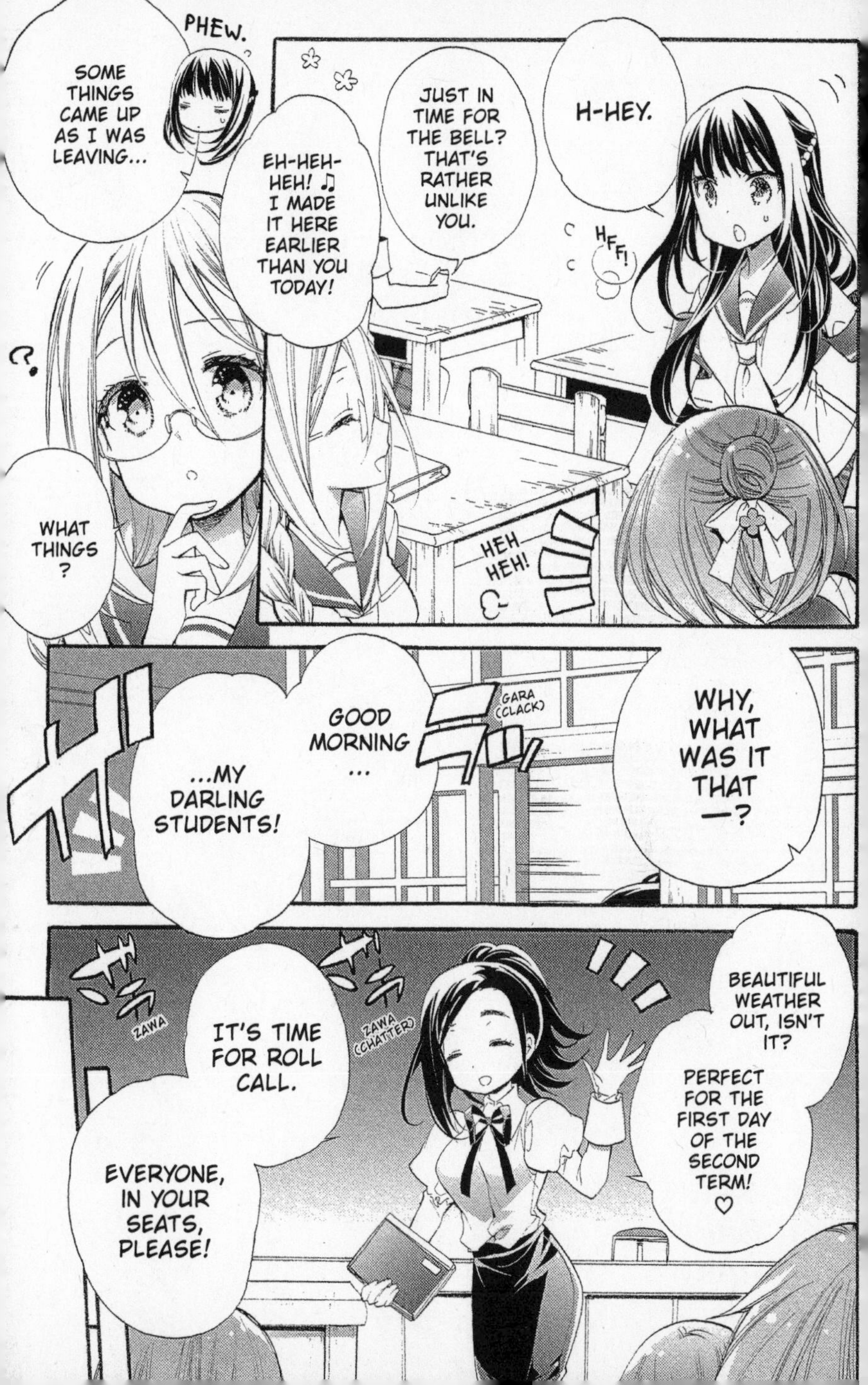
H-HEY.
HFF!
JUST IN TIME FOR THE BELL? THAT'S RATHER UNLIKE YOU.
EH-HEH-HEH! ♫ I MADE IT HERE EARLIER THAN YOU TODAY!
HEH HEH!
PHEW.
SOME THINGS CAME UP AS I WAS LEAVING...
WHAT THINGS?
WHY, WHAT WAS IT THAT—?
GARA (CLACK)
GOOD MORNING...
...MY DARLING STUDENTS!
BEAUTIFUL WEATHER OUT, ISN'T IT?
PERFECT FOR THE FIRST DAY OF THE SECOND TERM! ♡
ZAWA (CHATTER)
IT'S TIME FOR ROLL CALL.
ZAWA
EVERYONE, IN YOUR SEATS, PLEASE!

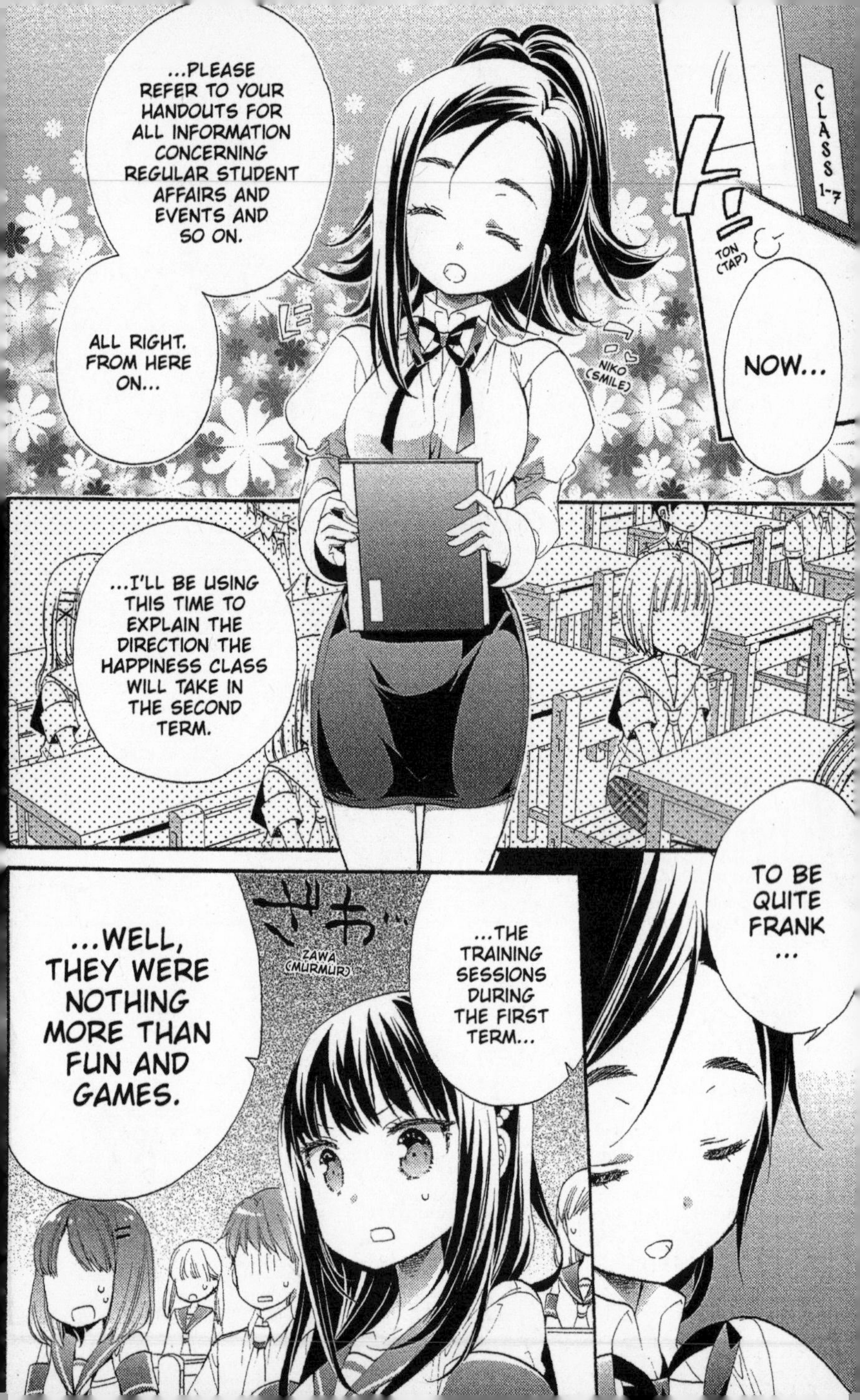
CLASS 1-7
TON (TAP)
NOW...
...PLEASE REFER TO YOUR HANDOUTS FOR ALL INFORMATION CONCERNING REGULAR STUDENT AFFAIRS AND EVENTS AND SO ON.
NIKO (SMILE)
ALL RIGHT. FROM HERE ON...
...I'LL BE USING THIS TIME TO EXPLAIN THE DIRECTION THE HAPPINESS CLASS WILL TAKE IN THE SECOND TERM.
TO BE QUITE FRANK...
...THE TRAINING SESSIONS DURING THE FIRST TERM...
ZAWA (MURMUR)
...WELL, THEY WERE NOTHING MORE THAN FUN AND GAMES.

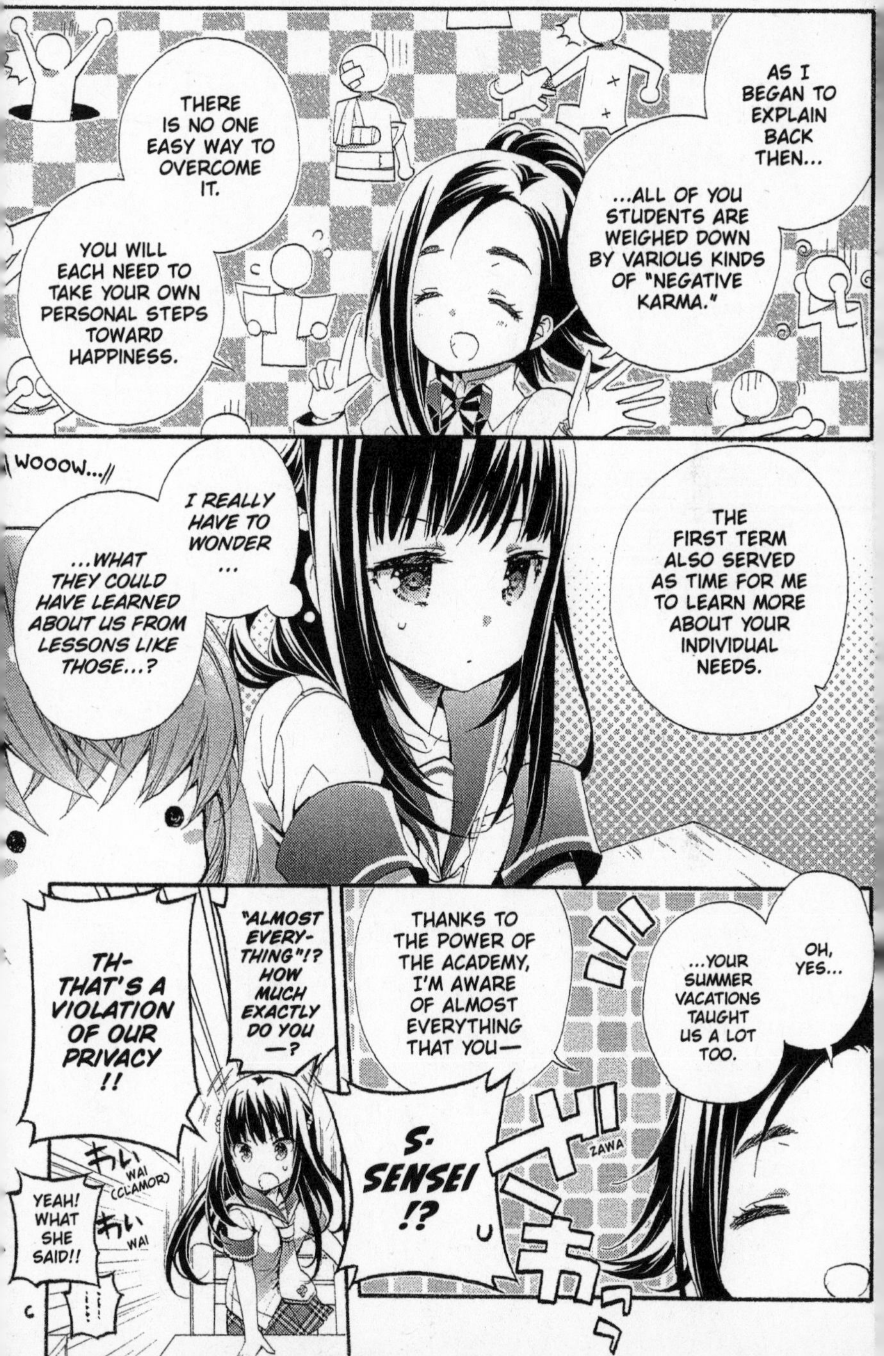
AS I BEGAN TO EXPLAIN BACK THEN...
...ALL OF YOU STUDENTS ARE WEIGHED DOWN BY VARIOUS KINDS OF "NEGATIVE KARMA."
THERE IS NO ONE EASY WAY TO OVERCOME IT.
YOU WILL EACH NEED TO TAKE YOUR OWN PERSONAL STEPS TOWARD HAPPINESS.
THE FIRST TERM ALSO SERVED AS TIME FOR ME TO LEARN MORE ABOUT YOUR INDIVIDUAL NEEDS.
WOOOW...
I REALLY HAVE TO WONDER...
...WHAT THEY COULD HAVE LEARNED ABOUT US FROM LESSONS LIKE THOSE...?
OH, YES...
...YOUR SUMMER VACATIONS TAUGHT US A LOT TOO.
THANKS TO THE POWER OF THE ACADEMY, I'M AWARE OF ALMOST EVERYTHING THAT YOU—
ZAWA
S-SENSEI!?
"ALMOST EVERY-THING"!? HOW MUCH EXACTLY DO YOU—?
TH-THAT'S A VIOLATION OF OUR PRIVACY!!
WAI (CLAMOR)
WAI
YEAH! WHAT SHE SAID!!

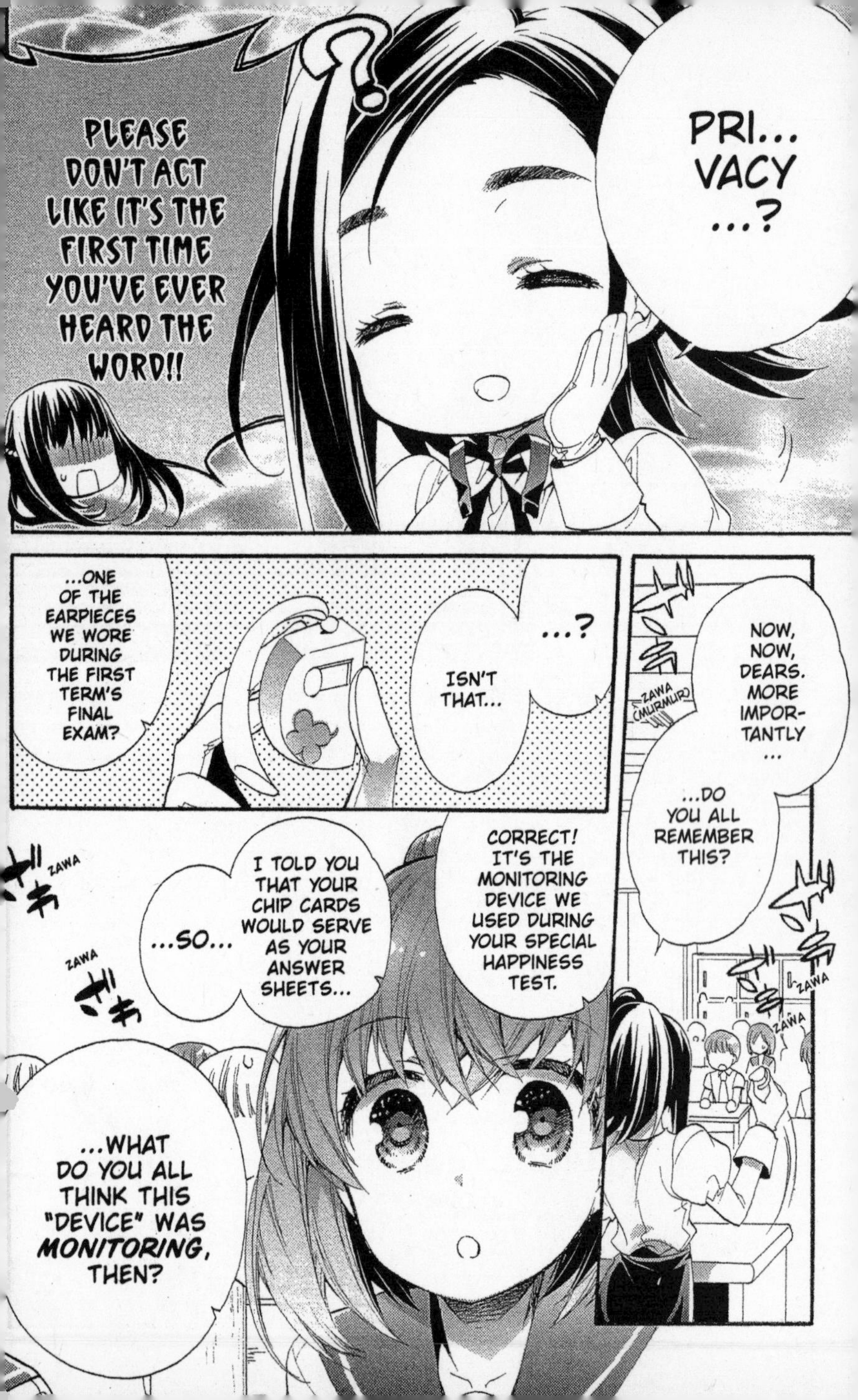
PRI... VACY ...?
PLEASE DON'T ACT LIKE IT'S THE FIRST TIME YOU'VE EVER HEARD THE WORD!!
NOW, NOW, DEARS. MORE IMPORTANTLY ...
...DO YOU ALL REMEMBER THIS?
ZAWA (MURMUR)
ZAWA
ZAWA
...?
ISN'T THAT...
...ONE OF THE EARPIECES WE WORE DURING THE FIRST TERM'S FINAL EXAM?
CORRECT! IT'S THE MONITORING DEVICE WE USED DURING YOUR SPECIAL HAPPINESS TEST.
I TOLD YOU THAT YOUR CHIP CARDS WOULD SERVE AS YOUR ANSWER SHEETS...
...SO...
ZAWA
ZAWA
...WHAT DO YOU ALL THINK THIS "DEVICE" WAS *MONITORING*, THEN?

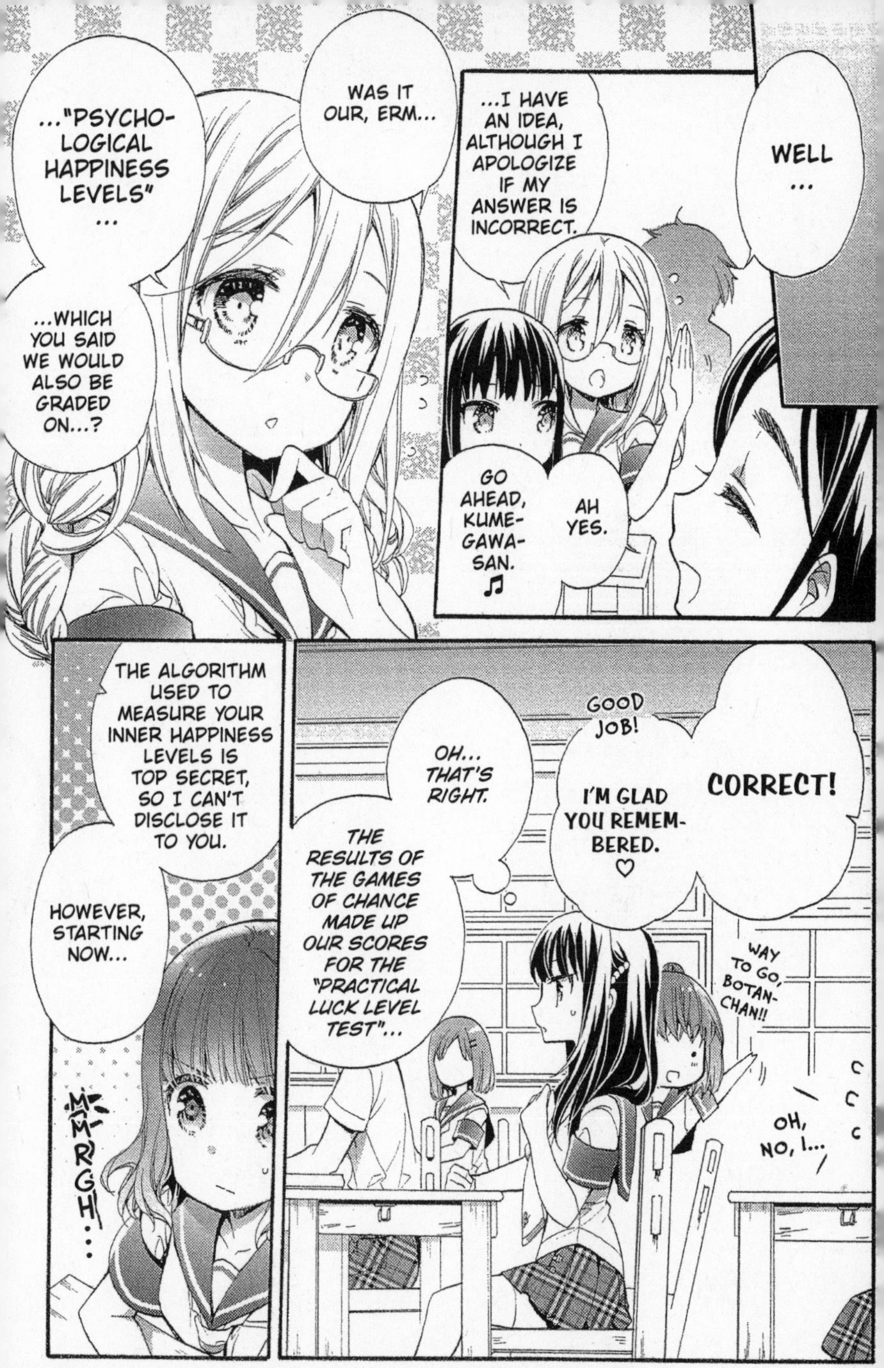
WELL...
...I HAVE AN IDEA, ALTHOUGH I APOLOGIZE IF MY ANSWER IS INCORRECT.
AH YES.
GO AHEAD, KUME-GAWA-SAN. ♫
WAS IT OUR, ERM...
..."PSYCHO-LOGICAL HAPPINESS LEVELS"...
...WHICH YOU SAID WE WOULD ALSO BE GRADED ON...?
CORRECT!
GOOD JOB!
I'M GLAD YOU REMEM-BERED. ♡
WAY TO GO, BOTAN-CHAN!!
OH... THAT'S RIGHT.
THE RESULTS OF THE GAMES OF CHANCE MADE UP OUR SCORES FOR THE "PRACTICAL LUCK LEVEL TEST"...
OH, NO, I...
THE ALGORITHM USED TO MEASURE YOUR INNER HAPPINESS LEVELS IS TOP SECRET, SO I CAN'T DISCLOSE IT TO YOU.
HOWEVER, STARTING NOW...
MMMRGH...

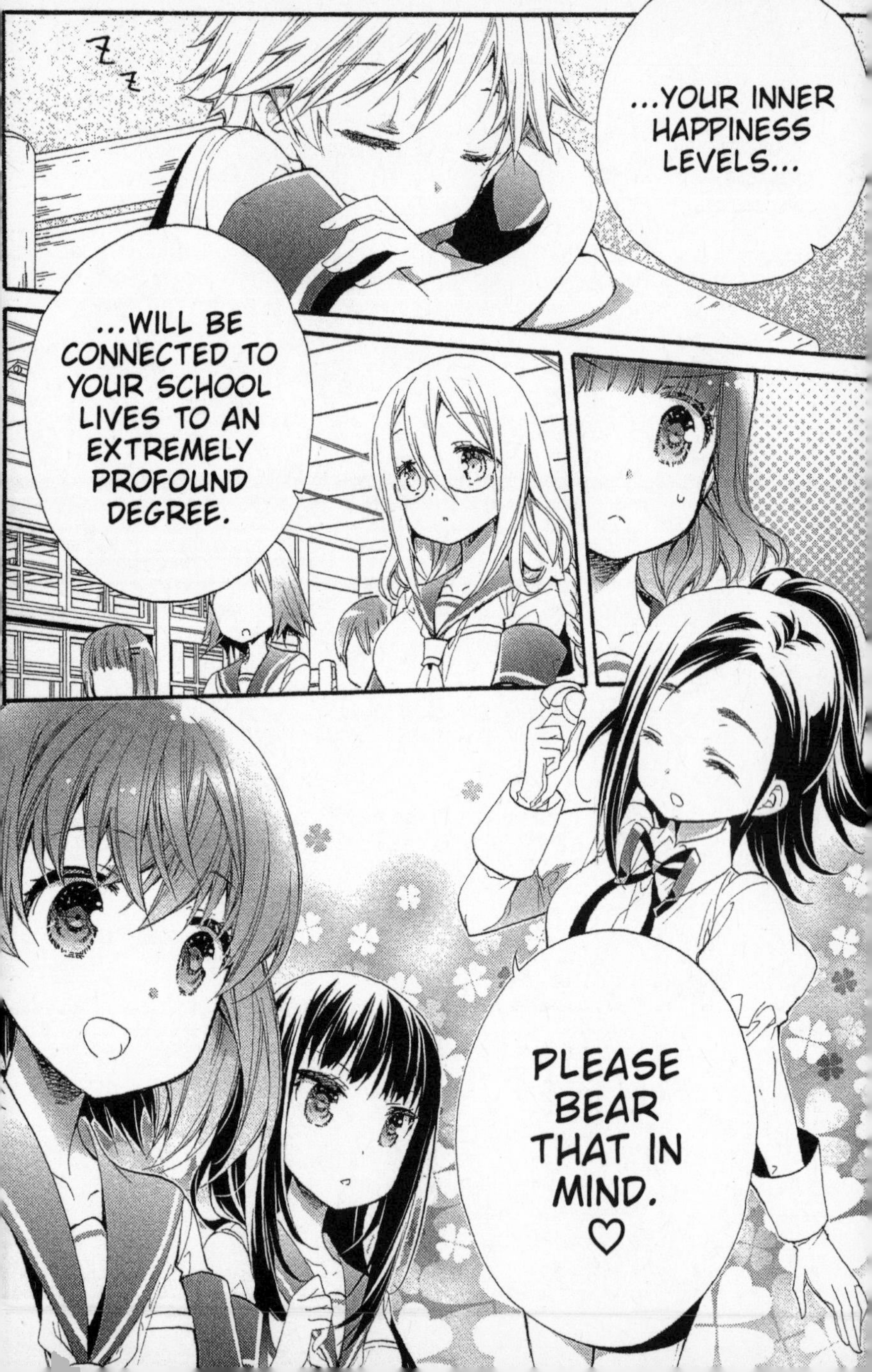
...YOUR INNER HAPPINESS LEVELS...
...WILL BE CONNECTED TO YOUR SCHOOL LIVES TO AN EXTREMELY PROFOUND DEGREE.
PLEASE BEAR THAT IN MIND. ♡

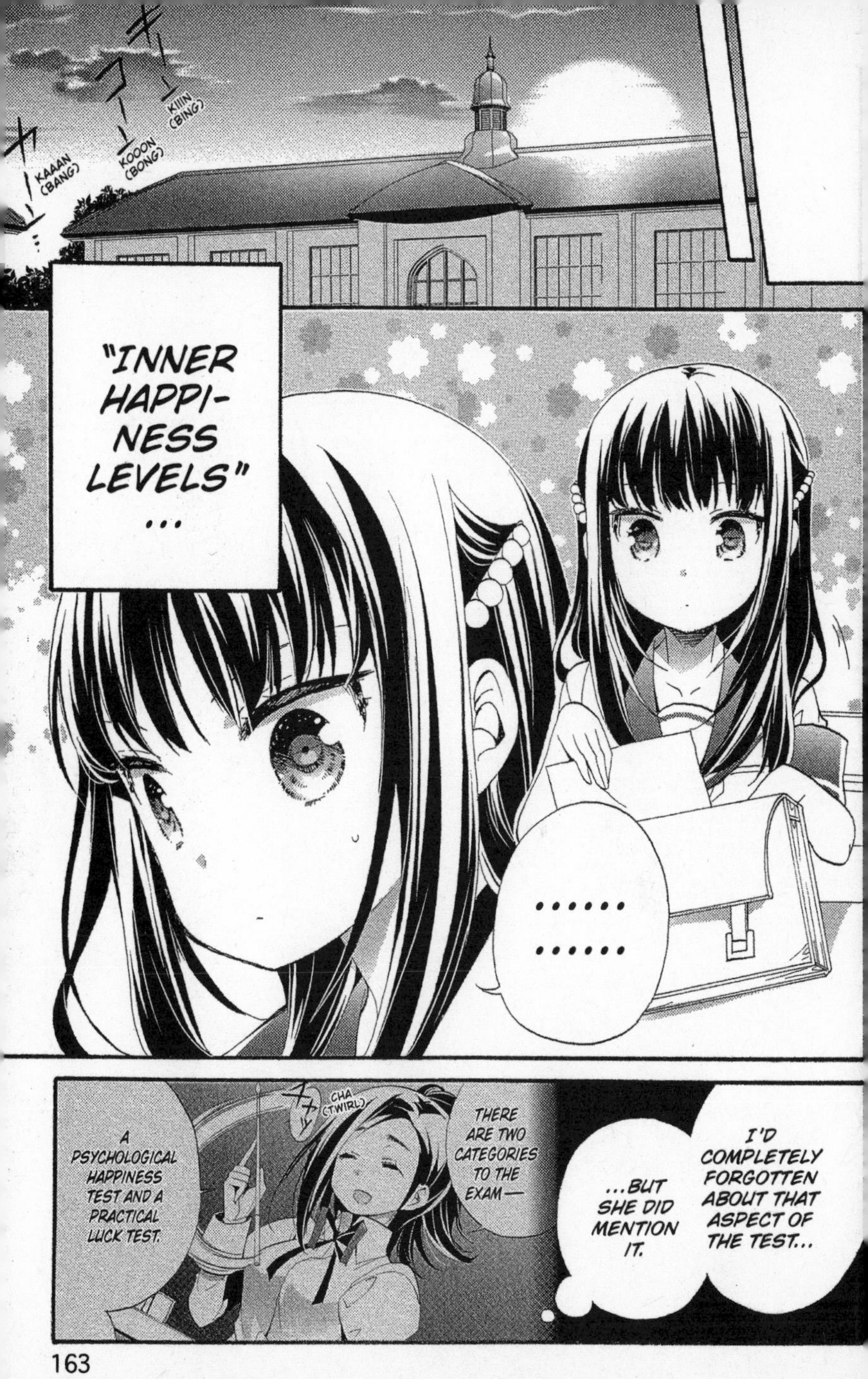
KIIN (BING)
KOOON (BONG)
KAAAN (BANG)
"INNER HAPPINESS LEVELS"...
......
......
I'D COMPLETELY FORGOTTEN ABOUT THAT ASPECT OF THE TEST...
...BUT SHE DID MENTION IT.
CHA (TWIRL)
THERE ARE TWO CATEGORIES TO THE EXAM—
A PSYCHOLOGICAL HAPPINESS TEST AND A PRACTICAL LUCK TEST.

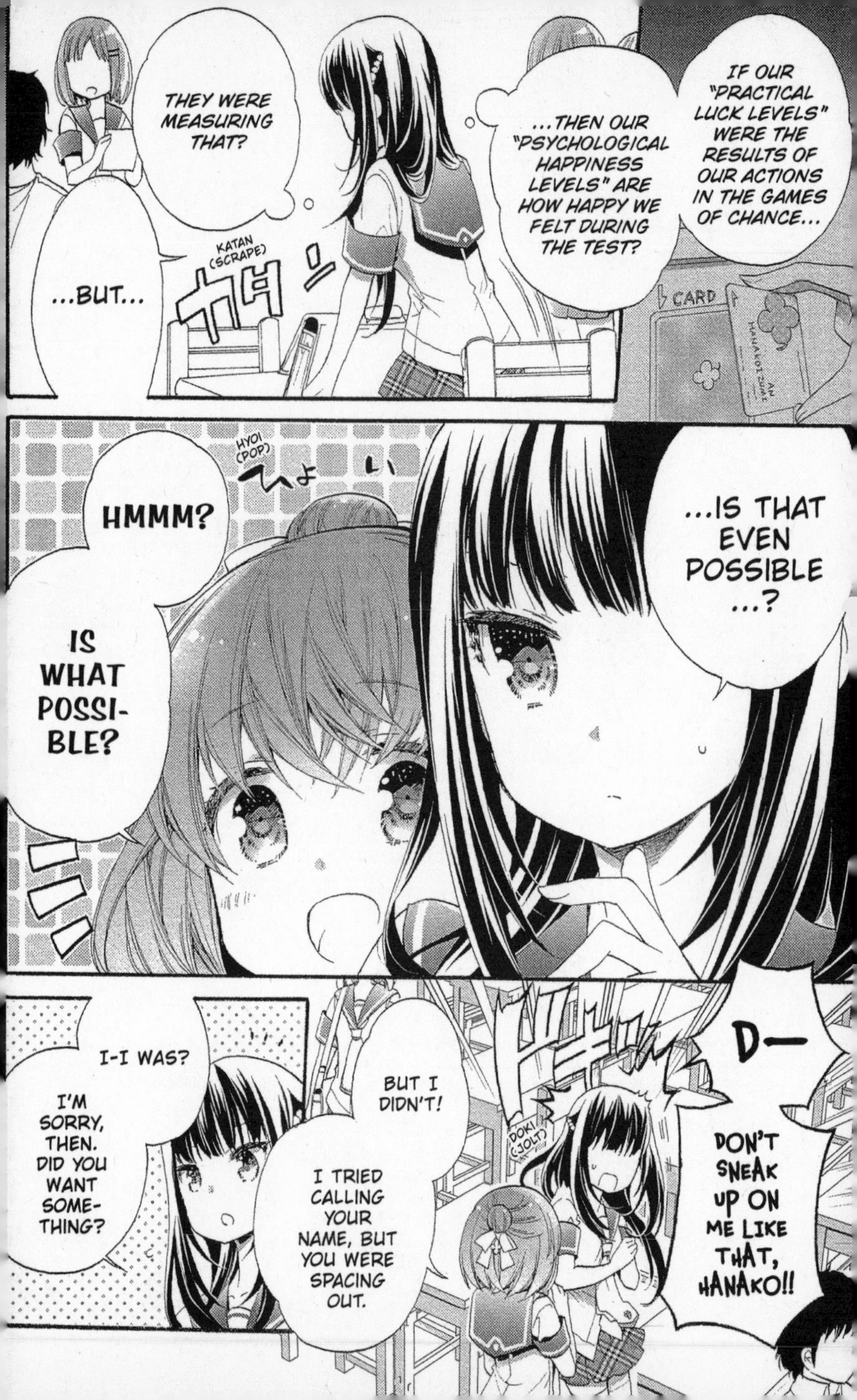
IF OUR "PRACTICAL LUCK LEVELS" WERE THE RESULTS OF OUR ACTIONS IN THE GAMES OF CHANCE...
...THEN OUR "PSYCHOLOGICAL HAPPINESS LEVELS" ARE HOW HAPPY WE FELT DURING THE TEST?
THEY WERE MEASURING THAT?
CARD
KATAN (SCRAPE)
...BUT...
...IS THAT EVEN POSSIBLE...?
HYOI (POP)
HMMM?
IS WHAT POSSIBLE?
D—
DON'T SNEAK UP ON ME LIKE THAT, HANAKO!!
DOKI (JOLT)
BUT I DIDN'T!
I TRIED CALLING YOUR NAME, BUT YOU WERE SPACING OUT.
I-I WAS?
I'M SORRY, THEN. DID YOU WANT SOMETHING?

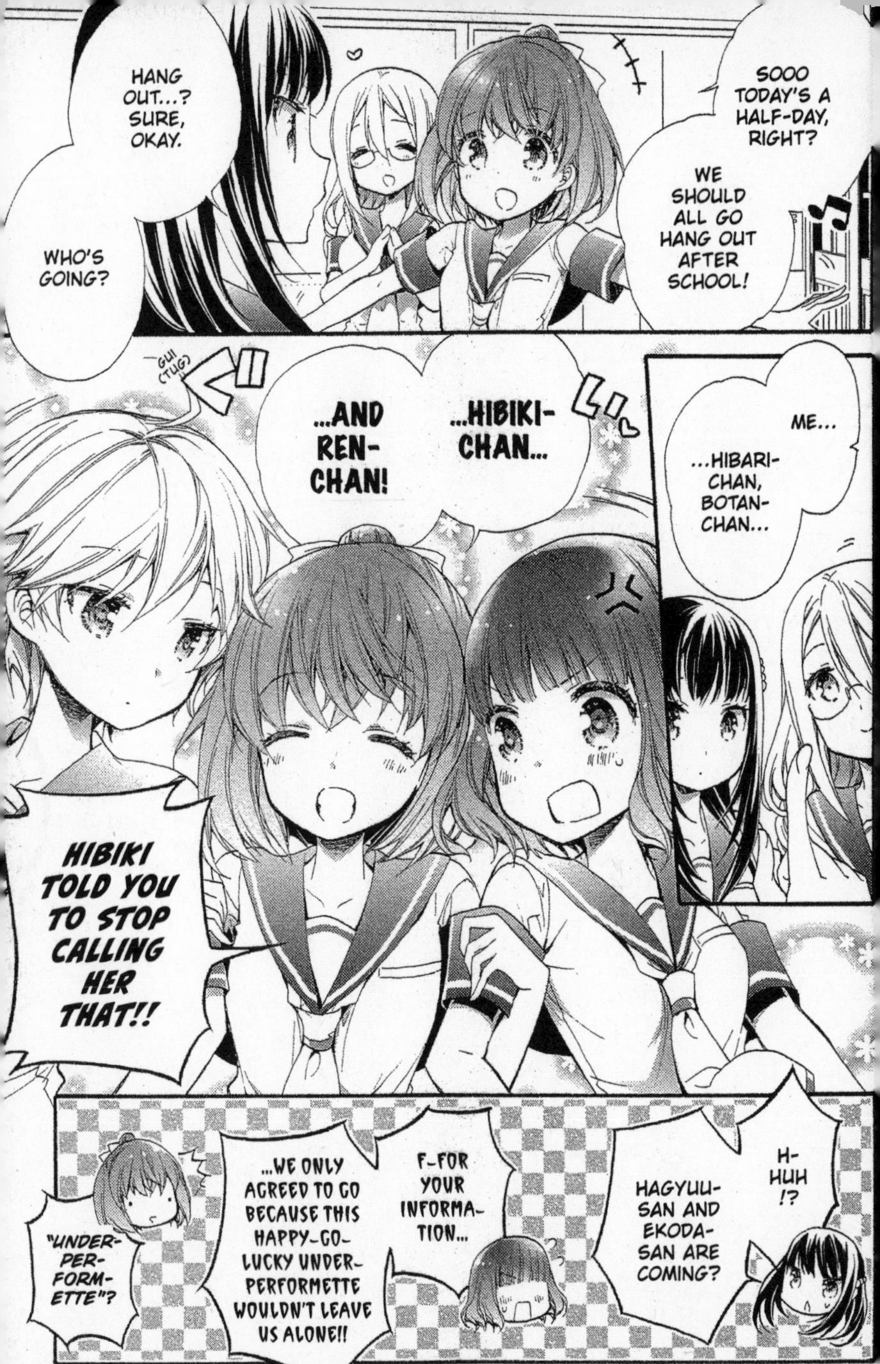
SOOO TODAY'S A HALF-DAY, RIGHT?
WE SHOULD ALL GO HANG OUT AFTER SCHOOL!
HANG OUT...? SURE, OKAY.
WHO'S GOING?
ME...
...HIBARI-CHAN, BOTAN-CHAN...
...HIBIKI-CHAN...
...AND REN-CHAN!
GUI (TUG)
HIBIKI TOLD YOU TO STOP CALLING HER THAT!!
H-HUH!?
HAGYUU-SAN AND EKODA-SAN ARE COMING?
F-FOR YOUR INFORMATION...
...WE ONLY AGREED TO GO BECAUSE THIS HAPPY-GO-LUCKY UNDER-PERFORMETTE WOULDN'T LEAVE US ALONE!!
"UNDER-PERFORMETTE"?

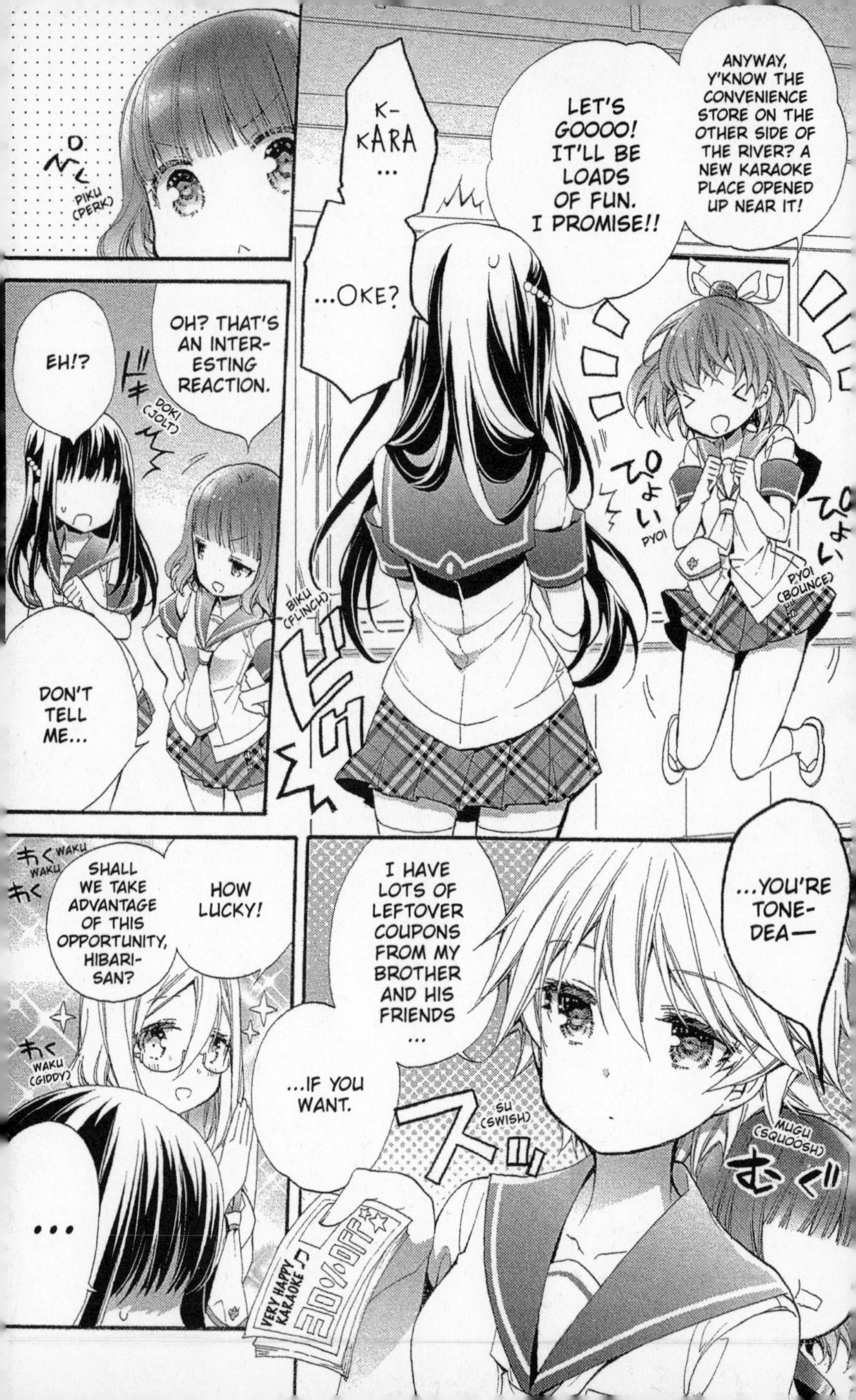

ANYWAY, Y'KNOW THE CONVENIENCE STORE ON THE OTHER SIDE OF THE RIVER? A NEW KARAOKE PLACE OPENED UP NEAR IT!
LET'S GOOOO! IT'LL BE LOADS OF FUN. I PROMISE!!
K-KARA...
...OKE?
ぴょい PYOI
ぴょい PYOI (BOUNCE)
BIKU (FLINCH)
PIKU (PERK)
OH? THAT'S AN INTERESTING REACTION.
EH!?
DOKI (JOLT)
DON'T TELL ME...
...YOU'RE TONE-DEA—
MUGU (SQUOOSH)
I HAVE LOTS OF LEFTOVER COUPONS FROM MY BROTHER AND HIS FRIENDS...
SU (SWISH)
...IF YOU WANT.
VERY HAPPY KARAOKE ♫
30% OFF
HOW LUCKY!
SHALL WE TAKE ADVANTAGE OF THIS OPPORTUNITY, HIBARI-SAN?
わく WAKU WAKU
わく WAKU (GIDDY)
...

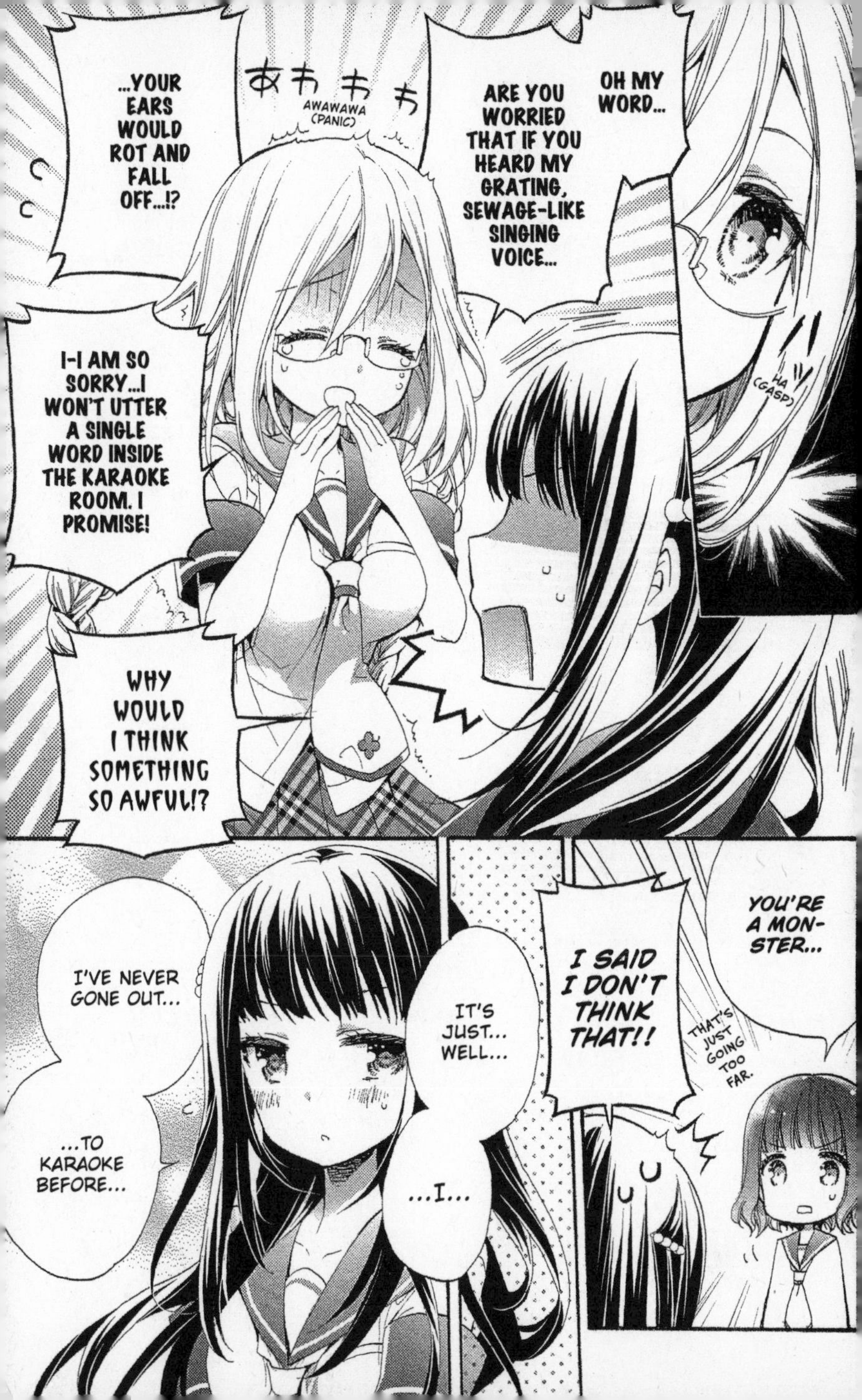
OH MY WORD...
HA (GASP)
ARE YOU WORRIED THAT IF YOU HEARD MY GRATING, SEWAGE-LIKE SINGING VOICE...
あわわわ
AWAWAWA (PANIC)
...YOUR EARS WOULD ROT AND FALL OFF...!?
I-I AM SO SORRY...I WON'T UTTER A SINGLE WORD INSIDE THE KARAOKE ROOM. I PROMISE!
WHY WOULD I THINK SOMETHING SO AWFUL!?
YOU'RE A MON-STER...
I SAID I DON'T THINK THAT!!
THAT'S JUST GOING TOO FAR.
IT'S JUST... WELL...
...I...
I'VE NEVER GONE OUT...
...TO KARAOKE BEFORE...

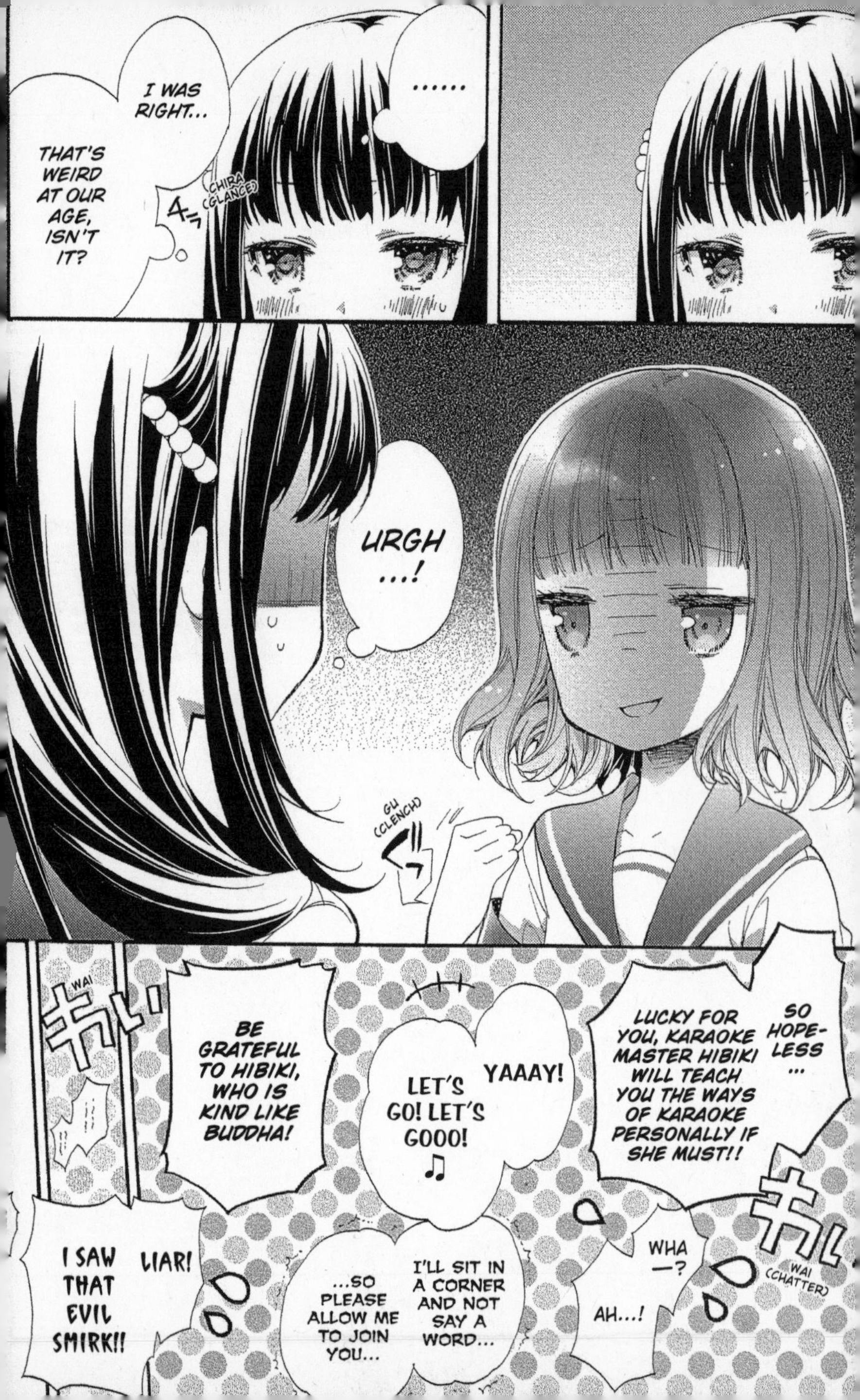
......
I WAS RIGHT...
THAT'S WEIRD AT OUR AGE, ISN'T IT?
CHIRA (GLANCE)
URGH ...!
GU (CLENCH)
SO HOPE-LESS ...
LUCKY FOR YOU, KARAOKE MASTER HIBIKI WILL TEACH YOU THE WAYS OF KARAOKE PERSONALLY IF SHE MUST!!
YAAAY!
LET'S GO! LET'S GOOO! ♫
BE GRATEFUL TO HIBIKI, WHO IS KIND LIKE BUDDHA!
WAI
WAI (CHATTER)
WHA —?
AH...!
I'LL SIT IN A CORNER AND NOT SAY A WORD...
...SO PLEASE ALLOW ME TO JOIN YOU...
LIAR!
I SAW THAT EVIL SMIRK!!

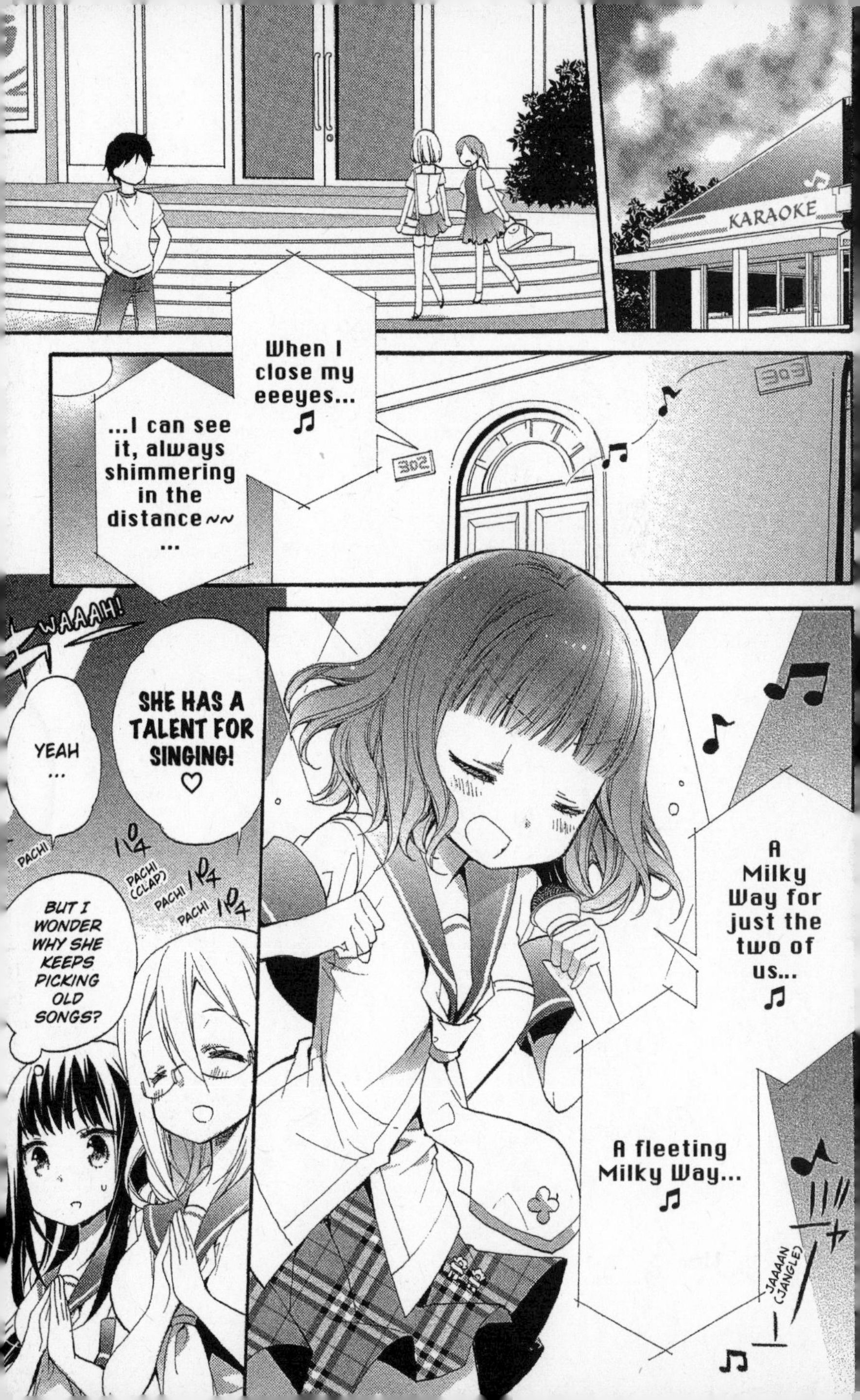
KARAOKE
When I close my eeeyes... ♫
...I can see it, always shimmering in the distance~~...
A Milky Way for just the two of us... ♫
A fleeting Milky Way... ♫
JAAAAN (JANGLE)
WAAAAH!
SHE HAS A TALENT FOR SINGING! ♡
YEAH...
PACHI
PACHI (CLAP)
PACHI
PACHI
BUT I WONDER WHY SHE KEEPS PICKING OLD SONGS?

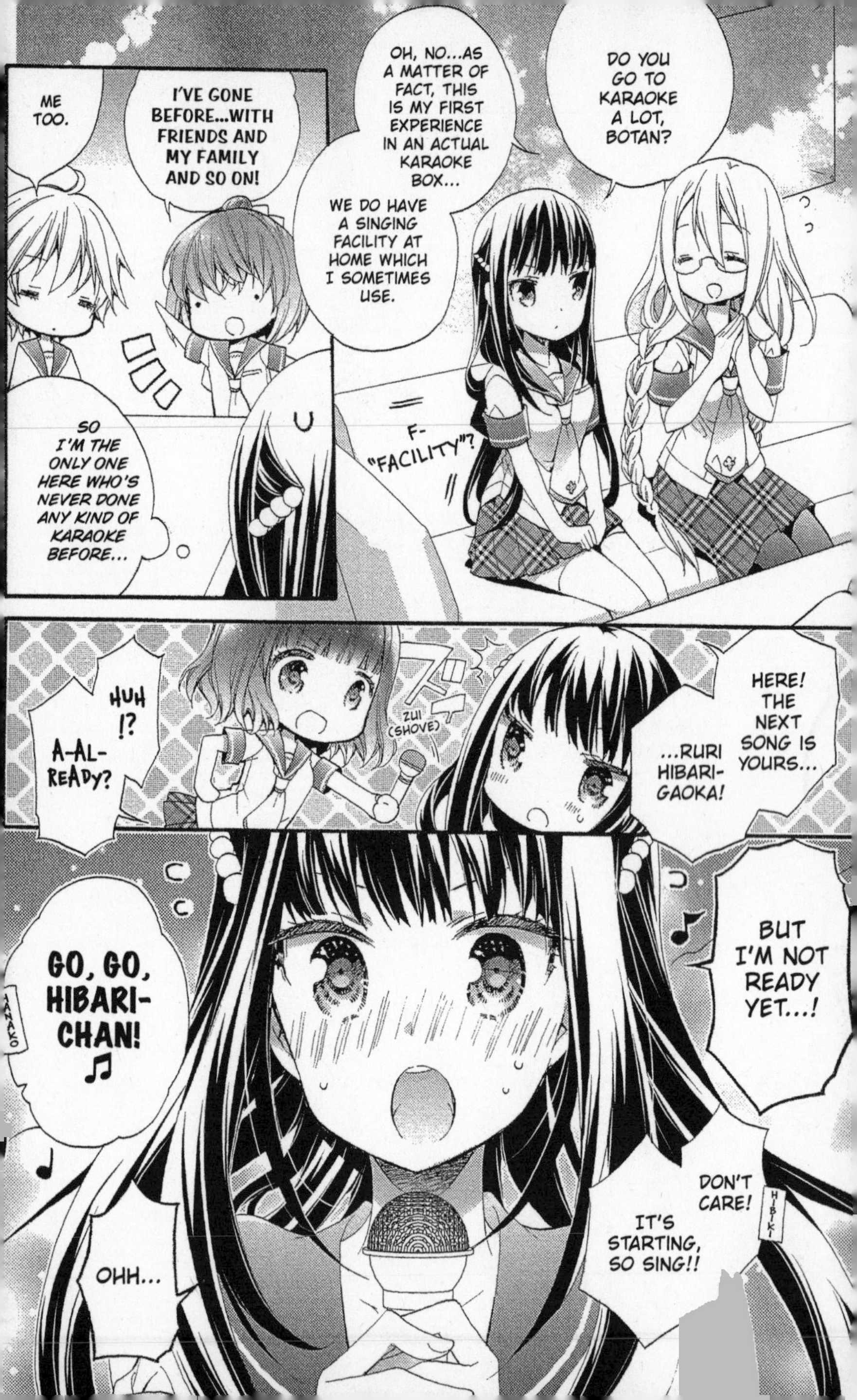
DO YOU GO TO KARAOKE A LOT, BOTAN?
OH, NO...AS A MATTER OF FACT, THIS IS MY FIRST EXPERIENCE IN AN ACTUAL KARAOKE BOX...
WE DO HAVE A SINGING FACILITY AT HOME WHICH I SOMETIMES USE.
F- "FACILITY"?
I'VE GONE BEFORE...WITH FRIENDS AND MY FAMILY AND SO ON!
ME TOO.
SO I'M THE ONLY ONE HERE WHO'S NEVER DONE ANY KIND OF KARAOKE BEFORE...
HERE! THE NEXT SONG IS YOURS...
...RURI HIBARI-GAOKA!
ZUI (SHOVE)
HUH!?
A-AL-READY?
BUT I'M NOT READY YET...!
NANAKO
GO, GO, HIBARI-CHAN! ♫
HIBIKI
DON'T CARE!
IT'S STARTING, SO SING!!
OHH...

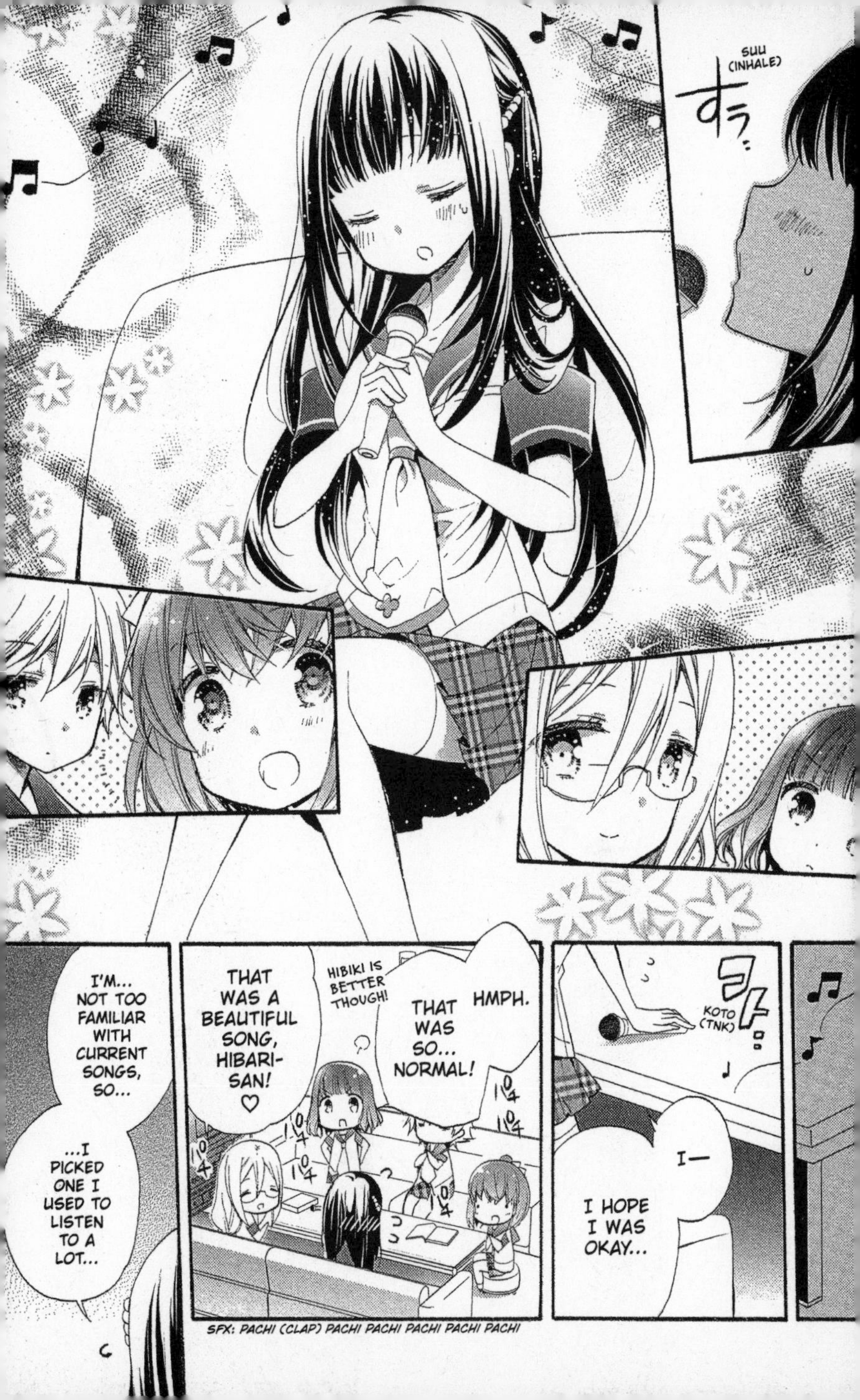
SUU (INHALE)
KOTO (TNK)
I—
I HOPE I WAS OKAY...
HMPH.
THAT WAS SO... NORMAL!
HIBIKI IS BETTER THOUGH!
THAT WAS A BEAUTIFUL SONG, HIBARI-SAN! ♡
I'M... NOT TOO FAMILIAR WITH CURRENT SONGS, SO...
...I PICKED ONE I USED TO LISTEN TO A LOT...
SFX: PACHI (CLAP) PACHI PACHI PACHI PACHI PACHI

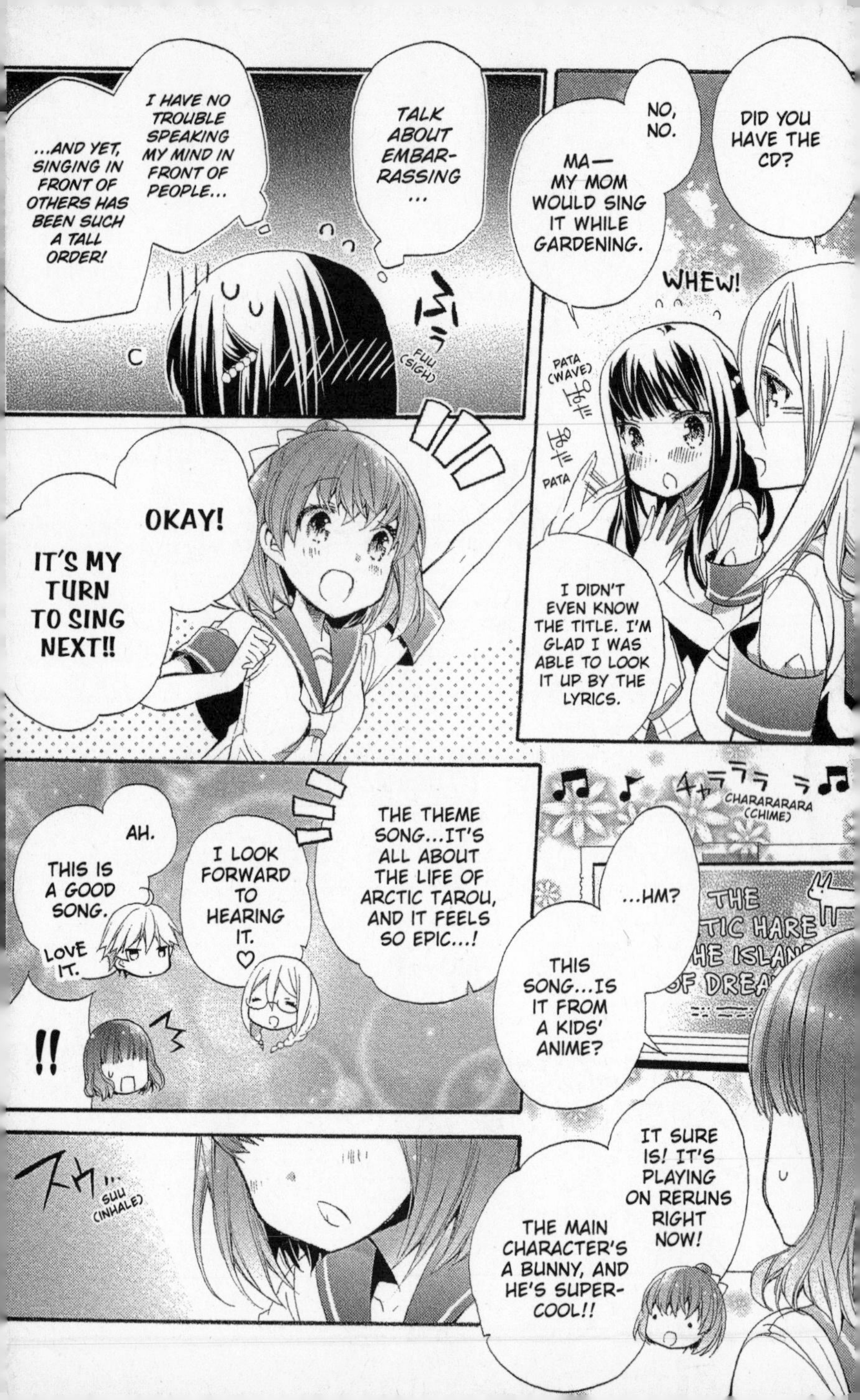
DID YOU HAVE THE CD?
NO, NO.
MA— MY MOM WOULD SING IT WHILE GARDENING.
WHEW!
PATA (WAVE)
PATA
I DIDN'T EVEN KNOW THE TITLE. I'M GLAD I WAS ABLE TO LOOK IT UP BY THE LYRICS.
TALK ABOUT EMBAR-RASSING...
I HAVE NO TROUBLE SPEAKING MY MIND IN FRONT OF PEOPLE...
...AND YET, SINGING IN FRONT OF OTHERS HAS BEEN SUCH A TALL ORDER!
FUU (SIGH)
OKAY!
IT'S MY TURN TO SING NEXT!!
CHARARARARA (CHIME)
...HM?
THIS SONG...IS IT FROM A KIDS' ANIME?
THE THEME SONG...IT'S ALL ABOUT THE LIFE OF ARCTIC TAROU, AND IT FEELS SO EPIC...!
I LOOK FORWARD TO HEARING IT. ♡
AH.
THIS IS A GOOD SONG.
LOVE IT.
!!
IT SURE IS! IT'S PLAYING ON RERUNS RIGHT NOW!
THE MAIN CHARACTER'S A BUNNY, AND HE'S SUPER-COOL!!
SUU (INHALE)

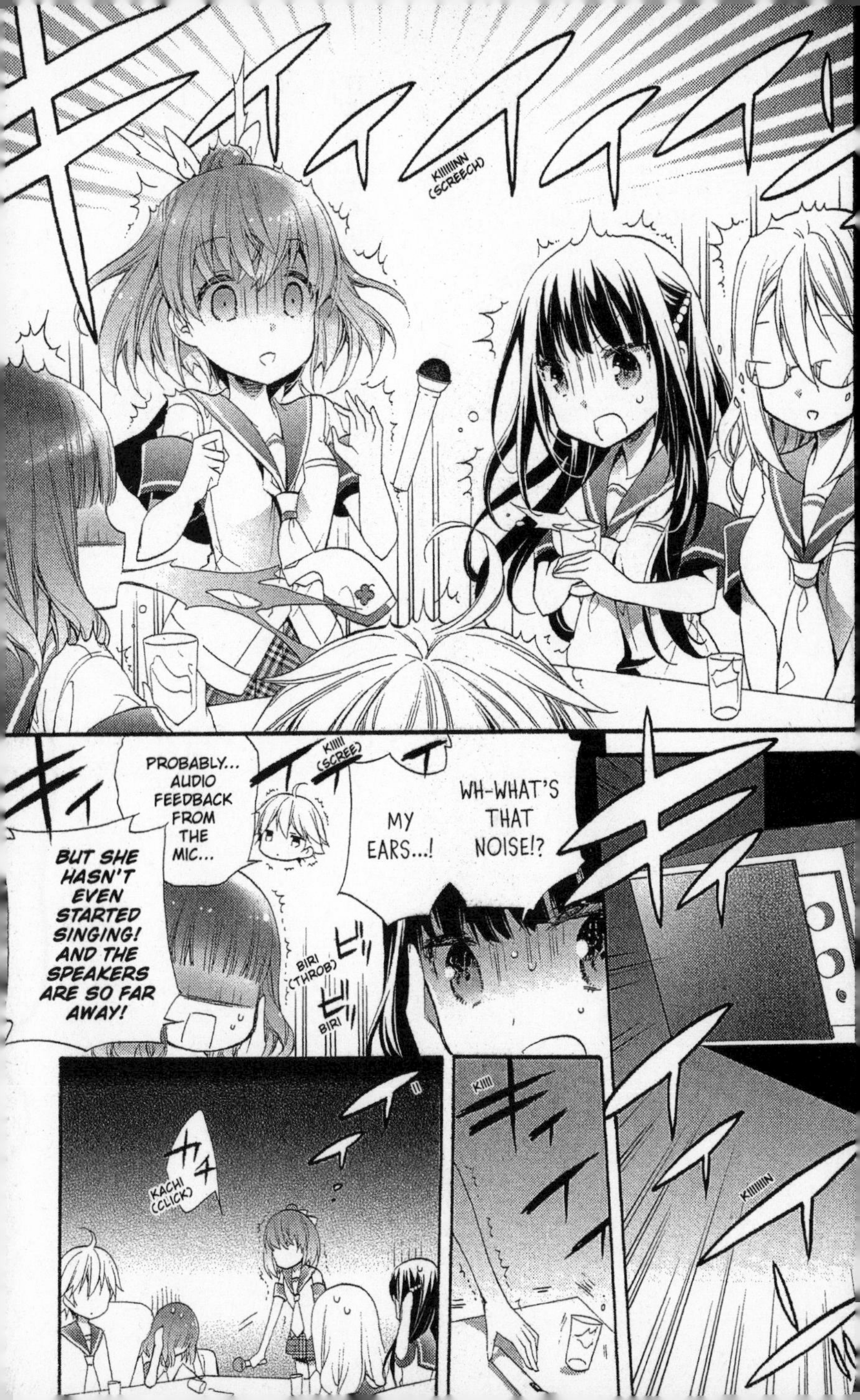
KIIIIIIINN (SCREECH)
WH-WHAT'S THAT NOISE!?
MY EARS...!
KIIII (SCREE)
PROBABLY... AUDIO FEEDBACK FROM THE MIC...
BUT SHE HASN'T EVEN STARTED SINGING! AND THE SPEAKERS ARE SO FAR AWAY!
BIRI (THROB)
BIRI
KIIII
KIIIIIIN
KACHI (CLICK)

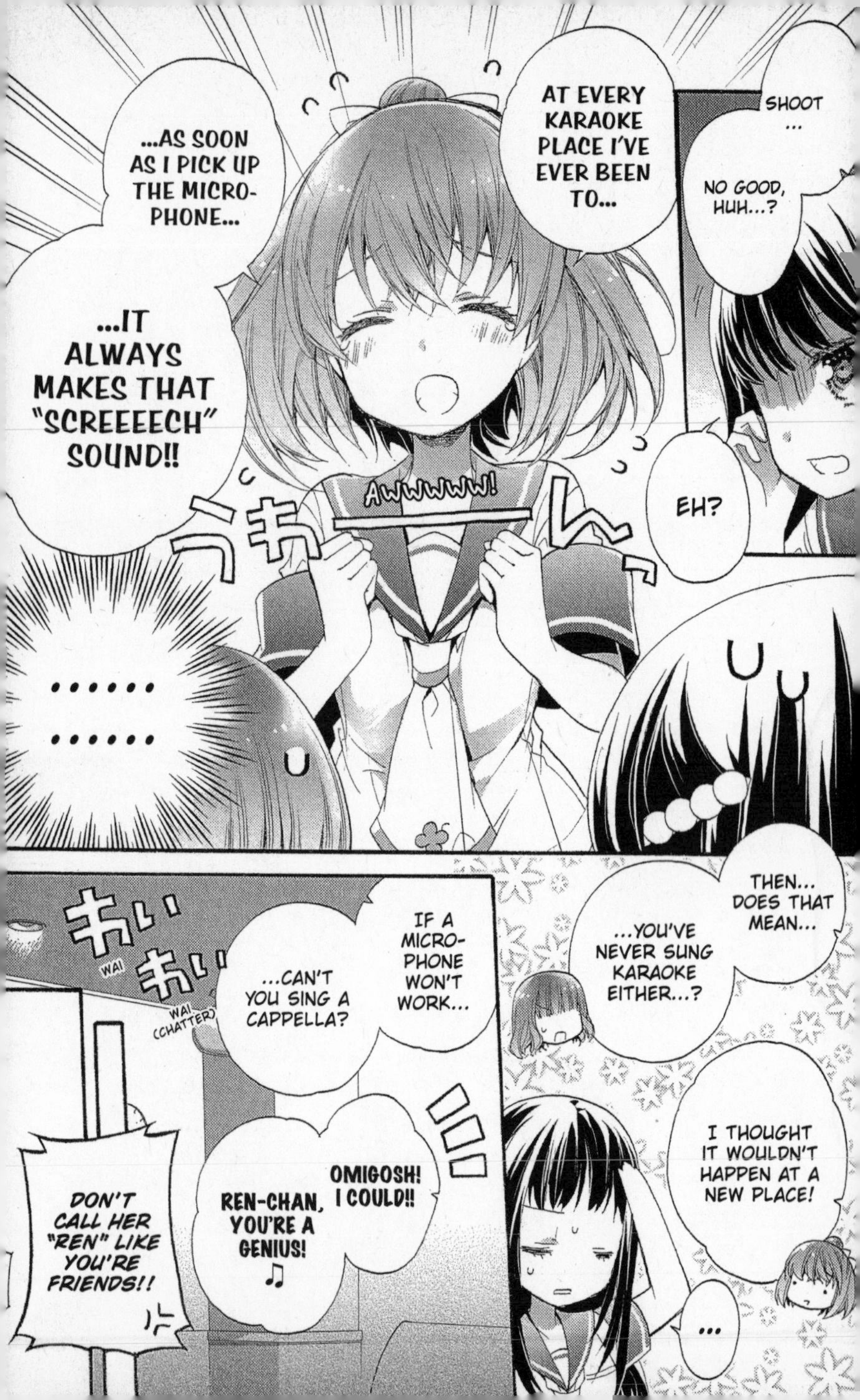
SHOOT...
NO GOOD, HUH...?
EH?
AT EVERY KARAOKE PLACE I'VE EVER BEEN TO...
...AS SOON AS I PICK UP THE MICRO-PHONE...
...IT ALWAYS MAKES THAT "SCREEEECH" SOUND!!
うわ～ん
AWWWWW!
......
......
THEN... DOES THAT MEAN...
...YOU'VE NEVER SUNG KARAOKE EITHER...?
I THOUGHT IT WOULDN'T HAPPEN AT A NEW PLACE!
...
IF A MICRO-PHONE WON'T WORK...
...CAN'T YOU SING A CAPPELLA?
OMIGOSH! I COULD!!
REN-CHAN, YOU'RE A GENIUS! ♫
わい わい
WAI WAI (CHATTER)
DON'T CALL HER "REN" LIKE YOU'RE FRIENDS!!

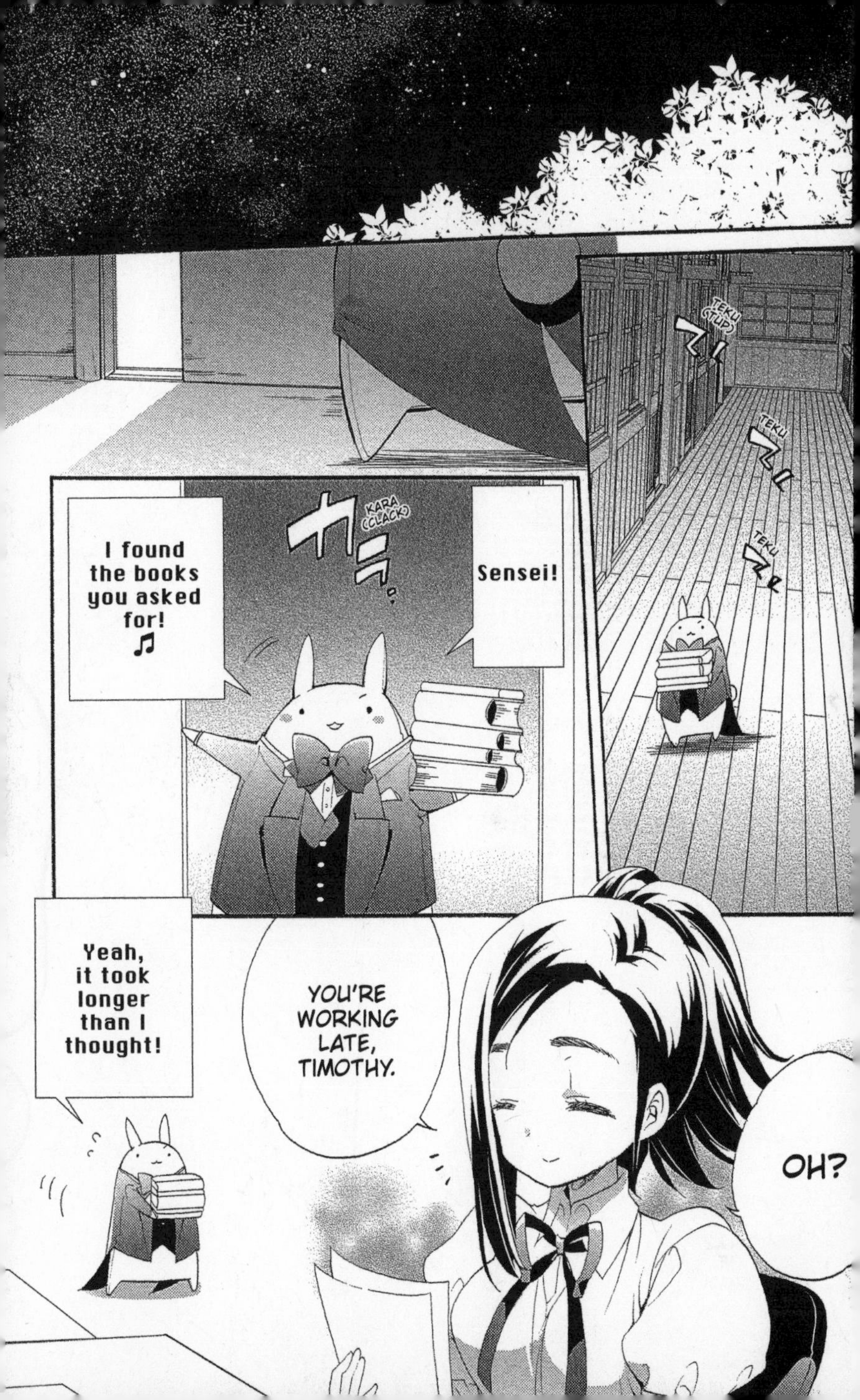

TEKU (TUP)
TEKU
TEKU
Sensei!
KARA (CLACK)
I found the books you asked for! ♫
OH?
YOU'RE WORKING LATE, TIMOTHY.
Yeah, it took longer than I thought!

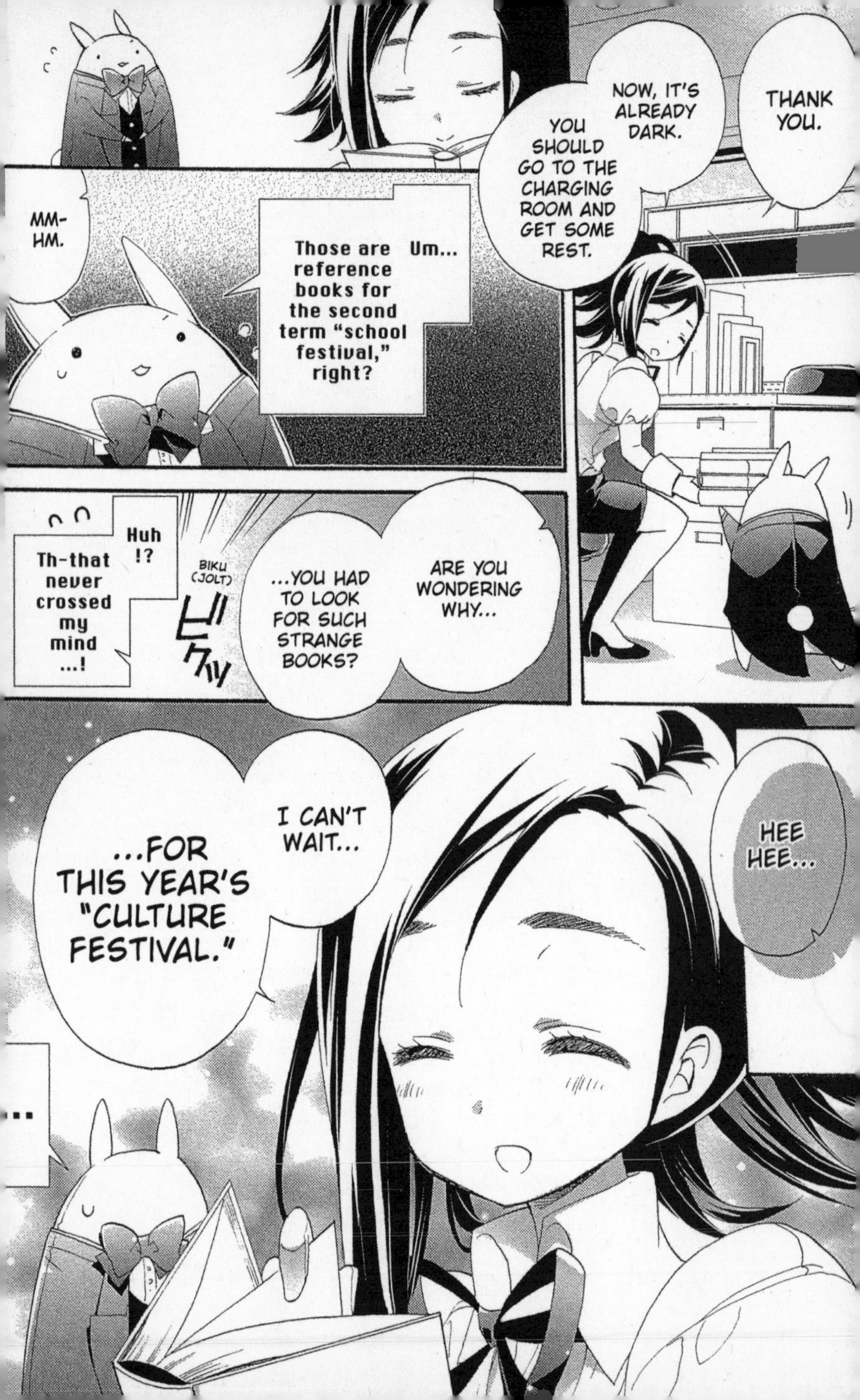
THANK YOU.
NOW, IT'S ALREADY DARK. YOU SHOULD GO TO THE CHARGING ROOM AND GET SOME REST.
Um... Those are reference books for the second term "school festival," right?
MM-HM.
ARE YOU WONDERING WHY...
...YOU HAD TO LOOK FOR SUCH STRANGE BOOKS?
BIKU (JOLT)
ビクッ
Huh!?
Th-that never crossed my mind...!
HEE HEE...
I CAN'T WAIT...
...FOR THIS YEAR'S "CULTURE FESTIVAL."
...

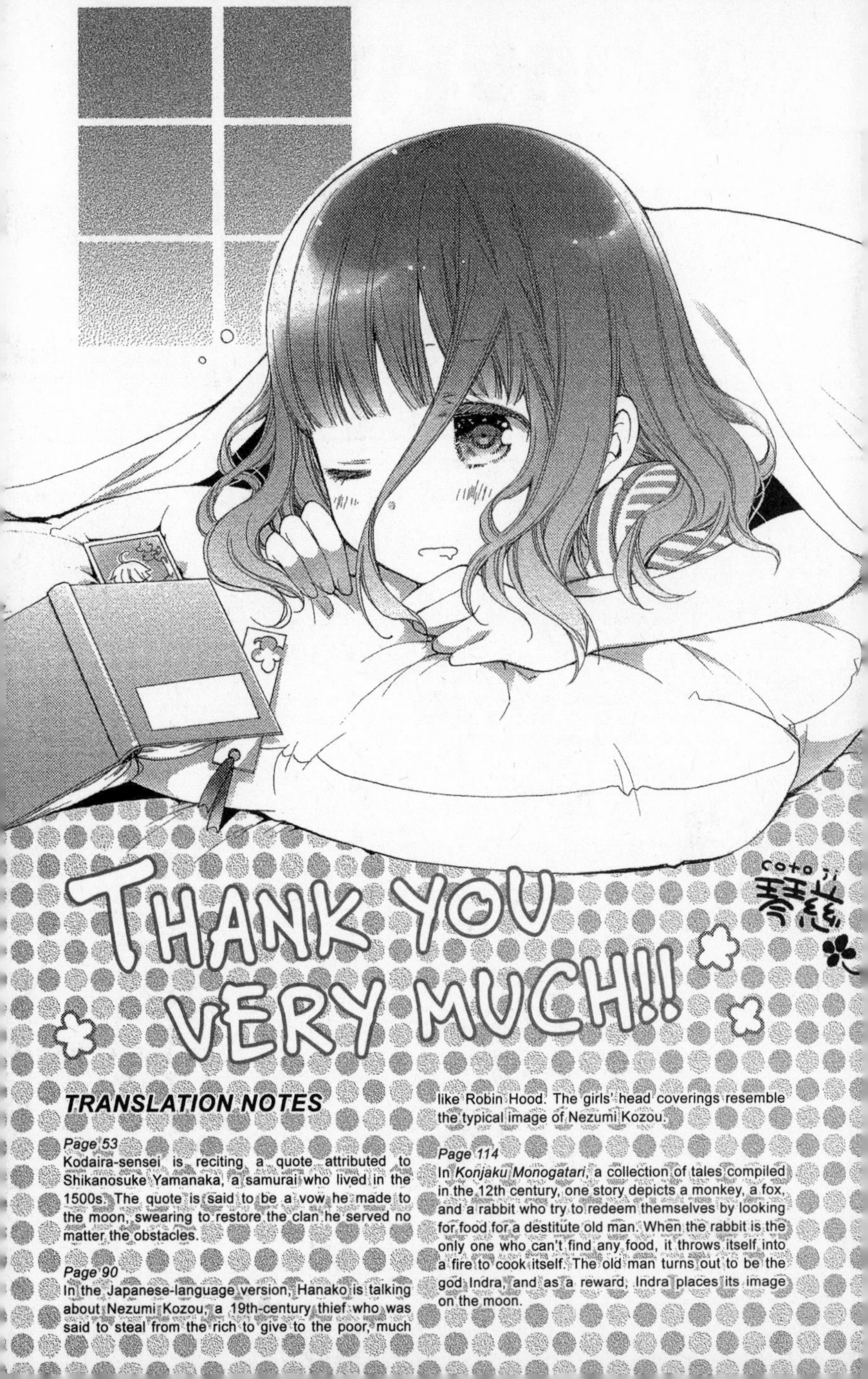
THANK YOU VERY MUCH!!
coto ji
琴慈

TRANSLATION NOTES

Page 53
Kodaira-sensei is reciting a quote attributed to Shikanosuke Yamanaka, a samurai who lived in the 1500s. The quote is said to be a vow he made to the moon, swearing to restore the clan he served no matter the obstacles.

Page 90
In the Japanese-language version, Hanako is talking about Nezumi Kozou, a 19th-century thief who was said to steal from the rich to give to the poor, much like Robin Hood. The girls' head coverings resemble the typical image of Nezumi Kozou.

Page 114
In *Konjaku Monogatari*, a collection of tales compiled in the 12th century, one story depicts a monkey, a fox, and a rabbit who try to redeem themselves by looking for food for a destitute old man. When the rabbit is the only one who can't find any food, it throws itself into a fire to cook itself. The old man turns out to be the god Indra, and as a reward, Indra places its image on the moon.

unhappy
go lucky!

COTOJI

Translation: Amanda Haley
Lettering: Rochelle Gancio

ANNE HAPPY ♪ VOL. 4
© 2015 Cotoji. All rights reserved. First published in Japan in 2015 by HOUBUNSHA CO., LTD., TOKYO. English translation rights in United States, Canada, and United Kingdom arranged with HOUBUNSHA CO., LTD. through Tuttle-Mori Agency, Inc., Tokyo.

English translation © 2017 by Yen Press, LLC

Yen Press
1290 Avenue of the Americas
New York, NY 10104

Visit us at yenpress.com
facebook.com/yenpress
twitter.com/yenpress
yenpress.tumblr.com
instagram.com/yenpress

First Yen Press Edition: February 2017

Yen Press is an imprint of Yen Press, LLC.
The Yen Press name and logo are trademarks of Yen Press, LLC.

The publisher is not responsible for websites (or their content) that are not owned by the publisher.

Library of Congress Control Number: 2016931012

ISBNs: 978-0-316-31788-7 (paperback)
       978-0-316-31790-0 (ebook)

10 9 8 7 6 5 4 3 2 1

BVG

Printed in the United States of America